Community in America

Community in America

The Challenge of
Habits of the Heart

EDITED AND INTRODUCED BY

Charles H. Reynolds and
Ralph V. Norman

UNIVERSITY OF CALIFORNIA PRESS
Berkeley   Los Angeles   London

University of California Press
Berkeley and Los Angeles, California
University of California Press, Ltd.
London, England
© 1988 by
The Regents of the University of California

Library of Congress Cataloging-in-Publication Data

Community in America: the challenge of Habits of the heart/edited
and introduced by Charles H. Reynolds and Ralph V. Norman.
  p. cm.
  Bibliography: p.
  Includes index.
  ISBN 0-520-06260-4 (alk. paper). ISBN 0-520-06262-0 (pbk.)

  1. Habits of the heart. 2. National characteristics, American.
3. Individualism. 4. Civics. 5. United States--Civilization--1945-
I. Reynolds, Charles H. II. Norman, Ralph V.
E169.12.H293C66 1988
973.92–dc19   88-15575
                                               LCIP

Printed in the United States of America
1 2 3 4 5 6 7 8 9

CONTENTS

ACKNOWLEDGMENTS

The authors of *Habits of the Heart* aimed from the very start to initiate a lively conversation about individualism and commitment in American life. They have been successful in this beyond any of their expectations. In gathering the essays for this reader, we have had the advantage of this growing conversation. We are most grateful to the authors of *Habits* for having set this all going and for their suggestions for this volume. They wanted, as did we, the sharpest and most cogent criticisms from friend and foe alike.

The idea for this volume grew out of a symposium on *Habits of the Heart,* organized by the editors of *Soundings* and held at the University of Tennessee at Knoxville in November 1985. Seven academic departments (English, History, Philosophy, Psychology, Political Science, Religious Studies, and Sociology) and five colleges (Business Administration, Education, Human Ecology, Law, and Liberal Arts), along with Provost George Wheeler and Chancellor Jack Reese, sponsored the symposium in cooperation with the Society for Values in Higher Education. Essays in this volume by Roland Delattre, Christopher Lasch, William May, and Ralph Potter were presented at the symposium, and earlier versions of their essays (as well as essays in this volume by Jean Bethke Elshtain, Jeffrey Stout, and Ernest Wallwork) were first published in the Spring/Summer 1986 issue of *Soundings*. The papers in this volume by Elizabeth Albert and Fredric Jameson were first presented in a colloquium on *Habits* at the University of Tennessee at Chattanooga in April 1987. Jameson's essay appeared in the Fall 1987 issue of the *South Atlantic Quarterly*. Vincent Harding's essay appeared in the Spring 1987 issue of *Crosscurrents*.

The editors are especially grateful to colleagues of the University of Tennessee at Knoxville and Chattanooga for their support in making this volume possible.

   The editors are deeply indebted to Allyson Lunden for her editorial assistance in preparing these essays for publication. We also want to thank Debbie Myers, Joan Riedl, and the *Soundings* staff (Mary Nietling and Nancy McCormack) for their work on the manuscript. Finally, we are grateful to James Clark, the director of the University of California Press, and members of his editorial staff, especially Barbara Ras and Amy Einsohn, for their superb assistance.

INTRODUCTION

The Longing for Community: Civic Ecology, Narrative, and Practices

Charles H. Reynolds and Ralph V. Norman

Habits of the Heart is the kind of scholarship that periodically kindles broad public interest because it catches and focuses something out there ready to be kindled, a widely shared but not yet fully articulated sense that something urgent and important requires attention. *The Lonely Crowd, The Feminine Mystique, The Culture of Narcissism,* and *Roots* immediately come to mind as books that similarly have captured the public imagination. These books differ considerably from a report of a commission appointed by the government or by a foundation. Such reports are often published under the names of distinguished persons who may have met each other only casually. In *Habits* we have a close conspiracy of like-minded and variously gifted colleagues. We will explain why "conspiracy" is an apt term, not simply "collaboration." *Habits* is a venture of shared hope; the collaboration is in this sense preliminary to a main event proposed but not guaranteed by the book: a public conversation by which concerned citizens will participate in renewing the hope for community and democracy in America.

CIVIC ECOLOGY

Habits renews expectations for democracy in our nation by proposing "narrative coherence" for a new "civic ecology." There are those who will find this a troublesome juxtaposition of terms. "Civic ecology" may seem the instance of a metaphor gone berserk. Ecologists, who like to think that theirs is a rigorous science of organisms in environment, worry that when the term is stretched too far from the life sciences it simply runs toward tautology and expires, like an army that has moved out beyond its supply lines. Throw any dozen items into the same bin (an "environment") and they start to form a system (an "ecology"). Thus family life

1

can be an ecology, corporate life another, the market a third. And why not a still life as an ecology of shapes and colors, or the west face of Chartres as an ecology of saints? The mind wearies just as the will to metaphor gets its second wind.

But other objections to the language of ecology run deeper. Since at least the days of Parson Malthus this language has been caught up in controversy over what may be called the final terms of social discourse. When Malthus introduced his bleak trajectory of the growth of population, he was rebuked not so much for his calculations, uncompromising as they were, as for the larger frame of nature and of history that had to be invoked in order to read those calculations properly. It was a frame of ultimate limitation; it bespoke an older, settled world. Into the ecology of that world, Malthusians would argue, something disturbing, destructive, and self-defeating had insinuated itself. If Malthus was right, the long-awaited partnership of Western rationality with Western conscience, which was supposed to break down every age-old oppression of humankind from slavery and starvation to warfare and ignorance, would bring no social salvation but rather our undoing. To many contemporaries of Malthus this doctrine looked as if it called for an end to humanitarian reform, still in its infancy, and for acquiescence in ancient injustice. The hideous truth behind the law of population was that an improvement in the conditions of human life could only make things worse in the long run, because science-and-conscience had begun to subvert the fragile ecology of the planet. Progress would be a mistake. If so, the story of Pandora should take center stage among the stories of the race, and Prometheus got what he deserved.

Whatever is to be said on behalf of this now familiar picture—and much is indeed being said in the late twentieth century that supports it—this version of the ecological imagination inescapably reinforces conservative polity, and it is no accident that spokesmen for the wretched of the earth have found the language of ecology signally uncongenial to the logic of revolutionary aspiration. They have sensed in the call for conservation of natural resources a call also for preservation of existing arrangements of power, whether within nations or among nations. They have sensed, with Pascal, that what passes for Nature may merely be a first Custom, the game played by those who got here first (or started winning first) and who mean to continue to win. No matter how good the intentions of the preservationists, the logic of preservation, insofar as it is a logic derived from ecology, seems to posit a largest environmental system in which all systems are internally related and in which the disturbance of any single part must imperil the accommodation of the whole. No matter, either, that the most radical critique of world culture derived from ecology tells the story of what went wrong when hunters and gatherers gave way to tillers of the soil and to founders of cities and settlements, when winners and losers in these establishments came to be identified and separated far more sharply. Sooner or later any story told on behalf of the world's dispossessed has to stop favoring a first, balanced whole and take to the valorization of conflict, rupture, and disintegration. At that turn we are into the collision of good systems and bad systems, and ecology does appear to have run out of any power of its own to keep the story going.

For these and for other reasons, which will shortly be obvious, the authors of *Habits* must be understood constantly to be testing all available languages of our culture against each other, checking the latent imperialism in each of them, blocking the rush of the mind toward the logical conclusions presumed to be entailed by any one of them. Terms like *civic, practical reason, religion,* and *ecology* take on new and unexpected meanings precisely in their juxtaposition. In this sense the discourse of *Habits* is like the discourse it recommends for America—open, supple, multivalent, a discourse of bricolage, words meant for an unfinished nation. Maybe this is our best warrant for taking ecology as one of the central metaphors of *Habits.*

If there is a hedonistic paradox, it might be argued, there is an equivalent ecological paradox. The paradox of hedonism is that pleasure too frontally intended is ruined; it needs to be off at the periphery of vision, never imprinted directly on the macula. The paradox of ecology is that wholeness—health, at-homeness, *Heil*—may not be forced; it must come in its own good time, an integrity always at the edges of the collectivity of particular conscious intentions.

The sense of a civic ecology in *Habits* is thus indirect; it works a little like the notion of a genetic reservoir. When ecologists worry about the disappearance of plant and animal species, their concern is in the first instance neither museological nor romantic. They do not see the Great Chain of Being coming unplugged, but they do fear damage, however dimly comprehended, to the living chains that support the things we value most. The urgency of protecting the reservoir lies in preservation of the primal brew, in the maintenance of the biological makings of food chains, as well as a vast array of other vital interconnections. In an American civic ecology the several traditions would represent the genetic resource, and they are related in unpredictable but profoundly significant ways. And so far they are what we have.

Traditions must be nurtured and protected, and this is why *Habits* may look quite conservative. But traditions must be living in change as well, and be nurtured in change; and this is why *Habits* also carries without much apology the look of a liberal manifesto.

Aristotle, never one to mix metaphors beyond necessity, would not have been bothered by the notion of a civic ecology. When he declared that the human is *zoon politikon,* a living city-creature, he had the germinal categories. Biology and politics he took to be separate but by no means unrelated spheres. It is true that he could not have used the phrase itself. In Athens *polis* and *oikos*, the public space of appearance and the private space of the household, did not mix. But *polis* and *zoe* did mix, and had to; humans could not survive in any other air than in that living space where speaking and acting sustained the city's narrative. According to *Habits* this "republican" tradition has existed in America alongside a biblical tradition that imagines the community as a household of the faithful and its members as brothers and sisters, the children of God. Hannah Arendt argued in *The Human Condition* that these traditions represent contradictory social imaginations. The bonds of the household are at best prepolitical; they are sustained by birth and blood. The city cannot be construed as a household, Arendt said, without inviting totalitarian versions of narrative coherence. But the America depicted in *Habits* betrays little disposition toward totalitarianism, and certainly not an emergency in that direction. On the contrary. Private liberty we have aplenty, public equality not so much, fraternity (a term drawn more from the house than from the city) hardly at all.

AS OTHERS SEE AMERICA

Liberty, equality, fraternity: the ideals of the French Revolution are not far below the surface of *Habits of the Heart,* and it is perhaps not surprising that the book's title was provided by a Frenchman. For the better part of a century Americans have turned first to Alexis de Tocqueville whenever it occurred to them to try to see themselves as others see them.

Not that Americans ever spent much of their very considerable introspective energy worrying about what other people think. It has been enough to send the country's best lights abroad and get the view from overseas through a long line of distinguished emissaries and temporary expatriates: Franklin, Jefferson, Adams and his progeny, the elder and younger Jameses, Hemingway and Fitzgerald, Du Bois and Baldwin, Thomas Eakins and Mary Cassatt, and Edward Hopper and Fairfield Porter, right down to such architects of the pax Americana as George Kennan, W. Averell Harriman, Charles Bohlen, and Dean Acheson. On their return to native soil, quite often well before their return, they could scan the moral landscape with a far sharper sense of the American difference, or so it seemed, than could the most sympathetic foreign observer.

For instance, Winston Churchill was in his time America's favorite English statesman. He had the advantage of a family tie, and many Americans were pleased to be included in his *History of the English-Speaking Peoples* and were even modestly instructed by it; but nobody supposed that it contributed something fresh or fundamental to the imagination of America. A century earlier one of the greatest British writers since Shakespeare had come over to read from his novels before grateful and admiring audiences, but when he stayed long enough to comment upon American cities and American character, Americans were not amused. What did Dickens know? At home he might flay Parliament and might well deplore the plight of London's poor, but American habits should have been off limits.

Henry Adams thought that this reluctance to hear from others might have sprung from the sheer intimidating immensity of the American project. In his history of the United States during the Jefferson administrations, Adams suggested that even in 1800, on the eve of Jefferson's presidency, well before the great waves of immigration gave rise to the image of the nation as melting pot, Americans were hard put to say much about themselves as a whole people:

> Only with diffidence could the best informed Americans venture, in 1800, to generalize on the subject of their own national habits of life and thought. Of all American travellers President Dwight was the most experienced; yet his four volumes of travels were remarkable for no trait more uniform than their reticence in regard to the United States. Clear and emphatic wherever New England was in discussion, Dwight claimed no knowledge of other regions. Where so good a judge professed ignorance, other observers were likely to mislead, and Frenchmen like Liancourt, Englishmen like Weld, or Germans like Buelow, were almost equally worthless authorities on a subject which none understood. (Adams [1889] 1986, 31)

Adams placed some of the blame for this absence of understanding on the low state of learning and of journalism, but he believed the vastness of American space and a corresponding diversity in American character to be the chief causes, even at that early moment in the history of the republic. With obvious relish, Adams cited one against the other the several contradictory descriptions of American character that were already available both from natives and from foreigners: Americans are temperate, they are hard-drinking; they are tactiturn, they are maddeningly talkative and curious; they are slovenly and boorish, they are clean and hard-working; no two are alike, they are all alike.

The hazard of generalization, and the still more dangerous hazard of theory: Adams's theme was to be repeated throughout the nineteenth century and on into the twentieth, and at no time more predictably than when foreign voices had delivered some characterization of America. It is a theme echoed several times in this volume, as social theory rooted in suspicious European antecedents is seen to spread down unevenly over a social reality knotted, dappled, and domestic, resistant to interpretation in foreign terms. The rhetorical power of *Habits* resides in its technique of vivid inspection, its evocation of neighbors and neighborhoods that white middle-class Americans quickly recognize. And the rhetorical failure of *Habits* appears to reside in setting up and then frustrating an expectation that all our neighborhoods, not simply those of the descendants of President Dwight, will be similarly evoked. *Habits* does not engage in a public conversation with dispossessed Americans or with people of color. A broader conversation is the proper test for the experiment urged in *Habits*. And if that broader discussion of *Habits* does not occur, the book—because of its focus on white middle-class Americans—could reinforce a "for whites only" vision of America. That would be a serious distortion of the vision the book attempts to present.

Habits focuses on the culture of white middle-class Americans. But before readers dismiss the book as provincial, sexist, or racist (as some people tell us they have done), they might want at least to see how the ecology proposed in *Habits* works, how it leads the authors to write:

> If the ethos of work were less brutally competitive and more ecologically harmonious, it would be more consonant with the ethos of private life and, particularly, of family life. A less frantic concern for advancement and a reduction of working hours for both men and women would make it easier for women to be full participants in the workplace without abandoning family life. By the same token, men would be freed to take an equal role at home and in child care. (*H*, 288)

Similarly, regarding desegregation and integration:[1]

> If the Civil Rights movement failed fundamentally to transform the position of black people in our society, it was because to do that would have required just the change in our social ecology that we are now discussing. So a movement to transform our social ecology would, among other things, be the successor and fulfillment of the Civil Rights movement. (*H*, 286)

Finally, this focus on white middle-class American culture does not entail a defense of the economic status quo. We read, "The litmus test that both the biblical and republican traditions give us for assaying the health of a society is how it deals with the problem of wealth and poverty" (*H*, 285). The authors go on to indicate that the biblical tradition makes it clear "that societies sharply divided between rich and poor are not in accord with the will of God," and that classic republican theory "rested on the assumption that free institutions could survive in a society only if there were a rough equality of condition, that extremes of wealth and poverty are incompatible with a republic."

NARRATIVE AND HABITS

"We in America need ceremonies is, I suppose, sailor, the point of what I have written"—this is the last sentence from a short story by John Updike that shows how fragile American ceremony is, how precarious its narrative, how loose its anchor in sponsored or shared memory. The title of the story is an emblem for this difficulty in rendering a single sense out of personal and collective experience: "Packed Dirt, Church-going, A Dying Cat, A Traded Car." That America needs ceremonies is one point of *Habits*. It is not that ceremonies or stories come hard out of this soil, for clearly they do not, but that the accounts Americans give of themselves are gnarled in recalcitrance to questions about a genuinely intended public texture, a convergence of narratives, a coalition that might stand up against and among the other, older coalitions of earth.

To be reminded that the older nations are themselves coalitions might help to correct the trick of perspective that makes these nations, sev-erally or in grand configuration, look like final unities of history, spirit, and place. It might qualify the notion that America is in this respect radi-cally unlike, say, Germany, France, Russia, or China. Poke at the nar-ratives of any of these and you find that historically they shiver into hun-dreds of competing stories and designs. If there is now a narrative that captures China, it was not always so, and never necessarily so, and may not be so tomorrow. Necessity is the trick that perspective plays when we look out on some far country and on other people's business. No; if Americans have neglected the task of a narrative for themselves, it can-not be charged up to their nature, much less to fate or to a destined role in history.

So the authors have recaptured the language of "habits." The term is helpful in its ambivalence as to factors like intention, freedom, and causation. In using the term, a student of human behavior acknowledges a certain potential complicity with that behavior, at least to the degree that the student can imagine a narrative embracing the observed behav-ior and her own. Can it be that Americans, insofar as they have listened at all to a foreigner, have listened to Tocqueville because they sensed this about the implicit narrative of *Democracy in America*? It was not travel literature he was writing. He was not making casual or witty observations about the folkways of another country. He described revolutionary cur-rents in which he and his countrymen were inescapably awash. To ask about the hearts and minds of Americans was at that moment to ask about the habits—that is, the customary disposition of resources, not least the disposition of the personal resource and therewith the disposi-tion of language—that would need to accompany this latest errand into the moral wilderness. France was not then comfortable with its own nar-rative, nor was Germany, nor was indeed any other of the old European coalitions. They needed as much help as anybody else.

AFTER TOCQUEVILLE: THE CITY ON A HILL

In recalling Tocqueville, the authors of *Habits* signal that they do not in-tend to perpetuate an isolationism of American self-consciousness. Tocqueville probed the prospects for the peculiar form of democracy he found in America in large part because he was concerned about the future political prospects of Europe, and especially of France. The authors of *Habits* draw extensively on Tocqueville as they explore their nation's future. An underlying angst of *Habits* is that the American prospect of maintaining a free and democratic society is directly related to our imagination as a people to discern an ecology appropriate to our history and adequate for our destiny. Our deepest challenge as a people is not our national economy, is not our inability to stop racial oppression, is not the prospect of a disaster in the natural environment, is not the oppression of women, and is not the control of nuclear weapons. But in part because each of these issues is so important, *Habits* invites us to examine a matter that must be attended to soon if the items on the nation's agenda are to be resolved: it is the cultural crisis of meaning and coherence, the state of the civic ecology. The appendix on method in social science (297–307) is the best place to begin a critical reading of *Habits*. Here we learn that "Tocqueville was following precedent when he wrote in the introduction to volume I of *Democracy in America*, 'A new political science is needed for a world itself quite new.'" The authors of *Habits* recognize that they, "too, have had to find a new way to deal with new realities," and they have approached this challenge "by consciously trying to renew an older conception of social science, one in which the boundary between social science and philosophy was still open."

Tocqueville figures prominently in *Habits* in large part because his "sense of American society as a whole, of how its major components—family, religion, politics, the economy—fit together, and of how the character of Americans is affected by their society, and vice versa, has never been equaled. Nor has anyone ever better pointed out the moral and political meaning of the American experiment." The authors of *Habits* share with Tocqueville an approach to social science that is at once "philosophical, historical, and sociological." And it is this perspective, opening up the boundaries between social science and the humanities, that distinguishes the authors of *Habits* from those social scientists who take the natural sciences "as the model for all disciplined knowing." The ethnographer's skills of participant observation and the interview empirically anchor the interpretive sociology of *Habits*. The interpretation of American culture, character, and society is also related at crucial points to the findings of other social scientists.

The purpose of *Habits* is to summon the American people to a recognition of our cultural crisis, to describe its origins, and to suggest ways that it can be overcome through conversations with one another and with America's formative religious and civic traditions.

By joining the conversation that shapes America's social and moral *ecology*,[2] by hearing and telling a story of how public conversations have continually re-created the interdependence of tradition, character, and society in America's civic ecology, *Habits* attempts to construe a narrative cultural coherence that Americans, with their cultural and ethnic differences respected, can affirm as one people. The narrative in *Habits* legitimates a complex normative coherence that cannot be duplicated by conventional social science or historical and ethical studies. And because this narrative unity is achieved through telling America's story of public conversation, other voices can (and in the spirit of *Habits*, should) join the conversation.

The opening sentences of the preface to *Habits*—"How ought we to live? How do we think about how to live? Who are we, as Americans?"—prepare the reader for the description of and the prescription for America's civic ecology that the book presents. Throughout, we encounter people (Brian Palmer, Joe Gorman, Margaret Oldham, Wayne Bauer, together with a host of other persons among the more than two hundred interviewed) and learn how they have struggled to find answers to these probing questions. We are constantly reminded of how Tocqueville described Americans of an earlier era in relation to similar questions. And we are reminded that John Winthrop, George Washington, Thomas Jefferson, John Adams, Ralph Waldo Emerson, Abraham Lincoln, and Martin Luther King, Jr., shared in and shaped the social and moral dynamic. They too struggled with the deep issues of individual moral identity and commitment to the common good. Because the authors locate America's formative heritage in the biblical, the civic republican, and the modern individualist traditions,[3] they recognize that these traditions at times provide conflicting directives.

A primary challenge to American public philosophy, as a new civic ecology is construed, is to do justice to the nation's extraordinary cultural resources. A critical reader of *Habits* is tempted to see this reliance on the biblical tradition, the civic republican tradition, and the tradition of individualism as itself too narrow. For instance, the tradition of individualism is read narrowly, in its negative self-interested formulations (as Hobbesian egoism). Individualism has more universalistic and liberal democratic formulations, as in the Kantian and classical utilitarian philosophical traditions, as well as in Dewey and pragmatism. Moreover, the book does not take sufficient account of America's distinctive pluralism of cultural traditions, or of feminist scholarship, and thereby does not take advantage of one of America's richest assets as a member of the international community of peoples and nations. As Bellah has eloquently argued (1978), if we can find a way to construe a normative public philosophy in America that takes account of our nation's cultural riches, America will be in a stronger position to contribute to a global public philosophy. This is a conversation that began early in American life and has never stopped. At moments, such as when the French, the Spanish, the English, and the Native Americans first went into competition for control of the land, it was not so much a matter of conversation as of hostility and open warfare. The American War of Independence and the creation of a federal government of states under a sophisticated constitution on the North American continent may have resolved the bloody aspects of these conflicts for a time. But it is a mistake to suppose that the question about ultimate loyalties ever went away, or that a competition of traditions should ever be expected to disappear. In the late twentieth century it is by no means clear that "America" is or ought to be the term designating the ultimate loyalty of Americans. The American Jewish community has its unique regard for the siting of the state of Israel on ancient holy ground; Afro-Americans have the dual consciousness that Du Bois identified; and Mexican Americans are caught inescapably between loyalty to a long-standing cultural heritage and immersion in the high-tech life of the U.S. For feminists, gender is the category for analyzing culture and male dominance is the enemy of authentic human community. There are Christians of every persuasion and eccentricity, loyal to the See of Rome, loyal to the book of Mormon, loyal to various imperatives of conscience that go beyond patriotism. Some Christians give sanctuary to illegal refugees; others demand sanctuary for their children from the harm of secular doctrine and scientific medicine. Some challenge Caesar when he charges off to Grenada, and others challenge Caesar when he goes soft on communism or abortion. The multinational corporations, replete with flags, philosophies and operations, are as fully international as the church itself, sprawling over the globe without special regard for national boundaries or historical loyalties. And there are the scientists: the physicist who feels as strong a kinship with colleagues in Bonn or Grenoble as with those in Seattle or Livermore, the biologist whose common cause on behalf of whales or dolphins or seaweed may be with Swedes, Japanese, Russians, or South Africans.

For many Americans today "my country, right or wrong" rings hollow; our most heartfelt allegiances often extend beyond any national boundary. At its best the public conversation envisioned in *Habits* is a global conversation in which everything—gender, constitutions, economic systems, boundaries, religion, ethnicity, traditions, and loyalties— is open to question, save only one thing: conversation itself. Readers of *Habits* must ask whether and in what degree the American experiment can be, as the authors want to argue, the chief emblem and model on this planet for that bedrock necessity of human community. Tocqueville pondered this possibility. It remains a breathtaking ambition. How much hubris does it contain, the City Set on a Hill?

THE CONSPIRATORS

We return to the thesis of *Habits* later, when we introduce the essays in this volume. But first we will review at least one major work by each of the five coauthors of *Habits*. For although *Habits* is profoundly indebted

to Robert Bellah, and has been associated primarily with him in the public mind, to study the writings of Richard Madsen, William Sullivan, Ann
Swidler, and Steven Tipton, and also to review some of Bellah's earlier
works, is to appreciate how much *Habits* is indebted to all five authors.

Richard Madsen

Madsen's *Morality and Power in a Chinese Village* (1984) is an engaging
study of the moral ecology (his term) of Chen village. Madsen probes
"the relationship between moral discourse, social predicament, and the
development of moral character among grassroots political activists in
rural China" (xvi) during and following Mao's cultural revolution in the
1960s and early 1970s. Madsen was introduced to modern China in the
1960s as a Catholic missionary in the religious society of the Maryknoll
Fathers. His superiors sent him to Taiwan and Hong Kong to study Chinese and serve as a missionary. He became interested, he says, "in trying
to understand what someone steeped in a Western Christian tradition
might learn about the meaning and purpose of life from people committed to a revolutionary Communist ideology like Maoism" (viii). Later
Madsen entered the graduate program in sociology at Harvard, where
Daniel Bell read Madsen's paper "Revolutionary Asceticism in Communist China," in which he analyzed the development of moral character
among the revolutionaries. This paper became the seed of Madsen's doctoral dissertation, a revised version of which was published as *Morality
and Power.*[4]

Morality and Power begins by asking, "What is a good society? What is a
good person? How should a good person act in view of the fact that the
society he lives in is inevitably imperfect?" Compare these lines with the
first sentences of *Habits;* the questions focus in both cases on the first
concerns of a public philosophy. Madsen early on introduces Chen
Quingfa, Chen Longyong, and Ao Meihua. We follow them throughout
his study, getting to know them in the same way that readers of *Habits*
get to know Brian Palmer, Joe Gorman, Margaret Oldham, and Wayne
Bauer. The Chen villagers struggle with how to relate their Confucian
heritage to Mao's teachings in ways that both honor family tradition (Confucianism) and serve the people (Maoism), two traditions more difficult to
integrate than the civic republican tradition and the biblical tradition are
in our nation. Finally, Madsen introduces us to a third type of moral reasoning, the utilitarian instrumentalism of revisionist Marxist-Leninists,
those who now rule in China.

In an extensive footnote Madsen says (17f.), "In analyzing the contrasting logic of the three paradigms for moral discourse presented
here, I have made use of a schema of four styles of moral reasoning
developed by Ralph Potter and recently applied to American religious
movements by Steven Tipton."[5]

Madsen found Potter's typology of moral discourse, as used and elaborated by Tipton, extremely helpful in his analysis of the moral ecology of Chen village, just as the authors of *Habits* found it helpful. This grammar of moral discourse is never explicitly formulated and argued in *Habits*. Instead, it is illustrated by stories and character types as the reader encounters Winthrop, Jefferson, Emerson, Franklin, and others, each of whom is culturally situated in relation to his view of America's civic ecology. But not all these formative figures by any means represent pure moral types. Lincoln and King, in particular, illustrate how the biblical and republican traditions can be mutually supportive for construing a new civic ecology. Madsen discovered that sensitive leaders in Chen village at times drew on Confucianism as well as Maoism to promote cooperation and reduce conflict among their people.

A balanced and inclusive system of cultural norms is essential for a healthy civic ecology. *Habits* places a major emphasis on America's need to recover the biblical and republican traditions, which are perceived today as overwhelmed by expressive and utilitarian individualism.

William Sullivan

In *Reconstructing Public Philosophy* (1982), Sullivan assesses philosophic liberalism, a set of "beliefs common to the Liberal and Conservative tendencies of post–New Deal American politics" (xii). He argues that liberalism is "deeply anti-public in its fundamental premises," and that if we are to realize "the nation's central value of popular self-rule, a renewed democratic political life of active citizenship and enlightened discussion is needed, and that in turn requires an expanded political culture, a public philosophy" (xii). Also,

> this public philosophy must be closely tied to the mores, the practical understanding of everyday life. If it is to maintain its authenticity and power to infuse the public acts of individuals with significance, it can neither be an intellectually detached theory about politics nor a mere set of slogans. Finally, a public philosophy is both a cause and an effect of awakened discussion of those things most important and at issue in the life of the nation. (10)

Sullivan sees philosophic liberalism (a liberalism shared by liberals and conservatives in America)[6] as a set of beliefs in which individual self-interests, an instrumental theory of value, and a managerial ethos of manipulating persons and things combine to create a crisis in contemporary American society. The constructive response to this crisis, he says, is a renewal of the civic republican tradition of public philosophy, which would feature at the very least: character formation; a sensitivity to the specific historical context in which the self is trained in the virtues; an appreciation for the formative power of culture; a theory of the interrelatedness of the ends and means of action; and a sense that shared goals and common goods can be pursued by individuals in community.

Sullivan criticizes philosophic liberalism, as typified in ways by John Rawls (1971) but more by Lawrence Kohlberg (1969a, 1969b, 1971), as having an inadequate appreciation for the social and moral ecology in which the moral agent is formed. In criticism of Kohlberg, he writes:

> The stage theory hardly speaks to individuals confronting the anxiety of nihilism. More clarity concerning our ways of thinking about moral principles is surely helpful, but it can in no way displace the character formation of a living culture, either by the schools or by the society at large. Finally, it is the *polis* which educates. The nature of the regime, the habits of the heart fostered in everyday life, these—as Tocqueville penetratingly saw—are the stuff of moral life. (153)

Ann Swidler

In *Organization Without Authority* (1979), Swidler focuses primarily on two free schools (Group High and Ethnic High), but she also relates her thesis about the interdependence of culture and organization to free clinics, communes, and collectives. She describes the animating idea of her work as an assumption

> that culture, in the sense of symbols, ideologies, and a legitimate language for discussing individual and group obligations, provides the crucial substrate on which new organizational forms can be erected. The ability to make altered patterns of social control effective depends on the development of new cultural resources. (viii)

To write this detailed ethnography, Swidler spent a year as a participant observer in each of the two schools. She was first interested in discovering how "organizations that reject authority find other ways to regulate social life" (3). She attends more to conflict and organizational dynamics than she does to stability or organizational survival. A second concern of her study is to locate these experiments in alternative organizations in a historical framework, to explore their social roots.

Swidler shows in detail how organizations that reject authority develop three new forms of social control to manage conflict and promote cooperation. She classifies these alternatives to authority as: (1) personal influence, or charisma; (2) collective incentives, or ideology; and (3) status equalization, or equality. Her discussion of ideology is especially instructive.

Recognizing that *ideology* is a much abused term, Swidler indicates that she uses it to denote how a group defines its legitimating assumptions, or understands the terms of debate. She argues that every group

> has some legitimate language, some set of shared assumptions about what demands people can make on each other. . . . Very often in political organizations there is some norm—like the ideal of "democracy"—which, while it may be violated repeatedly in practice, is irresistible when posed clearly in debate. Ideology in this sense is the set of arguments which, if

acknowledged by both parties to a debate, would be accepted as decisive. It provides the framework in terms of which people try to influence one another and the language in which they make claims and appeals. (100)

Seen in this light, *Habits* can best be construed as an attempt to reconstruct a language from the civic republican and biblical traditions that permits public goods, or the common good, to have a legitimating power in the moral arguments of public life. Swidler concludes her study in a spirit that animates *Habits*: "Thus charisma, group solidarity, and equality can each become disintegrative rather than integrative unless they are backed up by collective resources. And the capacity of groups and organizations to generate those resources depends in large part on culturally grounded meanings" (1979, 182). *Habits* summons us to recover two traditions of "culturally grounded meanings" that can legitimate placing restrictions on the pursuit of private goods by discrete individuals.

Steven Tipton

Getting Saved from the Sixties is perhaps an unfortunate title for an impressive work in descriptive ethics and interpretive sociology. This is essential background reading for a critical understanding of *Habits*. In the foreword to *Getting Saved,* Robert Bellah writes:

> Even before the book was completed, [it], through a series of fortuitous happenings, led to the formation of a collective project involving Tipton and several others, including myself, which we have entitled "The Moral Basis of Social Commitment in America." Using the technique of sociology as moral inquiry, with a central focus on the interview as a place where sociologist and citizen engage in active and concerned exchange, we are talking to Americans in a number of communities in various parts of the country. . . . We are approaching directly a variety of middle-class Americans in an effort to discover how they make sense of their society, how they view their participation in it, and what their hopes and fears are. . . . The books that this project will engender will all owe much to *Getting Saved from the Sixties.*

Tipton's study has not received the attention it deserves, in part because of its overly colloquial title and in part because the first fourteen pages seem to announce a book on ethical theory. For those who recall the sixties as a time when progress was made on civil rights, women's liberation, challenging the Vietnam War, and developing environmental awareness, the title of the book also connotes a historical amnesia of the kind now encountered among opponents of those moral struggles. But for Tipton (6of.) the period of the sixties was a failure insofar as liberalism did not fulfill its promises. Despite the reform movements, "racism persisted," "structural poverty persisted," and the Vietnam War represented "technical reason gone mad." Hence his efforts to construe, with the other authors of *Habits,* a new civic ecology for America.

Tipton studied three very different types of institutions and symbolic structures through which young people shattered by the sixties sought to renew the moral meaning of their lives: (1) the Living World Fellowship, a small charismatic Christian sect led by female Pastor Bobbi Morris; (2) the Pacific Zen Center, which involved participation in the rigorous discipline of meditation, with its rules and structure; and (3) the Erhard Seminars Training (*est*), a human-potential psychology movement, designed to help participants know and follow the rules necessary for achieving their version of the good life. As Bellah says:

> *Getting Saved from the Sixties* . . . is a book about central issues in American society—moral and political issues as well as religious ones. It uses the three movements chosen for study as lenses to look at the larger society at a particularly poignant moment in its historical transformation. It asks how young Americans from mainstream backgrounds were attracted to such exotic movements in the first place and what they came to make of their society after they experienced their conversions. During the course of the book Tipton sheds light on changing conceptions of family, community, occupation, and politics, and on the problems we are experiencing in each of these spheres. (ix)

In appendix 1 Tipton gives a thorough description of his theory of the four styles of ethical evaluation (borrowed in part from Potter, but extensively elaborated in relation to culture and institutions) referred to above in the discussion of Madsen's work. In appendix 3 he gives an account of the methods used in the study, including a detailed presentation of interview questions. The study is concretely related to the ways particular persons in actual circumstances understand their lives and their society. It documents how many counterculture youth went from a radical individualism, prior to conversion, to a new life of commitment following "getting saved." Tipton explains that he "has sought to engage individual members of these groups in the sort of moral conversation that focuses the felt truth of their own lives upon the wider society and culture. By beginning with moral biography and fastening on the crucial events, relationships, situations, and background social structures that frame an ethic, [this study] seeks to distinguish the social location and contours of particular ideas" (xv). An interview in Tipton's interpretive sociology becomes an opportunity for a conversation about the meaning and purpose of life, an occasion for one to share the story of her life, and has the potential for a holistic interpretation in that it permits the interviewer to frame the coherence of meaning and experience. In framing this coherence, Tipton and Madsen, in their respective studies, draw extensively on a grammar of moral discourse.

But the authors of *Habits,* when working together, frame coherence primarily through their narrative recovery of the biblical and republican traditions, with the grammar of moral discourse in the background (and illustrated with character types) rather than in the foreground (and explicitly argued). It should now be apparent how the authors of *Habits* practice historical, philosophical, and interpretive sociology as a form of practical reason.[7] Two interpretive schemes are at work in *Habits,* one a narrative recovery of the biblical and republican traditions, with their respective substantive commitments to historical and living moral ecologies, and the other a supposedly formal and content-neutral grammar of moral discourse.[8]

Tipton's book is an ethnography of moral discourse; it is by intention a work in descriptive ethics. *Habits,* in contrast, is a work in practical reason; in it one encounters the intentional use of narrative normative reason. There is not a direct distinction in Tipton's ethnography between a "first language" of individualism and a "second language" of commitment, as there is in *Habits,* although a similar distinction is used as he describes life prior to and following "getting saved." We can now understand why this distinction between first and second languages is present in *Habits.* Many persons interviewed and observed were interpreted as using the languages of expressive and utilitarian individualism, but as implying and searching for a narrative language to speak about the public meaning and coherence of their lives, concepts their "first language" of individualism could not adequately convey. The authors of *Habits* used the narrative "second languages" of the biblical and republican traditions to frame and flesh out the coherence of these implicit and intended public commitments.

In two earlier works by Bellah, to which we now turn, historical and sociological reasons are given for why these two living traditions should have a continuing role in shaping America's civic ecology.

Robert Bellah

In *The Broken Covenant* (1975) and in an essay titled "The Normative Framework for Pluralism in America" (1978), Bellah argues with passion that utilitarian individualism as an ethic represents both a breaking of God's founding covenant with this nation, a severance from a religious tradition that has secured the unity of American culture, and a radical departure from the civic republican tradition, a good cultural friend of the covenant tradition. These two living traditions are interpreted as carriers of a social ecology securing the common good of the people and their civic institutions, while also securing the dignity essential for equal respect of individual persons. In that distinctive social ecology the democratic experiment in America was born. And on a reconstruction of that ecology, Bellah argues, the future prospect for democracy in America depends.

Bellah (1975) interprets America today as in its third "time of trial" as a nation. He locates the first time of trial in the revolutionary era of the

nation's founding. Here the crisis was not simply the quest for independence, but the more demanding requirement to establish a constitutional polity to secure public goods and individual dignity. He argues
that Washington, Jefferson, Adams, and Madison conceived a democratic polity that remained faithful to Winthrop's understanding of
America's covenant tradition and simultaneously reaffirmed a continuity
with the civic republican tradition.

America's second time of trial was the Civil War. It was Lincoln,
America's greatest theologian, who, appealing often to "the providence
of God," provided the leadership that saved the union and freed the
slaves. As Bellah writes (1975, 54):

> The Civil War, like the Revolution, moved from liberation, in this case
> emancipation of the slaves, to the institution of liberty in the 13th, 14th
> and 15th Amendments. The most important provisions are contained in
> the 14th Amendment where Section 1 guaranteed the natural rights of
> man and equal protection of the laws and Section 5 authorized Congress to
> enforce these rights. Even though the radical meaning of these clauses was
> undermined for many decades by narrow court interpretations and a re-
> gressive political situation, their meaning can hardly be exaggerated. They
> are the charter under which many of the advances of the last twenty years
> have been made. They are the mandate for many more.

The rhetoric of this passage nicely illustrates Bellah's long-standing commitment to the "institutions of liberty." The "causes" of the black liberation struggle, the Native American, women, Hispanics, the environment,
peace, the control of technology, economic justice, and the necessity to
interpret America in an international perspective are all passionately supported by Bellah (1975, 1978).

An angst informing *Habits*, however, is that progress toward these
causes is in jeopardy unless the citizens of this nation recover and recreate a civic ecology that can sustain human community and culturally legitimate the "institutions of liberty." This ecology must be reinforced by
rituals and ceremonies that can provide meaning and coherence to persons and institutions sharing in communitarian practices. It must justify
broad-based social commitments to public goods.

With Durkheim lurking in the wings (and assuming that culture must
integrate a society), Bellah (1978, 368) cites John Adams: "We have no
government armed with power capable of contending with human passions unbridled by morality and religion. Our constitution was made
only for a moral and a religious people. It is wholly inadequate for the
government of any other." Now is the third time of trial for America,
says Bellah, for we live in an era in which Adams's fears of the unbridled
human passions are vindicated daily. Utilitarian individualism gives
these unbridled passions cultural legitimation. So to challenge utilitarian
individualism and to undermine its understanding of what makes hu-

man life meaningful, and of what legitimates public coherence, Bellah argues that we must strengthen an alternative ecology in conversation with biblical and republican traditions.

For Bellah, neither the nation's founders, nor Lincoln, nor Martin King were summoning citizens to a nostalgic return to an earlier era as they appealed to the biblical and civic republican traditions. They were, on the contrary, using those traditions to summon the people to join them in creating "culturally grounded meanings" to sustain new "institutions of liberty." They were in conversation with representatives of living cultural traditions as they forged a communitarian and democratic future for their nation.

Will America survive its third time of trial? The reception and discussion of *Habits of the Heart* represent a promising sign that many Americans are ready to explore alternatives to radical individualism, to reconsider their commitment to the common good, and thus to join in a common quest to reconstruct American culture.

THE STRUCTURE OF THIS READER

The essays in this reader present provocative criticisms, interpretations, and alternatives to *Habits of the Heart*. Vital public discussion requires that differences be aired openly and forthrightly so that reflective engagement can occur. These essays, together with the response by Robert Bellah, representing the authors of *Habits*, ensure that the broad public discussion the authors hoped to inspire will occur: a discussion through which concerned citizens participate in renewing the hope for community and democracy in America.

The structure of this reader reflects our understanding of *Habits*. Part One is on culture—the symbols and structures of meaning that shape how Americans live together and direct their common life. Part Two is on practical reason—how citizens discern (or fail to discern) a sufficiently powerful public morality to guide and coordinate their common life. Part Three is on civic practice—those activities in public life that are internal goods to the participants in a given activity while also contributing to the common good of all affected by the activity. Part Four is on religious practice—how religious convictions and orientations both shape and challenge our public visions of our common life and of the common good. And Part Five is the response by the authors.

CULTURE

Habits of the Heart is an analysis of American culture and a constructive proposal for strengthening and reforming American culture. The discussion of *Habits* has often been entangled in criticisms based at least partially on a misreading of its methodology and therefore of its intent. In the first essay of Part One, James L. Peacock notes that a schematic derived in large part from the work of Talcott Parsons informs *Habits*. For obvious reasons, the authors of *Habits* did not want to impose a heavy methodology upon the broad public readership to whom the book is directed. But, consequently, readers unacquainted with Parsons's working distinctions between natural, personal, social, and cultural systems have looked in vain for a discussion of America's social system (institutions, movements, processes, relationships). The authors, however, are primarily concerned to discuss the cultural system (fundamental values, ethos, commitment, purpose) in relation to civic practices, and they do not attempt to provide an extensive critique of institutional structures. Peacock's essay is helpful in sorting out some of the important strands of the discussion.

Peacock's clarification does not directly address criticisms of *Habits* generated by the concerns of black Americans or feminists. Such concerns, as we shall see, are vexing for the assessment of *Habits* because they do not easily fall under a single category of the cultural, the social, or the personal. Because social classes and churches so plainly are topics for social analysis, it is easier for Peacock to defend *Habits* in its apparent preoccupation with the middle class or in its apparent privileging of the Christian churches. Peacock shows that Bellah's earlier scholarship evinces a willingness to carry on such analysis, with respect not simply to America but also to other societies, such as Japan.

Peacock's reminder that *Habits* is primarily cultural rather than personal or social analysis is most clearly made in response to the complaint that *Habits* is unfair to therapy and therapists. He remarks that the authors do not mean to discourage therapy as a mode of treatment for people who are psychologically ill. What *Habits* faults is the degree to which a therapeutic model becomes generalized into a metaphor not simply for personal relationships but for the understanding of all human relationships. Once a language grounded in the analysis of the personal system comes to dominate our understanding of the social and cultural systems, it becomes impossible on the cultural level to construct a narrative intelligibly informed by public memory or hope.

Peacock observes that the interview technique may itself reinforce the bias of individualism. To hear from individuals what they find lacking in their personal lives or in their participation in a larger public life is not necessarily to find out what they do in fact lack or how they behave in public life. The student of culture must discover, often as participant observer, something about the social ecology of the larger habitat. We need to see what people do value, what in their "collective being" they do in fact trust—as members of a board of directors or the First United Church, as Red Sox fans, in contexts like the Elks Parade, the dance recital, the Memorial Day Sale, the company picnic. We may need, that is, to observe people in full dress—in their rituals—not simply behaving collectively, but thinking, believing, remembering, reenacting, and anticipating collectively. Is it through enacting the language of such ceremony, Peacock asks, that we are more likely to find Americans clothed in memory and hope? If so, looking for a sense of American community within the personal interview may be like looking for the church in the confessional booth rather than at the Mass, the Carnival, or the Feast of Our Lady.

The predicament of community in American life is nowhere more conspicuous than in the clash and incongruity, and therefore also the shallowness, of its rituals. If the authors had examined the variety of ersatz communities in American culture, they might have engaged earlier the issue of false versus authentic community, which critics such as Elshtain, Delattre, Harding, Jameson, and Hauerwas take up in this volume.

Jean Bethke Elshtain asks the interesting question, Who needs enemies? Her unhappy answer is: any coherent society with a strong sense of community, mission, and purpose. Elshtain cautions that *Habits* may too easily reinforce that venerable American tradition in which civic virtue is extolled closely in connection with the military strength and honor of the nation.

The affinity between cultural cohesion and armed defense against enemies has a long history. When Plato laid out the dimensions of his ideal state-self in the *Republic,* he believed it important to insert between the philosopher-scientist-rulers and the artisan-businessman-managers a class of protector-soldier-warriors. Not much attention has been given in Platonist scholarship to these "professional tidiers," as W. H. Auden called them, but clearly Plato did not believe that even an ideal society could live on bread and philosophy alone. The soldier class in the *Republic* corresponds to distinctively human emotions in the psyche, and especially to that most essential attribute of arms, Honor. The city must be armed to ensure inner and outer stability, and the soldiers cannot maintain this "defense" unless distinctive civic virtues like honor and courage are respected and this respect is focused and ordered in and through a distinct class.

America has lived nervously with such a class, preferring to think its defenders would be minutemen who could lay down the anvil, the plow, or the pen long enough to quell rebellion or resist distant affronts to national honor. It has required these services longer than a minute, and the distant affront has more commonly been to commerce than to honor. But Elshtain's point is that when the oil, computer, and financial interests need the protection of the American military, it is useful to have available a patriotic national purpose to which people will feel strong emotional ties. *Habits* begins by noting the absence of that kind of emotion in middle-class Americans. But the high moments in American history, insofar as it has coherence, have been the battles and wars, where national honor was at stake. The question raised by Elshtain is whether we can follow *Habits* in the search for viable community in America without falling victim to the old and very powerful logic in which arms and enemies are almost exclusively the context for the exercise of civic virtue.

Roland A. Delattre's analysis of addiction as a cultural phenomenon, or a "heartless habit," initially appears removed from the issues analyzed in *Habits*. In his characterization of the culture of procurement as constituted by addictive acquisitions, and as nourished and sustained by an interrelated cluster of addictions, Delattre provides an account of a fabric of meaning and a framework of interpretation that gives this cultural form such power for the dominant two-thirds of American society. As his essay unfolds, one senses that Delattre is describing a form of community that is perhaps the most meaningful community that many Americans experience, especially the expressive and utilitarian individuals of *Habits*.

Delattre suggests, in a way not fully developed, how both a tyrannical community and dependent individuals are shaped by the culture of consumption in our society. After depicting a form of community that is based on a pattern of economic relationships, he exhibits and unmasks the limitations of radical individualism in a consumer culture by showing how unfree radical individuals become when they are addicted to consumption and appearance. Furthermore, he argues, the culture of procurement inevitably leads to bloated Pentagon budgets and to "technological fixes" such as Star Wars.

"There is power in the blood." Like a theme in some chthonic fugue, these words run through Vincent Harding's saddened and impassioned letter to the authors of *Habits*. The letter moves on its own plane, keeping a steady and massive distance and yet taking the measure of *Habits* with an intimacy and exactitude obviously born out of long meditation on the questions about American life that *Habits* means to address. Harding is somehow convinced that these planes, which are now so tragically close and so inexorably distinct, will one day transect, and this is the hope that drives his argument. To suppose that it will be a pleasant or a happy conjunction is to confuse hope with optimism. Harding's words are full of hope, but they are not optimistic. In pondering Harding's distance from *Habits*, the reader is put in mind rather of great geologic plates pushing one underneath the other until such time as a third magnitude forces them upward, and the old accustomed crust bulges and breaks, and the self-confidence with which land used to greet sky is seen to have been in error.

In one obvious and most superficial respect, Harding's letter moves entirely past *Habits* without so much as a tremor and leaves its cultural argument untouched and unchallenged. Sympathetic to the critique of individualism, Harding supports the call for a new civic ecology and agrees that biblical and republican traditions are resources for an American spirituality. As for the first and second languages of moral discourse, he agrees with *Habits* that America is linguistically impoverished and incompetent. He knows the unspoken moral wisdom in the practice of many American communities. Nor does he have any discernible quarrel with the methodological moves made in *Habits*—the use of personal interviews, the discussion of representative figures out of the nation's past, or the blending of philosophy, sociology, and cultural analysis. He very much wants the conversation to continue. Harding agrees that America is hungry for a narrative that will sustain its best practices, and he believes in the indispensability of an informing set of stories. For all these reasons, on almost every page he addresses the authors as "Friends." He shares their hope for community and democracy in America.

Yet one thing is lacking: Harding cannot find in *Habits* the signal that can tell him how, when that hope is realized, Afro-American voices will have shared in the victory.

Harding's lament is not like finding that one's name has been left out of the telephone book or one's picture out of the school annual. It is not even like discovering that one's vote has been thrown away or disallowed. It is not, finally, as if a history has been written that is silent on the many fine contributions to society made by one's race. These are all corrigible mistakes and injustices that might be dealt with in the general economy of good intentions and revised editions. In a second edition the authors might add several extensive interviews with blacks. A new and expanded list of eminent Americans might include more distinguished persons from minority groups—blacks, Hispanics, Native Americans, and Orientals. These might be the appropriate corrections if in Harding's view *Habits* simply required a dose of intellectual equal opportunity.

The discrepancy that separates Harding from *Habits* will not be so easily overcome. That is because Harding says a sweeping narrative of the American experience is already available. We do not have to invent it, and we do not have to look far below the surface of American life to give it voice. This narrative has been in the making since the first ship left a New World port bearing its cargo of goods "grown in America"— tobacco, cotton, sugar, coffee—grown in America, to be sure, but planted, weeded, harvested, bundled, hauled, and loaded on board by Africans, and grown on land claimed from Native Americans for European uses. Already in the seventeenth century America's story had become a multiracial, transcultural, and international narrative. It is a story of world economy and of lonely exile, of the wealth of nations and the rights of Man, of unspeakable brutality and, in Harding's version, of redemptive suffering. It encompasses all four Parsonian systems: it touches personal lives, it touches social structures, it touches fundamental cultural values, and it touches Nature. "There is power in the blood," intones Harding, and in this phrase he suggests a single tragicomic impulse that runs through all the systems in terms of which America can be analyzed. We take Harding to be saying that American hope and destiny are tied to a rich inheritance of irrational variables—soil, genes, weather, money, emotion, race, custom, power, and powerlessness. *Habits,* he says, calls for the telling of this complex story, but cannot, for one grievous reason, hear it told.

The reason is that those who have suffered through this narrative are uniquely privileged to hear and retell the story, and in that hearing and retelling bear the story forward into the presence of their fellow Americans. Afro-Americans and Native Americans have long since won this privilege in their own appointed crucible, in the "lively, painful, beautiful ties of blood." If, as Harding suggests, the tale is one of "riches and shame," we all have much to win in telling it right, and much to lose if it continues to be mistold in the dominant myths of American imperial rectitude. The prospect alarming to Harding is the possibility that Americans might take *Habits* at face value and set about blending the old imperial mythology into a narrative for community in which, once again, the American truth born of suffering is invisible. That would be a tragic human loss for *all* Americans.

M. Elizabeth Albert says that the authors of *Habits* are genuinely ambivalent about feminism as a resource in reconstructing America's civic ecology; and she thinks that this ambivalence may be appropriate, for perhaps *Habits* argues an ethical and philosophical position that should lead to the reform of feminism. Albert asks, "How does the way the women's movement defines and works toward its goals limit its ability to transform our social ecology?" Her answer is that feminist theory and practice are commonly expressed in one or the other languages of individualism. That is, in challenging male domination, feminists leave the cultural premises of individualism unchallenged. They begin with the old dichotomy between individualism and community. Since *Habits* raises questions about this dichotomy, it may shed light on several current debates within feminist circles, such as the debate between Elshtain and Ehrenreich on the nature of social commitments.

Much feminist writing concentrates on the individual rights of women relative to husbands, parents, children, and institutions such as corporations, governments, and courts. The feminist claims equal-rights protections, challenges the fairness of traditional arrangements in the workplace (whether at home or at the office), and seeks redress for inequities in insurance rates, pension plans, and salary scales. All of these appeals can be accommodated within the language of utilitarian individualism. On these terms women continue to be seen atomistically as a neglected or persecuted class of economic agents such as classical liberalism describes. *Habits* does not deny that there is such a class, only that classical liberalism does not give us the most satisfactory terms for identification or analysis of that class.

Feminist theory is also frequently cast in terms of expressive individualism. In this mode, for instance, feminist language suggests as an unarguable first truth that women have a right to full, complete, and unimpeachable use, enjoyment, and disposition of their bodies, and that this right to self-realization comes before all other moral, legal, or social considerations. The fact that during pregnancy women share their bodies with persons other than themselves, who may have rights or claims not necessarily coterminous with their own, is not easily dealt with in the language of expressive individualism. This is only one of many moments when, says Albert (following Elshtain), the dichotomy between self and other, indeed between individual and community must be severely modified. Our language ought to be more supple than that. *Motherhood* is the traditional term used to denote an immense modification of solitary selfhood. This modification, or rather the need for it, seems, in the familiar language of liberal individualism, "unfair" to women and deserving of correction or compensation within a rational social system. The only legitimate role of community then would be to protect a woman's right to self-realization in general and to the disposition of her body in particular. While *Habits* does not explicitly elaborate an account of all this, Albert believes that the authors are calling for the middle terms that will enable us to say that communities are best made out of the "social compacts" where, as Elshtain says, there is "a solemn commitment to create something 'new' out of disparate elements—a family, a community, a polity—whose individual members do not remain 'as before' once they become part of this social mode of existence."

Fredric R. Jameson, like Harding, reads *Habits* from a great distance and works from within a relatively well-defined critical position. In style and derivation of thought, this position is basically Marxist, although in the present essay Jameson brings to bear only a few terms from that critical arsenal. To Jameson, as to Harding, *Habits* seems far too open-ended, unfinished, and methodologically pluralistic. Where *Habits* calls for the building of narrative and of conversation, Jameson is ready to suggest that this call is bound to fail because it has taken insufficient account of the quite concrete narrative that might be rendered of the complex relation between economic conditions and social and cultural developments. Though these are complex relations, in Jameson's view they are neither indeterminate nor abstract; nor can one be discussed without reference to the others. Jameson's criticism is that the book uses a variety of methodologies and models for exploration of American character and culture without any informing clues as to how the wider and (Jameson believes) determinate story might be told. Because there is no analysis of the relation of social and economic circumstances to cultural values, readers have no clear idea, he says, of what the success of the project would be like.

There is much in *Habits* that Jameson finds congenial. He applauds the analysis of discourse, the attention to first and second languages, and the suggestions about the mind-crippling limitations of ordinary American speech, which believes itself so down-to-earth but is in truth so falsely abstract. The reader is reminded of Hegel's challenge to the empiricists: "Who thinks abstractly? The citizen." However, Jameson sees *Habits* itself falling victim to these dangers of language. The resummoning of the republican and biblical traditions without analysis of the precise social history in which they found a place in American life, and of the specific contradictions in social existence that they in their own time both addressed and embodied, is, he believes, another version of nostalgia, the loss of the sense of history. Jameson likes the term *habits* as a mediation between attitudes and values on the one hand and social practices and institutions on the other.

Finally, however, Jameson sees *Habits* as another chapter in American exceptionalism. The authors did not take socialist thought or attitudes seriously, he says, because such perspectives have no wide or conspicuous purchase in America. What *Habits* fails to see is the much wider sweep of history in which America plays only one of the roles, and not necessarily, in Jameson's way of thinking, an exemplary one. It is unclear whether in this criticism Jameson is with or against Harding. They both allege that there is a wider narrative to be told, but it might be argued that Harding sees in the land itself, and in the mingling of voices within American space, a singular human exception.

PRACTICAL REASON

"How ought we to live? How do we think about how to live?" These first two sentences in *Habits of the Heart* are questions of ethics, questions of practical reason. An engaging public conversation about ethics, about how we ought to live, distinguishes *Habits* and gives rhetorical power to the book. When Ralph B. Potter applies his grammar of moral discourse to *Habits*, he has qualms because *Habits* engages in practical reason and does not merely describe the practical reason used by others. His "grammar" is a theory about practical reason and about the functions an adequate theory of practical reason must perform, but it is not a normative theory of practical reason: it does not specify the characteristics of a just society, the moral virtues of a good person, or the duties and obligations that moral persons have to one another.

Potter rightly sees the fourfold structure of Parsons's system at work in *Habits*. But Potter does not appear to realize that Parsons is in the background and a communitarian ethic is in the foreground. *Habits* is a story; it has a narrative; it engages in normative, practical reason. Apparently, Potter would have *Habits* engage in descriptive ethics only. And it might have done so—it could have been a good work in descriptive ethics and interpretive sociology. But that would have been a very different book from the normative critique of American life and culture the authors wrote. Thus although Potter raises his objections to *Habits* with an internal critique, he seems fundamentally to disagree with the concept of practical reason finding its voice in the book.

Jeffrey Stout is sympathetic to the notion of practical reason at work in *Habits*, even if he also has some disagreements with the book. Stout gives an alternative interpretation of the interviews with Brian Palmer and, rather than finding a "first language of individualism," Stout claims the interviewer asked Brian inappropriate and perhaps leading Socratic questions. After offering an alternative way of understanding Brian Palmer, and challenging the normative language used in *Habits* to interpret the interviews, Stout presents a devastating critique of Alasdair MacIntyre's *After Virtue*. He then draws on Richard Rorty to defend "pragmatic liberalism" against the critique of liberalism in *Habits*. It is not that the critique of liberalism in *Habits* is invalid for a certain version of liberalism, but simply that liberalism is more complex, and comes in more varieties, than *Habits* recognizes. Stout argues that normative discourse in a liberal society (where there is a limited but real agreement on the good) is also more complicated to interpret than either MacIntyre or *Habits* acknowledges. After showing how complicated our notions of morality and civility are, Stout returns to *Habits*, takes up its use of MacIntyre's concept of a social practice, and interprets that concept as a helpful way of distinguishing between instrumental goods external to an activity (for example, the fame gained from writing an essay) and goods internal to an activity (the writer's satisfaction while reading some good books and composing a good paper).

The authors of *Habits* largely agree with Stout's ten-point summary of his position as it relates to *Habits*. They rightly object to being labeled foundationalists. They remain unconvinced that liberalism in America is as complex as Stout claims. And Stout to the contrary, they believe the interviews support their view that utilitarian individualism is a "first language" most Americans use to talk about the good life or the good society. They argue that Stout has wrongly characterized as "Socratic" the style of the interviews they conducted to write *Habits*.[9]

In *The Flight from Authority* (1981), Stout defends tradition-based justifications for moral language in ways that buttress a normative appeal to the biblical and civic republican traditions. Stout and the authors of *Habits* are close to one another at the deep level of maintaining that a conversation with tradition is normative for practical reason. It remains unclear whether Stout's "pragmatic liberalism" belongs to the civic republican tradition. We require a concept of civic republicanism as a tradition and need to see how that tradition is formed, delimited, and carried forward. (Later we will see that Christopher Lasch's essay is helpful in thinking through this challenge.)

Bernard Yack assesses the communitarian critique of liberalism and argues that both classical liberal thinkers and contemporary communitarian thinkers (including the authors of *Habits*) dissociate individuals from their actual social attachments. Yack makes a critical distinction between philosophic dissociation and sociological dissociation. Liberal thinkers dissociate actual persons from the particularities of their social commitments and place them in a state of nature (or "original" situation) in order to gain a general point of view by which to provide a moral critique of the social order. This general point of view, which is frequently equated with the moral point of view, often makes a claim that moral reasoning is objective and universal.

Communitarian critics of liberal thinkers often complain that liberal thought denies that human life is always and inherently social. Yack counters this challenge by arguing that the philosophic dissociation among individuals in the state of nature assumed by liberal theorists need not entail a sociological dissociation among actual individuals living in a given social world. Hence, Yack insists, one cannot simply assume that a critique of liberal theory provides a good basis for a critique of liberal practice. Because all actual human beings are inherently social, individuals constituted by liberal society are also social beings with liberal attachments and commitments. Therefore, communitarian critics of liberalism cannot disencumber actual individuals from shared and acquired social characteristics without specific justification.

That all individuals are social does not help one evaluate competing forms of human community. The cultural preconditions of good political community are at issue between the defenders of liberal society and the advocates of communitarian society. And that is precisely what the authors of *Habits* recognize in their responses to Stout, Potter, and Yack. Indeed, success in focusing on culture as central to community, politics, and meaningful human life is what makes *Habits* such an important book.

CIVIC PRACTICES

Christopher Lasch argues against a republic of virtue and for a republic of practices. He agrees with Stout, and with the position we are taking, that civic republican thought does not need a strong agreement on *the* common good. If the state protects practices, rather than promotes a substantive notion of virtue (*the* common good), the authoritarianism of the republican communitarian tradition, which liberals rightly fear, can be minimized.

Rejecting the nostalgic quest for "the little community" of shared values as an adequate basis for communitarian thought, Lasch argues that public conversation is what builds social solidarity. He shows how it is possible to take a tradition seriously by being in conversation with it without adopting a "slavish, unquestioning attitude toward authority." His concept of tradition is a community of discourse perduring through time.[10] Lasch's communitarians are in conversation with the past and they come to understand their culture and themselves through conversation with it. Because communitarians understand themselves as tradition-shaped social and cultural beings, tradition, not the individual, is the locus of appeal for this form of practical reason. Tradition bestows, or fails to bestow, dignity upon the individual. As we interpret Lasch's argument, Stout, Dewey, Rorty, MacIntyre, and the later Rawls would all be communitarians. And with the exception of MacIntyre, who has a pre-liberal orientation, they all propose a post-liberal retrieval of the republican tradition.

Communitarian thought represents an understanding of civic ecology in which a theory of society and its living traditions always underlies moral reasoning. A conversation with living traditions is required as the present is interpreted and the future shaped, but not a substantive consensus on *the* common good, which has wrongly characterized its pre-liberal formulations.

A narrative account of society in which public reason is historically situated as a conversation with tradition delimits communitarian thought in *Habits* and characterizes the civic republican tradition as a communitarian tradition. Moreover, unless a society carries forward, and is carried by, a totally unified civic tradition, which has seldom (if ever) been true, communitarian moral reason will also be comparative, as it is in *Habits*. Such moral reason requires a conversation with disparate voices from the past (in *Habits*, the three major traditions). And before one dismisses this kind of thinking as inherently conservative, one might want first to study the prophets of ancient Israel who appealed to the covenant tradition and to the history of God's having called Israel into covenant, in making their radical criticism of contemporary social conditions. Amos, Hosea, Jeremiah, and Isaiah were communitarian thinkers who, in conversation with tradition, imagined a new moral ecology for their nation and its people. While this form of moral reasoning is narrative in structure and requires a conversation with tradition, it is not inherently conservative, in any ordinary sense.

Lasch's essay advances the argument proposed in *Habits*. Because *Habits* is such an ambitious book, it raises issues, such as the relation of communitarianism to civic republicanism, and each of these to varieties of liberalism, that will require a great deal of theoretical work. While Stout and Lasch take on these theoretical issues, much work remains to be done before this post-liberal option in social philosophy is as clearly formulated as certain versions of liberalism, Marxism, or classical civic republicanism.

In the spirit of *Habits*, William F. May offers a critique of liberal society. His focus is the professional-client relationship. Working from the Lockean myth of origins of the state, May finds the justification for the liberal state in the "cutting of a deal" that: (1) postulates an original condition of human autonomy; (2) orients society to the satisfaction of human wants and interests; (3) traces the origin of the state to supreme evil rather than supreme good: (4) encourages a passive rather than an active notion of citizenship; and (5) understands leadership as transactional rather than as transformational. May applies this analysis to the professional-client relationship and shows how it supports an adversarial notion of such relations. As an alternative, he proposes a collaborative relationship and points to hopeful signs that it may be emerging.

Ernest Wallwork agrees with *Habits* that therapeutic attitudes in their popular form are radically individualistic. Therapy tends to breed suspicion of community bonds as threats to self-autonomy and self-expression. The result is an individualistic understanding of human nature, in which a mysterious psychological self finds its fulfillment only by rejecting all personal and social commitments, including familial, religious, and community bonds as aspects of a shared morality. This highly individualistic model of therapy, as portrayed in *Habits*, is an eclectic mixture of indigenous American modes (Rogersian therapy) and imports (Gestalt) that most easily absorb the individualism of American life. Margaret Oldham (*H,* 14) reflects this therapeutic ideal.

Wallwork focuses on the difference between the individualistic understanding of human nature in popular American therapies and its alternative in Freud.[11] Wallwork shows that Freud consistently stressed the formative role of human bonds—from the mother-child relation of infancy through the mutuality of sexual intimacy to the adult goal of an ever-expanding network of libidinal ties with others. In Freud's view, the process of human development does not entail a movement toward a self-sufficient isolation from others, but a transition from a need-driven dependency on others to ego-active relations of interdependency with others. The myth of "radical individualism" was no more credible for Freud than it is for the authors of *Habits*.

Habits also presents the Freudian alternative as more social than individualistic. The one Freudian therapist who appears in the book (Ruth Levy, 136f.) represents strong community concerns and a social understanding of human development. Her views are characterized by the authors in the following way: "[Therapy can] help us recover the narrative unity of our lives woven through family ties into the social tapestry of communities situated in a given time, place, and culture. . . . Insofar as therapy reveals our identity to be inseparable from our history, and our personal history to be essentially social, it returns the separate self to communities of practical meaning" (*H,* 136). But beyond identifying some similarities between *Habits* and Freud, Wallwork argues for the unique contribution a Freudian perspective may bring to the discussion.

On the one hand, Wallwork holds that Freud is needed as a moral corrective for any uncritical affirmation of human bonds. In his view, any affirmation of the intrinsic goodness of bonds needs to be balanced by a Freudian insight into the always possible perversion of some bonds, especially the manipulation of the affections and guilt feelings of a weaker partner for the sake of the stronger. *Habits* hints at the legitimacy of a therapeutic critique of "traditional relationships and their moral basis" (140), but does not offer concrete stories of psychological manipulation, whether in marriage, neighborhood, religious communities, or politics. Wallwork (like Elshtain, Lasch, and Potter) reminds us of the "darker side" of pre-liberal civic republicanism, as of all communitarian bonds.

On the other hand, Wallwork contends that if the prospect held forth in *Habits* for renewing public life is to gain wide acceptance, it needs to be connected to several of the culturally dominant forms of human understanding: not only the biblical and republican traditions but also the therapeutic in its original Freudian form.

Wallwork, like Stout, invites the authors of *Habits* to enter a broader conversation with America's cultural traditions. His assumption is that an individualistic model of therapy can be reformed more appropriately by therapeutic insight gained from Freud than by moral argument based elsewhere.

RELIGIOUS PRACTICE

The four essays in this section concentrate on the prospect for religious practice in America as it affects and is affected by the broader cultural life. This culture, as we have seen, is by no means simple. It is a web of traditions, social classes, ideologies, and practical constraints, over which in some divinely guided way (as Americans have supposed) the Constitution casts a loose order and control.

American Catholicism has had the peculiar historical experience of being a minority community with the traditional conceptual resources of an established church. That is, it has had to forge its way as part of a pluralism of competing religious denominations and somehow make this experience intelligible in terms of a long intellectual inheritance in which church and state were close allies. What has developed has been a social and theological ethics as articulated by the bishops that capitalizes on the rich Catholic sense of layers or orders in any society and in laity, clergy, and public and private conscience in particular. In this tradition there are degrees of religiosity, of consensus, and of participation. It is, after all, a tradition built out of millennia of adaptation, compromise, decline, renewal, and reconceptualization. David Hollenbach shows how this tradition can be exploited in such a way that the bishops can appeal to and at the same time try to build a larger American consensus in social and moral issues than that represented simply by the Catholic church. Catholic theory can recognize that in one sense of American pluralism it is only one voice among many, but that no voice is simply one as each confirms what it has in common with others and seeks to establish a broader common ground. This possibility, which emanates directly from the kind of tradition that is the Catholic church, is obviously quite compatible with the ideal of conversation and of mixed, but cumulative, traditions central to *Habits*. Hollenbach's sense is that American Catholicism is in the main further along the way toward defining community within a pluralistic society than any other so-called minority voice. Whether the Church's voice remains in the minority, as one among many, is not known a priori. (In contrast, for Stanley Hauerwas it is a certainty a priori that the Church will remain one minority voice among others: evangelism or preaching may address social concerns but will not, or should not, move toward a Settlement, Constantinian or otherwise.)

How does an institutional posture like that of the Catholic bishops comport with the Constitution, and with the tradition of a separation of church and state? One answer, which Hollenbach and Richard Wightman Fox explicitly discuss and which is indirectly addressed by J. Irwin Trotter and Hauerwas, is that of John Courtney Murray, in whose view the separation places a limit on the claims of Caesar to command the conscience of any citizen. Separation means that there is a free, open forum for the discussion of the ultimate questions. The Catholic church (among the churches) can do its work in this arena. However, as Hollenbach suggests in his discussion of such recent ethical theories as those of Rawls and Michael Walzer, the arena encompasses both the "public square" of Richard J. Neuhaus and the smaller subpublics constituted by the various communities of American pluralism. In Elshtain's phrase, this space may be *contested*: it matters what voices speak and what gets accepted in the square.

Hauerwas systematically discounts the notion that Christians should be party to contesting a public space. For him Christianity has no essential claim on the space outside the life of the Church itself. This position is, in his view, reinforced by historical experience in which Christians become oppressors. He sees Jerry Falwell as the symptom of the kind of contention for the public space that has led to the persecution of Jews and has been, indeed, one of the sources of totalitarianism in recent Western history. Consequently Hauerwas is skeptical of any call, as in *Habits*, to civic virtue that is sponsored more broadly than by a confessional community.

Running through all these discussions is the troubled definition of liberalism. As Fox points out, the terms *liberal* and *conservative* have shifted and reshifted in such puzzling and spectacular ways in American life that great care has to be taken in using them at all. When *liberal* came to mean a person who believes in the government's solicitous use of expertise to solve large-scale social problems, the term had been stretched out of any relation to its use in the eighteenth and even nineteenth century. Yet it is possible to trace the route that led from the earlier to the later uses. Reinhold Niebuhr's intellectual career is examined by Fox in illustration of the way these fortunes of *liberalism* have their effect in theology. Niebuhr was systematically suspicious of "righteous" action, whether by the Church or by governments. He believed that society had its own deeply flawed logic and that the business of the theologian was to examine, in terms of the fundamental relation between God and persons, how this logic would always work itself out in the search for social justice or stability. In this respect he might have been taken to agree with the position argued here by Hauerwas, except that Niebuhr, according to Fox, never quite set aside the possibility of a moral consensus in the society. Less confident than Murray, he nonetheless found himself as a "liberal" theologian contesting the square. He would have appreciated a strong affinity between his finely nuanced sense of the ambiguities in individualism and community and the effort of *Habits* to display these ambiguities and the way through them in American practice.

According to Trotter, the move in the free churches toward use of a lectionary is much more than a piece of recent American church history. It signals that these churches recognize how fragmented, individualistic, atomistic, and therefore unsatisfactory has been the image of the Christian person in their preaching and in their liturgy. In the dissatisfaction with this aspect of the free church tradition and in the current movement toward certain Catholic emphases on the importance of community, Trotter sees signs of real sensitivity to the issues laid out in *Habits*. There is a sense in which the free churches provide the prime evidence for the central thesis of *Habits*, for it is precisely in these communities that the rootless, migratory, fragmented personal experience of so many Americans has found its religious expression.

PRACTICES IN HABITS

Robert Bellah concludes this volume with a substantial response to friends and critics of *Habits*. Bellah seizes this occasion to write an origi-

nal essay arguing that the idea of practices provides *Habits* with conceptual and thematic unity.

Bellah's response reflects the wide-ranging conversations, confer-
ences, and symposia in which the authors of *Habits* have been engaged
since the book first appeared. His essay demonstrates that the ambitious-
ness of *Habits*, its openness to the diverse methodologies abroad in
American cultural criticism, represents both rewards and hazards. The
rewards come from those whose voices have been heard in *Habits* and
who sense that some next steps toward a broader amassing argument are
now possible. These immediate friends of the book are represented in
this volume by Peacock, Stout, and Lasch. Bellah finds in May, Delattre,
and Trotter allies of a different kind; their essays, independent in derivation from *Habits*, he takes as supporting briefs for a new look at
American practices.

The hazards are more complex. They appear first in those critics
whom some readers might suppose to be friendly look-alikes whose own
vigorous cultural criticism may seem compatible with Bellah's diagnosis
but whose recommendations are more narrowly and schematically focused and perhaps (to Bellah's mind) headed in an opposite direction.
Yack, Fox, and possibly Hollenbach are among these. Bellah is careful to
identify the nuances that distinguish his argument from theirs, and he
chooses to do this by working through a fresh discussion of practices as
the key notion of *Habits*.

Another kind of hazard is the fear of insidious openings and sinister
implications. When *Habits* calls for a restored meaning of citizenship and
a new focus on the common good, does this represent, as Elshtain and
Jameson suggest, a potential opening to a dangerous new militarism, nationalism, or exceptionalism? When *Habits* deplores America's spiritual
confusion, does it, as Hauerwas implies, lend itself to the rhetoric of the
radical religious right? When it challenges the overgeneralization of the
therapeutic model, is Wallwork correct that we risk being drawn into
the latent agenda of know-nothings and welfare-baiters? When it attempts to rectify the weakness of tradition, are we being asked—as Albert and Harding fear—to abandon the freedoms wrestled out of tradition at such cost by the feminist and civil rights movements? When *Habits*
longs to restore a broadly shared second language of community, does it
invite what Potter sees as a sharper and more violent cacophony of the
several narrower communities of discourse that endure at present their
own uneasy truce and tolerance? These questions arise, Bellah claims,
from one-dimensional readings of a pluralistic argument. He points out
as prima facie evidence against such fears that neither the radical right,
the new militarism, antifeminism, nor racism has found any support on
a single page of *Habits*.

But, as we have seen, the sharpest naysayers to *Habits* are those who believe that its pluralistic commitment cannot do the work of a coherent and well-founded critique of the culture. They are represented here by Harding, Hauerwas, and Jameson, and it is to these three that Bellah devotes his most impassioned response. He reminds us that his own career has been marked by an active concern for social, racial, and economic justice.

The American longing for community will not be satisfied by any of the recent efforts that have laid claim to telling the story of the continent. The social practices that will create and sustain community will in Bellah's view be more subtle, more complicated in their relation to the biblical and republican traditions that have nurtured public commitment in this land than any beliefs or theories—religious, social, or economic— that have been nurtured in the modern spirit of radical individualism.

PART ONE

Culture

ONE

America as a Cultural System

James L. Peacock

"The primary focus of our research was not psychological, or even primarily sociological, but rather cultural" (*H*, x).

This statement, inserted without fanfare or elaborate conceptual exposition, defines precisely and comprehensively the focus of *Habits of the Heart*. The authors quite consistently hew to that mode of analysis which they term "cultural." They do not, however, spell out and emphasize what this kind of analysis entails and what it does not. As is appropriate to a work intended for a nonspecialist audience, *Habits* does not dwell on the conceptual apparatus that underlies it but moves straight to example and substance. Appropriate and necessary, this strategy nonetheless runs a risk. Understating their conceptual framework, the authors may be misunderstood by some who, failing to grasp exactly their intent and approach, take them to task for omission of what they properly exclude or misinterpret what they do say. Just such a misunderstanding is indicated by the comments of some readers, and a volume such as the present one can contribute importantly by highlighting the conceptual premises of the original work.

What, then, does the term *cultural* imply concerning the conceptual framework of the book? Following the prefatory allusion to "cultural," the term is more formally introduced in the second chapter, "Culture and Character: The Historical Conversation." "Cultural tradition" is defined here, albeit casually: "So long as it is vital, the cultural tradition of a people—its symbols, ideals, and ways of feeling—is always an argument about the meaning of the destiny its members share. Cultures are dramatic conversations about things that matter to their participants . . . " (*H*, 27). Culture, here termed "cultural traditions," then, is "symbols, ideals, and ways of feeling." Such a complex is seen not as a rigid framework, but instead as a dynamic process, part of "dramatic conversations

37

about things that matter." From these conversations, the authors abstract four themes. Two of these, the biblical and republican traditions, define a normative framework for American morality, while the other two, expressive and utilitarian individualism, at once derive from and oppose the traditions. These themes define the "symbols, ideals, and ways of feeling" that constitute the core of American culture. The book then proceeds to explore, graphically and provocatively, how these cultural themes, and the dilemmas they imply, are part of American "conversations," including especially the conversations the authors have with their informants, the Brians, Waynes, Joes, and Margarets.

Culture is of course a term widely used in the Western intellectual community, but only some of these usages correspond to that of *Habits*. The authors use the term in a way defined with some precision in sociology. Their notion of "culture" is quite close to that formulated most cogently by Bellah's mentor, Talcott Parsons, and now fairly pervasive in the social sciences. Although Bellah and his coauthors veer slightly from Parsons's original definition, nevertheless it is illuminating to review the Parsonian conception (see, e.g., Parsons and Shils, 1951).

Parsons, following Max Weber, saw human experience as "action," which is to say, meaningful behavior. For purposes of analysis, one can distinguish various aspects or "systems" entailed in all human action. The three major systems are the personality system, the social system, and the cultural system. The personality system includes those processes and traits that sustain the individual; Freud's image of the personality as constituted by id, ego, and superego is one way of conceptualizing this system, though Parsons added a fourth aspect, "identity," which defines the articulation of the personality with roles defined by the next level, the social system. The social system revolves around relationships among actors-in-roles and relationships among groups, and it prescribes these relationships by norms and social values. The cultural system is oriented toward formulating meaning and defining morality; its components are beliefs and existential conceptions as well as symbols, which express such conceptions and moral values that legitimize the more specific, institutionally focused values and norms of the social system.

Even in a simplified summary like this, the Parsonian conceptualization is rather dense; it is easy to see why the authors of *Habits* would not wish to refer to it directly or elaborate a similar schema in their book. However, such a scheme is useful in keeping our thoughts straight. Two points should be noted. One is that the three systems are not three separate things; they are three aspects of action, of the human experience. Usefully distinguished for some purposes, these systems are, in Parsons's term, "analytical," rather than concrete. The second point is that, of the three systems, the cultural system is ultimate. It delineates the premises that set the foundation for society and individual; it formulates the beliefs, values, and existential assumptions that underlie their thoughts and actions. From both these points it follows that social and individual behaviors necessarily involve cultural aspects. Conversely, it is difficult and perhaps not very useful to discuss culture in the abstract, separate from social and individual contexts. It is more telling and revealing to grasp culture in life—in action, or, as in *Habits,* in the conversations with informants.

My principal argument here is that *Habits* is quite consistent in emphasizing a cultural level of analysis, but that readers do not always understand, appreciate, or accept this. Consequently, they read the book as if it were working at the level of social or psychological analysis, or they read into the cultural analysis premises that were not intended.

How does one know what interpretation readers make of a work? Most readers are silent, except for those special ones singled out as reviewers. For my sources concerning readers' perceptions, I shall draw on a cross section. Occasionally I refer to written reviews, but most of my data come from comments heard from colleagues from a variety of disciplines who have discussed *Habits* in several forums.[1] Rather than cite the remarks of particular speakers, I summarize these remarks as three types of critique, which correspond to the three levels of Parsonsian analysis: the sociological, psychological, and cultural.

The sociological critique finds *Habits* lacking in its analysis of the social system. The work is taken to task for its vagueness in identifying the social structure of American society. What is the class structure, the community structure, the family structure, the religious institutional structure? How are relationships arranged and roles defined? What is the constitution of groups? In a society as large as America, what relationship is envisioned between the nation and the local communities? What are the roles of power and of economics? Moving toward activism, perhaps with a socialist cast, this line of criticism regrets not only the vagueness of *Habits'* sociological analysis but also the vagueness of its prescriptions for social action (especially in the final chapter). Paradoxically, this line also tends to criticize the book for too close a focus on, and perhaps identity with, a single social sector, the white middle class; the corollary is to dismiss the prescriptions for action that are given because the working class is neither canvassed nor mobilized in constructing them. According to these critics, one reason for scorning the book's focus is that the concerns and hopes of the middle class—for identity, purpose, and "feeling good about itself"—are abhorrently silly when compared to the desperate problems faced by most of the human species. More broadly, *Habits* is seen as Pollyanna-like in locating its hopes for social transformation in attitudes, in "habits of the heart"; realistically, it is argued, society will not change without movement at the level of political and economic forces, the *Realfaktoren.* Finally, at least one critic chides the book for ignoring the one social movement that offers any realistic hope of fulfilling its goals, socialism (Ehrenreich, 1985).

The psychological critique is, generally, that the psychological dynamics which explain apathy or other problems are not explicated. *Habits* is found wanting in the depth of analysis of its characters, who are treated superficially rather than engaged in sufficient depth to reveal their "total lives" (Gusfield 1986, 57). Of special concern is that the work denigrates psychotherapy. As one therapist stated, she was afraid the book would dissuade some people who had serious psychological problems from seeking the therapy they needed.

The cultural critique is of a different type than the others. Here the sin is of commission rather than omission. *Habits* is accused of a narrowly Christian apologetic. Harking back to the biblical tradition, *Habits* sees American culture too narrowly, as Christian in its base. In terms of action, it proposes, rather in the fashion of the Social Gospel or even the Christian Right, to diminish the separation of church and state and to transform America into a Christian state. If not that blatant, at least the book is sectarian, couched primarily within the domain of liberal Protestantism, addressing problems internal to that tradition; it is not sufficiently attuned to the totality of a pluralistic society that includes significant elements of non-Christians and non-Christianity.

All three of these critiques are cogent at some level. Nevertheless, each fails to grasp the level of analysis at which the book purports to work. Let us return to the text to review its arguments before considering these criticisms.

Regarding the social constitution of America, *Habits* counterposes two kinds of community, the "lifestyle enclave" and the "community of memory." The lifestyle enclave was once the domain of youth, but is now for adults at midlife and beyond. It is not a true community for it lacks what Max Weber would have called the "brotherhood of men" and Emile Durkheim, the "moral community"; it is merely a narcissistic, inward-looking enclave wherein the expressive self is expressed. The community of memory, by contrast, is—or was—a moral community, overly rigid perhaps, but bound by moral obligation grounded in tradition, such as the biblical and the republican traditions. In the past, such a community could be found in the small church-based town. In the present, a remnant of this community is found among the fundamentalists who, whatever their narrowness, at least have a moral basis; Les Newman, a Southern evangelical Baptist, has what Ted Oster of Silicon Valley lacks, a tentative community of memory—a church based on everyone sharing an experience with Christ (*H*, 155–57). The authors find that beyond the localized community, Americans have difficulty envisioning the total society. They may get involved and join everything, but they have no strong sense of obligation to a larger society beyond the enclave. Like Montesquieu and Madison, the authors see a need to transform private virtue into public virtue, to get good people into public life, to develop a commitment to the larger society. Retreat into the enclave simply creates a vacuum into which the bureaucrats, the experts, and the managers move, ultimately depriving Americans of their cherished individualism by substituting a kind of totalitarianism; economic liberalism is not liberating for it simply gives power to the experts. Among the directions of transformation proposed are that we be rewarded socially instead of simply monetarily, that moral ecology be treated as socially significant, and that in other ways Americans be integrated into a kind of movement toward reestablishing society.

Psychotherapy is the psychological phenomenon most explicitly analyzed. The problem with psychotherapy, according to *Habits*, is that therapeutic values are becoming cultural values. In America, "being good" becomes "feeling good." The objectified moral goodness of John Winthrop obeying God's will or of Thomas Jefferson's natural laws turns into the subjective goodness of getting what you want and enjoying it. Yet while therapy erects values implicitly, it actively distrusts morality, which it regards as mere "intellectualizing" (*H*, 129, 131). This antagonism is itself cultural, rooted in the "powerful cultural fiction that we not only can, but must, make up our deepest beliefs in the isolation of our private selves" (*H*, 65). Finally, even just "feeling good" is not really the end of therapy, for it smuggles into this seeming hedonism the asceticism of the rationalized Protestant-ethic culture; therapy is demanding in its "relentless insistence on consciousness and the endless scanning of one's own and others' feelings while making moment-by-moment calculations of the shifting cost/benefit balances" (*H*, 139). Here the calculating managerial style is extended, by a collusion of managerial and therapeutic values, into "intimacy, home, and community" (*H*, 48).

What place does *Habits* give Christianity? The biblical tradition is one of the two cultural traditions singled out as central to the American heritage. The Church is noted as one of the two institutions capable of challenging the popular culture of incoherence, the other being the University. Two particular kinds of churches are singled out for praise, as well as criticism, in terms of potential for defining a moral community. One is the evangelical church, which does maintain "a vision of the concrete moral commitments that bind church members" (*H*, 232) but is faulted for doing this too exclusively. The other is an Episcopal church, called St. Stephens, which is seen as more balanced. But it is suggested that an effective public church would need to bring all major Christian strands—church, sect, and mystical—into play to serve as a base for moral community.[2]

These, then, are the analyses. How just are the criticisms? My argument is that the sociological and psychological criticisms misconstrue the level at which the authors are working; cultural criticism gets the level right, but somewhat distorts the intent.

Emphasizing the cultural level of analysis, *Habits* delves into the social only to the extent necessary to demonstrate the problems that derive from America's cultural confusion: the loss of a community of memory, the lack of a sense of linkage between the local community and the wider society, the failure of good people to enter public life. It is true that the social analysis and the social proposals are not fully developed, but this could be interpreted as a result of the commitment to the cultural level of analysis.[3]

Similarly, it is true that *Habits* does not probe deeply into psychological terrain. For example, one would like to know more about the life histories and life cycles of the informants, not just to grasp their psychologies but to grasp the cultural models that guide these processes. The work justifiably limits its scope. Concerning the critique of therapeutic culture, the point of *Habits* is not to decry psychotherapy as such; the authors would doubtless agree that psychotherapy can be a valuable form of treatment for various individuals. Rather, their point is to expose the dangers that arise when therapeutic assumptions are incorporated into a society's moral ecology.

Finally, we consider the critique that the book expresses essentially a Christian viewpoint. It is true that the authors argue that the church and similar religious organizations are among the most viable institutions and value systems in America, and they are potentially a means for the regeneration of American culture. Such a conclusion does not, however, necessarily derive from Christian dogma.[4]

In fact, an analysis of the senior author's previous scholarship suggests that this conclusion could follow as much from a comparative religious sociology as from any sectarian creed. (This is not to claim that the two *are* necessarily independent but that logically they could be; the tack *Habits* takes can be explained by the sociology without recourse to the creed.) In support of this supposition, let us consider briefly some of Robert Bellah's previous work.

Bellah has done important work on Islam and other religions, but his first well-known study was of religion in Japan. In *Tokugawa Religion* (1957), he argued as follows. At a critical juncture in Japanese history, the Japanese were motivated to modernize by a kind of Protestant ethic. This Protestant ethic was not Protestantism as such but was forged from a mixture of Buddhism, Shintoism, and Confucianism. It harnessed a drive to work hard to an intense loyalty to groups—family, factory, nation—and their leaders, including the emperor. A task so lowly as making toothpicks became a glorious endeavor, a great task for the glory of the toothpick factory, the nation, and the emperor; such work was even an intensely religious experience, leading to something like salvation; but the salvation was firmly social.

Several years later, in an essay entitled "Religious Evolution" (1964), Bellah argued that world religions and associated societies pass through five types—primitive, archaic, historic, early modern, and modern. The early modern was exemplified by the Protestant ethic, European and American style, but with parallels in Japan and elsewhere. The essence of the Protestant ethic was to define a coherent ideal, believed to be grounded in an objectively existing otherworld, in terms of which one was driven to reform this world. Belief in the city of God incited continuous reform of the city of man—a transcendental base for social ethic.

With modernity, objectivism was replaced by subjectivism. Instead of truth there were truths; instead of an otherworld, there were as many worlds as there were persons to construct them subjectively. Thomas Jefferson foreshadowed this tendency by asserting, "I am a sect myself," and the individualistic sectarianism culminates in people like Sheila, who is quoted in *Habits* as saying, "I believe in Sheilaism." This mixture of individualism, subjectivism, and pluralism might engender a certain creative ferment, but it would not motivate the single-minded social reformism sustained by the Protestant ethic and the early modern type. However, viewing modernity in the abstract, in 1964, Bellah was more sanguine about it than when viewing it in the concrete, in America, today.

One can see in Bellah's early, cross-cultural studies the same hope pinned to a Protestant ethic, or something analogous, as is apparent in *Habits of the Heart*. Possibly this hope does reflect a liberal Protestant bias, as some have suggested, but this notion of the Protestant ethic is not a theological concept, drawn directly from Protestantism. Rather, it is a sociological concept, drawn from a sociological theory, based on cross-cultural analysis; the most influential theoretical framework is that set forth by Max Weber. From comparative studies of Asia and the West, Weber, like Bellah, argued that something like a Protestant ethic—some kind of transcendental system of values both metaphysically grounded and socially binding—was necessary for the kind of dynamic yet orderly social development that unfolded in the West, especially in England and America. Others, such as S. N. Eisenstadt at the University of Jerusalem (1968), have generalized the argument beyond Christianity and the West, as did Bellah in his study of Japan and in other studies.

The authors of *Habits* confine their analysis to America; but the basis of their argument is much broader. Their pained, though patient, dismay at the shortsighted narcissistic perspectives of their informants—the yuppies, the therapists, and even the activists—comes from these Americans' forsaking of not only the biblical and republican traditions of American heritage, but also a certain kind of human heritage. This human heritage is something like a Protestant ethic, not in a narrowly religious sense or merely as a social ethic, but as a cultural system.

Thus the argument in *Habits* must not be evaluated in terms of a narrowly American perspective; the authors are neither failed social scientists who lack the courage to go all the way with socialism nor doctrinaire proponents of liberal Protestantism. Though the authors draw on both socialism and Protestantism, it is in terms of an implicitly cross-cultural comparative framework that *Habits* proposes the Protestant ethic–like cultural revitalization of America.

If, as I have argued, *Habits* sustains an analysis at the cultural level, then the book should be evaluated at this level, rather than sociologically, psychologically, or in terms of an alleged creedal bias. As a cultural analysis, *Habits* is certainly cogent and telling, yet one can always discern biases. I shall mention two, the first trivial, the second perhaps more fundamental.

Sir Edward Evans-Pritchard once distinguished the cultural from the social level of analysis in the following way. He noted that Christians remove their hats but keep on their shoes when they pray, while Muslims remove their shoes but keep on their hats. That they are both showing respect is the relevant social fact. The difference in clothing, which Evans-Pritchard termed a "cultural" difference, is trivial, for it is a difference of style, not of basic pattern (1962, 16). One could argue against Evans-Pritchard that, in fact, such seemingly trivial differences in style may point to profound meanings; one can also argue that such small differences are often significant markers of identity with one group or subculture as opposed to another.

The issue is relevant in considering whether *Habits* adequately captures the cultural diversity of America. Obviously the research is localized in California, despite efforts at including some informants from the South and New England. This skewed localization is balanced by grounding the analysis in traditions central to American culture—the Jeffersonian and the Hamiltonian, for example—shrewdly chosen to represent not only different ideologies but different regional bases. Nevertheless, it is the style as much as the substance of the Californian informants— their language, their imagery, their expressions—that sets the tone of *Habits*, and these jar when placed beside certain other American subcultural styles. How different do my own informants, the Primitive Baptists of the Blue Ridge mountains, sound, as they preach the Institutes of Calvin in the language of the King James Bible (Peacock 1987). Granted, the Primitive Baptists may be at the extreme, and we know that even these mountaineers have Californianism beamed into their satellites, but the fact remains that ethnic, regional, and class differences in America are immense and the middle-class Californianism of *Habits* is only one stream of American culture. The problem with this criticism is, how could we have done better? Failing voluminous tomes that would defeat the purpose, the resort to a synthesis of central values and traditions exemplified by necessarily localized informants is probably the best solution. Every reader who feels not quite like Wayne, Joe, Brian, or Margaret must ask what the difference is, whether of style or of substance, and whether the central analysis is seriously affected by the difference.

A more serious question is whether the very conception and circumstance of the work predisposes it toward its conclusion.

An irony of *Habits*, which certainly does not escape the authors, is that their own methods manifest the same alienated individualism that they decry in their culture. One particular method especially illustrates this individualism: the interview.

Although the authors' primary data are interviews, these are not their only source. The interviews are taken as vehicles for expression of large cultural traditions and are then interpreted in terms of a range of other studies and insights. Still, the interview is the medium through which we are made to know American culture. While the interview is a staple of sociological research, it is worth considering how individual interviews abstract the informant from his or her social and cultural milieu. Might the interview itself predispose toward the expression of individualism? Surely, we should not leap to assert any simple equation between method and content, but we should be alert to such a possibility and at least consider alternative methods.

Anthropologists characteristically prefer not to rely on interviews. The favored anthropological approach to discerning culture is participant observation: the researcher lives in a community and from that experience constructs an interpretation of the cultural patterns the group actually follows, as distinct from those they merely profess. Indeed, a standard rule of thumb in ethnographic work is that there is always considerable discrepancy between verbalized ideals and actual behavior. A related anthropological precept is that cultural premises are frequently most powerfully expressed not in individual statements but in collective performances, such as rituals and ceremonies that affirm central values and beliefs; this insight is not of course original to anthropology, but was stated most forcefully in modern social science by Emile Durkheim.

The authors of *Habits* do cite anthropological participant-observation studies of American communities, and they make reference to collective performance in American life. While the values expressed in cultural performances might not have led the authors to different conclusions than those inferred from the interviews, it is suggestive that at least one study of American collective rituals (Warner 1953) has produced a picture of American culture as rather more cohesive.

Beyond the question of diagnosis, it is possible that an anthropological slant would have yielded additional recommendations and remedies. Notably lacking in the authors' prescriptions for "transforming American culture" are any suggestions for revitalizing rituals. Perhaps a concern with such cultural performance is dismissed as bread and circuses, in accordance with a modern post-Protestant view that the only viable social action is instrumental rather than expressive. But if Durkheim is right, America needs not only beliefs but also rituals: revivals, communions, rallies, and new forms not yet imagined. Revitalized rituals may require revitalized beliefs, but the reverse is also true.

In one sense, *Habits of the Heart* does better than to recommend revitalizing rituals. It has become one itself. The book is a cultural performance, or an essential text for such. Appropriate for this celebration of the one hundred and fiftieth anniversary of Tocqueville, *Habits* is inspiring serious discussion by concerned Americans who are sharing, often for the first time, the questions and hopes they have about the values and beliefs that are the foundation of our national culture.

TWO

Citizenship and Armed Civic Virtue: Some Critical Questions on the Commitment to Public Life

Jean Bethke Elshtain

No kind of greatness is more pleasing to the imagination of a democratic people than military greatness, a greatness of vivid and sudden luster, obtained without toil, by nothing but the risk of life.

ALEXIS DE TOCQUEVILLE, *DEMOCRACY IN AMERICA*

The authors of *Habits of the Heart* are interested in regenerating American public life, in reanimating civic habits. Their respondents, people interviewed at depth about the nature of their public and private lives and commitments, found it difficult to articulate any language of citizenship save misty metaphors of kinship and nearly impossible to conceive of a "common good" or "public interest" that recognizes economic, social, and cultural differences among people. Nevertheless, the respondents see themselves, all the same, as part of a "single society." Throughout *Habits* the authors deploy a strong language of *the* public good—or *the* common good—and of community. They would link local participation to a national dialogue and purpose; indeed, they speak of a *national* society. This, finally, is the question posed for our consideration: "Is it possible that we could become citizens again and together seek the common good in the postindustrial, postmodern age?" Clearly, the authors of *Habits* believe that it is. As one who has often expressed the same hope in strong and robust language, I nevertheless find myself being "nagged at" by doubts that coalesce into reservations as I consider the dream of a common good. This essay is about those reservations.

TOCQUEVILLIAN RUMBLINGS

That extraordinary Frenchman, Alexis de Tocqueville, haunts the pages of *Habits,* providing both framework and touchstone for critical and interpretive reflections. Thousands of words have been spilled analyzing Tocqueville's classic, *Democracy in America.* I turn to Tocqueville briefly not in order to buttress or debate various interpretations but to capture the lineaments of his assessment of nineteenth-century America's political promise and predicaments. My gloss does not differ markedly from

47

that of *Habits,* but the direction my interpretation pushes me requires that I take a hard look at what might be called the dark underside of evocations of civic virtue and the common good—something the authors of *Habits* fail to do.

It was never the intent of the American founders to create a classical republic along the lines of Jean-Jacques Rousseau's ideal of disciplined, restrained independent yeomen-citizens and their chaste wives for, argued James Madison in *Federalist Paper 10,* mankind can never achieve "perfect equality" in "political rights . . . possessions, their opinions, and their passions." For Madison, social homogeneity is both undesirable and impossible; "natural distinctions" are invariably augmented by "artificial ones." Rather than simply lamenting this fact, or perhaps seeking to eliminate distinctions altogether, one must provide for the more or less orderly working out of compulsions to distinguish and to divide.

Rousseau's republics of civic virtue are impossible to achieve in practice, in the Madisonian view, because they require of individuals the ability to transcend competing interests in the name of some common good. Perhaps, in previous epochs, human beings living within small, homogeneous societies could attain or approximate an ideal of civic virtue. But the modern era has unleashed forces, individual and collective, that undercut such older ideals. The modern world is heterogeneous, driven by interest, dedicated to commerce; societies intermingle through trade and populations migrate—these and more are incompatible with the discipline, restraint, and education to citizenship demanded in the classic civic republican vision.

Tocqueville, however, resists junking the republic ideal altogether. Why? Because the empirical reality of American democracy, in his view, even as it frees individuals from the constraints of older, undemocratic structures and obligations, also unleashes atomism, individualism, and privatization. His fear is not that this invites anarchy; rather, he believes that the individualism of an acquisitive bourgeois society will engender new forms of social and political domination. Individual disassociation invites the tyranny of mass opinion and centralized political authority. The lure of private acquisitiveness spawns political apathy and invites democratic despotism. All social webs that once held persons intact having disintegrated, the individual finds himself isolated and impotent, exposed and unprotected. Into this power vacuum moves "the organizing force of the government," the centralized state.

This is pretty bleak stuff and it is one side of the ledger limned by the authors of *Habits.* But, with Tocqueville, they insist that American democracy has the means to avoid this fate, to respond to atomization and disassociation. The cure may be found in political liberty, remnants of civic republicanism, and the moral ethos of religious identity that invite, in turn, civic participation. Tocqueville noted the plethora of voluntary political and beneficent associations in which Americans participated as well as structured guarantees of genuine power at municipal and state levels. His is an early vision of participatory democracy in which the "moment" of civic virtue is sustained in loose and diverse forms in a variety of associations pursuing multiple, not singular, ends. Participation that begins locally may be transformed and a genuine public-spirited citizenship may, in turn, loft upward toward a more inclusive, universal possibility (Elshtain 1981; 1986).

Nineteenth-century America, as captured by Tocqueville, was a society whose ideals bred simultaneous strengths and weaknesses. A new world, freed from the orthodox and corporate constraints of the old, American democracy would either fulfill its bracing promise of liberty with equality or sink in a surfeit of privatized, individualistic apathy accompanied by an unchecked momentum toward centralization and ultimate despotism. Tocqueville's political hope rested in a society honeycombed by multiple, voluntary political associations, checkmating tendencies toward coercive homogeneity. The centralized state must be curbed and limited just as social atomization must be muted and mediated through the coming together of citizens for self-interested *and* public-spirited ends. For the authors of *Habits* the latter involves a moral ecology that can carry the weight of "sustained and enduring commitments" involving a language of "fixed moral ends" that rescues individuals from sinking in a sea of subjectivity. Here the language of *the* public interest, or *the* common good takes over. And here I find I must demur, as much as I would like to concur.

Tocqueville issues additional cautions that go unmentioned in *Habits,* strictures of the sort embedded in the epigraph to my essay. Tocqueville discusses the virtue of the Roman republic on its road to Empire, a virtue or *virtus* wholly absorbed within notions of military prowess and prized as the valor of the ideal man, *vir.* This "singular community," in Tocqueville's locution, was sadly lacking in other civic habits, for the notion of virtue itself was assimilated into the glory of conquest. Although Tocqueville did not see America as a new Rome, he warned of the fatal lure of military greatness and that combination of rapacity and aggressive innocence as to one's own intentions and purposes which it spawns.

ARMED CIVIC VIRTUE AND ITS DISCONTENTS

These are troubling thoughts. I shall pursue the lines of reflection they suggest along two prongs. First, I shall take the measure of civic virtue as called up by the civic republican tradition in which both Tocqueville and the authors of *Habits* repose much of their hope. Second, I shall carve out the cultural space within which we might recapture what John Diggins (1984) has recently called the "lost soul of American politics," a form of civic life that resists the strong language of *the* common good and virtue flowing from civic republicanism as it was transformed historically into nationalistic statism.

The problem with the tradition of civic virtue can be stated succinctly: that virtue is *armed*. In the beginning politics gave birth to war. Better put, in the beginning politics *was* war. For the Greeks, war was a natural state and the basis of society. The citizen-warrior of the polis served the ends of the collective. For the great civic republicans of the early modern era—most importantly Machiavelli and Rousseau—the virtues of the ancient world are called upon to instruct their own epochs (Elshtain 1987). Tocqueville understood this nexus in a way *Habits* ignores. The first duty of Machiavelli's prince is that he be a soldier and create an army of citizens prepared to defend and to die for the *res publica*. His goal is civic self-sufficiency; his ideal is that of a polity that is akin to a singular armed body. The Machiavellian citizen must dedicate his life and actions to the republic or the city; the civic good is paramount.

When Jean-Jacques Rousseau, writing two centuries after Machiavelli's death, proclaims that "true Christians are made to be slaves" and ill suited to citizenship, he, too, reverberates to Machiavellian echos. The terms *Christian* and *republic,* he insists, "are mutually exclusive. Christianity preaches nothing but servitude and dependence" (Rousseau [1762] 1978, 128). The plangent note sounds: the polity must be as one; the national will must not be divided; citizens must be prepared to defend civic autonomy through force of arms; whatever puts the individual at odds with himself is a threat to "la nation une et indivisible."

Rousseau's animus is meted out to any *particular interest* that might block the general interest or will, driving a wedge between the citizen and the wider social body. The *citizen* is not to be confused with the bourgeois, a man given over to private interest and commerce. The transition from private to public person is ritualized by Rousseau as a rite of passage analogous to religious conversion, on the one hand, marriage on the other. Mimetically, the pre-citizen puts "his will, his goods, his force, and his person in common . . . and in a body we all receive each member as an inalienable part of the whole" (163). We strip off the old and put on the new person, not in Christ, but in the body politic. Citizenship is constituted in the interstices of the self, inscribed in the flesh, felt in the bones.

Rousseau was one of the great prophets of armed civic virtue. His ideas were absorbed by leading thinkers and activists of the French Revolution and, in turn, became constitutive of the creation of the modern nation-state. A demanding vision of total civic virtue requires the presence of enemies within and without. The chief process that drew men out of their localities and regions and made them conscious of belonging to a wider community—a *national* community—was military conscription (Howard 1984). (And it was *men* given the nexus between soldiering and citizenship.) If Rousseau's Geneva was an ideal republic surrounded by *real* walls, the nation-state encompassed no such palpable barrier, being fortified instead by mytholegalistic grandeur—all the vast pretensions of sovereignty that are essential, not accidental, to the nation-state as we know and experience it. Borders have been militarily and legally established that others dare not transgress, just as to breach the walls of the earlier fortified city was an act of war.

The *national* identity that we assume, or yearn for, is historically inseparable from war. The nation-state, including our own, rests on mounds of bodies. America escaped some of the wrenchings that accompanied the emergence of the *Kriegstaat* in Europe in this sense: our local identities, on which Tocqueville and *Habits* place such heavy reliance, were not seen as the deadly threat to national unity as they were perceived by European architects of nationalism. But, finally, no people escaped altogether the militarization of citizenship as the story of armed civic virtue marched into the twentieth century. The turning point for us, we Americans, was World War I. The authors of *Habits* do attend to the era—a bit—but not to the war itself. That is, they spend some time articulating alternative visions of the *national society*, linking this ideal with our continuing and as yet incomplete quest for *the public good*. They find one notion of the public good in the era "after World War I," in the opposition between the Establishment and Populism. I will not rehearse their argument here; rather, I want to question it because of what they omit from the story. As they go on to discuss the Progressives, the authors of *Habits* both praise and challenge—praise the search for a common good, challenge the commitment to rationality and science, the triumph of management over politics.

All this is well and good, but the stuff of genuine historic torment and tragedy goes unmarked. Given the insistence in *Habits* that "communities of memory" are essential to the completion of the quest for an American civic virtue, their historic insouciance concerning the seamy side of our national aspirations seems a rather serious lapse. For what made possible, in the minds of nearly all Progressives with the brave exceptions of Jane Addams and Randolph Bourne, the *national* community was World War I itself.

Nation-states can exist *on paper* before they exist *in fact*. Such is the story of the United States. For a *united* United States is a historical construction that most visibly comes into being as cause and consequence of American involvement in the Great War. Prior to the nationalist enthusiasms of that era, America was a loosely united federation with strong local and regional identities. The state's long arm did not yet reach everywhere, although a centralized federal government did exist.

More important, perhaps, in the telling of this particular tale was the presence on American soil of millions of immigrants who had flooded

her shores in great waves throughout the late nineteenth and early twentieth century. Such "hyphenated Americans" were a source of concern to
many "true Americans" and nationalizing politicians alike: Italian-
American, Irish-American, German-American, Polish-American—who
or what were "they" really? Could they be trusted to be loyal to their new
home or had their hearts remained in the old? These questions kept
various individuals and groups awake at night, fretting over the infusion
of too many alien and alienating people and philosophies into the American bloodstream. World War I "solved" the problem. America became
America as a society-in-arms.

Walt Whitman's nineteenth-century dream of inseparable cities and
an indissoluble continent glow with an essentially pacific democratic purpose. But indissolubility continent-wide is a tough dream to embody in
and on the bodies of recalcitrant, diverse human material. We as a
people did not come close to this dream until the Great War, and then it
was as much a nightmare as the stuff of democratic utopias. The discourse of armed civic virtue is the creation of nationalizing, progressive
liberals, those who championed universal military training and conscription as a homogenizing agent in what they regarded as a "dangerously
diverse society." Shared military service, one advocate argued, was the
"only way to 'yank the hyphen' out of Italian-Americans or Polish-
Americans or other such imperfectly assimilated immigrants" (Kennedy
1980, 29). When President Wilson committed himself to universal conscription, one explicit purpose was to help mold a new nation.

I cannot detail all the many excesses of that era—the wartime assaults
on dissenting opinion and persons, the mobilization of America's school
system for war in the conviction that armed civic virtue required a bold
plan. These were the years of nationalizing American schools, homogenizing the curriculum, establishing the "service" ideal. But the service
was to the *state*, not to the society. Service was to bolster our greatness,
not to enhance our character. The grand ideal of American civic virtue
was born. We should not be at all surprised that when Americans living
today point to a period when our virtue and commitment as *one* people
was highest, they do not speak of the 1960s Civil Rights movement or
any other essentially unmilitarized effort; rather, they hark back to the
days of World War II.

CHASTENED PATRIOTISM: A NONBELLICOSE PUBLIC HOPE

No country can leap out of its historically determined dimensions. What
I have done, thus far, is to make visible a dark dimension of our civic life
that *Habits* glosses over. I do so because I mean to suggest an alternative
to strong notions of civic virtue and a common good—ideals inseparable
historically from war and preparation for war. But there is that space I

alluded to earlier within which we might recover features of an American community of memory that would locate us as civic beings, not within the frame of a common good but through a shared sense of pathos and tragedy. For the latter, I believe, better serve us in an age riven by Hiroshima and the Holocaust.

There must be *within* a people a capacity, however inchoate, that an appeal can help to forge into something discernible as an identity. Of American social identity it can be said that it is not only profoundly individual, it is also intensely linked to the belief that being an American means or ought to mean "something." It means one has claims against a society if it refuses to treat one with respect. It means this country has stood for certain worthy ideals, however imperfectly realized. A revitalized political discourse must be neither abstract nor ahistorical but concrete, available to social participants, involving a potentially transformative dimension, a critical edge.

Liberal, republican, and "nativist" elements commingle in this American civic stew. The discriminating values of the republican ideal (in which citizenship is armed, as I have noted already, and, as well, the property of a minority) evolved over time to a more solidly egalitarian democratic ideal of citizenship. Never easy with the presumptions of the *primacy* of politics—and that is the direction civic republican virtue pushes—Americans modified, even mollified, that ideal by the countervailing pressure of Christian ideas, including the teaching that freedom *from* politics could also embody an ideal of a way of life.

From our present site, appeals either to old notions of a robust, coherent community as large as *the* nation *or* to the robust, coherent individualist fall short of mapping the terms of a civic ethos that might ongoingly sustain us and form both personal and civic identities. But there are luminescent recognitions that infuse a deep moral seriousness and an awareness of the inherent *tragedy* of political action available to us as individuals and "a people" through the life and words of Abraham Lincoln.

Recently, John Diggins (1984, 315) has argued that Lincoln helped heal the Machiavellian moment of severing politics from morality by "reintroducing into political discourse the Christian moralism that Machiavelli had purged from the theory of statecraft. Although there are elements of Machiavellian sensibility in Lincoln's conviction that he too was experiencing a universe eclipsed in moral darkness . . . , Lincoln was convinced that ultimate moral questions did not admit of relativistic interpretations"—even though they might require trimming one's actions and going for less than one's interpretation, taken neat, insists upon. Slavery *is* wrong. But ridding a nation of it involves a series of tragic encounters.

Lincoln instructs us today, chastening the arrogance of rationalist managers of events, shaming the insipid ramblings of watery psychologisms, challenging the proclaimers of *the* common good in a statist order. Rejecting Machiavellian instrumentalism and the "logic of success," Lincoln hopes more for the goodness of the nation's soul than for the greatness of the state. This means that grand visions of *civic unity* fall through the cracks of Lincoln's tragic recognitions. A nation must learn how to endure defeats, better that by far than to crow in victory and war-bought unity.

A people is well advised to "renounce heroically the very things that enslave the spirit" rather than to seize aggressively at a greatness that corrodes its soul (Diggins 1984, 327–28). The Civil War was not fought between one side that was righteous and another that was not; rather, as Lincoln said, "Both read the same Bible, and pray to the same God" and "But let us not judge, that we be not judged." Diggins may be right—this is a remarkable stance for a political leader—but it is the stance of our greatest political leader, one continuously reinscribed on the American conscience, helping to shape our political consciousness. This means that *power* and *interests* alone, as the authors of *Habits* also insist, must not and need not define our politics. We can, with Lincoln, open our hearts to pity, recognizing, among other things, that there is no redemption through the triumph of war, only the possibility of redeeming a defeat.

As I write these words, we Americans are in the midst of a period of civic rejuvenation many choose to call "the new patriotism." To me, much of it looks suspiciously like the old nationalism, an aggressive self-identity that invites arrogance through our identification with the state's awesome preserve of force and calls up dreams of a unified society—highly mobilized and ready to do battle, a chimera that invites the ecstasies of nationalistic excess. The language of nationalism is like the language of war, drastically oversimplified, deployed, in George Orwell's words, either in "boosting or in denigrating," classifying whole peoples as "good" or "bad."

Patriotism is part of our repertoire of civic ideals and identities. The excesses of patriotism may be lamented, but it cannot, and should not, be excised, for love of country also yields civic concern *for* country. We cannot practice patriotism as a civic virtue in the ways available in pre-state societies characterized by relative homogeneity and moral consensus. Attached more to the sense of a moral community than to a "state," patriotism nevertheless can be, and has been, evoked to bring out the best as well as the worst in us.

For example, we all have some shared sense of what is at stake to describe Martin Luther King, Jr., as a Christian and a "great American patriot" who had the courage to criticize his "beloved country" in time of war even as he affirmed his ties to the country. It makes no sense at all to think of King as a "great American nationalist." His "I Have a Dream" speech, also invoked in *Habits,* is a dream of a multinational, racially and regionally diverse, plural democracy united in a covenant for essentially pacific purposes. In his "Beyond Vietnam" speech, King makes a plea to

> my beloved nation. This speech is not addressed to Hanoi or to the National Liberation Front. It is not addressed to China or to Russia . . . but rather to my fellow Americans who, with me, bear the greatest responsibility in ending a conflict that has exacted a heavy price on both continents.

These are the words of a patriot, not a nationalist, speaking in the language of transcendent vision—a dream of democracy, not an argument of obligation.

I have in mind, as I bring these reflections to a close, the image of a *chastened* patriot as a civic ideal—for the language of public good and public interest will not get the civic juices flowing. This is a risky business, to be sure, but we are currently in rather deep trouble and the risks we do not run may be the possibilities we do not explore. The citizen I have in mind is both committed *and* detached: enough apart so that he or she can be reflective about civic ties and loyalties, cherishing many commitments rather than valorizing one alone. Rejecting a counsel of cynicism, my chastened patriot modulates the rhetoric of high civic purpose by keeping alive the distant voice of ironic remembrance and recognition of the way patriotism can shade into the excesses of nationalism; recognition of the fact that civic identity in the form of Rousseauian civic virtue cannot be reconstructed for our time.

THREE

The Culture of Procurement: Reflections on Addiction and the Dynamics of American Culture

Roland A. Delattre

My subject is related in several ways to themes opened up in *Habits of the Heart*, not least of which is the fact that people bring into their performance in the conduct of public affairs the habits of mind and the patterns of behavior shaped by their social and cultural formation. I want to consider the cultural roots of one such pattern of behavior in public life that is reassuring to its practitioners in the short run but dangerously self-destructive—to the rest of the world as well as to themselves—in the long run, a long run that stands in daily risk of being cut very short indeed. This cultural pattern—addiction—bears heavily upon modern individualism and the important corollary issues that the authors of *Habits* invite us to consider with them.

With the title of that book in mind, I was tempted to call this paper "Reflections on a Heartless Habit." Addiction is among the most heartless of habits, and its importance as a feature of the culture in which most Americans participate goes a long way to help explain the mindlessness as well as the heartlessness of so much of our common life. I intend to shed some explanatory light on the extraordinarily high tolerance among Americans for the recent extravagance of our national budget deficits and especially the growth in military expenditures that makes for so much of that deficit—a phenomenon that is particularly striking in view of the commitment to reduced federal expenditures so fundamental to the program that brought Ronald Reagan into the presidency and that remains so central to the rhetoric of his administration.

Our nation's deficit-financed military buildup cannot be understood in anything less than cultural terms. That is, it is not simply a question of political ideology or of policy decisions and military strategy. It has to do with the fundamental symbolic forms and activities through which we make sense of our world, the habits of the heart through which we work out our identity and achieve some orientation in the world. More specifically, I want to explore the proposition that what I am calling the culture of procurement—and I quite deliberately employ an ugly term that connotes both acquisition and prostitution—of compulsive or addictive acquisition, is a perverse intensification of addictive dynamics that are an important part of the culture of consumption in which the dominant two-thirds of American society so largely participates. This dominant American culture, I submit, continuously nourishes and rewards addictive behavior and attitudes. No longer can we dismiss addiction as simply a refuge from failure in our society, though millions of Americans do seek relief from pain, stress, and failure—or, more importantly, their *sense* of failure—in some variety of addictive behavior. (And thereby they both confirm and accelerate the process of failure in their work or in their personal lives.) But addiction has also become one of the most likely conditions and ingredients of socially and culturally defined success in the dominant regions of American society. Some kind of addictive dependence—of which there is an endless variety—is commonly experienced by Americans as essential to survival, and especially to those intent on making it in the dominant social system. Addictive behavior and dependency are among the socially available and culturally encouraged ways of trying to handle the demands of success—perhaps especially of exceptional success. The level of stress, loneliness, and emotional denial endured by those who rise to leadership in the corporate culture of professionals, experts, and managers—pressures often experienced as dehumanizing—makes some pattern of addictive dependence a virtual condition of success at the upper levels, though not only at those levels, of our society. But because from below the possible rewards are more evident than the costs, there is no lack of candidates intent on working their way up the corporate ladder.

When I characterize the dominant American culture as addiction-nourishing, I have in mind more than behavior involving commonly recognized addictive substances—from coffee and sugar to alcohol and cocaine. Use and dependence on such substances form a part of the system of addictive activities and attitudes that supports the culture of procurement, the compulsive acquisition nourished by the dominant culture. Closer to the center of my subject are addictions that have as their object an activity rather than a substance—compulsive dependence on work or sex, for example, but more important even, compulsive dependence on spending and acquiring. All these addictions, whether to substances or to activities, contribute in various ways to the formation of the culture of procurement.

The key to addiction is not found in the substances or activities that are the objects of addiction, but in the experience and the pattern of dependence. The logic and dynamic of addiction is an ever-increasing dependence on an ever-narrowing source of reliable satisfaction—the increasing dependence flowing from the need to escalate the dosage in order to achieve the same level of satisfaction, together with an increasing incapacity to deal with other needs and alternative sources of satisfaction.

The culture of procurement, constituted at its core by addictive acquisition, nourished and sustained by a whole network of addictions, is a powerful presence in the life of the nation. It is a culture in itself, not merely a cultural theme. It offers a fabric of meaning and a framework of interpretation, a sense of how the world is and of how things are done among us. In evidence throughout the dominant two-thirds of American society, this culture achieves its quintessential expression in the military-industrial complex, which Max Stackhouse (1971) has so ably analyzed and named Necropolis, the City of Death—and in which we seem to have very generally taken out citizenship papers.

The logic of procurement as a culture is not the logic of need, even though there are real needs to be met in, for example, providing for the national defense. It is rather the logic of addictive dependence on acquisition, with procurement as the most reliable way to respond to the need for security. That logic is built on broader culturally defined expectations for *more*—though "more" is rarely experienced as sufficient—together with a haunting fear of inadequacy. Those cultural pressures are in tune with a formative theme long present in the dominant cultural version of what America is about: the conviction, so illuminatingly explored by Sacvan Bercovitch in *The American Jeremiad* (1978), that faithfulness to the founding covenants of the nation means never merely replicating but always exceeding the achievements of predecessors. It means expecting more, doing more, getting more, and in its pathological form, getting high on more. An explicit corollary is, If it is possible to acquire, then it is necessary; an implicit corollary is, Enough is never sufficient but always requires more. This culture of procurement governs—or "possesses"—the military establishment and its political base in Washington and around the country. Similar cultural dynamics are at work throughout the dominant society, accounting for the high tolerance Americans display toward the Pentagon budget and the federal deficit, and accounting also for our collective difficulty in extricating ourselves from the powerful dynamics of the culture of procurement. To break the cycle of addiction requires much of an individual and will surely require even more of a whole society. Such a development seems unlikely unless our nation finds itself in a major economic crisis or a spiritual revolution, though the prospect of our weathering the one or experiencing the other is closely related to the adequacy of our response to the political and cultural challenge so keenly analyzed for us by the authors of *Habits*.

Research on addictive behavior in individuals can, I believe, shed light on the dynamics of the culture of procurement. To understand this self-destructive cultural form, I begin with Stanton Peele's (1981; Peele and Brodsky 1975) description of addiction, a condition that he regards as normal rather than abnormal in our society.[1] The addict, Peele says, is a person who has not learned to come to grips with his world and who therefore seeks stability and reassurance through some repeated ritualized activity. This addictive activity is reinforced in two ways: first, by a comforting sensation of well-being induced by the addictive object; and second, by the atrophy of the addict's other interests and abilities and the general deterioration of his life situation while he is preoccupied with the addiction. As satisfying alternatives become fewer, the import of the addiction grows larger, until it is all there is. An activity becomes addictive, according to Peele, when it makes it increasingly difficult for a person to deal with his real needs, thereby making his sense of well-being depend increasingly on a single external source of support. The key to addiction does not reside in the object per se, but in the release from fear that the object provides. Unable to believe in his own adequacy, the addict welcomes the freedom from responsibility that submission to an external control affords.

Lawrence Hatterer also concludes that addictive behavior has invaded every aspect of American life today. Hatterer (1980, 17) states that: "A person should be considered addicted when an overpowering, repetitive, excessive need exists for some substance, object, feeling, act, milieu, or personal interaction at any cost, along with a denial of the destructive consequences to one's physical, emotional, and social well-being and, in some instances, to economic survival. In true addiction there is always excessive use of pleasurable activities to cope with unmanageable internal conflict, pressure, stress, and confrontation." Typically, addictive behavior begins pleasurably, involves increasing activity to achieve the same effect, and eventually results in injury or harm to the addict's health, work, family, and social relationships. The addict, however, denies any detrimental effects on self or others. If forced to stop, the addict suffers withdrawal pains, both physical and psychological. Hatterer distinguishes between "hard" addictions, those involving alcohol, narcotics, or barbiturates, from which the harmful effects are immediate, and "soft" addictions such as compulsive smoking, gambling, running, spending, or work, from which the harmful effects are not so immediate. In his view, addictive behavior is so omnipresent in our society that "we all feel the cloud of concern about becoming addictive—preoccupation with weight, smoking, drinking too much, or being caught in an excess of spending, acquiring, gambling, sex or work."

For most Americans, the process of addictive behavior begins early in life with the socially available and culturally encouraged dependence on sugar. Children incorporate—literally "take into their bodies"—first a tolerance and then quickly a craving for nutritionally exorbitant doses of sugar, especially in breakfast cereals, soft drinks, and candy. Colas, the most popular of our soft drinks, also introduce children to caffeine and prepare them for coffee and tea. The message to young people is that there are reliable packaged sources of pleasurable experiences readily available as relief from boredom and stress. Over time, nonsugary foods and drinks seem boring by comparison; more importantly, the pleasure of sweets becomes secondary to the reliability of the relief and escape such foods provide from pain, emptiness, and a sense of inadequacy. By the time children have grown into adults they know to use substances to deny the reality of these and other negative experiences.

Teenagers discover other substances, such as tobacco, alcohol, and marijuana, that seem to facilitate social interaction and relief from a sense of inadequacy. To cite one measure of the extent of our nation's addictive behavior: Traffic in cocaine alone exceeds $100 billion a year— about twice the sum Americans give annually in voluntary support for religious, educational, social, and cultural philanthropy, and about one-third of the annual Pentagon budget.

Important as they are, these addictive dependencies on substances are but a part of the backdrop for the culture of procurement. Now I want to turn to the addictive activities of the culture of consumption itself. Ours is not flat out a consumer culture. As Jackson Lears points out in *The Culture of Consumption* (Fox and Lears 1983), the ethos of production—with its high value assigned to work, sacrifice, saving, and deferred satisfaction—is still powerful. But it is recessive by comparison with the ethos of consumption—characterized by periodic leisure, compulsive spending, apolitical passivity, and a morality of individual fulfillment. The dream of abundance has a long history among Americans, though it has sometimes been at odds with dreams of freedom and justice. At least since the middle of the nineteenth century, most Americans have increasingly come to regard abundance rather than scarcity as natural and, especially since 1920, to want and expect regular access to more things, better things, and newer things.

These expectations have been based on experience as well as promises. It is easy for those of us well positioned in our society to forget how radically distinctive that pattern of consumption is. Consider just one set of figures. Measured in BTUs (British thermal units), energy consumption in the United States, which had not risen significantly during the nineteenth century, rose from 110 million BTUs per capita in 1900 to 185 million in 1920, languished through the Depression, and then rose rapidly to peak at 360 million BTUs per capita in 1973—more than tripling in seventy years. In 1971, when the United States consumed 330 million BTUs of energy per capita, the rate for Japan was 98 million, for

France 117 million, for the Soviet Union 136 million, for Great Britain 165 million, and for the world as a whole only 58 million.[2] Related sets of expectations are woven into the fabric of meaning and the interpretive patterns by which we live—which is even true for many Americans who are systematically denied access to abundance.

The culture of consumption is so powerful that it has invaded every region of our experience. The family, once a unit of production, has become primarily a unit of consumption. We practice the politics of consumption, entering political life less as citizens than as consumers. As C. B. Macpherson argued some years ago in *The Life and Times of Liberal Democracy* (1977, 43) the governing assumption is "[that] man is an infinite consumer, that his overriding motivation is to maximize the flow of satisfactions . . . to himself from society, and that a national society is simply a collection of such individuals." Accordingly, citizens are treated and come to treat themselves "as simply political consumers," for whom political candidates and parties are "suppliers of political commodities," and for whom, as Robert Westbrook (1983) put it more recently, the act of voting is not so much making a choice as it is buying a product. Schools have come to resemble training camps for consumer consciousness, encouraging a passive dependence on experts, who preside over every portion of the curriculum, and prompting premature and restrictive specialization so that students will be qualified for certification into one of the priesthoods of experts. Family. Politics. Education. There is no need to survey all the important regions of our experience that we enter as consumers, our habits of heart and mind formed by the culture of consumption. It is not everything, but it is nearly everywhere.

To consume, to consume abundantly and as a birthright, is not in itself an addictive behavior or evidence of addictive attitudes. But as a fabric of meaning and power, the culture of consumption has in several ways become a generator and an enabler of addictive dependencies and attitudes. For the culture of consumption does not simply nourish the expectation and desire for more, newer, and better things and circumstances. It nourishes the conviction that more and newer is better and necessary, and that nearly every need can be met, every anxiety relieved, by acquiring more, newer, or better things. We come to expect a "fix" by fortunate acquisition, even if it is only a newer model of something we already have. Most members of the dominant two-thirds of our society are acquisition addicts, people who rely on spending—a little or a lot— to boost their spirits. Buying is a reliable source of good feelings, of some satisfaction, and of spinoff satisfactions if a purchase also pleases or impresses others.

Such reliability is a hallmark of addictive behavior. Shopping, spending, and acquiring are not as reliable in what they deliver as a cigarette or a cup of coffee. But even if the goods or services purchased are sometimes disappointing, the activity of spending and acquiring seems to provide many consumers with predictable pleasures: a sense of freedom, choice, and control as one selects one's purchase; a sense of well-being and independence from being able to pay for—or charge—the selected objects; a sense of good judgment from having consulted experts and done comparison shopping—or a sense of excitement from an impulse purchase.

In *The Simple Life,* David Shi very nicely describes the vicious cycle inherent in modern consumer culture: "Although we have more and more time, money, and products at our disposal, these are swiftly overtaken by endlessly rising expectations and expanding appetites" (1985, 225). The problem is not simply one of individual greed; the institutions of the culture of consumption and procurement encourage and facilitate addictive levels of consumption. Highly congenial to the escalator effect of addictive dependence is the credit card, which facilitates yielding to the addictive demand for increasing the dosage while simultaneously postponing the need to reckon with the cost of one's habit. Credit cards do have nonaddictive uses. But things can get out of hand, and they probably have. Consumer installment debt continues to hit new records, and savings as a percentage of disposable personal income has dropped in recent years noticeably below the fairly steady, though low, 5 to 7 percent rate to less than 3 percent. In response, economists puzzle over new incentives to reduce spending and increase savings. An analogous addiction to living beyond our means shows up in the federal deficit as well.

The culture of consumption also lends support to addictive dependence by ministering to an addict's inordinate concern with keeping up appearances. We are all familiar with the role of appearances in a social system informed by consumption, but for an addict the common concern with appearances is raised to a higher power. As addictive dependence grows, the addict becomes obsessed with keeping up appearances and with not being found out. Significant others are drawn into the act. Especially if things are not going well, resources and alibis are mobilized, generally in the hope of buying time for the addict to recover, but usually serving instead only to enable the addiction to intensify. This concern with appearances is in part an effort to compensate for a sense of bewilderment about the realities of the world, a feeling accentuated by the experience of addictive dependence.

That sense of bewilderment points to yet another feature of the culture of consumption that nourishes addictive dependence: remystification of the world. The most powerful institutional carrier of this remystification is the corporation, the principal artifact of industrial society, together with the corporate cadres of professionals, experts, and managerial elites who staff the vast bureaucratic organizations, both public and private. The cultural as well as social significance of this process is best described by Alan Trachtenberg in *The Incorporation of America* (1982), where he traces the genesis in the latter half of the nineteenth century of what we now call the corporate culture. Jackson Lears and Richard W. Fox, in *The Culture of Consumption* (1983, ix–xvii), have perhaps best caught the symbiotic relation of mutual dependence between the culture of consumption and the corporate culture of professionals, experts, and managers. We experience that symbiotic connection as a curious and disorienting conflict. On the one hand, as participants in the culture of consumption, we are encouraged to seek individual satisfaction and fulfillment, to place ourselves at the center of our world—a world in which the consumer is the very image of fully realized humanity, someone of importance and power, one whose attention is widely sought. On the other hand, we experience the world from which our goods and services come to us, the world controlled by the corporate culture, as complex and mysterious beyond comprehension. Even if we occupy an important place in it—as a professional, an expert, or a manager—our experience of much of the rest of that world leaves us feeling incompetent, powerless, and dependent. We feel dependent not only upon the experts and professionals who preside over the mysteries of various regions of our experience but also upon the managers and bureaucrats who seem to understand and to control the processes of production and the service institutions upon which we rely. In the ceaseless pursuit of the good life, consumers are constantly reminded of their powerlessness.

This experience of dependence, powerlessness, and incompetence, which is symbiotically related to more self-affirming features of the culture of consumption but which systematically undermines those experiences, tends very strongly to feed and nourish an important feature of addictive behavior—namely, a kind of all-or-nothing disposition that swings between grandiosity and a sense of one's own insignificance, between a sense of near omnicompetence and complete incompetence. One extreme makes for dangerous flights of overreaching ambition; the other makes for resignation, submission, and passivity. When persuaded of his own incompetence, an addict is more likely to grant omnicompetence to the system.

Theodore Roszak writes of people "convinced of their own absolute incompetence and equally convinced of the technocracy's omnipotence" (1972, 427). This is of a piece with the dynamics of addiction: one experiences a deep sense that something is wrong, one assumes that it must be oneself, and one sublimates or denies the dis-ease and discomfort: Stick it out, try harder, and trust the experts who preside over the highly mystified world. In such a world the consumer reigns but does not rule; rule is assigned to the corporate order. Harry Angstrom, the protagonist of John Updike's novel *Rabbit Is Rich* (1981), is a model fictional realization of the occupant of this world—a lower-level functionary of a corporate culture who experiences his world as mystified and shares in the culture of consumption with nervous uncertainty about his own competence.

A final characteristic of addictive behavior exhibited within the culture of procurement is related to the remystification of the world and the feeling of passive dependence on the expert agencies controlled by corporate culture. During the advanced stages of addictive dependence, the addict feels a growing sense of the inevitability of developments, of having no alternatives, of the world closing in, of being trapped. Unable to imagine conditions being different or ways of making them so, lacking confidence in his capacity to do otherwise, the addict responds by, in effect, throwing oil on the fire, escalating his dependence by turning to larger doses—a strategy that seemed to work at earlier stages of addiction. Increasingly unable to deal with other needs and alternative sources of satisfaction, the addict becomes progressively isolated and alienated until *in extremis* he is entirely alone with his addiction.

Can these characteristics of addictive dependence nourished by the culture of consumption be applied to the culture of procurement at the Pentagon and related institutions? I believe they can, for at the Pentagon, as elsewhere, the habits of cultural formation are carried forward as natural. The management of military policy and procurement is approached by its practitioners in ways that have come to be taken for granted by themselves and by their constituents. Let me sketch out this dynamic.

First, those who participate in the culture of procurement approach problems by looking for a "fix" by fortunate acquisition. Thanks largely to the efforts of a few political leaders and of a relatively free press, we know the extent to which military procurement follows less from a careful assessment of needs than from an addiction to acquisition. The support system that enables the maintenance of that habit is carefully cultivated so that every state and most congressional districts have a stake in supporting the practice.

Second, the procurement addict turns to reliable sources of relief from the problems of foreign policy and military preparedness. But the reliability of relief—that something is being done to meet a perceived threat—is quite different from the reliability of effectiveness in dealing with the perceived threat. Hence the need to escalate the dosage, the investment in procurement, once the measures taken prove ineffective.

Third, we can see the escalator effect at work as every new weapons system promises more than it can deliver except at the price of sometimes dramatic cost overruns, and as each stage in weapons development, once in place, leads to yet more sophisticated systems, the adoption of which drives the defense budget yet further beyond our means.

Fourth, we see in the culture of procurement an obsessive preoccupation with keeping up appearances, a preoccupation that is disguised in the language of national interests and national credibility.

Fifth, perhaps no region of our national life has become more thoroughly mystified than defense. Much like patients in the presence of doctors, both leaders and constituents are confounded by the impenetrability of military language and terminology. As civilians, we tend to defer passively to the military experts. Since experts disagree, it may be a matter of which one can appeal to our deepest fears or wishes.

Finally, addictive dependence leads to a sense of being trapped and having no alternative but to try harder in the same old way. In an illuminating essay, "The American Millennium" (1985), Frances FitzGerald sees something like this spirit at work among our national leaders. She conjures up the ghosts of FDR and George Marshall observing the temper of the nation's leaders today: "Instead of a jaunty self-confidence or a benign paternalism, they would encounter a defensive churlishness combined with adolescent self-promotion—a tendency to brag and strut." She goes on to associate that spirit also with the Manichean grandiosity and the search for an all-powerful "fix" with which the addict hopes to bring in the millennium. Her language is different from mine, but she describes a pattern of leadership engaged in grandiose metaphysical battles in which the stakes are represented as total victory or total defeat.

We can also see the sense of entrapment and absence of alternatives at work on a smaller scale. Just as we find it easier to continue a subsidy for the tobacco industry than to find alternative sources of livelihood for those employed in it, so also, hooked on defense contracts, we seem unable to generate even contingency plans for the reallocation of human and material resources to meet real and demanding needs. The familiar refrain "I'll quit tomorrow" is heard from the procurement addict, aware of a growing danger and the need to change, but postponing action and begging for "just one more" fix.

The addictive culture of procurement is not a sufficient explanation of Pentagon behavior or federal deficits, but it is a powerful contributing factor that deserves careful study. I am aware that I dwell in a glass house and am reluctant, from my doorway of vulnerability, to throw stones at procurement addicts. But it might be a good idea if we, in all seriousness, formed an organization once proposed by Kurt Vonnegut: a new WPA, War Preparers Anonymous, modeled after Alcoholics Anonymous and its twelve-step program for recovery. If my analysis of the culture of procurement is correct, such an organization would make an effective contribution toward creating world peace and a sane society.

We must attend to the dynamics of American culture and the quality of American life in the wake of the social, economic, and cultural developments of the past century. The project I have sketched here requires much more development. But it bears some close parallels to issues and themes raised by *Habits of the Heart*. That book comes to us as a distinguished and (I expect) enduring contribution to a tradition of important studies which focus on matters related to the cultural developments I have described. None of those cultural developments are more significant than the transformation of American society into one of mass production and mass consumption. This transformation has been driven by, and has reinforced, the utilitarian individualism that *Habits* characterizes. My argument has been that those who participate in the dominant two-thirds of our society, that portion of our society to which *Habits* is directed, find their principal resources for personal meaning, identity, and orientation to the world more in terms provided by their relation to processes of consumption than in terms of production. Their solidarity comes from their mutual participation in the community of consumption.

The relationship of the culture of consumption to a mass, economic-based form of community is a complex subject worthy of study. The culture of consumption does not subsist independently of the culture of production; nor does the economic community of mass consumers exhaust the forms of community that Americans experience. As Christopher Lasch (1984, 23–59) has shown, the two cultures of consumption and production are systematically related and their contemporary forms have developed in symbiotic relation. And as Daniel Horowitz (1985) has indicated, ordinary people as well as elites have played an active role in shaping consumer culture. But neither Lasch nor Horowitz nor *Habits* offers an analysis of how the culture of consumption leads to a new form of economic community in which individuals are isolated, alone in a community that fosters habits of addiction and transforms individuals into dependent mass consumers with insatiable wants and cravings, which then are identified as needs. The possibility of creating a new form of public community, which can strengthen a healthy individualism, is the prospect we find explored and proposed in *Habits*. This cultural transformation will require the reconceptualization of individuals as citizens, rather than consumers.

FOUR

Toward a Darkly Radiant Vision of America's Truth: A Letter of Concern, An Invitation to Re-Creation

Vincent Harding

*Your country? How came it yours? Before the Pilgrims landed we were here. . . .
Actively we have woven ourselves with the very warp and woof of this nation.
. . . [a]nd generation after generation have pleaded with a headstrong, careless
people to despise not Justice, Mercy, and Truth.*

W. E. B. DU BOIS, *SOULS OF BLACK FOLK*

Dear Friends,

Near the end of *Habits of the Heart* you issued a generous invitation to all of your readers. You said that your work was intended "to open a larger conversation with our fellow citizens, to contribute to the common dialogue." Thus, you encouraged a person like myself to "test what we say against his or her own experience," to "argue with us when what we say does not fit" (*H*, 307). I have chosen to respond, to enter the conversation with you and to engage in the larger dialogue. Appreciating the spirit of your invitation, I have decided to address you directly in the form of this letter.

In light of my own encounters with the history and present experience of this nation, I must argue with you. I find *Habits* a work that is clearly informed by the best of intentions, but a work that is fundamentally and sadly flawed. It is because I am so fully committed to your quest for "a new social science" that will help us to deal with "new realities" in our nation and world; because I also resonate with your sense of urgency about our need to create a "public philosophy" that will free us to move toward humane understandings of the "common good" in America— because I stand firmly with you in all this, it has often been very painful for me to recognize and be jarred by the critical disjuncture I sense between your intentions and your creation. But the disjuncture is real, and I want to share my sense of its nature and sources, as well as some thoughts concerning its possibility for correction.

At the very beginning of *Habits*, you provide what I believe to be the key to understanding the open wound that runs throughout its pages.

There, citing the restraints of "a small research team and a limited budget," you say "we decided to concentrate our research on white, middle-class Americans" (*H,* viii). You then make an arguable, but cogent case for your emphasis on the middle class as central to American life; however, you make no case at all—except for budget and staff—for the decision to exclude middle-class people who were not white. From your perspective, it appears that the only real problem created by such a decision was that "we were not able to illustrate much of the racial diversity that is so important to a part of our national life" (ibid.).

I want to suggest that the problem you have created is far more profound. Illustrations of racial diversity are not the primary loss. What you have missed is a major portion of the painful reality, the ambiguous richness, and the anguished integrity of this nation's past and present—as well as a full sense of the magnificent possibilities of its future. In other words, I believe that your choice of a white middle-class focus has distorted the picture of America you have seen and projected, thereby defeating some of your own best hopes. I have chosen four elements of *Habits* to illustrate and elaborate my concern.

I

Let me begin with the problems created by your methodology. For me, there is something fundamentally appealing about a book that promises to be "based on conversations with ourselves, our ancestors, and several hundred of our fellow-citizens." In spite of what I know about your unquestionable integrity and intentionality, the appeal literally paled (the pun is only slightly intended) when I realized with whom and to whom you are really talking. For instance, the conversations "among ourselves," refer essentially to four white middle-class men and one white middle-class woman. There is no way to avoid the problem that this presents. You claimed to be researching and writing a book whose primary focus is cultural, whose fundamental questions have to do with what it means to be an American. Carrying out that task in the midst of one of the most fascinating and frustratingly multicultural and multiracial nations in the world, you are severely limited and confined by your chosen base of white middle-class Euro-Americans. Carefully reading your text, I can see no other conclusion.

This is no judgment on you, friends; but it may well be a judgment on your judgment, on your decision concerning how best to study America and Americans in the 1970s and 1980s. For instance, had your own research team included one or two similarly sensitive, skilled, and concerned nonwhite social scientists, do you think they could have possibly made a decision to look at the questions of "Who are we as Americans? . . . What is our character?" without including a significant body of Americans of color in their quest for answers?

While it is true that your group's basic composition almost forces you to miss the richness of our nation's multivocality, I think more is at stake. As I shall continue to say in a number of ways, this is far more than a matter of diversity. In a society still suffering from major residues of white supremacist thought and action—a terrifying blindness in a largely nonwhite world—it is imperative for our nation to break out of its prison of whiteness. *Habits* honors Martin Luther King, Jr., for his leadership in this work, but your own grouping, in its self-constitution, failed to follow that leadership. Thus your concern for the "common good" was severely compromised by your failure to expand yourselves, to enrich your own primary community. As a result, you missed one of the major lessons of our history: middle-class white America has never been able to heal itself without a major rediscovery of its interdependence with the rest of this nation. (Isn't it only natural that the search for the common good should be a common enterprise?)

In light of your self-definition, your "conversations with our ancestors" are similarly flawed. Indeed, I found the woundedness of this aspect of the work very painful. As I read your book, there could be no doubt that the ancestors of the white middle-class Americans carrying out this important inquiry were also white and middle class. Do you understand the pain? What does it mean for this American, and others like me, to come upon a roster of "exemplary Americans" from the past and find only Benjamin Franklin, Thomas Jefferson, John Winthrop, Abraham Lincoln, and Walt Whitman? Surely these are all honorable men in their way (although I say that with some ambivalence). But what does it mean for our children to be told by scholars of your caliber and reputation that these are the "exemplars" of America? The later introduction of Martin King does little to erase the impression that exemplary Americans are, by example, *white men.* Friends, this is not simply an absence of diversity, this is a distortion of truth.

Let us take one ancestral case in point: Thomas Jefferson. In discussing America's biblical and republican traditions, you touch very lightly on the reality of American slavery as the major antebellum contradiction to those worthy traditions. And when you refer to slavery, you tell us that Jefferson, one of your exemplars, "vigorously opposed slavery in principle" (*H,* 30). You then cite his marvelous words concerning the first requirement of a democratic government: "'Equal and exact justice to all men, of whatever state or persuasion, religious or political'" (*H,* 31). Wouldn't your work have been far richer and more faithful to the difficult truth of America had you found some way to discuss and illumine the continuing presence of that clamorous contradiction in Jefferson's own life and in the lives of most of your white male democratic exemplars?

Even better, in your search for representatives of the biblical and republican strands in eighteenth- and nineteenth-century American life, how much more American your work would have been had we been introduced to Frederick Douglass, Sojourner Truth, David Walker, Harriet Tubman, or Henry Highland Garnet. Here were exemplary Americans who lived the biblical and republican traditions. Steeped in those traditions, these were the ancestors who opposed slavery not only "in principle" but in full practice, often at great jeopardy to their lives. These were women and men (along with many nonconformist white sisters and brothers who did not manage to become exemplars either) who lived out the great American ideals while carrying on a faithful struggle against the most powerful threat to democratic community and biblical faith in the America of their time. In the process, they transformed the faith and tradition, becoming creators and bearers of the seed that eventually produced Martin Luther King, Jr., and his companions in the freedom movement. These are *my* exemplary Americans. I trust them and their freedom-obsessed white allies much more than a group of white men who too often managed to carry biblical and republican traditions in one hand and acceptance of slavery in the other. For reasons that I will later explain, I consider *all* of them my ancestors, but, for the transformation of America, I choose my models (exemplars) from among those women and men who were moved by their religious and democratic faith to become active participants in the long and risky struggle against slavery.

One last word on ancestors may be appropriate, friends. I think there is a revealing irony in the fact that your preeminent "ancestor" was not an American, but the brilliant French lawyer, social critic, and author of *Democracy in America,* Alexis de Tocqueville. You claim him as "the predecessor who has influenced us most profoundly in thinking about life in America." But what did you do with Tocqueville's harsh and powerful commentary on the destructive relationships between white Americans and their black and Indian co-inhabitants of this land? That aspect of his work seems totally absent from your treatment of the American past.

On the basis of what he had seen, heard and felt in the United States, Tocqueville wrote, "The European is to the other races of mankind what man is to the lower animals . . . he makes them subservient to his use; and when he cannot subdue he destroys them" ([1835–40] 1855 1 : 362). Perhaps even more directly related to our conversation is Tocqueville's subtle sensitivity to the contradictions at work among the white lovers of democracy and freedom. At one point, as you probably recall, he compares the Spanish settlers and the North Americans in their deadly approach to the natives of the hemisphere. His conclusion was:

> The Spaniards were unable to exterminate the Indian race by those unparalleled atrocities which brand them with indelible shame, nor did they even succeed in wholly depriving it of its rights; but the Americans of the United States have accomplished this twofold purpose with singular felicity; tranquilly, legally, philanthropically, without shedding blood [surely an

overstatement—even before the "winning of the west"] and without violating a single great principle of morality in the eyes of the world. It is impossible to destroy men with more respect for the laws of humanity. (Ibid., 385–86)

I find it sad and problematic that in your fascination with Tocqueville and your exemplary Americans you have nothing to say about this visitor's trenchant criticism of the oppression of the children of Africa and the despoiling and destruction of the natives of the land which were being carried out by—or at least under the aegis of—a number of your heroes. Even the Constitution, which you admire for creating "a machinery of national government consciously adapted to the social reality of expanding capitalism and the attendant culture of philosophical liberalism" (*H*, 254–55), requires re-visioning. For at the heart of its "expanding capitalism" was the business of speculation in the lands of the Indians and speculation in the bodies of the Africans. And the philosophic liberalism of that time, as in our own moment of history, was usually adjusted to accommodate and justify such profitable "social reality."

If one takes Tocqueville seriously, just as when one listens to Douglass, Walker, and Truth, it seems to me that the argument can be made that the contradiction between your exemplars' purported love of freedom, on the one hand, and the real destruction of the lives and freedom of nonwhite men and women, on the other, has been at least as much a major theme in American history as the conflict between individualism and community. (Of course, when somewhat more fully interpreted, white supremacy can be seen as a form of racial individualism, clinging to the prerogatives of whiteness, denying the larger community of the peoples of creation. Do you see the pernicious dangers of a continuing focus on the white middle class in the light of such a history as ours?) Ironically enough, your failure to pay any serious attention to this *other* American tension may be connected to the same problem Tocqueville faced when he was unable to see white-black relations in America as a crucial manifestation of his own majority-minority theme. That is, neither you nor he included black people in your definition of the American community. Friends, I do not mean to be harsh, and I am not ignoring the contrary commitments of your personal lives. But if I move solely in the context of your book (which is all the evidence most readers will have), then, in spite of its important references to Martin Luther King, Jr., I can come to no other conclusion.

Unfortunately, the essential method of exclusion also continued into the heart of your "conversations with our fellow citizens," thereby shaping—and limiting—the definitions you would give to "matters of common interest." As I reflected on your decision to omit black people and so many others from the class of "fellow citizens," my mind went to Richard Wright's *Twelve Million Black Voices*, a work now almost half a century old. Both asking and declaring his question, the powerful black artist wrote: "If we had been allowed to participate in the vital processes of America's national growth, what would have been the texture of our lives, the pattern of our traditions, the routine of our customs, the state of our arts, the code of our laws, the function of our government!" Immediately he provided a response: "Whatever others may say, we black folk say that America would have been stronger and greater!" (Wright 1941, 145).

In the forty-five years between Wright's book and yours, social scientists who are concerned with a new "public philosophy" must surely have learned that black people have participated deeply "in the vital processes" of this nation's post–World War II development and have affected its traditions, its culture, and its law. And yet, at this point in history, you still decided that you could explore fundamental questions about the nature of Americans and their character without including black citizens in your essential conversations. Beyond the pain evoked in me by your choice, I can only join with Wright and the nameless others who must say of your work as he said of America, it "would have been stronger and greater," had you understood the necessity of engaging black fellow citizens in your conversations. Indeed, many of the questions you were raising about the American "character" are questions that have been consistently forced into the public arena by the freedom-seeking, community-creating activities of your black fellow Americans. To reverse Wright's question, can you imagine what post–1945 (to say nothing of post–1776) America would have been like without the insistent challenge we blacks mounted to the republican and biblical traditions of this nation? Was it primarily a failure of your budget and staff or a failure of imagination that excluded us?

I am convinced that the very questions you posed to your contemporary white fellow citizens would have found a richer and more complex set of responses had you also raised them in the presence of the nonwhite middle-class people in America. Among them are surely keepers of a profound set of tensions. Many of them have been reared (to use an old-fashioned word) in communities where the extended family, the clan, or the tribe continues to make powerful claims on the person and does much to shape that individual life. What would they say about individualism and community, about the need to leave family and grounding? What would the resilient and fascinating phenomenon of black family reunions contribute to the discussion?

Within the black community, there are many persons who are deeply ambivalent about the American middle-class mainstream in which they now move. They still have lively, painful, beautiful ties of blood and commitment to that vast, burdened body of non–middle-class Americans who are totally absent from your work. Indeed, each of the nonwhite middle-class groups bears its own set of ambivalent feelings about movement into the American mainstream and what it does to structures of family, community, and memory. What is the therapy they are experiencing for their divided hearts? Their stories are a crucial element in the continuously developing narrative of America. Can you afford to ignore them in your work?

So, too, when you tried to explore the lives of those men and women who are participating in "newer forms of political activism that have grown out of the political movements of the sixties," could you imagine the richness that might have been available to you? For instance, what is happening with the black Americans whose freedom movement did so much to shape the new, post–World War II American realities? How do middle-class black activists now relate to the "system" that has traditionally been the source of such ambivalent responses? Are we in it? And if so, what difference does it seem to make? Are we black folk bearers of a new vision of the public good or simply more stylish copiers of all the dangerous flotsam that drifts in the mainstream? Do we have a second (or first?) language that is more adequate than others to probe our experience? Has not the language of faith, emotion, and community been one of our strengths in the past? Where does it stand now? Wouldn't it have been fascinating to listen, to compare? Indeed, wherever you turn, whether to love and marriage or to religion, the experiences of peoples of color (even in their middle-class manifestation) are surely necessary to provide a true sense of what America is now and what it is yet to be. How could you have come to another conclusion—especially in light of your concern for the "riches" of culture, for the largeness of method? I am really puzzled.

That, friends, is at the heart of much of the pain I experienced as I read your book. First, methodologically, I felt that when you decided to go white you had separated yourselves from some of the most vibrant, complex, and truly "American" middle-class experiences in this country. Of even more importance, though, was my sense that you were cutting off yourselves (and, perhaps, many of your readers) from authentic encounter with the future of this nation. For while some persons do not know it, surely you must: We are not now and never have been a white middle-class nation. And in our own perilous times it seems absolutely essential that all of us who write for the public about the definition of America must make it powerfully clear that our *only* humane future as a nation is located in a multicultural, multivocal, multiracial territory. Indeed, to ask in the 1980s what is an American, and even to begin to try to answer the question on exclusively white grounds is, in my view, both backward and dangerous. It is to deny a truly public philosophy.

Surely our fellow citizens need to receive a much more useful vision from some of their most compassionate scholars. As it now stands, *Habits* is too great a temptation to all the old white fantasies that gave Euro-Americans the sole right to define the past, present, and future of the nation. In today's world this is a dangerous, perhaps suicidal, misperception. On this matter, I think it is worth quoting Martin Luther King, Jr., at length, partly because he is your one black exemplar, but more because his wisdom is very much to the point on the matter of the dangers of extending and encouraging the white fantasy. Shortly before he was assassinated, King was involved in the preparation of an article for *Playboy* magazine that did not appear until months after his death. In it he reminded Americans that "Integration is meaningless without the sharing of power." (Is the publication of such a book as *Habits* an act of power?) Then he extended his concern, saying:

> The implications of true racial integration are more than just national in scope. I don't believe we can have world peace until America has an "integrated" foreign policy. Our disastrous experiences in Vietnam and the Dominican Republic have been, in one sense, a result of racist decision-making. Men of the white West, whether or not they like it, have grown up in a racist culture, and their thinking is colored by that fact. They have been fed on a false mythology and tradition that blinds them to the aspirations and talents of other men. They don't really respect anyone who is not white. But we simply cannot have peace in the world without mutual respect. (Washington 1986, 317–18)

Such is the ultimate danger of all-white perceptions of America and Americans.

I am sure you had no intentions of encouraging the image of an essentially white America, of a nation that can be defined primarily in terms of its European-derived middle class; but I am afraid that is one of the images cast into the public mind by your work. (I cringe to read such statements as "America was colonized by those who had come loose from the older European structures, and so from the beginning we had a headstart in the process of modernization" (*H*, 276). And I wondered where in this generalization were *we* who were *cut* loose by the modernizers from the even older African structures; where were *we* who were dispossessed by the modernizers from the even older native American structures?) As a result, in my eyes, it is not hard to see you standing in Joe Gorman's shoes, filled with what you called "a fundamental generosity" of character, but also setting forward "a mythical past" of white "representative" men, and white, racially insensitive (sometimes supremacist) social movements. In the process, we are given a sanitized study, which, as you described Gorman's beliefs, "provides little help in understanding" how our beloved, misguided nation "might work out its contemporary problems and almost no framework for thinking about . . . the larger society" (*H*, 13), a society erupting all around us in many colors and conditions—most of them neither white nor middle class.

II

In addition to the methodological dilemma created by the narrowly white middle-class focus, your decision to limit the sources of your history and your ancestry leads to other serious difficulties as well. In your important and commendable search for "new visions of the public good" that might help us resolve some of the problems created by destructive individualism, you look to the nation's post–Civil War history for possible guideposts. In the process, you identify "six distinct visions of the public good" that have emerged in the United States over the last century and suggest that "all have developed as responses to the need for citizens of a society grown increasingly interdependent to picture to themselves what sort of a people they are and where they should be heading" (H, 257). Placing the visions in pairs, you see "each pair emerging in a period of institutional breakdown and subsequent reintegration of the national economic order." You begin with what you identify as the "alternative visions . . . of the Establishment versus Populism" and, in what can only be called misinformed nostalgia, you characterize Populism as "the great democratizer, insisting on the incompleteness of a republic that excluded any of its members from full citizenship" (H, 259). I find this very strange and very sad—for several reasons.

First of all, friends, it seems to me that if there is a logical, historical beginning point for exploring institutional breakdown and the rise of alternative visions, it is surely at the supreme national crisis of the Civil War. Out of that war came two clearly opposing visions for the post-slavery American nation. The vision of the overwhelming majority of the nation (the Establishment?) called for the continuation of white supremacy and domination. The other vision—carried primarily by black Americans (and such nonexemplary whites as Wendell Phillips)—aspired to shared power in a democracy of black and white "fellow citizens." While it was not the only major choice after the war, the option for the creation of a just and multiracial democracy was central. Indeed, those critical alternatives and our various American responses to them provide a powerful motif of continuing tension in the nation's life, a tension you seem to miss or to ignore. Thus you do not include in your understanding of visions of the public good such a succinct and magnificent statement as the one by Frances Ellen Watkins Harper, the exemplary black American poet, activist, and stirring freedom lecturer. She set the critical question before the nation in 1875 when she said:

> The great problem to be solved by the American people, if I understand it, is this: Whether or not there is strength enough in democracy, virtue enough in our civilization, and power enough in our religion to have mercy and deal justly with four millions of people but lately translated from the old oligarchy of slavery to the new commonwealth of freedom; and upon

the right solution of this question depends in a large measure the future strength, progress and durability of our nation. (Foner 1972, 431)

Harper's vision was typical of much that can be found in any serious examination of nineteenth-century black social, political, economic, and religious thought. It preceded the Populist vision and was far more faithful to the democratic vocation of America. In confining yourselves to white exemplars, you miss this source of so much of the nation's best democratic and anti-individualistic history. For instance, you seem not to know the voice of W. E. B. Du Bois, who proclaimed at the beginning of this century that:

> The problem of the twentieth century is the problem of the colorline, the question of how far differences of race . . . will hereafter be made the basis to denying over half the world the right of sharing to their utmost ability the opportunities and privileges of modern civilization. (Meier, Rudwick, and Broderick 1971, 56)

Had you claimed the voices of such ancestors, then you would have recognized how deeply flawed were your three favored historical carriers of the vision of the Public Good—Populism, Welfare Liberalism, and Economic Democracy. For, beginning with the Populists, each of the movements and participants roughly grouped under these headings displayed a fundamental refusal to choose a multiracial democracy over a white supremacist vision of America.

Thus, only from the most narrow and racially insensitive (or historically uninformed?) position could you possibly declare that the Populists and progressives "wanted a national community that would be genuinely democratic and inclusive." Both groupings, and others like them, betrayed the black-held vision of a new multiracial society, and none of them led naturally to Martin Luther King, Jr., your own most-favored hero of the recent struggles for a new America. You cannot get to King in any organic way if you totally neglect the matrix of the black struggle for freedom, if you ignore the Afro-American biblical and republican traditions—or if you present an entire chapter on religion in America and keep it stunningly white. Of course, this is not to say that other American—and non-American—traditions did not contribute to the flowering of King and the modern black movement for a new Public Good. But it is to say that nothing in *Habits of the Heart* helps us to trace the essential Afro-American Christian democratic roots of the man and the movement. In other words, your choice of focus ironically cuts you off from the heartland of your/our major twentieth-century exemplar.

III

Indeed, my friends, I think it is unavoidably clear that your important search for the way to "create a new social science for new realities" is seriously hindered by your own narrow definitions of both the old and the new American realities. As I have tried to indicate in this missive, America has always been much richer, more multivocal, more colorful—and far more painful—than you have pictured it in your dealings with history or with contemporary society. And, even more important, America is now and must become far more varied in its visions and traditions (even when we confine our view to middle-class manifestations) than you have suggested. Essentially, moving from past toward future, I am inviting you to expand, radically expand, your vision of ancestors, friends, and fellow citizens. For if you, among the best and the brightest in American academic life, cannot discover and reflect such powerful lively realities in your work, how can we hope for a new social science, at least, and a new nation at best? Wasn't it this new reality that Martin King was trying to encompass in his last years—breaking beyond the middle classes, calling men, women, and children of all colors and conditions? Building on the many American traditions of democratic struggle, he was helping to shape a new public philosophy, moving toward a new society, inviting *all* of his fellow citizens to become exemplars in the perilous, beautiful quest for a new community in America. (By the way, friends, it seems to me that King was also raising serious questions about certain matters of community and chaos that you touch lightly, if at all. For instance, by the end of his life he was engaged in an unrelenting critique of American racism, materialism, militarism, and their companion, "paranoid anti-communism," making it clear that he saw all these leading to our government's policy of attacks against revolutionary movements of the poor all over the world. Indeed, his serious search in his last days for a way toward nonviolent revolution of the poor and their allies both encompassed and transcended the best in the American biblical and republican traditions. He was setting out on a path that you do not explore at all.)

I am calling upon you to open your hearts and expand your horizons, to develop new habits of vision, connection, and hope. Without such an enlarging process, your work carries a series of tragic ironies from the past into the present, threatening our future possibilities, leading you to become the objects of your own harshest critiques. For instance, in your helpful appreciation of the role of authentic community as a source of true individuality and interdependence, you raise a valid warning about disabling communities. You noted that "there are authoritarian groups in the United States," who differ from "genuine communities [in] the shallowness of and distortion of their memory and the narrowness of what they hope for" (*H*, 162). Is this a social and intellectual trap toward which you have unintentionally moved? Because of the unfortunate selectivity in your choice of ancestors, friends, and fellow citizens, is there not an inauthentic sense of "American" community at work among you, one that tends toward shallowness and distortion in your view of the past and narrowness in your hope for the future?

And when you criticize Ted Oster and other modern American individualists, do you sense the possibilities of the critique being turned on your work? You say,

> When thinking of the imperative to "love thy neighbor," many metropolitan Americans like Ted . . . consider that responsibility fulfilled when they love those compatible neighbors they have surrounded themselves with, fellow members of their own lifestyle enclave, while letting the rest of the world go its chaotic, mysterious way. (H, 179)

I must ask, Who are *your* neighbors of past, present, and future? Is that gathering of *relatively* compatible middle-class white people who form the core of your partners in dialogue really true to the fundamental meaning and mystery of our chaotic, multiracial nation and our largely nonwhite and non–middle-class world? Or are they part of an "individualism" of race and class?

As it stands now, friends, it may be that Mike Conley of Suffolk (181–85) is closer to you than you have dreamed. He opposes an influx of nonwhite people into his community and does not excuse himself, but says, "'I don't want them living near me, causing trouble for me.'" In a sense, Mike seems to reflect the reality (rather than the good intentions) of your work. To deal with human subjects—past and present—who are not white and middle class would have simply caused too much "trouble" for your research design, the makeup of your team, and your budget constraints. So we have a book in which the choices made by your team and the decisions made by Mike actually lead to the same outcome: there are no nonwhites (except for a deracinated Martin Luther King) in the world of *Habits*, no troublesome presence. As a result, the verdict you pronounce on "people such as Mike" becomes a verdict for you to ponder: "There is no rationale here for developing public institutions that would tolerate the diversity of a large, heterogeneous society and nurture common standards of justice and civility among its members" (H, 185). Could this not be said of *Habits*? Do my nonwhite students mistake the work when they say, "I just don't see myself here"? In spite of your best intentions, I think the problem is real.

IV

But I cannot leave you here, just as you must not leave my students outside the ambit of your questions and explorations concerning who *we* Americans really are. Personally, I deny that you can even begin to forge an answer to those questions while we are locked out of the arena of your research and your memory (to say nothing of the debilitating absence of all the other Americans who are not now and never have been middle-class white people). As I trust you have gathered by now, I am seriously asking you to re-vision your work, to change your habits and to enlarge your hearts.

Obviously, this is no simple task, but neither is the redefinition of America and Americans. In our generation, people like King and Fannie Lou Hamer, Clarence Jordan and Viola Liuzzo, Malcolm X and Diane Nash, Bob Moses and Cesar Chavez, Paul Robeson, Micky Schwerner, and Roy Sano—to name only a familiar few—have taken up the un-simple task that has obsessed freedom-loving Americans since the nation began: To re-create, again and again, a vision of America and Americans worthy of the terrible grandeur and the heart-rending agonies of our unique and common pilgrimages. In that tradition, Langston Hughes called us to "make America again." In a sense, it is a call—is it not?—to re-create our habits, our institutions, and our hearts.

I would suggest that one possible beginning point for those of us who are committed to re-creation is a new recognition of who *our* ancestors really are. To claim Tubman, Truth, Walker, and Douglass, to recognize such beautiful ones as Lame Deer and Ida B. Wells-Barnett as our fore-bears is crucial to the development of a truly public social science, as well as the establishment of a sound basis for a wide-ranging and profound vision of the public good.

And it is also absolutely necessary to redefine and give public mani-festation to our understanding of who our fellow citizens are. So, let the conversation that established this important and deeply flawed book continue. But now it shall include others whose truth must inform and reshape the heart of American life. We widen our circle (and I use the first-person plural now because the rebuilding, healing, re-creative task belongs to us all), not in a quest for modish "diversity," but out of a deeper hunger for authenticity. In that spirit, I would suggest at least four groups whose voices must enliven the conversation and reinvent the book:

Speak to your black fellow citizens. We may well be the American middle-class community that has made the single most powerful contri-bution to the creation of a new, justice-seeking public philosophy since World War II. Speak to them and discover the organic setting out of which King came. Recognize through them the necessity of the struggle for a redefinition of the American biblical and republican traditions. Work with what it means to claim both Jefferson *and* David Walker, Lincoln *and* Frederick Douglass, Whitman *and* Frances Ellen Watkins Harper. Allow Sojourner, Harriet Tubman, and Ida B. Wells-Barnett to open us up to a host of sister ancestors—like Angelina Grimke, Pru-dence Crandall, and Susan B. Anthony—who have not even appeared on your list of exemplary white Americans. Speak to black citizens, rec-ognize how many of this middle class live on the edges of all the ear-lier, harder, more brutal times. Understand the pain that often seeps through the newly constructed, flimsy walls of class among us. Touch the sensitivities, often dulled, but sometimes filled with razor-sharp memories of poverty, joblessness, protest, and despair, qualities of life so clearly missing from the rather bland America you have drawn for us. Listen to them and discover again that there is no character to American life without the anguish, the blues, and the harrowing, democratizing victories of its strangely radiant communities of blackness.

Speak to Asian-Americans. (How could you, often based in California, have ignored them in your plans? What would it have been like for you to have worked with a Japanese-American social historian like Ronald Takaki?) Especially be certain to move among those hundreds of thousands who have been thrown up on our shores in the wake of our nation's latest imperialist ventures in Southeast Asia. Literally taste the differences in the ways they identify themselves as Americans; recognize the fascinating variety and depth of their cultural, religious, and political experiences as they become part of the continuing transformative drama, recreating the American "self," deepening the American story. Who are we becoming as we absorb not only their foods, but experience their family lifestyles, explore their spiritualities? Who are we Americans, as these Asian ancestors become ours, as the lotus lines are crossed? Was it not you who said "if we are ever to enter that new world that so far has been powerless to be born, it will be through reversing modernity's tendency to obliterate all previous culture" (*H,* 283)? Did you not declare: "We need to learn again from the cultural riches of the human species and to reappropriate and revitalize those riches so that they can speak to our conditions today" (ibid.)? The new world is already upon us, friends. Our wealth in human resources is beyond every past dream. Enter and listen, teach and learn. Let there be new dreams, worthy of our new realities.

Of course, the new world that has been borning among us demands that we speak and hear Spanish. Speak to those who are part of the steadily surging millions of our Hispanic fellow citizens. They are totally absent from your first visions—again an amazing omission by scholars who have lived in what was once Old Mexico. Listen to those who have crossed the rivers—reawakening memories of North Stars that once filled the skies and hearts of our exemplary ancestors. Surely they raise more than philosophical questions about the nature of our "second language." Indeed, as so many of these children of the hemisphere move into our common body politic from such places and Central and South America, they bring us the gift of new ways to ask the question: "Who are we, as Americans?" They insist on reminding us that the only singular geographic entity that is justly called "America" is the hemisphere itself. They force us toward our riches and our shame, opening the possibility that the peculiar agony now wrenching the poverty-crushed, his-

torically disdained Central nations of this America is one that our ancestors, our fellow citizens, and we ourselves cannot ignore. For the pain
is in our heartland, and it does not have to continue. Speak to those
who come from there. Ask them about the past and future meanings of
America. And listen.

Then, my brothers and sisters, as you dream the new world in richer,
deeper hues (and wilder moods) than you ever knew before, if you never
speak another word, if you never hear another song, listen to the natives
of this land. (Were there any songs among your fellow citizens, your ancestors, yourselves? Can Americans ever be known without the songs we
sing in our hearts?) Hear the chants and whispers, listen to the dyings
and the rising again, let the drums sound, enter the lodge, welcome the
sun, dance, be still, join the eternal birthing that does not require a second language of logical words, that emerges from the deep places of our
Grandmother and sings wordlessly in the center of our expanding heart.
Do such things. First as acts of respect, as lessons in humility. For how
dare we think that we can define the meaning of America, of American-
ness, without entering the world of those who were here before the land
was named, before our other, European, ancestors had even awakened.
(And you speak of "modernity's tendency to obliterate all previous culture"!) Listen and beware.

Listen as well to learn. For was it not you who wisely dreamed, "if we
are to enter that new world that so far has been powerless to be
born . . ."? Do you, do we, really want to find the power to be born?
Again? Listen to the natives of this land. For though they themselves
speak with many voices from many places of great pain, they surely open
to us deep, powerful wisdom as well, especially concerning our search
for the relationships between individuality and community. For who has
suffered the ravages of America's individualism more fully than they?
And who among us has experimented for more millennia to develop
creative expressions of the common wealth? Listen to Dakotas and Ojib-
was, to Hopis and Navahos; listen to Black Elk, Chief Joseph, and Chief
Seattle. Listen to the echoes and the shouts. Listen to the mourning in
the wind. There is power in the blood.

Listen. For survival and transcendence. I must assume that you know
there can be no twenty-first-century definition of the public good that
does not find some way to include the reality of our interdependent relationships with the life forms around us—whose health and well-being we
need at least as much as they need ours. Our ancestors, the Chinooks,
our ancestors, the Creeks, our ancestors, the Kiowas—all our Indian ancestors knew this. (Just as our African ancestors knew it.) To ignore their
cries and their love calls, to live and interview and write as if they did not
exist is madness. Extend the dialogue. Deepen the definitions—for the
sake of our sanity. Let your new insight become: A social science con-

cerned with the whole of society would have to be historical and environmental, multivocal, as well as philosophical.

Then listen to Chief Seattle, an exemplary American, and receive the
most profound levels of his gift and his promise, beyond the words, as he
says:

> . . . when the last Red Man shall have perished, and the memory of my
> tribe shall have become a myth among the White Men, these shores will
> swarm with the invisible dead of my tribe, and when your children's chil-
> dren think themselves alone in the field, the store, the shop, upon the
> highway, or in the silence of the pathless woods, they will not be alone. At
> night when the streets of your cities and villages are silent and you think
> them deserted, they will throng with the returning hosts that once filled
> and still love this beautiful land. The White Man will never be alone.
>
> Let him be just and deal kindly with my people, for the dead are not
> powerless. Dead, did I say? There is no death, only a change of worlds. (in
> Turner 1977, 253)

Here is American religion, American wisdom, American hope. Listen
and receive it. (There is power in the blood.)

Let it enter your circles as an invitation and a challenge, sister, brothers, fellow citizens, friends. For it calls you away from the dangerously
constricted arena of your methodology, your history, and your hope. It
announces that white Americans, whatever their class (or profession),
are not alone, cannot be alone, cannot survive or overcome alone (cannot be trusted alone?). The word from Chief Seattle announces that
you are surrounded, undergirded, covered, and pierced through by
the hands and hearts of all those ancestors of every kind who also love
this land and who have experienced "a change of worlds." You are surrounded by life, my friends, and you are challenged by the children of
these life-givers, children who now invite you out of your racial individualism into the darkly radiant, expanding community of all those Americans who are changing, recreating this world, your world, our world, for
the common good.

To receive such a word is to be given some guidance for our largely
uncharted journey together toward the meaning and mystery of this
chaotic and magnificent nation we share. Perhaps now you will understand why I wanted you to hear the chastening words my exemplar, Du
Bois, offered to your unlistening ancestors—our ancestors—almost a
century ago when he wrote:

> Your country? How came it yours? Before the Pilgrims landed we were
> here. Here we have brought our three gifts and mingled them with yours:
> a gift of story and song—soft, stirring melody in an ill-harmonized and
> unmelodious land; the gift of sweat and brawn to beat back the wilderness,
> conquer the soil, and lay the foundations of this vast economic empire two
> hundred years earlier than your weak hands could have done it; the third

a gift of the Spirit. [And I would add a fourth: the gift of an insistent determination to wrest the realities of freedom and justice from the promises of this land.] Around us the history of the land was centered for thrice a hundred years; out of the nation's heart we have called all that was best to throttle and subdue all that was worst; fire and blood, prayer and sacrifice, have billowed over this people, and they have found peace only in the altars of the God of Right. Nor has our gift of the Spirit been merely passive. Actively we have woven ourselves with the very warp and woof of this nation. . . . Our song, our toil, our cheer, and warning, [our love of freedom] have been given to this nation in blood-brotherhood [and sisterhood]. . . . Would America have been America without her Negro people? (Du Bois [1903] 1961, 185)

Without her Hispanic people? Without her natives of the bloody land? Without her new and old Asian re-creators? Your country?

Let the questions break open the circle, redefine our common task. And let them end this missive, for I am sure that I have never written and you have never received so long a letter before. But that is surely part of the danger and the promise of open invitations and open hearts. With gratitude for your initiative, I now offer my openness to you.

In search of our new nation,
Vincent Harding

FIVE

In the Interest of the Public Good?
New Questions for Feminism

M. Elizabeth Albert

When I first read *Habits of the Heart,* I was, as I still am, enormously sympathetic to the authors' general argument that our individualism makes it difficult to think about our commitments to other people and to live our lives in the interest of the common good. However, I was uncomfortable about the authors' specific treatment of women's issues, though I was hard pressed to say exactly why. I hardly considered the book sexist; in fact, pointing to the work of feminist thinkers like Carol Gilligan, the authors even grant that the very "moral sensitivities" necessary to the common good may have long been nurtured in women (*H,* 111). Yet while—or perhaps because—the book seemed so sympathetic to women in certain respects, I could not shake the feeling that the authors had, if nothing else, simply not considered feminism fully enough. Yet as I examined the authors' treatment of feminism, I also found myself asking questions about feminism itself.

My main problem with the authors' treatment of feminism is simply that they pay only very brief attention to it. They do not anticipate questions feminists might ask not only about the implications of their analysis, but about the thinking that went into the analysis itself. Why, for instance, though they appear to take a position that is consistent with a certain strand of feminism, do the authors confine most of their discussion of women's issues to the chapter "Love and Marriage"? That seems to leave their otherwise liberal-minded book open to charges of relegating women's issues to the "woman's sphere"—the very problem the chapter argues against. But I was more troubled by the authors' failure to acknowledge that the women's issues they discuss in "Love and Marriage" have been given voice in the women's *movement* and that the women's *movement* is and has been active in bringing about social change. Although the women's movement fits the authors' own definition of a social movement—in that it seeks "new visions of social life" founded on the ideal of democratic equality (*H*, 212)—the authors seem almost not to regard the women's movement as a social movement at all. On two separate occasions, when the authors discuss social movements that have acted in the interest of the common good, they do not mention the women's movement—though they do mention Prohibition. The authors express regret that no significant social movement has been active at the national level since the civil rights movement of the 1950s and 1960s. And yet the National Organization for Women and other feminist groups have been active throughout the 1970s and 1980s, so much so that if we substitute "sex" for "race," what the authors say about the Civil Rights movement characterizes the women's movement as well. Couldn't we say that the women's movement has "permanently changed consciousness, in the sense of individual attitudes toward [sex], and . . . altered our social life so as to eliminate overt expressions of discrimination" (*H*, 286)?

I have to admit that my manipulation of rhetoric here isn't entirely fair, for I think a problem of the book is precisely that the authors seem to put the women's movement in the past tense. Although they acknowledge that feminism has not accomplished all of its goals, the fact that the authors never discuss the activities of women's organizations—like the National Organization for Women, the Women's Legal Defense Fund, the National Women's Political Caucus, or the American Association of University Women (Hawkes 1986, 379)—nevertheless suggests that they no longer see the women's movement as an imperative. The lack of interest among college-educated people, who have been most supportive of feminism, appears to be becoming more prevalent, as an article reprinted in the winter 1986 issue of *Social Policy* suggests. The article, which originally appeared in *The Daily Pennsylvanian*, the University of Pennsylvania's student newspaper, is Andrea Levine's response to Betty Friedan's *New York Times* article, "How to Get the Women's Movement Moving Again" (3 November 1985). Levine, a senior at Pennsylvania, writes "I hadn't been thinking about feminism much lately, which was one of Friedan's many on-target points" (1986, 58). Levine goes on to remind her fellow students that while the women's movement has accomplished a great deal, its task is not over:

> On the whole, today's college women have grown up in a society that encourages us to do anything we want. We no longer feel privileged that we can be doctors or lawyers—of course we can. And yet, liberation in the professional arena is not in itself livable; new opportunities pose new problems, problems that remain unresolved. (Ibid.)

We need to remain conscious of the women's movement, Levine argues, not just because gains have brought new problems—like how to manage a career and a family without, as she puts it, "making tradeoffs

detrimental to either"—but because the gains themselves are threatened. As Levine points out: "the Reagan Administration has voiced proposals for eradicating the ban on government contracts to companies
practicing sex discrimination. The legal support systems we've grown up
with could crumble as we enter the real world" (ibid.).

Thus, because women's rights are still so at stake, I cannot help feeling
that the authors are obliged to speak more directly for the movement
that seeks to win and protect these rights. But the authors are frustratingly silent: "feminism" and "women's movement" are not even listed in
the index. Furthermore, the authors openly and explicitly support the
Society for Economic Democracy—why not the National Organization
for Women? Admittedly, the aim of the book is not to champion particular causes (in fact, that contradicts one of its main points), and of course,
the authors cannot include every example. What I see as an "omission"
could be simply the luck of the draw. But the women's movement has
been so long-lived and addresses such basic concerns that it deserves
more attention—even more so because some of Levine's "problems that
remain unresolved," are exactly the problems addressed in *Habits*.

The authors' overall silence on the women's movement is just one in-
dication of what I believe is their genuine *ambivalence* toward the movement. This ambivalence surfaces in several details of their argument. In
the chapter "Love and Marriage," when the authors appeal to the findings of feminists like Carol Gilligan and Sara Ruddick, they also note,
"There is anxiety, not without foundation, among some of the opponents of feminism, that the equality of women could result in complete
loss of the human qualities" that Gilligan and Ruddick point out have
"long [been] associated with the 'woman's sphere'" (*H*, 111). Obviously,
for the authors to lend this anxiety a degree of validity suggests they
share the anxiety themselves. In their analysis of Cecilia Dougherty's involvement in public life, the authors argue that while Cecilia's involvement *began* in a women's consciousness-raising group, the group was not
among the "determining factors in [her] activist commitments" (*H*, 160).

More importantly, in the section "Reconstituting the Social World,"
the authors insist that in order for society to change for the better, we
cannot just change a social policy here and there—we cannot just provide government-funded child care or mandate fair housing; rather, we
must "transform our social ecology" (*H*, 286). Obviously, because the authors call for a *new* social movement with this wide-ranging transformation as its goal, they do not think the women's movement is going to accomplish that goal. The women's movement may parallel the Civil Rights
movement, but it will not, as the new movement would, be its "successor
and fulfillment" (*H*, 286).

But in each of these cases, the authors merely *imply* their ambivalence.
And of course, since they do not openly acknowledge their ambivalence,
they do not explain it. They do not explain why the "equality of wom-

en" may threaten the "human qualities . . . associated with the 'woman's sphere.'" They do not fully account for the reasons Cecilia Dougherty's feminism was not as important as other factors in bringing out her sense of civic responsibility. But more significantly, because this issue really entails the other two, they do not explain why the women's movement is limited. They leave us asking, How does the way the women's movement defines and works toward its goals limit its ability to transform our social ecology?

I have argued so far that the authors of *Habits* are curiously silent about the women's movement, and that their silence seems to indicate their ambivalence toward the movement. I have argued, furthermore, that because their ambivalence is unexplained, it raises significant questions about the women's movement. It is those questions I would like to explore now.

A difficulty we all encounter when we think about the women's movement is that its ideology has been notoriously ambiguous. Few people— "feminists" or "antifeminists"—are completely sure what the term *feminist* means or what exactly feminists want. This ambiguity produces stereotypes of feminists and antifeminists alike—stereotypes that center on attitudes toward family. Antifeminists believe that feminists hate men and children, while feminists believe antifeminists are accomplices in the oppression of women. It is the antifeminist *stereotype* of the feminist which seems to motivate the authors' worry that the women's movement may undermine the "human qualities" embodied in traditional female roles.

Ironically, however, *Habits* offers a vocabulary for dispelling the stereotypes to which the authors themselves fall prey. And dispelling these stereotypes is the first step toward resolving the larger conflict between feminists and antifeminists. *Habits* suggests that the stereotypes feminists and antifeminists use against each other result from the ambiguities in the languages of individualism and commitment. The split between feminists and antifeminists, in fact, is almost completely equivalent to the ideological split between individualism and commitment (again, commitment expressed in terms of the family). The authors even suggest that women have been more conscious of the conflict between the two ideologies than men have been: "Traditionally," they note, once again pointing to work like Carol Gilligan's, "women have thought more in terms of relationships than in terms of isolated individuals. Now we are all supposed to be conscious primarily of our assertive selves" (*H,* 111). The conflict is intense for women because—as I have often felt myself— being an individual and being committed appear to be mutually exclusive ways of defining oneself. But as the authors continually argue, there needn't be so rigid a dichotomy. In fact, I believe that if we are to maintain the drive for social equity, feminists must actively seek to soften that dichotomy.

In "Feminism, Family, and Community" (1982), Jean Bethke Elshtain attempts to negotiate the middle ground between the poles of individ-ualism and commitment. In this article, and in the debate it sparked in subsequent issues of *Dissent*, we can see being worked out in feminist terms precisely the issue posed in *Habits* of how we can envision a society that grants each of us our "individual dignity" but does not allow us to lose sight of our connections to each other.

The beginning of Elshtain's article echoes the concern of *Habits*. Elsh-tain worries that feminists' emphasis on women's independence is wear-ing away what she sees as the primary link between ourselves and other people, the family: "The need to write this piece," she says,

> derives from my discontent with the way "the family" has been treated in much feminist and radical argumentation since the 1960s, and with the way "community," while celebrated, has remained mostly an empty term—for there is no way to create real communities out of an aggregate of "freely" choosing adults. (1982, 442)

Elshtain then criticizes feminism for embracing individualism too un-critically and defines her own position as "social feminism." Social femi-nism is opposed to, in Elshtain's words, a "starkly contractual" society (1982, 446), or as the authors of *Habits* explain it, a society based on a "social contract" that arises from "negotiation between individuals acting in their own self-interest" (*H*, 107). Elshtain's social feminism espouses instead the "social compact," which in fact evokes the republican and biblical virtues valued so highly in *Habits*:

> The social compact . . . is inseparable from ideals of civic virtue and retains a hold on working-class, religious, and rural culture. A compact is no con-tingent agreement but a solemn commitment to create something "new" out of disparate elements—a family, a community, a polity—whose indi-vidual members do not remain "as before" once they become part of this social mode of existence. (1982, 446)

Elshtain's idea of social feminism is similar to the ideal society called for in *Habits* in more ways than its appeal to republican and biblical virtues. Elshtain's "social mode of existence" calls to mind our authors' idea of "a form of individualism that is fulfilled *in* community rather than against it" (*H*, 162). And like our authors, though perhaps to a greater extent, Elshtain believes commitment to others finds its primary expression in the family. The family, she says, is the "prerequisite for any form of so-cial life" (1982, 447). Elshtain's notion of the family is also anticapitalistic. The family is at the base of her ideal society because it "incorporates val-ues that implicitly challenge corporate power and antidemocratic, man-agerial elites" (Elshtain 1982, 443).

Despite her openly anticapitalist bent, Elshtain's emphasis on the fam-ily as the base of society sparked passionate attacks on her article by other self-proclaimed radical intellectuals. I will discuss one of those arguments—Barbara Ehrenreich's—at some length, first because the issues Ehrenreich raises are exactly those she might have raised against *Habits,* and second, because the debate between Elshtain and Ehrenreich can clarify the position of *Habits* as well.

Ehrenreich's emotional reaction to Elshtain's article is motivated by Ehrenreich's sense of history: the right to individual dignity. Ehrenreich attacks Elshtain for not acknowledging the ways the traditional family has been implicated in maintaining oppressive capitalistic, patriarchal institutions and ideologies. Ehrenreich argues that Elshtain

> and others who romanticize the traditional family as a haven for non-market values consistently overlook the economics of the situation. The wife's dependence on her husband—whatever feelings may or may not be involved—is also a financial dependence. The husband, in turn, is dependent on his employer, so that the family as a whole might as well be married to capital. (1983, 104–5)

While Elshtain does not deny that the institution of the family can function to maintain the powers-that-be, she argues that to define the family in purely economic terms is too simplistic and reductive. A purely economic definition like Ehrenreich's, Elshtain argues, "ignores the family as the locus of deep emotional bonds and ethical imperatives" (1983, 107). In other words, while Ehrenreich thinks Elshtain ignores the problems embodied in the traditional family, Elshtain thinks Ehrenreich lets those problems blind her to the positive characteristics of the family. Clearly, I think, what both women want to support, and what *Habits* wants to support as well, is a critical view of the family—something Elshtain more explicitly proposes when she says we should aim to "draw feminism and traditional notions of family life into a mutual relation in a manner that does not see earlier terms of women's oppression as the only way to restore family life" (1982, 446).

Tradition is as important a term in Elshtain's ideology as it is in *Habits.* A call for a return to tradition is often understood to indicate a reactionary political stance. For this reason, Ehrenreich finds Elshtain's emphasis on tradition disturbing. But Ehrenreich overlooks Elshtain's statement, "my aim is to *contest,* not to abandon, the grounds of tradition, a terrain thus far handed over to the right" (1982, 446; emphasis added). To contest tradition, not to idealize it naively, is at the heart of the distinction drawn in *Habits* between *tradition* and *traditionalism.* Paraphrasing Jaroslav Pelikan, the authors declare, "tradition is the living faith of the dead, traditionalism is the dead faith of the living" (*H,* 140). Ehrenreich does not seem to understand that tradition, not traditionalism, lies behind Elshtain's vision of society.

As the debate between Ehrenreich and Elshtain illustrates, when individualism is seen as an either/or proposition, not only do feminists and antifeminists part company, but so do feminists themselves. Ehrenreich's

understanding of Elshtain's position is simplistic. Ehrenreich does not
see that Elshtain's feminism, informed by tradition, not traditionalism, is
both more complex and, importantly, more self-critical than her own
position. Elshtain's feminism, in fact, shows promise as a means to realize
the goal outlined in *Habits*. Her form of feminism may help us to "reappropriate a language in which we could all, men and women, see
that dependence and independence are deeply related, and that we can
be independent persons without denying that we need one another"
(*H*, 111).

It is precisely in the interest of *tradition* that feminism, specifically the
work of feminist scholars, has much to contribute. Yet in this respect,
Habits most overlooks feminism. Perhaps the authors believe that the
feminist critique merely deconstructs or rejects tradition. However, that
is not an accurate view of the feminist scholar's aim. As Lillian Robinson
explains in "Treason Our Text," feminist literary criticism, for example,
desires to *create*, not destroy, our tradition—feminist theory simply provides us a tool to evaluate our tradition critically. The point in feminist
literary criticism, Robinson argues, "is not to label and hence dismiss
even the most sexist literary classics, but to enable all of us to apprehend
them, finally, in all their human dimensions" (1985, 118). Robinson is
calling for a more honest version of our cultural tradition. Just as a
smaller community of memory must include in the story of itself an account of the suffering it has *inflicted* (*H*, 153), so we must acknowledge
the elements of our tradition of which we may not be proud. That does
not, however, mean that feminist scholars turn their backs on tradition
altogether.

Feminist scholarship, furthermore, is crucial to reviving the admirable strands of our tradition. Literature by women, which feminist literary critics have only recently brought to serious attention, may in fact
offer just the alternative visions of society that "speak to our condition
today" (*H*, 283). Jane Tompkins describes one such vision in "Sentimental Power," her well-known essay on *Uncle Tom's Cabin*. Harriet Beecher
Stowe, according to Tompkins, presents a vision of society which does
not pit self-interested individuals against one another. In Stowe's society,
the home becomes the center of all human life. "Motivated by self-
sacrificing love, and joined to one another by its cohesive power,"
Tompkins explains, "people [in this society] will perform their duties
willingly and with pleasure: moral suasion will take the place of force"
(1985, 97). Stowe's vision, unfortunately, has been dismissed by scholars
as a sentimental retreat from the public sphere into the private sphere.
Tompkins argues much to the contrary: Far from sentimental, Stowe's
novel is a political expression calling for a new society. In fact, Tompkins
insists that *Uncle Tom's Cabin* meets Sacvan Bercovitch's definition of the
"jeremiad," literature that acts as a "mode of public exhortation . . . de-

signed to join social criticism to spiritual renewal, public to private identity, the shifting 'signs of the times' to certain traditional metaphors,
themes, and symbols" (cited in Tompkins 1985, 95).

Stowe's vision of society, in this respect, is "revolutionary," Tompkins
says. Private life *is* public life. Public institutions disappear. As Tompkins
elaborates:

> The image of the home . . . is in no sense a shelter from the stormy blast of
> economic and political life, a haven from reality divorced from fact which
> allows the machinery of industrial capitalism to grind on; it is conceived as
> a dynamic center of activity, physical and spiritual, economic and moral,
> whose influence spreads out in ever-widening circles. (1985, 100)

Tompkins's essay on *Uncle Tom's Cabin* is just one of the feminist
sources from which the authors of *Habits* might have drawn to evoke the
sense of tradition that checks the ideology of strict individualism. But
unfortunately, by not considering more work by women writers and intellectuals as they draw from our artistic and intellectual past, the authors leave themselves open to the charge of being somewhat traditionalistic in their thinking about our cultural tradition. Though the authors'
failure to make use of the resources of feminist scholarship in defining
our tradition is for me the most troubling aspect of their argument, ironically, it has been in anticipating their reaction to a particular piece of
feminist scholarship—Tompkins's essay—that I've been most able to see
valid reasons for their ambivalence toward the women's movement.

While the home as the "dynamic center of activity" eliminates the conflict between individualism and commitment, it maintains problematic
relations between people. *Uncle Tom's Cabin,* at least in Tompkins's interpretation, pits men and women against each other in a struggle for
power. Tompkins says that in Stowe's vision of society "men are inciden-
tal"; the society is "not . . . controlled by men but by women" (1985, 100).

The themes of control and power and their attendant images of men
and women as adversaries do run through feminist rhetoric and are, I
think, a valid source of concern. *Habits* makes it clear that when political action is motivated by a desire only to increase one person's or one
group's control and power, it does not work toward the common good.
Much of what I've read on women and politics, unfortunately, suggests
that feminists frequently conceive of their political action in just such
limited terms. Studies of women and politics are often obsessed with determining the numbers of women in office and the numbers of women
who vote, but devote little attention to analyzing what those women actually accomplish for the society.

Such single-minded striving for power leads the women's movement
into practicing the politics of interest, where one enters politics "to get
what one or one's group needs or wants, rather than because of spon-

taneous involvement with others to whom one feels akin" (*H*, 200). As Ellen Hawkes points out in *Feminism on Trial: The Ginny Foat Case and the Future of Feminism*, in the 1984 presidential elections, people within and outside the National Organization for Women worried that NOW was becoming "an arm of the Democratic party" (1986, 378), supporting the Democrats, Hawkes suggests, simply to get Ronald Reagan out of office and Geraldine Ferraro into office.

The feminists' desire to claim power for women can be so strong that in some feminist ideologies men become trivial, even invisible. As we saw earlier, the vision of society that Tompkins admires in *Uncle Tom's Cabin*, though it may perhaps not be "limited to purely personal concerns" (1985, 100), nevertheless leaves no room for men. Tompkins argues that Stowe's image of Simeon Halliday's shaving represents how Stowe "reconceives the role of men in human history: while Negroes, children, mothers, and grandmothers do the world's primary work, men groom themselves contentedly in a corner (ibid.). Neither Elshtain nor Ehrenreich says much about the moral and social roles men play in their visions of society. Ehrenreich portrays men as the almost stereotypical enemies to be overcome and forgotten, and while Elshtain values men at least for their roles as breadwinners, her social feminism, it seems to me, is based primarily on the metaphor of motherhood. In fact, while a great deal of feminist work I have read praises the virtues of motherhood, very little even mentions fatherhood or marriage. In asserting the value of women and of female roles, we sometimes seem to define men completely out of a role in the family.

Thus, while feminism cannot be emphasized enough for its role in maintaining a "self-revising" sense of tradition (*H*, 283), it does contain elements that make it appear, at least, to work toward a separated society rather than an integrated one. I believe that this is the deepest source of the authors' ambivalence about the women's movement. Instead of bringing men and women to understand their fundamental need for one another, the women's movement appears instead to make it easier and easier for men and women to do without each other. As the authors point out, "the present ideology of American individualism," of which they imply feminism is very much a part, "has difficulty . . . justifying why men and women should be giving to one another at all" (*H*, 111).

A symptom of the tendency of men and women to do without each other is today's high rate of divorce. While its ultimate cause may be the ideology of individualism, divorce has more directly and more immediately affected our thinking about the family than any other factor. Because it often requires people to develop nontraditional lifestyles, divorce even challenges our very definitions of the family.

How we define the family as we move toward a revitalized social ecology is no minor task. Definitions of the family were, in fact, a source of bitter contention between Ehrenreich and Elshtain. Though Elshtain declares that family has "its basis in marriage and kinship" (1982, 447), she does not elaborate which particular relationships she considers family relationships. The specific reforms Elshtain calls for, however, suggest that her image of the family is the very traditional one-income, two-parent family. (Elshtain wants men to be paid a family wage so that women can stay home to care for children if they so choose.) Hence, in her response to Elshtain, Ehrenreich worries that Elshtain implicitly degrades nontraditional households, particularly the single-parent household. And Ehrenreich's worry does have some basis. While I do not believe Elshtain intends to degrade living arrangements that result from divorce, neither does she seem to consider these arrangements ideal: they are the symptoms of a problem.

How does *Habits* define the family? While the authors describe what a family feels like, so to speak, they do not, as Elshtain does not, list the particular relationships that might fall under the definition of family. For all their emphasis on maintaining ties across generations, the authors' ideal seems to be the traditional, two-parent nuclear family: they do not include interviews with people who define their families as extended families, nor do they present single parents' descriptions of their family lives. But like Elshtain, in presenting the two-parent nuclear family as an ideal, the authors mean, I am convinced, to do anything but degrade nontraditional families. However, defining the family in terms of particular relationships may be more important to their argument than they explicitly acknowledge—for a compelling reason suggested by Elshtain's argument. Like the authors, Elshtain believes that the ideology of what she calls "possessive" individualism, expressed in economic terms as capitalism, renders traditional family relationships extremely fragile. When ties to the family break down, people attempt to create surrogate relationships by loosening the definition of the family, by applying it indiscriminately to any "ad hoc collection" of individuals—to unrelated people who happen to live under one roof, or even to the large impersonal institutions that undermined the family in the first place (1982, 448). (This is where the notion of the "corporate family" originates.) According to Elshtain, we cannot so easily give up the traditional definition of the family if we are to challenge the market-system and move toward a society that does not drive people apart. Unfortunately, however, Elshtain's definition comes across as more rigid than she perhaps intended. As *Habits* points out, alternative definitions of the family have in some important respects *improved* our social and moral climate. In this new "more tolerant atmosphere," the authors argue, "alternate forms of committed relationship long denied any legitimacy, such as those between persons of the same sex, are becoming widely accepted" (*H*, 110). This development, the authors explain, is praiseworthy: "To the extent that this new atmosphere creates more sensitive, more open, more intense, more loving relationships, as it seems to have done, it is an achievement of which Americans can justly be proud" (ibid.).

Besides the fact that Elshtain's definition of the family comes across as more rigid than she perhaps intended it to, a second problem is that her fundamental metaphor for family relationships, and thereby social relationships, is the parent-child relationship, particularly the mother-child relationship. Again, the rhetoric of feminism, by overemphasizing the mother-child relationship, makes it easy to define men out of the family. And in this respect, feminism can be seen implicitly (though unintentionally) to make it difficult to think about how people are related through marriage. This is a significant problem, for I would argue that marriage is the more important family relationship through which we should understand our civic lives. Unfortunately, marriage is also the family relationship that seems most at risk. The ties of birth and kinship do not seem nearly as threatened. Many of my friends, men and women, have said that while they look forward to being parents, they aren't nearly as enthusiastic about being wives and husbands.

But why is marriage the more important relationship for us to consider in our thinking about the family as a model for civic commitment? Marriage is our most personal experience of committing to another person to whom we aren't joined by blood kinship—of committing to a person who is most distinctly "other" than ourselves. Marriage, furthermore, is an obligation we must assume; to be married, we can no longer be absolutely "freely choosing." Because we are not born to a community the same way we are born to a family, we need a metaphor for the act of making a commitment. Marriage—without its sexual and romantic elements, of course—provides that metaphor.

I should stress here that I believe my idea of marriage is not at all traditionalistic. Nothing will be gained by returning to the old patriarchal institution of the family. But neither will anything be gained by allowing to stand in its place the notion of marriage that the authors describe as "the expression of the choices of the free selves who make it up," free selves who may end the relationship as soon as it no longer meets their needs (*H,* 107). If marriage is to provide a model for civic relationships, as I believe it can, it must be based on a belief in individual dignity and equity, and it must ultimately put the common good of the relationship before the separate needs of the individuals—before the separate needs of men *and* before the separate needs of women.

I have argued so far that the absence of a discussion of the women's movement in *Habits* implies a critique of feminism, a critique I have tried to bring to light. While the authors' ambivalence toward the women's movement is sometimes based on what appears to be misunderstandings of feminism's aims, the fact that they have those misunderstandings in the first place nevertheless indicates legitimate problems in the women's movement. Most of those problems arise from feminism's aligning itself too closely with individualism in the strictest sense. Despite these problems, I believe feminism does, underneath it all, work toward the common good and can still lead the way toward a transformation of our social ecology—feminist thinkers like Elshtain lead me to believe as much (though as I've just suggested, her ideas are not without their problems, either). But feminism can bring about a transformation only when it can speak to the consciences of more people—starting with the women who have so far been ambivalent or hostile to the movement.

Ironically, one of the reasons the women's movement has alienated women in particular from its cause is not that it embraces individualism too wholeheartedly, but that it does not uphold the principles of individualism highly enough. Ellen Hawkes argues that the women's movement became obsessed with the "women-as-victims" mentality, in which women were not seen as freely choosing individuals, but as passive puppets in the hands of male oppressors. Women who fought this image, arguing that they were not unhappy as wives and mothers, that their senses of themselves had not suffered in their relationships with men, were accused of not being feminists. Such thinking, however, flew in the face of the positive aspects of individualism in denying women the very individual identities feminism claimed to be winning for them. As Hawkes explains:

> Feminism doesn't confer instantaneous identities; women bring individual characters, pasts, loves, hates, emotional ambiguities, private and public needs, and multiple concerns to feminism. But they will only come to the women's movement when feminism doesn't deny or obliterate or rewrite as "correct" the lives from which they've forged those identities. (1986, 413)

Habits does not—as perhaps it should have—engage in an open dialogue with feminism, for it asks that feminism radically reevaluate its aims. The authors' ambivalence about the women's movement, which I have argued sometimes seems based on stereotypes, makes it clear that feminists must make dispelling those stereotypes a priority. And as I proposed much earlier, the language that integrates individualism with commitment may be just the tool feminists need to dispel those stereotypes that ultimately limit their effectiveness in bringing about important social changes. The large goal for feminism, furthermore, must be, as our authors put it, to sustain "what is best in our separation and individuation, our sense of dignity and autonomy as persons" (*H*, 286) and, at the same time to continuously remind us that while men and women may have genuine differences, we cannot forget John Winthrop's idea that we share "'our community as members of the same body'" (*H*, 285). With this integrated ideology behind it, the women's movement will surpass the politics of interest and may even realize the dream of the Civil Rights movement: to bring about a "national community that . . . respect[s] both the differences and the interdependence of its members" (*H*, 249).

SIX

On *Habits of the Heart*

Fredric R. Jameson

It is probably inevitable that *Habits of the Heart* should first be approached
as a continuation of Robert Bellah's own work, whose operative distinction between *religion* and *belief* (as in the title of his most famous book,
Beyond Belief) informs it. In the earlier work, Bellah was able to propose
the persistence of a form of "modern" religion in our time, which disen-
gaged itself from the formal dogma (and institutional structures) of what
we used to think of as "religion" in general. *Habits* will then "apply" this
notion to late capitalism in the U.S., with a twofold agenda: to show, on
the one hand, that something like a "modern religion beyond belief" still
persists here, and on the other, to suggest that it is a force upon which
we can build (the mixed metaphor can serve as an emblem of the problem), in other words, that "modern religion" (what might, in analogy to
certain new philosophical schools, be termed *weak* religion) is the most
plausible candidate for the correction of those psychological and social
defects critics of any number of ideological persuasions have come to deplore in the North American superstate.

Yet *Habits* is a collective volume whose production process the authors
describe at several points for us. While it is certainly not a collection of
essays and does have organization and stylistic coherence, its conceptual
unity ought not to be overestimated, since the chapters offer a play of
differing emphases and slight variations of positions on the basic themes.
What is more significant, however, than such relative ideological variations are fundamental slippages in the authors' basic models, and it is to
these that I want to draw attention. (It should be clear, however, that
such slippages can perfectly well take place within the thought or exposition of any one of the writers and need not reflect methodological or dis-
ciplinary differences among them, although those may also be present.)

These slippages can, however, be understood only within the fundamental unity of the project, which can be characterized as a powerful onslaught on what the authors, adapting the term from Philip Rieff, call "therapeutic" values and ideologies: something I will for the moment call a *turn back,* in the gradual waning of absolutes or objective values, toward the self and its immediate feelings of well-being for the basis of judgment and action. Christopher Lasch's "culture of narcissism" is, as we will see, another way of coming at this so-called me-generation reality, which as these very terms and their currency suggest, is one of our most popular stereotypes for describing the psychological state of things in the United States today (by calling it a stereotype I do not necessarily mean to imply that it is *wrong*). But "therapy," as the authors of *Habits* use the term, does not have to be a *psychological* concept (even though the hesitation or oscillation between psychology and a different conceptual status is among those slippages that interest me here). It is, rather, the final form of individualism, and as the subtitle of the book suggests, is thereby reintegrated into the major theme of the work, which can be better characterized as a critique of individualism in the name of an absent, yet powerful, empty conceptual space the authors term *community.*[1] The originality of their project is therefore to have linked a traditional dualistic critique based on the opposition between individualism and community with a much more contemporary cultural and sometimes psychological diagnosis of American therapeutic narcissism today. Or, if you prefer a somewhat different description, as a discourse this text seeks to combine the language of an older political science (drawing largely on Tocqueville) with that rather different language of the contemporary "culture-critique" or pop-psychological diagnosis.

The essential question that any radical or Marxist reading *Habits* will wish to pose about this text is whether, despite the great power of the critique of individualism to be found here, the alternative possibilities—designated as "community"—ever fully come into view. "Community" is after all a pious word (and the pieties of this text are not among its most attractive features); it is also a word congenial to the right as well as to the left, one whose history contains some deplorable pages as well as some inspirational ones. But I do not ever recall finding the alternative language of the collective or of collectivity in these pages, which seek to stage an "evenhanded" critique of both left- and right-wing activism and ideology. I therefore have many questions about the eventual uses and effect of this book, and they do not always presuppose the identification or unmasking of the authors' own personal intentions and ideologies, about which I am often also uncertain.

Before I explore these points in more detail, however, let me return to the interesting matter of conceptual slippages, of the insensible drift from one theoretical model to another. The most interesting of these slippages in my opinion is that which can be observed within the concept of individualism itself. The authors offer a complex, interesting, and not at all simplistic history of this phenomenon: from what they call the biblical and republican moments in the colonial period and the early Republic, through the two distinct stages of utilitarian or market individualism, and then the expressive or "personal" private-life individualism, these last intersecting in complex ways with the economic moments of the entrepreneur, the manager, and the therapist. Not the least interesting feature of this historical account is the judicious manner in which the authors refuse a facile opposition between the managerial (or organizational-man) moment and the various logics of individualism in its multiple forms, showing that these last are often unexpectedly consistent with the later monopoly structures. What is missing here, however, is not merely a theoretical account of how economic structures generate character types but also, in a more general way, any theoretical sense of how models function and how they may be inconsistent with each other, an inconsistency we can already begin to detect in this first historical account.

For a certain distance and reflection begins to suggest a basic problem even here, and in particular a distinction between the mode of explanation used in describing the biblical and republican moments of individualism, and the later market type. This second group of phenomena are economic, while the first ones can only be described—in some expanded sense—as cultural. Surely the determination of character by religion is cultural through and through (including not merely specific beliefs, but a specific text, the Bible itself, read in specific, historically new ways). But "republicanism," although it might at first glance seem to bring into play more properly political values and although, on the other hand, a few conventional appeals to yeomen farming would seem to link it to the economic, is also a cultural phenomenon: something evident when one begins to consider the role of classical texts, such as Plutarch's *Lives* in the formation of these ideals, and the role of classical education and reading in the transmission of those texts. We have here two distinct models of the formation of character types: in a first moment, "character" is formed by cultural mechanisms, in a second and later moment by the new economic circumstances of the market itself. I am not necessarily suggesting that this inconsistency is itself historically flawed, though one could imagine a more complex justification for the shift from the cultural to the economic, in which it would be argued that different modes of production generate precise, dialectically different mechanisms of character formation. But the authors do not make that kind of argument and do not seem aware of the theoretical issue itself: the result is that, particularly since theirs are relatively familiar explanations, the authors represent a complicated historiography as "natural" and as "realistic," along the lines of a history manual, and the reader takes it for granted that this discussion is a representation of historical reality and a narrative of historical change, when, to the contrary, it is neither a representation nor a narrative, but rather an explanation of certain kinds of data. The authors are here generally concerned to shock the contemporary American reader into some new and disturbing self-consciousness about his or her situation and values; it therefore does not seem too much to ask that they should not score their effects by foreshortened and oversimplified background narratives of this stereotypical kind, particularly when their own central problem here will turn out to be precisely the issue of the relative power of the cultural versus the economic.

This is, however, something of a footnote to the principal exhibit I want to offer in the matter of models and the slippages among them. For it turns out that there is here yet another (a third?) model of the origins of individualism, which is neither cultural (or educational) nor economic, but derives from what we may loosely call the history of ideas. (Let me add in advance that this explanation is no less traditional or stereotypical than the other two.) Here, it is a question of the determining influence of great ideas, and of the Western philosophical tradition generally, in the formation of character, and I quote briefly: "This notion of an unencumbered self is derived not only from psychotherapy, but much more fundamentally from modern philosophy, from Descartes, Locke, and Hume, who affect us more than we imagine" (*H,* 80). This concluding reminder and warning is surely either disingenuous or tactically manipulative: for we surely "imagine" just that, and the history of ideas has insisted in a laborious and repetitive fashion on the supreme inaugural conceptualization of the "self" by Descartes and in the extraordinary success story of this "idea" all the way down to modern times. That the authors have little enough time for a whole range of contemporary countertheories of the dispersal of the self and the decentering of the centered subject (only Erving Goffman is mentioned) is a pity; but their exclusively North American focus, to which I will return later, evidently excludes such foreign, French, poststructural imports and curiosities, which might have lent a new richness and depth to their discussions of the contemporary therapeutic character. Indeed, I will observe in passing that many of those European theories are, in reality, secretly North American in their content if not their form. The hidden reference point of much postcontemporary speculative description of the decentered self or ego, the schizophrenic consciousness, is not European psychology, but North American psychology and behavior as that fascinates the European intellectual: Gilles Deleuze and Felix Guattari's extraordinary *Anti-Oedipus* (1983), for example, seems to me best grasped sociologically as an attempt to theorize a North American counterculture, for which the Europeans had no social equivalent. I am tempted to recall Hegel's description of his own project, namely, to recreate in pure thought for a

Germany that had no revolution what the French themselves achieved concretely in revolutionary praxis. But I prefer to end this digression with a wonderful sentence of Regis Debray on the subject: "these Columbuses of revolution," he says of the European 1960s political culture, "following Godard's *La Chinoise,* imagined themselves to be discovering China at the moment at which they were in reality landing in California" (1979, 58).

Still, theories of the decentered or schizophrenic subject, like those of the Cartesian ego or consciousness, present similar methodological problems insofar as they attempt to wish away the gap between philosophy and daily life or lived experience. However you decide to handle it, I cannot but think that there is a fundamental problem in asserting the determining influence—particularly over a period that spans many generations—of an abstract idea of some sort, particularly one that is less a value than a description. Can the Cartesian cogito be imagined to have produced new kinds of human subjects, new types of individualistic selves? How can a philosophical innovation transform character structure, produce new kinds of human animals? Even if you feel yourself able to conceive this kind of influence and to feel no great problems in accepting as unproblematical the essentially idealistic model it presupposes—the shaping power of sheer philosophical abstraction over concrete life—there remain two other questions and historical problems to be resolved. The first is that of the historical emergence of the crucial concept: Why Descartes, and why that particular moment in historical time, and not some obscure medieval genius, or some unsung sage from another, more exotic culture? Any explanations you offer of the relative fit and match between Descartes's discovery or intellectual invention and his own historical context—the science of his time, for example, or its technology, or the changes in its social life—will at once begin to undermine the model of the history of ideas here presupposed and move us into some other kind of determination—a more social or economic one.

But the other question is more serious, particularly given the nature of the present project. It is simply this: Even allowing for the power of the Cartesian (or the Lockean or Humean) concept, even supposing that it was able to play some determinant role in its own social moment, how does one go on to account for the transmission of this intellectual influence over a number of generations? How is it that thinkers at their widest read by specialist groups and evoked in passing in potted philosophy courses continue to "affect us more than we imagine"? Notions of intellectual tradition, or of Western philosophy or rationalism or whatever, are peculiarly unexamined concepts that on close inspection prove to be ways of avoiding the dilemma and papering it over, rather than genuine solutions. Let me name this problem, which will be of significance to us throughout, or rather let me mention one of its possible theoretical names, which is simply that of *social reproduction*. Even if a society manages to produce a certain kind of dominant personality—such as that of individualism—and even if it does so by means of some luminous new abstraction, such as the Cartesian cogito (something I cannot really understand, as I've suggested), it remains for such a society to solve the problem of reproducing that character structure and of ensuring its persistence and reproduction across generations of new human individuals and organisms. "Tradition"—a now rather meaningless word—is sometimes explained in terms of collective memory and storage, and of the transmission in various ways of selected features, facts, narratives, valorized concepts, and the like. Even tradition, however, surely presupposes something else, namely the existence of institutions which secure that transmission; and with the introduction of the notion of institutions, we are surely once again well outside any explanation by way of the history of ideas and squarely once again within the social and the economic.

The concept of institutions, however, does not exactly solve the problem at stake here, but merely enlarges it and makes it more comprehensive. An older dialectical language would have described this problem as one of mediations: that is, the difficulties of linking concepts or realities of one order—in this case, something I will vaguely call "character," if not national character or dominant character structure (for example, individualism)—with concepts and realities of a quite different nature, namely abstract ideas (Cartesian reason) or, as with my last proposal, social institutions. And this is also a question of the multiple languages of the concepts themselves, or the multiple codes of the various disciplines: trying to make links between character and social institutions, for example, also involves devising languages or codes that compute in various specialized disciplines, an operation I have called *transcoding*.

As to the issue of national or collective character—a theoretical construct whose problems are often ingeniously alluded to by the authors—it may be worth making some observations on it before proceeding. One of the crucial solutions to the matter of what a social or national character is and how it is perpetuated involves an idea that one is astonished to rediscover in the *title* of the book (taken from a phrase of Tocqueville), but nowhere else, namely the concept of *habit*. I remind you, in passing, that in Lenin's brief remarks on cultural revolution in *State and Revolution*, "habit" already played a fundamental role: communism will have become a reality, Lenin says in effect, when the new socialist values and morality, the new socialist behavior, have become a *habit*—that is to say, are no longer ideals but are rather taken for granted. "Habit" thus usefully envelops abstract conceptions of value and concrete forms of behavior or social practice: it is already, then, we might say in a more dialectical language, a mediatory term. This is the spirit in which, in the *Outline of a Theory of Practice* (1977), Pierre Bourdieu has revived and reinvented this concept as the central mechanism for social reproduction, the form of the so-called *habitus,* which inscribes abstract values spatially, in the form of practical trajectories that individuals are called upon to traverse, trajectories that describe and define the limits of social choices. Extrapolating from Bourdieu's ideas here, I may say that a dominant social character is to be analyzed as a complex of such habits.

The nagging question that remains unresolved is the status of this concept and the doubts which may still remain as to whether the notion of habit solves the theoretical problems of accounting for the existence of a dominant social character or simply names the problem and thereby merely *seems* to resolve it. Does not then, one begins to wonder, the very concept of habit or *habitus* itself become a new problem to be resolved? At this point I want to read into the agenda some notions of Jean-Paul Sartre, from the *Critique of Dialectical Reason* (1976, 77–318), which seem to open up new avenues for exploration. For Sartre, social praxis— which always involves solving problems and confronting contradictions— also always tends to leave a kind of residue, what he calls the *practico-inert.* This residue, this dead mark or trace of a now extinct praxis, then survives to form a part of the new situation, the new dilemma or contradiction, which people confront in their new historical present. Would it therefore not be plausible to suggest that what is called social character is to be seen as just such a residue, just such a form of the practico-inert, just such a scar left in the present by the outmoded and forgotten practices of the past? We may conjecture, for example, that in a certain communal situation certain kinds of character traits prove necessary and effective in overcoming specific concrete social difficulties and dangers: forms of puritanism, for example, or authoritarian family structures organized around a patriarch. When the problems in question are surmounted, these specific collective stances—something like the muscular contraction of a body resisting a specific weight and pressure—do not go away but persist without function, in the forgetfulness of the purpose they once served (and I may add that this forgetfulness of the crucial role of forgetfulness in social reproduction is not the least problem with contemporary appeals to social memory). Social "character" would then be this persistence of traits that have lost their function and now exist as givens or data, as elements of a new situation and as themselves problems that must be overcome (as in various efforts to alter collective habits that have become counterproductive).

Whatever one thinks of this kind of approach to the question of national or social character, it is at the least useful in making clear what the authors of *Habits of the Heart* do not do and also what is missing from even more psychological theories, such as those of Christopher Lasch or David Riesman. These last are undialectical, there is no conception in them of contradictions that societies must overcome, or of social history as a struggle to overcome contradiction. Nor is there any conception of dialectical survival, of unequal development, lag, interference, or reification. Nor, finally, is any role blocked out for amnesia, forgetfulness, oblivion, and repression in the social process (alongside the functions that may be attributed to memory).

As far as memory is concerned, indeed, another observation may not be inappropriate here: the authors are most dialectical when they suggest that the opposition between older forms of character structure and the new individualisms is not to be grasped as the presence or absence of a tradition (that is, of a form of collective memory). On the contrary, they show that individualism is itself a kind of tradition, albeit of an invisible type (and that it is with that specific and more recent kind of *tradition* of individualism that its critics must struggle). Still, it seems to me that the very concept of "memory" or "collective data storage" will not be dialectical unless we grasp it as functioning in different ways at different social moments and indeed as taking on radically new and dialectically original forms. If collective memory is a function of social structure, then we need to take into account the possibility that the newer forms of data storage (and the institutions which secure those) have gradually made some of the older forms of collective memory unnecessary and archaic. I would like to suggest that a book which so ambitiously grapples with contemporary North American social and psychological realities today is seriously deficient if it does not (as this one does not) acknowledge and formulate one of the most significant symptoms of contemporary or postmodern North American society and culture—namely, the loss of historicity, the loss of a sense of the past (as well as a sense of the future), the waning of any sense of that radical difference of the past in terms of which alone we might achieve some sharper sense of the uniqueness of our own present.

Culture remains a privileged area in which to witness this evaporation of history, which may be linked to the fate of the extended and then the older nuclear family, but is certainly also related to the structure of late or multinational capitalism itself. The appetite for images of the past, in the form of what might be called simulacra, the increasing production of such images of all kinds, in particular in that peculiar postmodern genre, the *nostalgia film*, with its glossy evocation of the past as sheer consumable fashion and image—all of this seems to me something of a return of the repressed, an unconscious sense of the loss of that past, which this appetite for images seeks desperately to overcome. Such forms of compensation offer remarkable material for juxtaposition and comparison with those older cultural forms in which a living sense of history was able to express itself (as, for example, in the traditional historical novel). I raise this issue of the dynamics of historicity for reasons of form as well as of content: *Habits of the Heart* seeks to make its effects and do its cultural work by way of a juxtaposition of the present with the historical past that may not any longer be possible in the contemporary situation in and about which they write. As for their central theme—the possibility of community or collectivity today—it is hard to see how its unique and unparalleled difficulties can even begin to be measured without taking into account the vicissitudes of that sense of the past and of the future which has traditionally been felt to be the fundamental precondition for genuine community in the first place.

Now, however, I want to return to my starting point in order to close an enormous parenthesis I there left open and to rectify the misapprehension I may have left that the authors of *Habits* disposed of only one model for accounting for the causes of individualism. This was what I described as an idealistic model: namely, the suggestion that philosophical conceptuality—and in particular Descartes's conception of consciousness—was somehow ultimately responsible for the emergence of the modern individualist character as such. But that discussion began by an exploration of what I called slippages in the authors' explanatory models. It is now time to say that alongside this philosophical and idealistic conception of causality the authors also propose a very different and far more contemporary (or postcontemporary) one—a model that, turning upon language itself, seems to me to escape many of the problems we have raised about the older model of the history of ideas and to break interesting new ground.

In their alternative description (which coexists uneasily with the idealizing one), the authors treat individualism not as a form of consciousness or as an idea, but rather as a particular kind of language or of *discourse* (to use a word that is not theirs but which has come into theoretical currency in various places today). For what they offer here is in reality the beginnings of something like discourse analysis: It turns out that the most effective way of staging a critique of individualism is to be found not in a critique of its philosophical "ground," nor even in what would necessarily be a moralizing (if not social and political) critique of the kinds of behavior it produces, but rather in its limits as a language or discourse. In this, one of the most remarkable features of the authors' work, "individualism" is grasped as a "first language" into which we are all in one way or another locked, and through which we sometimes imperfectly attempt to express truths inaccessible to that first language (as, for example, vague intimations of the nature of community, in other words, of what we lack, what is missing from our daily lives in this system). The first language or discourse of individualism, then, powerfully deflects and deforms everything that passes through it; like a system of cartographic projection, it translates the content offered it into the style and specificity of its own volumes and contours, with the Wittgensteinian consequence that whatever it cannot express falls outside of social reality. "Most of the people that we talked to over the past several years, particularly the more affluent and better educated, used a language influenced by therapy to articulate their thoughts about interpersonal relationships" (*H*, 138). This means the exclusion of alternatives, of visions of radically different kinds of social arrangements, which cannot compute in the dominant discourse or language. It means that the authors are, in effect, engaged in a kind of "language experiment" in which, minimally, they seek to make us aware of the asphyxiating confines and limits of the language into which we are locked; at their most ambitious, they seem themselves to strain to produce a new language capable of bursting the seams of the older one and making new realities and new possibilities appear. The word *community* is evidently the locus of this attempt, which is unsuccessful for reasons shortly to be enumerated.

For this first dominant language not only restricts visions of alternatives, it also limits what can be grasped about the present: "The extent to which many Americans can understand the workings of our economic and social organization is limited by the capacity of their chief moral language to make sense of human interaction" (*H*, 204). Here we touch on both the convergences and the differences in emphasis between this new linguistic model and what has become current in other forms of poststructuralism generally—that is, a determinism by language itself, if not even a production of reality by language. But these authors posit a wordless reality that is not altogether covered or fully organized by the existing language—the language of individualism and therapy is here in some sense productive and determinate, since it generates new forms of consciousness, behavior, and relationship in its own image; yet some features and dimensions of that reality do not fit and cannot be explained or expressed—making their presence felt in the mode of mute contradiction, nagging unease, nonarticulation.

Meanwhile, the other tendency of poststructuralism—the positing of some total system of control, some total or totalizing "synchronic" power (à la Foucault, for example) over our horizons of discourse—is surely present in *Habits,* but it is checked and nuanced by an equally poststructural sense of the heterogeneous and of inner distances within the system. Thus the authors stress the survival, within the single dominant or hegemonic discourse, of older secondary inherited languages, which as you will have guessed are those of older American moral, religious, or republican values. Like the ancient Romans, therefore, or the great civilizations of the Far East, which knew and acknowledged several distinct official and unofficial religions at the same time, North Americans today generally dispose of several optional absolutes and tend to be traditionally wedded to this or that second language while functioning in the dominant force-field of the first, which powerfully filters and deforms those residual values and discourses and often—as in both religious and political, left- or right-wing value systems—tends to translate their terms into its own therapeutic truths. It would seem that what is necessary under present circumstances is some third language: some new form of discourse capable of struggling for legitimacy against the first one, but not marked by the past in such a way as to make it vulnerable to the residual second languages as they range themselves subordinately in the force-field of the currently hegemonic or dominant one. The authors' concept and "language" of "community"—let me now suggest openly— cannot serve as that new third language, since it is itself residual and traditional, and more than that, since its very concept is organized around the merely retrospective: their full designation for this concept is "communities of memory," an emphasis that strategically foregrounds that indispensable sense of the past that has already been touched on to the exclusion of the other fundamental dimension of time—namely the future. Everything changes, one would think, when, for the static conception of "community," we substitute the active slogan of the "collective project" (a term I owe to Henri Lefebvre), which suddenly reorients our thinking around the praxis that gives a collectivity its form and meaning. Even the very conception of religion itself changes when—returning to its etymological sense—one grasps it as the badge of community membership and of group adherence, rather than as a set of inert doctrines and "beliefs" (on which more below).

The point is not, once again, what the authors really had in mind when they lent their formulation its retrospective cast, nor where their ultimate social and political sympathies lie. Even on their own operative conception, what counts is the degree to which they think they have been able—within what they call our "first language"—to forge a code and to articulate a vision which seeks to break radically with that imposed by that dominant language or discourse from within which they necessarily write (and we necessarily read).

The problem is, I fear, that they are not necessarily prepared to break completely with that dominant discourse. "We do not argue that Americans should abandon individualism—that would mean for us to abandon our deepest identity" (*H,* 142). But given the pervasiveness of the therapeutic, they have also powerfully, if perhaps unwittingly, demonstrated that nothing can be achieved without such a radical break. Their assertion—"Indeed it may be only in terms of those older [religious and political] traditions that the deeper meaning of our individualism and the aspirations it embodies can be salvaged at all" (*H,* 141)—rings like an admission of failure if not an anticipation of defeat. These are, perhaps, peculiar words to use about an enterprise in connection with which it is not at all clear what its success would mean; and they are also, perhaps, ungrateful words to use about a project that is full of new materials both for a critique of individualism and a theory of community to which I have not yet done justice. Some concluding remarks, therefore, on both these areas.

I have mentioned the kinship of the linguistic features of *Habits of the Heart* with what is often called discourse analysis: it may now be the moment to say a little more about this last (and I draw here essentially on the recent work of Stuart Hall).[2] The political forms of discourse analysis turn fundamentally on the conception of legitimacy or legitimation, which we owe to Max Weber (or, in a more contemporary guise, to Jürgen Habermas): the idea is that viewed from this angle, as a struggle between competing discourses (or what used to be called ideologies), discursive politics is essentially to be grasped as the conquest of legitimacy by one discursive system, which then becomes the dominant or hegemonic "language." Although this element of struggle is missing from the historical viewpoint of *Habits*, the notion of a dominant or hegemonic discourse (in this case, that of individualism, or in its late form, of the therapeutic) is certainly present. What is less clear in this work is the status of the other competing discourses, the story of what happens to discourses that lose their legitimacy or fail to gain it in the first place. The authors' conception of "second languages" only blocks out a special case of that failure, reserved for residual languages, discourses of the past, which have been superseded and, as it were, mummified and preserved like museum pieces within the new hegemonic language. There are, however, other possible outcomes.

Stuart Hall has analyzed at great length the triumph of Thatcherism in Britain as a supreme example of discursive politics at work, and of the way in which a new and newly legitimized language manages, through struggle, to displace and discredit an older legitimate language, in this instance, that of the welfare state (or what we would here call liberalism). What Hall suggests is that it is not objective circumstances that have changed—deficit funding and Keynesian economics function as well or as poorly as they always did—but rather the legitimacy of welfare-state language, which people are increasingly reluctant to use. Thus, no liberal politicians in the West now seem willing to attack the principle of "fiscal responsibility" or the ideal of the balanced budget, even though excellent social reasons could be given for resisting these doctrines. Meanwhile, although it is clear that distinct ideologies are in play, the analysts of so-called discourse theory, like Hall, maintain that their perspective allows us to see features of the struggle which are not visible or articulable when we limit ourselves to the older language of "ideology" as a form of consciousness or as a variant of the history-of-ideas approach. This struggle, they maintain, takes place within language and is best explored as a local series of conflicts and contests around words, terms, charged figures and the like.

The crisis of social democracy, of the welfare state, or of Keynesian liberalism in general as a discourse is surely not unrelated to the crisis in what is properly a "third language" here: namely, the discourse of socialism or Marxism. Discourse analysis enables us to underscore features of these discursive struggles or crises that are rather different from classical forms of censorship or outright repression; it is not, in other words, that "third language" books are banned or the conceptual features of socialist discourse are unknown or unfamiliar. The silence or absence is of another type, best exemplified, perhaps, by the way in which socialist ideological or conceptual positions are always missing from sample offerings or a range of commentaries on current events. The media frequently cover themselves by allowing a range of commentators to state public positions—but this range is always limited, spanning only the ideological spectrum from old or new conservatives to left-of-center liberals. Marxist commentaries are omitted, although there is no lack of qualified Marxist analysts. This discursive absence, this limitation of the public sphere, is not exactly censorship, nor is it damaging only for the left. One of the weaknesses of contemporary liberalism, for example, is surely the absence of any pressure from more radical positions behind it. But whatever your own ideological positions, genuine Marxist analyses of current events are both more unusual and more interesting than the vacuous and turgid right-wing statements to which a media sampling of positions customarily resorts. Marxist discourse is illegitimate, it lacks legitimacy, it is discursively disqualified (something that has little enough to do with the viability of its alternative solutions and concepts). I have dwelt at some length on this matter because it seems to me that *Habits* is also incapacitated or debilitated by the exclusion from it of any kind of socialist or Marxist perspective. One of the case studies presented here deals with a sixties leftist: the authors' point is essentially that this activist's language is as contaminated by therapeutic individualism as the language of the other "subjects," who represent different ideological positions, from yuppie-ism to more classical nostalgic conservatism. One might well agree with this judgment on 1960s radicalism, without drawing the antipolitical consequences which seem to flow from it and which I want to spell out in a moment.

This is the moment to pursue the most interesting of the authors' points a little further: I refer to their description of the social fragmentation and atomization of late capitalist society, whose older classes (or in cultural and political terms, class publics and clienteles) seem to have been exploded and dispersed. Theirs is not a novel diagnosis, and we all feel its force in various ways. But traditionally the process has been understood as a reversal of larger social groups to isolated individuals in the grip of this or that form of *anomie*. What is clearer today is that the isolated individual of that type has also disappeared: myths of the lonely rebel or nonconformist are patently antiquated. The larger class group-

ings have in fact given way to new types of micro-groups, as they are
sometimes called. This is what the authors powerfully register by their
conception of what they call "lifestyle enclaves" (a term whose ugliness
befits its object), new types of subgroups organized around partial features of everyday life—"shared patterns of appearance, consumption,
and leisure activities, which often serve to differentiate them sharply
from those with other lifestyles" (*H*, 335). Their point about left political
activism in the United States is that it also seems to correspond to just
such a lifestyle enclave, and the diagnosis is pertinent, sobering, and
"therapeutic" (in the other, more positive sense of that term). One would
think, in any case, that it is the emergence of these new social forms
which poses the greatest practical and theoretical problems for the reinvention of any new concept of "community," and also that the new
institutional frameworks of such lifestyle enclaves would be the most
immediate issue on the agenda. But in elaborating this new analytic concept, the authors stage it in a somewhat different way, as a revision and
repudiation of the older stereotypical and still widely current notions of
public and private associated with Hannah Arendt. Arendt had argued,
you will remember, that the specificity of contemporary society sprang
from an enormous expansion of private life, such that it ultimately encompassed and extinguished the older traditional forms of public life
and public space. The authors of *Habits*, however, sharply reinvert this
formulation and reintroduce the "public" (in the form, now, of economic relations) back into the heart of what Arendt thought of as the
private: "The problem posed by therapy is not that intimacy is tyran-
nically taking over too much of public life. It is that too much of the
purely contractual structure of the economic and bureaucratic world is
becoming an ideological model for personal life" (*H*, 127). This is a
shrewd and telling objection, which might take us far, indeed farther
than the authors often seem willing to go.

But I have not yet offered what seems to me the ultimate reason that
genuine left alternatives play no part in a book whose thrust would seem
to be a radical or at least an antihegemonic one. The language of the
sixties radical is classed as an example of the therapeutic—not the Marxist or socialist or communal—for a reason that is never mentioned but
which seems to me finally inescapable: it is that this is a book about
Americans, and Marxism and socialism alike are not American, whatever else they may be; they do not belong in a work that too strategically
and systematically limits itself to American (I prefer to say North American) social and psychological life. The attitude is familiar, but I want to
deplore its larger formal effect on the resonance and implications of this
interesting book as a whole. I will therefore suggest that for all its merits
and great interest, and very much in the spirit of its acknowledged
predecessors, from Tocqueville on, *Habits* still leaves us locked into the

confines of that familiar old idea, American exceptionalism. America is special, Americans are unique: therefore a boundary is drawn that automatically excludes any comparison with the experience of other peoples and nations in the world today (including their politics) and universalizes its subject matter by parochialization. But if we were forced to recognize that other parts of the world have different experiences of community or collectivity and a different history of the penetration of individualism (and of forms of the therapeutic), then everything would change. We would have a new ballgame in which forms of praxis become conceivable that would render unnecessary the moralizing appeal to pious American values and ideals of "community" for which no objective preconditions can be discovered in "actually existing" capitalism today. I am tempted to suggest that American exceptionalism is indeed as noxious and as deserving of ideological critique as the American individualism which is the authors' target (and probably has intimate links with the latter as well).

Discussions of *Habits of the Heart* can thus ultimately open up in two relatively distinct directions: that of its reading of late capitalist society today (and its assessment of the latter's possibilities and limits), and that of the question of Bellah's evaluation of the powers of contemporary religion.

Of the first, the most damaging thing that can be said is that diagnoses and critiques of the "therapeutic" in our time tend themselves to be forms of the therapeutic and are locked into its thought patterns as into a mirror image. Whether religion today—Bellah's "modern religion"—is any more than the simulacrum of religion, religion transformed into its own image, is at least a damaging possibility that is never entertained in *Habits*.[3] "Cultural revolution"—even the mild reforming variety proposed there—does not involve the substitution of culture (including religion) for revolution, but rather presupposes this last, namely radical, systemic transformation, a concept and a vision for which words like *socialism* once existed, but which the enlargement of the parochial framework of *Habits* would have demonstrated to be in full crisis everywhere in the world today (including the socialist countries). What is wanted, then, is the reinvention for late industrial society of a new form of the utopian project, about which I have suggested elsewhere that its most judicious beginning might lie in a self-punishing enumeration of all the blocks that make the reimagining of utopia today a difficult, if not to say a well-nigh impossible, task.[4]

As for religion—"modern" or otherwise—its possible contributions to the utopian process are of course hotly debated by the left today, as they could not but be after the tremendous social explosion of the Iranian revolution, the practical-political role and effects of liberation theology, the historical studies of the function of the Protestant sects in earlier English revolutionary history by Christopher Hill and E. P. Thompson, the discovery in the Anglo-American language zone of the philosophy of Ernst Bloch, and any number of very different social, political, and intellectual developments of that kind. My own sense is that the plausible distinction between religion and belief may be misleading here, and not merely because the hypostasis of something called "belief" tends to restore those old stereotypes of "ages of faith" and "ages of skepticism" to which a social and materialist historiography seems preferable. In that case, let's simply agree that "belief," grasped in that way, as the consciousness and the "values" of the Other, has never existed in the first place, at any time in human history.[5] Rather, my point is that opposition of religion and belief excludes what must necessarily be the decisive feature in any ultimate judgment as to whether religion, today or in the past, is "progressive" or "reactionary": namely, social practice itself, and in particular the question of the priest and the church, the institution and the community of the faithful, of the central text as well, and of its specific "interpretive communities"—in short, the whole matter of *agency* in historical change, and of the various types of agency at work or possible in a specific social formation. But the form agency takes for us— both readers and writers of *Habits*—is that of *intellectuals,* another old-fashioned concept whose contemporary enfeeblement and tendential extinction is a symptom of the problematic structure of late capitalism as well as the bad faith and "therapeutic" oblivion of the people to whom that designation used to apply. Questions of religion fully as much as questions of social change demand a rethinking and a reinvention of the role of the intellectual as such; and the enthusiasm with which *Habits of the Heart* has been greeted by right-wing intellectuals in the U.S. today is certainly not the least reason why—for all its interest—one continues to feel no little malaise about the ultimate uses to which the book is destined to be put.

PART TWO

Practical Reason

SEVEN

Qualms of a Believer

Ralph B. Potter

It did not take long for the authors of *Habits of the Heart* to seize the interest of a professor of social ethics. The preface opens with a classic question of my discipline: "How ought we to live?" The pace is sustained as they note that "Our inquiry can thus be located in a longstanding discussion of the relationship between character and society" (*H*, vii). For members of my profession, it is a great occasion when someone addresses such ancient questions with the intention of being both historically and sociologically informed. It is sensational news when book reviewers pay attention and numbers of lay persons actually read and discuss such a volume!

STRUCTURAL CONSIDERATIONS

There is a twofold focus in *Habits*. The analysis of the inadequacy of our moral discourse moves back and forth from the level of the individual to the level of society. An adequate moral language must first enable an individual to ground choices in a large framework of meaning. Secondly, at the social level, it must serve as a medium for adjudicating disparate visions of how our major institutions should be arranged. It will be helpful to pause for a moment to consider the repercussions of the failure to fulfill each of these functions of an adequate moral language.

At the individual level, Brian Palmer best represents the moral malaise analyzed by the authors. They report that "when Brian describes how he has chosen to live . . . he keeps referring to 'values' and 'priorities' not justified by any wider framework of purpose or belief" (*H*, 6). Brian "lacks a language to explain what seem to be the real commitments that define his life, and to that extent the commitments themselves are precarious" (*H*, 8). Thus, his moral reflection is unable to provide him with comprehensive and coherent practical guidance. The parts of his life do not fit into a stable and harmonious pattern, rooted in a reflective appreciation of the way things are and are meant to be.

Without a vision of "a morally coherent life," no stable sense of self can emerge. Without such a stable self, we are unable to establish and maintain cooperation and commitment with others. Without the capacity to elicit cooperation and commitment, we forfeit many ways of relating and many eminently choice-worthy ways of life. The impoverishment of our moral language leaves us, as individuals, bereft of the resources needed for deliberation concerning the way in which our own lives are to be formed.

At the social level, our impoverished moral language leaves us vulnerable to civil strife and tyranny. The authors make clear the reasons for concern:

> Where moral views are seen as rooted only in subjective choice, there is no way of deciding among them except through coercion or manipulation.
> . . . The fear is that where the interests involved are incommensurable and therefore almost impossible to adjudicate, interest politics must inevitably break down into coercion or fraud. (*H*, 203)

The discussion in *Habits* shifts back and forth between these two focal points, from the individual threatened with an aimless isolation born of a failure to root preferences in a wider sense of meaning, to a society suffering the breakdown of the mechanisms for moral adjudication and menaced by the forceful imposition of arbitrary sets of preferences.

But the underlying structure of *Habits* is not merely twofold; it is, in fact, fourfold. In order to repair the impoverishment that endangers both self and society, four elements must be linked into a coherent understanding of our condition, and an adequate moral language must enable us to speak about these four dimensions of our existence. In a discussion of the limitations of American religion, this fourfold pattern is made explicit when the authors note that we are "deprived of a language genuinely able to mediate among self, society, the natural world, and ultimate reality" (*H*, 237). We have, in this passage, a faint echo of the life work of Talcott Parsons, as well as, I believe, the underlying logic and central doctrine of *Habits*. To envision and attain "a morally coherent life," we must be able to speak a language that orients the self in relation to the natural order, society, and ultimate reality.

THEORETICAL AND PRACTICAL PROBLEMS

This formula may sound simple enough, but it entails immense complications: the theoretical problem of encompassing all four dimensions within a coherent account of the world, and the practical problem of countering the confusion arising from the coexistence of a number of rival moral languages.

First, let us speak to the theoretical problem of integrating all four dimensions in a single, adequate moral language. The authors specify that we need a "language genuinely able to mediate among self, society, the natural world, and ultimate reality." A tiny bit of juggling puts these tasks back into the order in which Parsons generally treated the functional prerequisities of any social system: adaptation, goal attainment, integration, latent pattern maintenance (Parsons 1951). First, an adequate moral language must relate us to the natural order through "economic" and "ecological" doctrines. Second, it must provide a psychological account of how a stable sense of self is created and maintained. Third, it must yield a political philosophy to guide our reconstruction of a just and sustainable society. Fourth, it must express a common sense of what life is about and, ultimately, the terms of our human existence. Further, let us add a point that will become important later. It is the assumption that the elements of such a pattern of justification fit together as a cybernetic system of control and constraint. The "higher-order" elements, the vision of what life is about and the reflections upon the right ordering of society, provide templates or paradigms for the specification of appropriate patterns of personality and suitable means of adaptation to realities imposed by our natural environment. Such a logic lies behind the priority granted to the biblical and the republican traditions.

Unlike the authors, I am unwilling to concede a privileged status to the biblical and republican traditions on the grounds that they perform functions their rivals do not. As I see it, each of the four major orientations—utilitarian individualism, expressive individualism, the republican tradition, and the biblical tradition—must be looked upon as an effort to encompass all four dimensions. Each can be made to serve the task of relating the self to society, the natural order, and to ultimate reality.

In the indictments the authors bring against utilitarian and expressive individualism, the words "large" and "small" are prominent. Yet though the worlds of the therapist and the manager may be "small," they are quite well furnished: "While the culture of manager and therapist does not speak in the language of traditional moralities, it nonetheless proffers a normative order of life, with character ideals, images of the good life, and methods of attaining it" (*H,* 47). Exactly what more is needed? Just how large does a larger whole have to be? It would be helpful to see a philosophical footnote explaining why being linked to a small world is, in theory, inferior to seeing oneself as part of a large world. All four perspectives are put to use to orient us in the universe. The issue is whether some do the job better than others. We would profit from a more amplified discussion of what it means to do such a task "better."

Second, let us consider the practical problem of establishing a widely shared "first language" as the vehicle for discussing aspects of the common life that concern us all. By my account, *there is no first language available in America*. Discussion of the fundamental matters to which the authors would have us turn can be conducted only in terms borrowed from one or another of the four living languages carried and renewed by those who have embraced one of the ways of life characterized by the labels utilitarian individualism, expressive individualism, republican virtue, or the biblical tradition.

These moral languages are embedded in ways of life precious to subgroups occupying specific locations and determined to protect the possibility of living according to their lights. Each draws life from a living community. The very forms of consciousness, capacities for experiencing and communicating, have been decisively shaped by the forms of life that are generated and sustained by occupation, education, income, and social class groupings of the four major orientations. Thus, the four living languages provide the framework for organizing and expressing our reactions to the world. They enable us to communicate and to establish forms of solidarity with those who share a similar perspective.

At the same time, they also estrange us from those who speak other languages. A way of life has crystalized around each of Parsons's four functional prerequisites of any social system and, in so doing, has given rise to a distinctive language. Economic individualism crystalizes around the necessities of mastering the natural order for the sake of economic productivity and material welfare. Expressive individualism is the cultural precipitate of granting priority to concern for the personality system. Republican virtue has been defined out of an integrative concern for the right ordering of the major institutions of society. The biblical tradition preserves and protects a cultural pattern of meaning, enabling us to envision the origin, purposes, and destiny of human life.

Each of the four central styles or orientations may be understood as specializing in one or another of the four types of mediation called for. Each offers a partial language, a skewed vocabulary, an incomplete vision of the common life as a candidate for the common mode of discourse through which we decide how to settle the arrangements of our life together. But no one of them is able to do justice to each and all of the four dimensions that must be integrated: "It is an outstanding feature of industrial life that these sectors have become radically discontinuous in the kinds of traits emphasized and the moral understandings that guide individuals within them" (*H,* 45). In the absence of an adequate first language that might serve as the basis for adjudicating questions of the common life, the interplay of the four living languages in our public life is like a zero-sum game in which the stakes are the facilitation or hindrance of one or another of the four ways of life rooted in specific social settings.

QUALMS: THE PRICE OF CONVERSATION

This analysis thus brings us to an impasse. We are in the perilous condition of not being able to talk about dimensions of our lives that we cannot afford not to talk about. In order to settle the arrangement of our common life, "to mediate among self, society, the natural world, and ultimate reality," we must discuss matters as profound and uncertain as the meaning of our lives, the justice of major institutions, the purposes of our common undertakings in the world, our obligations to coming generations, and our respect for the natural order upon which we depend. We skirt such questions purposively, out of an awareness that they are explosively divisive. It is not simply shallowness that prevents the type of public conversation the authors recommend. Reticence grows also out of awareness that, given the deep pluralism, the alignment of philosophical differences with other cracks in American society, and the dominance of institutions (e.g., political parties, churches, and schools) that are not designed to accommodate conversation as a specific mode of edifying interaction, the effort to relate policy decisions to fundamental principles would be more likely to intensify and harden differences, rather than to raise the level of public political discourse.

By my account, if these issues were to be genuinely taken up, they would have to be discussed using words and concepts borrowed from one or several of the four living languages. Readers and reviewers of all stripes may pause to be edified by *Habits.* Many of them may praise it heartily. But, when they resume their debates concerning specific issues, they will find themselves still divided by the distinctive languages they must use to express their most deeply rooted convictions.

If one of the languages were to prevail as the vehicle for public discussion, its native speakers would reap advantages while others would find it difficult to express their vision of life in an unfamiliar idiom. If two or more languages were patched together, to create a sort of political Esperanto, new confusions would pervade our public discourse. The only available languages rest upon different visions of the world and our place in it. Debate upon such fundamental issues would lay bare profound discrepancies that have been muted, and the plausibility and justification of each way of life would come to be at stake. Each of us can sense that should matters come to be settled on the basis of a view of the world other than our own, the prospects of our being able to live out our sense of what we would like to be and do would likely be diminished.

The authors sense these kinds of dangers, yet downplay them: "We have been afraid to try for a more substantial consensus for fear that the effort may produce unacceptable levels of conflict. But if we had the courage to face our deepening political and economic difficulties, we might find that there is more basic agreement than we had imagined"

(*H*, 287). Or, I must add, we might find that we have the potential to be a Northern Ireland or a Lebanon. As a WASP professor living in a blue-collar Italian and Irish Catholic neighborhood, I do not find it wise to bring all my analytical skills into play to lay bare the latent discrepancies in the world views that shape daily choices. I can imagine that if I lived in a setting in which I could be more confident that my way of seeing things might prevail, I would be more enthusiastic about establishing the links between self, society, the natural world, and ultimate reality as a prelude to the formulation of more coherent policy.

Nevertheless, we are assured by the authors that "strongly held differences do not undermine the debate about our common future as long as it is pursued through civil discourse and we seek to persuade, rather than coerce, our fellow citizens" (*H*, 246). It would be helpful to have an elaborated answer to the question, What keeps discourse "civil"? What kinds of people, in what types of settings, can discover, in the midst of a joint enterprise requiring close cooperation, that their views of life are fundamentally different and still live and work together "happily ever after"? The coexistence of four imperfect languages, each rooted in a way of life and each a candidate to serve as the dominant idiom for discussion of the common life, creates an American moral tradition that is versatile but volatile, flexible but explosive. It creates a genuine dilemma for both ethicists and social commentators. One wants to clarify certain grounds of decision by laying bare the logic of different orientations, but in so doing fundamental differences may be intensified rather than transcended.

There is no neutral, transcending, overarching "first language." The authors acknowledge that because analysts are part of the society they are analyzing, "in framing their problems and interpreting their results, they draw on their own experience and their membership in a community of research that is in turn located within specific traditions and institutions" (*H*, 302–3). All of us are in that condition, all the time. The authors hedge about their introduction of the idea of a "first language," noting that all of their subjects "draw from different traditions." But they go on to say that:

> beneath the sharp disagreements, there is more than a little consensus about the relationship between the individual and society, between private and public good. This is because, in spite of their differences, they all to some degree share a common moral vocabulary, which we propose to call the "first language" of American individualism in contrast to alternative "second languages," which most of us also have. (*H*, 20)

I take that to be a misstep which dampens a full appreciation of how radical our moral pluralism actually is. What appears to the authors to be a "first language" is simply an area of overlap in four different vocabularies that belong to four very different languages. It is, strictly speaking, a mere coincidence. Let us examine a specific case.

The chapter titled "Individualism" opens with an accurate and important observation: "Every one of the four traditions we have singled out is in a profound sense individualistic. There is a biblical individualism and a civic individualism as well as a utilitarian and an expressive individualism" (*H*, 142). If one wishes to induce greater awareness of the meaning of individualism in the lives of Americans by making them more self-conscious of the reasons for their conduct, there is no way to do so apart from increasing their understanding of how their reasons for the affirmation of individualism *differ* from the reasons brought forward by those differently situated. Thus, the very process the authors hope to stimulate moves toward the intensification rather than the diminution of differences. They are asking people to link their particular judgments to their general way of seeing things. Different ways of seeing things form the bases of four different languages growing out of four different ways of life.

To speak of a "first language of American individualism" is confusing. The phrase projects the error of "value-free social science" (to which the authors are resolutely opposed) onto a wider screen, as if at some level of civic discourse there were an overarching neutral language available to us that would not confine us to our specific, everyday ways of speaking. In practice, if we want to explore the meanings and grounds of individualism, or any other significant theme, we are pushed back into reliance upon four distinctive languages that have at least as much power to estrange as to unite.

It is difficult for a professor to be against more penetrating reflection, self-awareness, and profundity. But I am not certain we can evoke the gods without increasing the risk of a war among the gods.

PRESCRIPTIONS

What, then, are we to do? I wish to take a hard look at the prescriptions provided in *Habits* for our moral ailments. Mindful that the authors have made important links between social settings and forms of belief and action, let us try to discover precisely what they would wish us to do. Then we can ask, What pattern of belief is necessary to make such action meaningful? and, What social arrangements would have to exist in order to undergird such forms of belief and action?

The authors remind us that the social embeddedness of ideas and patterns of aspiration prevents any simple recapitulation or return to ways that were rooted in social settings now past.

We thus face a profound impasse. Modern individualism seems to be producing a way of life that is neither individually nor socially viable, yet a return to traditional forms would be to return to intolerable discrimination and oppression. The question, then, is whether the older civic and biblical traditions have the capacity to reformulate themselves while simultaneously remaining faithful to their own deepest insights. (*H*, 144).[1]

Yet when one gathers up the texts of *Habits* that touch upon our responsibilities and opportunities, there is a notable instability and vagueness in the specification of what we are to do. I propose that the reason for this instability and vagueness is that the understanding of what is to be done is itself a function of one or another of the four primary orientations or ways of life. The authors' own prescriptions are largely drawn from the republican tradition. But the other orientations generate different understandings of the tasks confronting us, and it is easy to fall into speaking in terms that make the most sense in different frameworks of meaning.

In *Habits* the terms used to express what we are to do range from a passive hope for revival (*H*, 271) to a more vigorous effort actively to reform (*H*, 294). In between are terms such as *seek, find, discover, recover, reverse, reconsider, reform, renew, reappropriate, reformulate,* and *cultivate.* Sorting these out a bit, one can ask among which groups are particular forms of renewal likely to take place? Again, what ideas would one have to hold to have such action make sense? And, what forms of life and social institutions would be necessary to sustain such action?

According to one reading of the biblical tradition, true revival comes only by the Will of God and not as a result of any exertions upon our part. It is incumbent upon us to watch and to pray, for we know not the day nor the hour at which His Spirit may descend anew. Nevertheless, one can observe, after the fact, that God has chosen to send His Spirit, not upon sophisticated readers, but upon those who are able to sustain a naive belief and an urgent sense of their own need of redemption. In the biblical tradition, it is among the simple, the poor, and the dispossessed that we must look for a renewal.

The creation of a "first language" to aid in the discussion of our public life requires a balanced habit of mind, and it is not likely to be the work of those seized by the Holy Spirit and embued with holy enthusiasm. Conversely, anyone likely to read *Habits*, let alone join us in discussing the book, has, most probably, lost a capacity for naive and simple belief and is not a serious prospect to unleash a new outburst of religious energy in the world. There is much that churches and church members may do to serve the common good and to contribute to the revival of republican virtue. But theological virtues and the revival of true religion are gifts of God's grace that cannot be forced or earned by our exertions.

Words such as *reappropriate* and *renew* seem to fit nicely with the intui-

tive mode of judgment that underlies the ethic of expressive individualism. Devotees of the therapeutic ethic would be good prospects to enter
empathetically or "get the feel" of ways or thought appealing to them.
Reform has an active ring. It would seem to be the likely approach of
those accustomed to projects, to shaping and reshaping things. Utilitarianism entered the world as a doctrine of reform.

It is the republican tradition that is the home of such activities as civil
discourse, conversation, and cultivation of civic virtue. The authors report that "We have taken the position that our most important task today
is the recovery of the insights of the older biblical and republican traditions" (*H*, 303). Since true revival will be God's gift and not our accom-
plishment, our efforts appropriately focus on the resuscitation of republican virtue. We are reminded that, "in a free republic, it is the task of the
citizen, whether ruler or ruled, to cultivate civic virtue" (*H*, 270). But
how is this to be done, by whom, and in what social setting?

The republican tradition, like each of the other orientations, proves
upon close inspection to be internally diverse. "The longstanding discussion of the relationship between character and society," within which the
authors mean to place their study, has given rise to an immense literature upon the right formation of the self. One must assume that the authors mean to subsume this steady torrent of counsel under the heading of the republican tradition. It could not be ignored completely. Traces
of it crop up in the discussion of *The Federalist Papers* (*H*, 254). There we
read of ideals of character that derive from "integrity, grace, and excellence," a constellation of virtues that does not loom large in the biblical,
utilitarian, or expressive individualist accounts of ideal character.

In this literature of self-perfection, which purports to guide, is the application of will toward the choice of the type of person we shall be. Various mixes of the active and the contemplative life yield ways of life ranging from the politically and militarily engaged "man of action" to the
reflective "cultivated" person free to spend days enjoying leisure conversation amid a circle of friends. Epicureans tilted to the contemplative
side. Staunch republicans, such as Cicero, lived out an alternating style
of engagement and retreat. Perhaps I am pressing too hard in asking
which strand of the republican tradition the authors of *Habits* wish to
emphasize. But it would be helpful to know, because we would conduct
ourselves differently, seek to engender different combinations of virtues,
and recast the structure of our institutions in different forms, depending
on the answer given to such an odd question.

For example, the authors represent the Civil Rights movement as
"combining biblical and republican themes in a way that included, but
transformed, the culture of individualism" (*H*, 249). One may, indeed,
get such an outcome by combining Ernst Troeltsch's category of sectarian Christianity with what I have characterized as the politically or mili-

tarily engaged version of the republican tradition. On the other hand, if one makes an amalgam of Church-type Christianity and the more contemplative side of the republican tradition, the result is, in effect, the nineteenth-century Anglo-American model of the Christian Gentleman. It is important to read the fine print on the labels before mixing up such brews.

Both sides of the republican tradition have an appeal for the authors. At times they summon us to exhibit the courage and engagement of the politically engaged wing of the tradition. At other points they urge us to pursue the task of cultivation, an activity that imposes the virtues of care and patience. The invocation of courage suggests that we are entering a battle. In calling for a balanced renewal of commitment and community, they declare that "such a renewal is indeed a world waiting to be born if we only had the courage to see it" (*H,* 277). And again, after noting that "we have been afraid to try for a more substantial consensus for fear that the effort may produce unacceptable levels of conflict," they suggest that "if we had the courage to face our deepening political and economic difficulties, we might find that there is more basic agreement than we had imagined" (*H,* 287). Clearly, we are at times being summoned to join in a struggle. We are called to a more vigorous participation in public life, because that is the arena where the effective definition of what the nation and its citizens shall be is hammered out, blow by blow. At the same time, we are being asked to maintain the unusual stance of being very aggressively well-balanced. That is not a posture from which one generates much emotional or political clout.

But the main voice of *Habits* is not a battle cry. It is as if the authors, whenever they might have been tempted, turned away after contemplating the virtues we need to stand firm in battle, the organizational forms best designed for such a mission, the personal relations suitable for those engaged in such an undertaking, and the fate of truth and simple honesty in the midst of battle.

The contentious side of the republican tradition, with its demand for courageous engagement, is present in *Habits.* But so is the other strong wing, that which centers not upon stimulating courage to be tested in battle, but upon the cultivation of the arts of civil conversation. The more peaceable wing of the republican tradition has thrived among those possessing leisure to become versed in the liberal arts and practiced as gardeners. Those who have enjoyed the luxury of peace have frequently had recourse to the metaphor of cultivation, a term which acknowledges that life-giving energies come from elsewhere while affirming our responsibility to prepare the ground, uproot choking overgrowth, and tend new sprouts with care.

How are we to go about preparing American soil for the cultivation of civil discourse? What forms of life must we establish if we are to bring forth an adequate first language, maintain civil discourse, and cultivate civic virtue through conversation? This is a request to turn the analysis around to point the other way, as it were. We have received a post facto interpretation. Certain ways of viewing and speaking about the world have been observed and have then been attributed to certain social conditions.

STRATEGIES

I want to reverse this reasoning. If we know that a certain way of viewing and speaking is necessary, can we specify what form of life might nourish and bring forth such a perspective and moral language? Is there anything we can do to favor the emergence of such ways of living and to contribute to the evolution of a more adequate language?

The most basic enterprise the authors urge upon us is "to raise the level of public political discourse" (*H*, 287). The aim is to enable persons to reflect upon their choices in the wider framework of their fundamental ideas concerning the nature of society and of ultimate reality. Do we have the materials necessary to formulate a sort of sociology of reflective reappropriation? What type of social settings and relations are most likely to stimulate this exact kind of reconsideration? How do we raise the *level*, not simply the intensity, of public debate?

I agree wholeheartedly with the authors' assertion that "any living tradition is a conversation, and argument in the best sense, about the meaning and value of our common life" (*H*, 303). I wish they had said much more concerning the preconditions of having a conversation, since it is through conversation that people can be engaged to do the type of moral reflection likely to raise the level of their philosophy rather than simply hardening it to withstand assaults. What moral qualities must one possess in order to converse rather than instruct? How many persons can be engaged in an activity the very name of which points to an equal and alternating balance of participation?

Conversation, the practice of turning a topic around and around as the opportunity to speak is passed from person to person within a circle, has been the principal medium of philosophical reflection among those who have taken Socrates to be a model. Conversation is a very particular practice, different in its requirements and in its "yield" from meditation or direct, pragmatic action. The process of recasting one's thoughts by referring them to larger frameworks of meaning requires a highly individualized form of interaction. It is something that cannot happen when one person is doing all the talking. It cannot be done in mass meetings. It takes time. It even requires a form of architecture that permits people to meet on the same level and to be heard, each by the other. Most of our major institutions are not designed to encourage the kind of conversation that is central to the vision behind *Habits*.

Less obviously, conversation requires the background contribution of types who may not be eager to be directly engaged. It demands a measure of leisure gained, at best, as the by-product of the economic productivity of practitioners of economic individualism. It requires a skill in listening and a willingness to hear, which have been given greater respectability through the influence of expressive individualism. Humility and patience are virtues to be learned from one strand of the biblical tradition.

Historic representatives of republican virtue have, for the most part, been eager to talk only to their own kind, even when they have been willing to spend much energy talking at and instructing more benighted souls. If the authors wish a resurgence of republican virtue, they will first have to provide the correction of the republican tradition itself by broadening the conversation.

A start in that direction can be made by revising the underlying conceptual scheme of *Habits* to build in the authors' intention of "respecting differences based on morally intelligible commitments" (*H*, 287). We need to keep working on a better way to talk about the four strands that constitute the fabric of our tradition. The image of a woven fabric is, if you will pardon the pun, too tightly knit. The suggestion of a hierarchy, with the biblical and republican traditions at the top, does not do justice to the independent vitality and indispensable historical contribution, on the side of freedom, of the economic and expressive individualisms. What is needed, I believe, is a way of looking at the four types within American society that is analogous to Troeltsch's typology of religious associations, cited in *Habits* (243–46). For Troeltsch, the church, sect, and mystical types each had biblical warrant. None could claim to be more primitive, more authentic, or more adequate than the others. There could be no appeal backward to some more pristine or powerful tradition. There is only the perpetual dynamic tension of the several types, correcting one another in the midst of the battle to control the brutality that lurks below and within (Troeltsch [1911] 1931, 1013).

It is difficult to discern the inner mechanisms of this mutual correction. One gropes for images. Maybe it is like squeezing a balloon. You can stretch it this way and that, but when it is too far distended forces come into play to pull it back into shape. Or perhaps one should refer to a hanging mobile, turning this way and that, but always finding a new balance, a new position of momentary equipoise. Of one thing I am certain: all four ways of life must receive their due. Each is needed as a counterweight to the mischief of those who would be willing to do without them.[2]

EIGHT

Liberal Society and the Languages of Morals

Jeffrey Stout

"We have reached the point," wrote Livy long ago of ancient Rome, "where we cannot bear either our vices or their cure." Livy's message may come from another epoch but, according to *Habits of the Heart*, it applies to us here and now. We speak not one moral language but several, and they serve us poorly, at least as they stand. The primary language in which we understand ourselves is shot through with individualism, and is therefore ill suited for public discourse on the common good or for shaping meaningful lives. Our secondary languages of morals, which hark back to older traditions, have begun to wither away, thus losing their power to hold public discourse together. As a result, "the time may be approaching when we will either reform our republic or fall into the hands of despotism, as many republics have done before us" (*H*, 294).

As Alasdair MacIntyre argues in *After Virtue*, that time has come, for "the new dark ages . . . are already upon us." Our moral premises are like so many incommensurable fragments of lost languages. The moral concepts we use, deprived of the contexts in which they formerly made sense, have become mere means of expressing our feelings and manipulating others. Where once there was coherent discourse on the virtues and the common good, we now have the assertion of Nietzschian wills, masked by moral fictions, managed by bureaucrats. The barbarians, MacIntyre says, "are not waiting beyond the frontiers; they have already been governing us for quite some time. And it is our lack of consciousness of this that constitutes part of our predicament" (1984, 263).

Our predicament must be very dire indeed to merit such pronouncements. Not so dire, perhaps, as to erode all ground for hope, but very dire nonetheless. Yet is our predicament in sufficiently clear focus to warrant such conclusions? In this essay I shall pursue this question, starting off by raising doubts about *Habits of the Heart* and *After Virtue*. I will then examine two attempts—by Richard Rorty and Gilbert Meilaender—to defend liberal practices and institutions against the kind of criticism these books espouse. My conclusion will be that we are likely to profit less from sweeping pronouncements, either for or against "liberal society" and its characteristic forms of moral language, than from a willingness to borrow freely from both its critics and defenders while descending to the level of detail. It is time to begin working out a more balanced and nuanced account of our situation and recasting our normative questions in more specific terms.

I

Habits of the Heart portrays our predicament as an impasse: "Modern individualism seems to be producing a way of life that is neither individually nor socially viable, yet a return to traditional forms would be to return to intolerable discrimination and oppression" (*H*, 144). Individualism is our "first language," the moral vocabulary Americans share, but it feeds an illusory "quest for purely private fulfillment" that "often ends in emptiness" (*H*, 163). Moreover, it "often implies a negative view of public life" and lacks the conceptual means we would need for addressing ourselves to the public good. Our only hope, then, lies in our ability to reclaim and reform the "second languages" of biblical and civic republican traditions, thereby striving to keep our individualism in check, even as it places limits on their tendencies toward discrimination and oppression.

This picture has considerable appeal, and it is anything but completely unfamiliar. We need to ask, however, what it might mean to say that individualism is our *first language* of self-understanding and why we should believe that this is so. The authors of this book do not answer these questions directly, so we shall need to tease out answers from the use they make of their interviews with white middle-class Americans.

In describing the form and style of these interviews, the authors state:

> Though we did not seek to impose our ideas on those with whom we talked . . . , we did attempt to uncover assumptions, to make explicit what the person we were talking to might rather have left implicit. The interview as we employed it was active, Socratic. (*H*, 304)

Consider an example of the Socratic interview in action. Ann Swidler, "trying to get Brian Palmer to clarify the basis of his moral judgments," was told that "lying is one of the things I want to regulate." "Why?" asked Swidler.

A. Well, it's a kind of thing that is a habit you get into. Kind of self-perpetuating. It's like digging a hole. You just keep digging and digging.

Q. So why is it wrong?

A.   Why is integrity important and lying bad? I don't know. It just is. It's just so basic. I don't want to be bothered with challenging that. It's part of me. I don't know where it came from, but it's very important.

Q.   When you think about what's right and what's wrong, are things bad because they are bad for people, or are they right or wrong in themselves, and if so how do you know?

A.   Well some things are bad because . . . I guess I feel like everybody on this planet is entitled to have a little bit of space, and things that detract from other people's space are kind of bad . . . (*H*, 304–5, ellipses in original)

It is the final answer in this series, of course, that sounds to Swidler and her colleagues like the language of American individualism. Swidler, like Socrates, kept on probing—asking why? and, how do you know? —until Brian produced something resembling a moral principle. And this, presumably, is to be taken as "the basis for his moral judgments" about lying and perhaps therefore as evidence of what constitutes Brian's *first* language of self-understanding.

There is, however, another way to read this interview. Brian's first inclination is not to invoke a moral principle. In fact, he initially sounds downright Aristotelian. Why does he want to regulate lying? Because lying is a bad habit. Every act of lying reinforces the habit, makes things worse. "So why is it wrong?" Brian seems both puzzled and put off by the question. Aristotelian answers seem not to wash with this questioner. So he rephrases the question, as if searching for a real doubt to address. Finding none, he confesses that he doesn't know why lying is wrong, "It just is."

Evidently, like C. S. Peirce, Brian doesn't know how to answer questions that aren't connected to real doubts. When Brian says that the wrongness of lying is basic, I suggest a Wittgensteinian gloss reminiscent of *On Certainty*: he can't think of anything more certain than the wrongness of lying that might be introduced to support the idea that lying is wrong. He'd rather not be bothered with the sort of challenge the question implies. This, for Peirce and Wittgenstein, shows wholesomely pragmatic philosophical instincts. But his interviewer won't stop. Her next question is worthy of the *Euthyphro*, a question that would be hard to answer without invoking a principle for Socrates to pounce upon. And like poor Euthyphro, Brian plays along.

Habits of the Heart places Brian Palmer front and center. It is his case with which the book begins. Brian, we are told, "recalls a youth that included a fair amount of hell-raising, a lot of sex, and considerable devotion to making money" (*H*, 3). After marrying at twenty-four, he threw himself into his career, hoping to support his family and achieve success. Nearly fifteen years later, his wife left him, and Brian began to reexamine and reorient his life. He has since remarried. Here is Brian describing his second marriage:

"To be able to receive affection freely and give affection and to give of myself and know it is a totally reciprocal type of thing. There's just almost a psychologically buoyant feeling of being able to be so much more involved and sharing. Sharing experiences of goals, sharing of feelings, working together to solve problems, etc. My viewpoint of a true love, husband-and-wife type of relationship is one that is founded on mutual respect, admiration, affection, the ability to give and receive freely." (*H*, 5)

This is how Brian talks when not interrupted by Socratic questions. Reciprocity, involvement, shared goals, and mutual respect define for him what makes his second marriage better than his first. Is this the language of individualism? Surely, not in any sense of "individualism" that should give cause for concern. "Yet despite the personal triumph Brian's life represents, despite the fulfillment he seems to experience," our authors hasten to add that "there is still something uncertain, something poignantly unresolved about his story" (*H*, 5). For Brian has trouble, they say, explaining why his new life is better than his old one:

His description of his reasons for changing his life and of his current happiness seems to come down mainly to a shift in his notions of what would make him happy. His new goal—devotion to marriage and children—seems as arbitrary and unexamined as his earlier pursuit of material success. Both are justified as idiosyncratic preference rather than as representing a larger sense of the purpose of life. (*H*, 6)

Yet Brian does not sound like an individualist when he tells his story. Nor does he seem to be appealing to arbitrary or unexamined preferences. The only evidence *Habits* offers to support the conclusion that there is something uncertain or unresolved about *his story* is generated not by his storytelling but rather by Swidler's Socratic questioning. Only at the end of a chain of Socratic questions does he produce what our authors redescribe as "the ultimate ethical rule . . . that individuals should be able to pursue whatever they find rewarding, constrained only by the requirement that they not interfere with the 'value systems' of others" (*H*, 6). The language of individualism seems, if anything, to be less his first language of self-understanding than it is his language of last resort—a set of slogans he reaches for (with obvious reluctance) when somebody won't take storytelling or unprincipled talk of habit and happiness as sufficient for the purposes of justification.

Brian's story takes shape as what MacIntyre (1977) would call a dramatic narrative. He narrates the major transition of his life as a comedy, not a tragedy. Only if character traits, actions, and outcomes are depicted, within the evaluative framework of the narrative, as good or bad, happy or unfortunate, can the plot take the dramatic form it does. The story implies moral judgments. If Brian were unable to render this sequence of events convincingly as a comic triumph, that would constitute powerful evidence against the judgments implicit in his narrative. The story does not portray Brian's conversion as arbitrary; it portrays it as a reasonable response to crisis. It shows us how Brian, when faced with an unhappy situation for which he can now recognize his own responsibility, reoriented himself in a way that made him happy.

When Swidler asks Brian why he finds the outcome happy, he says that he just finds "'more personal satisfaction from choosing course B over course A'" (*H*, 8). It makes him feel better about himself. Swidler and her coauthors treat these remarks as if Brian were advocating a moral principle of the form, One ought always to choose the course that will maximize one's own satisfaction. Brian can, however, just as easily be read as offering his own experience as evidence for the claim that one course is objectively better than the other and therefore *should* be preferred to it. He may be saying, in effect, I have lived in each of these ways; the first way made me miserable, while the second way, with its shared goals and mutual respect, made me happy. He does not say that merely feeling happy *makes* that way right. And if Swidler had asked him whether somebody who derived "personal satisfaction" from cheating or raping people should be deemed morally upright, I suspect he would have said no.

Brian reoriented his life not by appealing to principles but by identifying his problems and solving them. Swidler and her colleagues complain that within the context of Brian's life, "Solving conflicts becomes a matter of technical problem solving, not moral decision" (*H*, 7), but "technical" is their word, not his, and he does not contrast his attempts to solve problems with *moral* decision-making. He identifies the problems that brought about the crisis in his life by saying that he had disordered priorities. Reordered priorities solved his problems. Far from employing merely technical reason, in the sense that treats ends as morally indifferent or arbitrary and seeks only the most efficient and appropriate means, Brian seems to recognize the importance of reordered ends or loves in a quest for the good life.

I can sum up the doubts I am raising about the portrait of Brian Palmer in *Habits of the Heart* as follows: Brian's justification of his life does not, as the authors think, rest on "a fragile foundation" (*H*, 8), for it does not rest on a foundation at all. It rests in the details of his story. It is by telling his story and implicitly invoking its evaluative framework that Brian initially understands his life and justifies his current commitments as superior to his old ones. *Habits* seems to assume, without argument, that what Brian's life needs, if it is to count as justified, is a philosophical foundation—a principle that will stop the regress of answers to Socratic questions or perhaps a reflective view of the purpose of life. Only if we make this assumption does the material quoted from Swidler's interviews support the conclusion that Brian "lacks a language to explain what seem to be the real commitments that define his life" (*H*, 8).

Brian Palmer's case is only one of many discussed in the book, and I have too little space to examine others in any detail. But I have similar doubts about other cases. When Margaret Oldham says, "'I just sort of accept the way the world is and then don't think about it a whole lot'" (*H*, 14), I take her to be showing resistance to the search for foundations. When she says that things will turn out well if she is the best person she knows how to be according to her "'own lights'," I don't take her to be treating her values as given, "whatever they might happen to be" (*H*, 15). When Wayne Bauer has trouble defining, in response to Socratic questions, what a better society would be like, I find him predictably puzzled by the abstract turn of the dialogue, not "strangely inarticulate" (*H*, 19). And when the authors characterize all these people as "confused about how to define for themselves such things as the nature of success, the meaning of freedom, and the requirements of justice" (*H*, 21), I recall poor Euthyphro and wonder whether Socratic questions are bound to make nearly anybody from whatever time or place seem inarticulate.[1]

II

We have reason to doubt, then, that *Habits of the Heart* succeeds in justifying its conclusions about the "first language" of American individualism. Let us now turn to a book that influenced the authors of *Habits*, MacIntyre's *After Virtue*, according to which the disorder of our moral discourse leaves us "all already in a state so disastrous that there are no large remedies for it" (1984, 5).[2] MacIntyre begins his defense of this claim by inviting us to notice that "The most striking feature of contemporary moral utterance is that so much of it is used to express disagreements" (1984, 6). No doubt, moral language in our period is often used to express disagreements. Why, though, should this seem striking or surprising?

We do not debate whether it is just to torture people for fun. The matter is hardly trivial, but it is not something we disagree over or entertain serious doubts about, and we therefore have little reason to mention it unless it can be made relevant to the resolution of some disagreement. Public discourse, at least under conditions of freedom, tends to concentrate on controversial matters, the better to resolve them, leaving platitudes to one side. It would be more striking and perhaps even disturbing, I would think, if this ceased to be so and moral language came to be used in public settings only or largely for the ceremonial expression of widespread moral agreement.

Moral platitudes do play a role in our use of moral language outside of public ceremonial expressions of consensus, but one needs to look in the right places to find them. Once such place is the nursery, where we begin to initiate our children into the moral consensus we share, such as it is. MacIntyre's attention is fixed, however, on those points at which we most obviously lack consensus, and he cites our public debates over warfare, abortion, and the tensions between equality and freedom. He finds, moreover, that "the most striking feature" of these debates is "their interminable character." "There seems," he says, "to be no rational way of securing moral agreement in our culture" (1984, 6).

The reason we have so much trouble securing moral agreement on such issues, MacIntyre suggests, is that the various premises from which people argue are conceptually incommensurable. The premises from which argument proceeds employ concepts originally at home in quite different moral languages. We know how to construct valid arguments using one set of premises or another, but we do not know how to appraise the significance of the concepts used in any given argument without begging the question. From our rival conclusions we can argue back to our rival premises; but when we do arrive at our premises argument ceases and the invocation of one premise against another becomes a matter of pure assertion and counterassertion.

As a result, our public discourse becomes "an unharmonious mélange of ill-assorted fragments" (1984, 10). We speak as if we were appealing to impersonal criteria, but each of us in fact typically fails to do more than express his or her unreasoned decision to adopt some set of premises as a starting point. Nor have the philosophers fared any better than the rest of us. They too have failed "to provide a shared, public rational justification for morality" (1984, 50).

MacIntyre does not conclude from this failure that there can in principle be no such thing as moral knowledge. He holds, to the contrary, that in earlier stages of our history, stages in which there was widespread agreement on "man-as-he-could-be-if-he-realized-his-*telos*" (1984, 54), people were capable of engaging in rational public discourse on conduct, character, and community. It is only by recovering something like an Aristotelian teleological framework and tailoring our inherited moral languages to fit, he thinks, that we shall be able to render moral discourse rational again.

Any such recovery is not, however, a merely philosophical undertaking: it cannot succeed, according to MacIntyre, without being embodied in the habits, dispositions, shared assumptions and goals of a living community dedicated to the common good. Since liberal society is not such a community and is not likely to become one in our lifetimes, the only hope for moral rationality is the "construction of local forms of community within which civility and the intellectual and moral life can be sustained" (1984, 263). The salient characteristic of liberal society, on this view, is that it is not unified by a *telos*. Liberal institutions attempt to manage collective life in the absence of agreement on the good. In such institutions, politics cannot help being "civil war carried on by other means" (1984, 253).

I am prepared to grant that complete absence of agreement on the good would render rational moral discourse impossible. I am also prepared to grant that our agreement on the good falls well short of perfect harmony. Furthermore, liberal institutions are plausibly viewed as an attempt to manage collective life in the absence of perfect agreement on "man-as-he-would-be-if-he-realized-his-*telos*." What MacIntyre has not shown, it seems to me, is that moral discourse in liberal society cannot itself be understood as held together by a relatively limited but nonetheless real and significant agreement on the good.

We are not united in consensus around a particular theory of human nature or man's true *telos*, and our disagreements about certain particular moral issues have therefore proved especially difficult to resolve, but our disagreement about what human beings are like and what is good for us does not go all the way down. In fact, it is hard to see how it could. As Donald Davidson (1984, chap. 13) has argued, if you start pushing disagreement about some subject matter down too far, it tends to disappear by becoming merely verbal. Complete disagreement about something leaves us unable to identify a common subject matter to disagree over. It therefore makes sense to speak of disagreement, in morals as much as elsewhere, only if we are prepared to recognize a background of agreement.[3] It would be a mistake, then, to think that our disagreement on the good is total or that the areas of apparently intractable moral disagreement to which MacIntyre calls attention could be the whole story.[4]

This line of reasoning suggests a picture of liberal society both more complicated and less dismal than MacIntyre's: Even though we no longer share a single theory of human nature and despite the fact that Aristotelian teleology has long since passed out of philosophical fashion, most of us do agree on the essentials of what might be called the provisional *telos* of liberal society. What made the creation of liberal institutions necessary, in large part, was the manifest failure of religious groups of various sorts to establish rational agreement on their competing detailed visions of the good. It was because people recognized putting an end to religious warfare and intolerance as morally *good*—as rationally preferable under the circumstances to continued attempts at imposing a more nearly complete vision of the good by force—that liberal institutions have been able to get a foothold here and there around the globe.

In other words, liberal society can be seen as justified by a self-limiting consensus on the good—an agreement that it would be a bad thing, that it would make life worse for all of us, to press too hard or too far for agreement on all details in a given vision of the good. Our shared conception of the good consists in moral platitudes and habits of judgment too numerous to mention. Admittedly, it does not extend far enough to eliminate disagreement on some matters of importance. Where we do disagree on such matters, that is where we should expect the complexity of our conceptual heritage to show itself, both as a resource and as a problem. But while there are times when, in response to Socratic questioning or an especially knotty dilemma, we are unsure how to carry on with our reason giving, there are vast regions of moral terrain in which we carry on perfectly well.

If something like this alternative picture can be sustained, we should be less tempted to see moral discourse in our culture as simply incapable of supporting rational argumentation. Our failure to provide philosophical foundations for the premises we use in arguing long-disputed points will be less likely to elicit far-reaching doubts. No form of discourse need exhibit either philosophical foundations or means for resolving all disputes before being deemed fully respectable. Any criterion of respectability that implies otherwise itself deserves suspicion.

III

Standard philosophical defenses of liberal society take some such criterion for granted and then try to provide the wanted philosophical foundations and means for resolving disputes. As Richard Rorty points out in a recent unpublished essay, "The Priority of Democracy to Philosophy," this strategy plays right into the communitarian critic's hands. For, as MacIntyre never tires of pointing out, the various proponents of foundations for liberal society are very good at wrecking each other's proposals. They do not need help from communitarian critics. And the disputes they are trying to resolve prove every bit as intractable after a new proposal is made as before.

Rorty's recent writings defend liberal society in a nonstandard, pragmatic way.[5] A pragmatic liberal like Rorty does not begin by trying to establish a philosophical foundation, like an individualist theory of human nature or a Kantian critique of practical reason, and then construct upon it an apparatus for resolving disputes by cranking out liberal conclusions. He is apt to be as suspicious of such attempts as any communitarian. But he does not see liberal society as dependent on foundations. Rorty defends liberal society in part by deflecting the demand for foundations, as I have in the previous sections of this essay, and in part by pointing out contingent features of liberal society that make it the best available set of arrangements we can get under the circumstances, at least by "our" lights.

Much of Rorty's argument in "The Priority of Democracy" is an attempt to reinterpret John Rawls's *A Theory of Justice* (1971) as the great contemporary expression of pragmatic liberalism, thereby defending that book against those like Michael Sandel (1982), who sees Rawls as founding a liberal theory of justice on an incoherent metaphysics of the self. Actually, I think this struggle over *A Theory of Justice* is beside the point. Both Rorty and Sandel probably make the book seem more coherent and self-conscious than it is. Rorty is reading it backwards, from the vantage point of Rawls's subsequent, consistently pragmatic and antimetaphysical writings. He has little trouble finding passages in the book that prefigure the later, Deweyan Rawls of the "Dewey Lectures." But Sandel would have equally little trouble finding passages to support a more metaphysical reading. My own view is that Rawls had not yet worked out all the implications of his pragmatic conception of justification when he wrote *A Theory of Justice,* with the result that the book is fundamentally ambiguous.[6] He got clear, and achieved his true greatness as a philosopher, only later.

The irony of Rorty's reading of Rawls, as he himself seems to realize, is that it is hard to see why Rawls would have spent so much time elaborating on the technical details of the original position—the feature of the book for which it is best known—if he had started out with something like the Rortian pragmatism one finds in his recent essays. As Rorty says, "It is tempting to suggest that one could eliminate all reference to the original position from *A Theory of Justice* without loss, but this is as daring a suggestion as that one might rewrite (as many have wished to do) Kant's *Critique of Pure Reason* without reference to the thing-in-itself" (n.d., 19). If Rawls had started out as a Rortian, he would have written a much shorter book we would remember mainly for the idea of "reflective equilibrium." Or perhaps he would have written something more like Michael Walzer's *Spheres of Justice* (1983).

Actually, Walzer's book strikes me as not only a clearer example of pragmatic liberalism than Rawls's but also a much more helpful one. Rawls gave us a valuable trope for saying what liberal justice is all about, but Rawls and others immediately pressed it too hard in the hope of finding something difficult and technical for liberal moral philosophers to do, and the resulting rigor was almost entirely misplaced. Walzer, who has been criticized for being impressionistic, gives us something more useful. He helps us see moral philosophy as reflexive ethnography. For Walzer, participant observation begins at home, and it aims for thick description. The anthropologist's thick descriptions discern the difference between a wink and a blink in some foreign culture. Walzer's thick descriptions discern the difference between an apt application of a principle and an application that takes a principle outside its proper sphere. The culture in question is ours, and if interpreting "to one's fellow citizens the world of meanings that we share" (Walzer 1983, xiv) is impressionistic, that is because it has to be.[7]

In any event, we can easily set aside the issue of what to make of Rawls and take Rorty's main point to be that we should shift attention away from "the claim that the social theory of the liberal state rests on false philosophical presuppositions" (n.d., 40).[8] When we follow this advice, he thinks, our attention naturally shifts *toward* such questions as whether liberal institutions can be "combined with the sense of common purpose which pre-democratic societies enjoyed" (ibid.) and whether "the sort of human being who is produced by liberal institutions and culture is undesirable" (n.d., 6). These are better questions, in no small measure because they are more concrete, but Rorty has thus far done little to answer them, aside from insisting that no one such question has to be viewed as prior to all the others that might occur to us. Rorty is quite prepared to say, for example, that a sense of common purpose may just have to be given up if we want to enjoy the benefits our society produces or "that even if the typical character-types of liberal democracies *are* bland, calculating, petty and unheroic, the prevalence of such people may nevertheless be a reasonable price to pay for political freedom" (n.d., 33).

If communitarian critics of liberalism stuck to questions like these and stayed clear of questions about the putative philosophical foundations of liberalism, Rorty says, they would at least "avoid the sort of terminal wistfulness with which their books typically end" (n.d., 40). He cites the conclusion of *After Virtue*, with its talk of the new dark ages and its reference to the need for another St. Benedict, as an example of such wistfulness. But the terminal wistfulness, I think, has little to do with concentration on questions about philosophical foundations. It is rather a function of everybody's inability to imagine a full-blown alternative to liberal society that would be both achievable by acceptable means and clearly better than what we've got now. No one has trouble *imagining* a way of life that, by his or her lights, would qualify as an improvement upon the current order. But it always turns out to be a way of life in which everybody, or nearly everybody, comes to see the light—that is, comes to see things by *my* light, in light of *my* conception of the good in all its detail. If imagined utopias are to generate more than terminal wistfulness, we will need also to be able to imagine in realistic terms how to achieve them by acceptable means, how to make them nonutopian.

The problem with most communitarian criticism of liberal society, then, is its implicitly utopian character. The critics do succeed, at times, in articulating quite reasonable misgivings many of us feel concerning life in liberal society. Yet they very rarely give us any clear sense of what to do about our misgivings aside from yearning pensively for conditions we are either unwilling or unable to bring about. Liberal responses to communitarian criticism, on the other hand, often show what seems to be smug insensitivity to those misgivings.

Rorty occasionally acknowledges the force of communitarian misgivings, but only very rarely and in passing. For instance, in a passage meant to extol the liberalizing changes that increased "people's sense of themselves as free citizens of free countries," he adds an aside to the effect

that "Weber was of course right in saying that some of these changes
have also worked the other way (to increase our sense of being controlled
by 'them')" (1985a, 169). And he speaks of the "sort of 'shock' we get
when, reading Foucault, we realize that the jargon we liberal intellectuals
developed has played into the hands of the bureaucrats" (1985a, 173).
But these concessions will not lessen the impression of smugness until
they are developed.[9]

What we need to find, it seems to me, is the mean between smug approval of the *status quo* and wistful alienation from it—the mean between
liberal apologetics and implicitly utopian criticism. I think all the authors
I have been discussing would like to find this mean, but I am convinced
we won't be able to find it until we set aside such polar oppositions as
liberal versus communitarian and invent more detailed ways to flesh out
reasonable misgivings about our predicament. A misgiving counts as
more than merely wistful, and thus worth being fleshed out, if it can be
connected with something more than vague yearning, some relatively
concrete proposal about what to do.

                                    IV

Pragmatic liberalism is not the only nonstandard defense of liberal society. Like Richard Rorty, Gilbert Meilaender (1983) defends liberal arrangements as the best—or rather, the least bad—available and dissociates himself from the typically individualist premises found in standard
forms of philosophical liberalism. Also like Rorty, he is wary of communitarian proposals. Yet his reasons come not from Dewey's pragmatism
but from Augustine's theology.

The most we can hope for from the earthly kingdom at its best, according to Meilaender, is a measure of order that can secure private
space in which we can form friendships and families and voluntary associations. In these spheres, not in the sphere of political doings, we find
the closest thing to true happiness one can find in this life—analogues to
the forms of association the blessed enjoy in God's Kingdom. Politics at
its best makes room for such happiness and such associations. It also
opens up the space in which individuals can pursue the spiritual life as
they understand it. Politics is no substitute for that and always goes sour
the moment we begin thinking of an earthly political community, whether
actual or potential, as our real home.

Meilaender defends the liberal state, then, not because he considers
its arrangements truly just, for there is no truly just state in this life, but
rather because it is the form of political life best suited to proper recognition of the limits of politics. Communitarians are to be distrusted because they call us into a kind of solidarity with others in public life that
would have a disastrously totalizing effect upon us. Much of what they

say in criticism of liberal society is true enough, from Meilaender's point of view, but this should not be surprising. Liberal society is not the Kingdom of God. So, like all forms of political association in this life, it is radically imperfect. It is to be preferred not because it approximates the ideal but simply because its recognition of the limits of politics makes it not quite as bad as the other forms.

Meilaender in fact goes out of his way to call attention to what he sees as liberal society's limitations and dangers—in particular, its tendency to allow the language of the capitalist marketplace or the ethos of minimal decency to "seep" into the parts of our lives where they don't belong:

> When enshrined at the center of our public consciousness is the minimal virtue which asks only civility, when our common life acknowledges a plurality of forms of the good life and the need for freedom to pursue our private visions of the good life—when these are the beliefs upon which our community is founded—it will be difficult to prevent a belief in the primacy of private interests from seeping down into and dominating our understanding of virtue. Serious moral education, serious training in virtue, may then become difficult to sustain. We may even have difficulty sustaining the common life of smaller groups upon which we are relying to transmit those "higher" elements of our moral vision. (1983, 7)

Meilaender can sound like *Habits of the Heart* when he says that "the individualism of our world often seems destructive, that we demonstrate little willingness to sacrifice private desires for public ends" (1983, 5). He readily grants that the liberal state is not a true home for its citizens.

But things would be much worse, according to Meilaender, if we overthrew the liberal state and replaced it by an earthly political community, of our own making, meant to be our home. What we need, instead, is "a Chalcedonian politics":

> a form of the liberal tradition which does not attempt to overcome the tension between ethics and politics, yet does recognize that there is indeed a tension. This form of the tradition claims that the public realm—the political—exists *not* just to support and make possible individual pursuit of private goals and projects, *nor* to foster fraternal solidarity. Rather, the political realm exists to foster *private, social* bonds—to make space in life for families, friendships, clubs, faiths, neighborhoods. (1983, 9)

Meilaender is saying that the Chalcedonian public realm exists to create space for families, friendships, and so on, not *just* to serve the "individual pursuit of private goals and projects." The word "just" is meant to leave some room for the language and values of individualism, while the word "not" puts unrestricted individualism in question. I introduce Rorty and Meilaender partly to show that liberalism comes in forms, both pragmatic and Augustinian, that owe little to individualism as a metaphysics of the self or as an unrestricted philosophy of life. Nor are these forms of liberalism recent historical developments. They can be traced

well back into early stages of liberal thought. The picture of liberalism as
dependent upon radically individualist philosophical foundations does
justice to neither liberal society nor liberal thought.

Meilaender's Chalcedonian public realm aims to protect private *bonds*,
and thus forms of association in which the virtues might flourish and be
taught, not merely the "individual pursuit of private goals and projects."
It seems not at all concerned to promote fraternal solidarity among the
citizenry. Meilaender does not say, "nor *just* to foster fraternal solidarity," but simply: "nor to foster fraternal solidarity." Suppose, however,
we try to split the difference between Meilaender's "Augustinian vision"
and the totalizing tendencies he fears in communitarian politics as follows: first, by granting that the political sphere ought to leave room for
both private bonds and the individual pursuit of private goals and projects; and second, by adding that yet another legitimate purpose of politics is to foster a sort of public life in which members find *some part* of
their identity as citizens of a republic directed to the *common* good.

By splitting the difference in this way we can avoid seeing complete
identification of oneself with one's political roles as the only alternative to
Meilaender's virtually exclusive emphasis on the private sphere. The
truth in Augustinian liberalism can then be reformulated as the idea that
every sphere of earthly human life, from the most public to the most private, has its temptations and dangers. No sphere can rightly occupy the
position of be-all and end-all in our lives without throwing the rest out of
proper proportion—neither vocation, nor family, nor voluntary association, nor private projects, nor politics.

This formulation allows us to say, for example, what remained deficient about Brian Palmer's life after he remarried. He has, we sense,
simply traded one disproportionate preoccupation, his dedication to his
career, for another, his dedication to his family. His life is better than it
used to be, somewhat less narrow in orientation. He has recognized the
limitations and miseries of life dedicated wholly to the individual pursuit
of private goals and projects. And he has found considerably more happiness, not merely greater subjective satisfaction, in private bonds. But
there remains a sense in which his life is narrowly focused, a sense in
which one aspect of life has acquired a disproportionate importance.
This is what I take the authors of *Habits of the Heart* to be trying to get at
in their discussion of his case, but it has little to do with his stammering
in response to Socratic questions or his apparent commitment to individualism as an ultimate principle.

Meilaender has not established a special deficiency in political life that
would disqualify it as a realm in which we might, and perhaps *should*,
seek some measure of our fulfillment as people. He has simply drawn
attention to features of communitarian solidarity that, if allowed to take
over our entire lives, would make things much worse than they are now.

Atomistic individualism and totalitarian solidarity do not exhaust our options. They are more like obviously undesirable extremes than like options anyway, and none of the authors I have been discussing is proposing either. My question at this point is not exactly Rorty's question of whether liberal institutions and practices can be "combined with the sense of common purpose which pre-democratic societies enjoyed," but rather how we might enhance the sense of common purpose we already have, limited as it may be, without acting unjustly or making things worse.

Communitarians and liberals alike tend to view liberal society as centered in the idea that we can get along without what Cicero called "an agreement with respect to justice and a partnership for the common good." Meilaender sees this idea as rooted in good Augustinian theology, suspicious of any this-worldly attempt to instantiate a truly excellent form of political community. Pragmatic liberals see the same idea as rooted in contingent features of modern societies, where diverse populations are crowded into the same territories and no group succeeds in imposing its own conception of the good. Communitarians see the same idea as an especially telling expression of what is wrong with the liberal order. I wish now to raise the possibility that this picture of liberal society, so widely shared by its defenders and its critics, is seriously misleading.

My reasons for thinking so were already implicit in the treatment of MacIntyre offered in section II. There I suggested that while it goes without saying that people in liberal society fall well short of complete agreement about matters pertaining to justice and the common good, it does not follow that they do not agree at all about such matters. If my argument in that section was correct, their disagreement on such matters could not be total. We should therefore be less impressed by the opposition between Cicero and Augustine or by overly sharp contrasts between societies that agree on such matters and societies that do not. If we think of liberal society as having a provisional *telos*, a self-limiting consensus on the good, we should be able to avoid thinking of the question, Individual freedom or common purpose? as presenting an exclusive choice. We have so little *sense* of common purpose in part because we have become so accustomed to a picture that hides the actual extent of our commonality from view. We need also to remember that preserving a healthy degree of individual freedom inheres in our common purpose and helps define our conception of justice.

Having "an agreement with respect to justice and a partnership for the common good" is hardly an all-or-nothing affair. Most of us would be happy to expand our agreement with respect to justice and enhance our sense of common purpose provided we could do so without unacceptably displacing private bonds, curtailing our freedom to pursue private projects and goals, or imposing our preferences by force. If someone asks where we should draw the line between acceptable and unacceptable displacement of private bonds, curtailment of freedom, or imposition of preferences, we have nothing that is both highly general and highly illuminating to say.

We can say "Imagine yourself needing to agree with others while meeting behind a veil of ignorance . . ." or "Count as acceptable whatever can be justified to others on grounds they could not reasonably reject" or "Suppose yourself to be conversing under conditions of undistorted communication. . . ."[10] Yet no such saying helps very much in abstraction from what Dewey (1957, 212) called the meaning of the daily detail.[11] We help determine our fate not by choosing for or against liberal society as such, nor by finding the right general principle of acceptability, but by drawing the line here or there in countless particular cases, given our sense of the daily detail. MacIntyre is surely right in this: There is no substitute for *phronesis*.

V

It would be good, of course, to have a better sense of the daily detail than we do. *Habits of the Heart* is at its best when it uses interview material to bring the daily detail of marriage or career or therapy to life instead of probing Socratically for ultimate principles. *After Virtue* covers too much ground to dwell on any detail for more than a moment, and I have criticized its picture of moral discourse in liberal society because of its abstractness and one-sided emphasis on discord. It needs to be added, however, that MacIntyre's book does offer the sort of conceptual tools we need to correct that picture, if only we put them to use. *Habits of the Heart* puts some of these tools to good use—namely, MacIntyre's descriptions of the Rich Aesthete, the Manager, and the Therapist as stock "characters" in liberal society. Still more valuable, for reasons I can only sketch here, is MacIntyre's distinction between *social practices* and *institutions*.

By a social practice, MacIntyre means something quite particular:

> any coherent and complex form of socially established cooperative human activity through which goods internal to that form of activity are realized in the course of trying to achieve those standards of excellence which are appropriate to, and partially definitive of, that form of activity, with the result that human powers to achieve excellence, and human conceptions of the ends and goods involved, are systematically extended. (1984, 187)

The crucial notion here, for my purposes, is that of goods *internal* to a form of activity, as distinct from goods *external* to it. Internal goods are such that they can be specified only in terms drawn from the activity itself, recognized only by people experienced in the activity, and realized only by participating in the activity well, as judged by its standards of excellence. External goods, in contrast, include prestige, status, and money—which one can in principle achieve for reasons having little or nothing to do with excellence as judged by the standards implicit in a specific form of activity.

You can of course win prestige, status, and money by participating well in a genuine social practice like chess. But you can also achieve such goods by cheating at chess or by participating in some other form of activity. The goods internal to chess, goods Anatoly Karpov has achieved and I have not, cannot be identified without invoking the language of chess. Karpov could not have achieved them by cheating at chess, and he could not have achieved them by becoming an excellent architect. The prestige Karpov has won by playing chess as well as he does can be won in other ways.

Medical care is a social practice in MacIntyre's sense. It requires the cultivation of virtues, including skills of caring and discernment specific to medicine as such. Some, though not all, of these skills are technical. Doctors and nurses pursue goods internal to the practice of medical care, goods that cannot be achieved in any other practice or by any other means than by being a good doctor or nurse, exhibiting the forms of excellence peculiar to those roles. This practice is embodied in institutions—in our society they include the hospital, the professional association, the medical school, the partnership—and is closely related to such broader institutions as the capitalist marketplace and governmental agencies. Unsustained by such institutions, the practice would change dramatically for the worse, if not collapse altogether.

Institutions, MacIntyre says, trade heavily in external goods, and necessarily so:

> They are involved in acquiring money and other material goods; they are structured in terms of power and status, and they distribute money, power and status as rewards. Nor could they do otherwise if they are to sustain not only themselves, but also the practices of which they are the bearer. (1984, 194)

Yet it would be foolish to neglect the moral threat institutions typically pose to the social practices they make possible. For goods like money and power and status, which have no internal relation to a social practice like medical care, can compete with and perhaps even engulf goods internal to the practice.

We are right to worry about a system in which the proliferation and distribution of external goods makes doctors and prospective doctors lose sight of the goods internal to medical care. The practice of medical care tends increasingly to be dominated in our society by the modes of interaction and patterns of thought characteristic of the marketplace and the bureaucracies that make the practice possible. Without the marketplace and the bureaucracies, the practice would undoubtedly suffer terribly. With them, it tends to be overwhelmed by goods and roles alien to its own *telos* of caring for the sick.[12]

It is in this kind of tension between internal and external goods that many of the deepest problems of our society lie. The same pattern shows up everywhere—not only in medicine but also in other extraordinarily valuable practices, from sports to humanistic education. Newspapers everyday run stories about the extent to which drugs, money, and status threaten to dominate goods internal to the practice of sports. Commencement speakers annually bemoan the extent to which undergraduate concern over advancement to careers in corporations and bureaucracies threatens to dominate goods internal to humanistic education.

With these thoughts in mind, I can bring this essay to a close and bring some of its themes together by making the following points:

1. Anxiety over the language of individualism as a corrosive element in our lives, like that expressed in *Habits of the Heart*, can be reinterpreted as the fear that our thought and speech are more and more dominated by external goods. A life lived merely in pursuit of external goods, a life like the one Brian Palmer used to lead, is morally empty. A society of people living such lives, a society in which people did not learn the virtues in social practices, would be morally blind.

2. The idea that liberal society lacks any shared conception of the good is false, but that does not mean that all is well. It could still be the case that politics, as the social practice of self-governance directed toward the common good, has begun to give way to merely bureaucratic management of competition for external goods. It is therefore right to worry about becoming despots and barbarians. On the other hand, the social practice of politics is *always* being threatened in some such way. All genuine republics, not just the liberal kind, are fragile things, susceptible to corruption by external goods.

3. Rorty's shock, upon reading Foucault, that our vocabularies are playing into the hands of the bureaucrats, Meilaender's talk about "seepage," MacIntyre's descriptions of merely manipulative modes of interaction, and the widespread dissatisfaction with technical rationality echoed in *Habits of the Heart* all tie into this problem: the uneasy relation between social practices and such institutions as the capitalist marketplace and large-scale bureaucracies.

4. We do not need help from Rorty's light-mindedness toward traditional philosophical problems to help make "the world's inhabitants . . . more receptive to the appeal of instrumental rationality" (n.d., 39). If we take instrumental rationality to be the kind of reasoning we use in the pursuit of external goods, the world's inhabitants are already all too receptive to its appeal. Light-mindedness toward traditional philosophical problems might do us some good, however, if it helps us stop judging our moral discourse by the ultimate principles we utter in response to Socratic questions.

5. It would be foolish to wish for a world in which we had only social

practices and no institutions, a world in which external goods posed no temptations, for there can be no such world. Any such wish would be mere wistfulness. As MacIntyre says, "no practices survive for any length of time unsustained by institutions" (1984, 194). Nor can we reasonably hope for a world in which nothing like our current institutions had a place, for such a world would also have little or no place for many of the social practices we find most enriching and meaningful.

6. We can, nonetheless, reasonably hope for a world in which the proliferation, distribution, and merchandizing of external goods is subject to just political control and in which the goods internal to social practices, including the practice of self-government, are granted the right to life and given room to flourish. The hope that social practices, not simply private bonds and the individual pursuit of external goods, be protected is not an expression of terminal wistfulness, for it is neither nostalgic nor utopian. There are in fact countless specific things one could do to improve the prospects of a particular social practice.

7. We shall not bring our predicament into clear focus until we learn to see liberal society as a single interlocking network of social practices and institutions. Our social theorists know how to talk about the marketplace and the bureaucracy. They also know how to talk about sectarian and revolutionary protests coming from the margins. Yet they barely know how to talk about social practices, in MacIntyre's sense, at all. This means, if I am right, that our social theory tends to leave out of the picture precisely the features that would help us understand what makes liberal society worth caring about, as well as the resources it makes available for its own transformation. We know how to describe a clinic in the idiom of Foucault or a university in the idiom of functionalist sociology, but everything comes out looking like a system of external goods in which people are moved only by status, money, and the will to power. A sociology that included social practices would look different. It would also help connect institutions to the meaning of the daily detail.

8. The languages of morals in our discourse are many, and they have remarkably diverse historical origins, but they do not float in free air, and their name is not chaos. They are embedded in specific social practices and institutions. We need as many different moral concepts as we do because there are so many different linguistic threads woven into a fabric of practices and institutions as rich as ours. It is a motley: not a building in need of new foundations but a coat of many colors, with problems here and there that require the best attention we can give.

9. We can make good use of Aristotelian and civic republican talk of virtues and the common good without supposing that this sort of moral language requires us to jettison talk of rights and tolerance. We can do this by thinking of liberal political institutions as oriented toward a provisional *telos*—a widely shared but self-limiting consensus on the highest

good achievable under circumstances like ours.[13] But this *telos* justifies a kind of tolerance foreign to the classical teleological tradition. And it also allows us to think of rights as a type of property assigned to people by whatever arrangements count as justified, relative to the highest achievable good.

10. Our task, like Thomas Jefferson's or Martin Luther King's, is to take the many parts of a complicated social and conceptual inheritance and hammer them together into a pattern that meets the needs of the moment.[14] It has never been otherwise. The creative task of every generation, in other words, is moral bricolage. It is no accident that Jefferson and King were as eclectic as they were in using moral languages—and no shame either.[15]

NINE

Liberalism and its Communitarian Critics: Does Liberal Practice "Live Down" to Liberal Theory?

Bernard Yack

Liberalism, like its chief rival, Marxism, has come to refer to a variety of practices and institutions, as well as to a set of political theories. Its critics usually focus their attention on either liberal theory or liberal practice and then go on to reject both. Recent communitarian critics of liberalism are no exception. They concentrate on identifying the limitations of liberal theory and then point to the ways in which these limitations are embodied in liberal practices and institutions. Their arguments thus prompt the question posed in the subtitle of this essay: Does liberal practice "live down" to liberal theory?

A critique of liberal theory need not entail a critique of liberal practice. Nor need a critique of liberal practice entail a critique of liberal theory. Just as one may accept the goals of liberal theory and deny that liberal practices adequately realize them, one may approve of liberal practices and deny that liberal theories adequately justify them. In this essay I argue that recent communitarian critics of liberalism, such as Alasdair MacIntyre, Michael Sandel, Roberto Unger, and Benjamin Barber, as well as the authors of *Habits of the Heart,* cannot move so easily from their critique of liberal theory to a critique of liberal practice. In particular, they cannot use the dissociation of individuals assumed in liberal theory to characterize liberal practices and institutions. I argue further that they now appear able to move back and forth between their critiques of liberal theory and practice only because they blur the distinction between two clearly different conceptions of dissociation.

My aim in distinguishing between these two conceptions of dissociation is to clarify some of the implications of the communitarian critique of liberal theory—much of which I find soundly argued—rather than to provide a new justification for liberal practices and institutions.[1] In the first two sections of the essay I argue that contemporary communitarians, such as MacIntyre and Sandel, ignore many of the implications of their own theoretical positions when they try to justify their rejection of liberal practices and institutions.[2] In particular, they ignore the fact— implicit in their own critique of liberal theory—that the concepts and categories devised by liberal theorists cannot adequately describe or account for the behavior of individuals who participate in liberal practices and institutions. Members of liberal societies must be constituted, like all other real individuals, by their shared sentiments and institutions, while the individuals discussed by liberal theorists (in a hypothetical state of nature or "original position"), lack many socially constituted characteristics. Nevertheless, communitarian critics often describe participants in liberal practices as "unencumbered selves," selves pushed relentlessly toward complete isolation from the sentiments and standards of their fellow citizens. Moreover, sociological evidence of the alienating and atomizing effects of liberal individualism, such as that presented in *Habits of the Heart*, encourages them to do so.

The alienation and anomie noted by observers of modern societies must, according to communitarian theory, be part and parcel of a form of communal life, unlike the hypothetical dissociation discussed by liberal theorists. Consequently, when communitarian critics of liberal practice demand the *reconstitution* of community among modern individuals, they are also, implicitly, demanding the *deconstitution* of the communal ties that presently shape modern lives. To criticize liberal practice, as opposed to liberal theory, communitarians must justify *disencumbering* individuals of shared and socially acquired characteristics. They must justify the assertion that we should uproot many of the communal standards we already share, rather than merely justify the claim that we need shared standards. In the final section of this essay, I argue that when communitarians, such as Benjamin Barber or Roberto Unger, attempt such justifications they run into many of the same problems that have plagued liberal theorists.

I

Alasdair MacIntyre's *After Virtue* (1984) is the most celebrated and influential of the recent communitarian critiques of liberalism. It combines a neo-Aristotelian critique of all modern political and moral theory with a lament about the collapse of moral virtue in the modern world. Although the main focus of the work is the inadequacy of modern theory, MacIntyre argues that modern practice suffers from the same limitations he finds in modern theory. "We have," he claims, "—very largely, if not entirely—lost our comprehension, both theoretical and practical, of morality" (2–3):

Modern systematic politics, whether liberal, conservative, radical or socialist, simply has to be rejected from a standpoint that owes genuine allegiance to the tradition of the virtues; for modern politics itself expresses in
its institutional forms a systematic rejection of that tradition. (1984, 255)

"The tradition of the virtues" is impossible, according to MacIntyre,
outside of a community constituted by a set of shared stories about virtue
and vice. To the extent that we act and relate to each other, MacIntyre
argues, we try to live according to characteristics, noble or base, with
which we become familiar through the stories that we tell to each other.
The sharing of stories creates a moral community; moral actions are
those that live up to the virtues described by our shared traditions. If we
deprive a society of either these traditions or the ability to tell stories
about the characteristics it admires, we dissolve its moral character. We
deprive that society of its theoretical and practical comprehension of
morality:

> . . . man is in his actions and practice, as well as in his fictions, essentially a
> story-telling animal. . . . We enter human society with one or more im-
> puted characters—roles into which we have been drafted—and we have to
> learn what they are in order to be able to understand how others respond
> to us and how our responses to them are apt to be construed. It is through
> hearing stories about wicked stepmothers, lost children, good but mis-
> guided kings, wolves that suckle twin boys, . . . that children learn or mis-
> learn . . . what the ways of the world are. Deprive children of stories and
> you leave them unscripted, anxious stutterers in their actions as in their
> words. (1984, 216)

Liberal theorists, like all modern moral theorists, fail, MacIntyre com-
plains, to recognize the dependence of moral action on the particular
stock of shared stories that individuals inherit. They recognize only "impersonal criteria" as proper justifications for action. As a result, they
sever individuals from the "context of utterance" that gives meaning to
their viewing individuals outside of this context. As dissociated beings
appealing to impersonal universal principles, they must fail in their attempts to account for and justify moral action (8–9).

Liberal practices and institutions, like virtually all modern practices
and institutions, according to MacIntyre, also express "a systematic rejection of that tradition" (255) that sustains moral virtue. He claims that
a moral "catastrophe sufficient to throw the language and practice of
morality into grave disorder" (3) has occurred. The disdain for past traditions and stories as criteria for describing and judging moral actions
underlies all of our practices and institutions. That disdain has tri-
umphed to such an extent that the major alternatives to liberalism in the
modern world, Marxism and Nietzscheanism, share liberalism's devalua-

tion of tradition. We cannot recognize the catastrophe that has befallen our moral lives because modern theory fails to give us adequate language to comprehend moral activity. But this catastrophe is so complete that MacIntyre suggests there is no possibility of reforming modern practices and institutions. He proclaims that "the new dark ages . . . are already upon us" and advises us on the means of keeping the tradition of moral virtue alive in "the coming ages of barbarism and darkness" (263).

Let us assume MacIntyre is correct in his description and critique of modern theory. What justifies his conclusion that modern theory's hostility to storytelling and particularized moral communities actually destroys communal traditions? Apart from a brief discussion of bureaucracy, MacIntyre offers little analysis of the way in which liberal institutions and practices work in the contemporary world. His argument appears instead to rest on an unjustified conflation of theory and practice:

> . . . the transition into modernity was a transition both in theory and in practice and a single transition at that. It is because [of] the habits of mind engendered by our modern academic curriculum . . . that ideas are endowed with a falsely independent life of their own on the one hand and political and social action is presented as peculiarly mindless on the other. This academic dualism is of course itself the expression of an idea at home almost everywhere in the modern world; so much so indeed, that Marxism, the most influential adversary theory of modern culture, presents what is just one more version of this same dualism in the distinction between basis and ideological superstructure. (1984, 61)

MacIntyre comes to such a conclusion because he assumes that "every action is the bearer and expression of more or less theory-laden beliefs and concepts; every piece of theorizing and every expression of belief is a political and moral action" (ibid.). His assumption here should not be confused with the uncontroversial assumption that theory and practice condition each other. Few philosophers would deny the assumption that theory, especially through its influence on concept formation, helps shape moral judgment and action, and that moral and political practices contribute to the form and content of theory. MacIntyre, however, assumes much more than this. He assumes that the theory and practice of an age embody one another. Great political figures from the Medici to Napoleon, MacIntyre insists, can be

> . . . understood as expressing in their actions . . . the very same conceptual changes which at the level of philosophical theory are articulated by Machiavelli and Hobbes, by Diderot and Condorcet, by Hume and Adam Smith and Kant. . . . [For] abstract changes in moral concepts are always embodied in real, particular events. (Ibid.)

As a result of this assumption, MacIntyre is able to read modern institutions and practices as a text that embodies the texts of the great modern philosophers. Modern theory provides us with an adequate guide to the description, if not the evaluation, of modern practice. Mac-Intyre rails against the academic separation of intellectual and institutional history, but he fails to search beyond intellectual history for adequate resources for his own description of modern institutions.

In an early article MacIntyre defended an extreme version of this rather idealistic approach to social analysis and interpretation. He argued that "to identify the limits of social action in a given period is to identify the stock of descriptions current in that age" (1962, 60). Such a position seems to rule out the possibility of social practices for which we do not yet have any adequate concepts and descriptions. Ernest Gellner, among others, has subjected this position, which he described fifteen years ago as the "New Idealism," to a withering critique. He suggests that because "our world is concept-saturated (which is true), it is falsely and absurdly argued [by MacIntyre and others, such as Peter Winch] that therefore our conduct can only be explained in terms of our concepts" (Gellner 1973, 143–44). In other words, MacIntyre uses an uncontroversial assumption about the interpenetration of theory and practice as if it were equivalent to the extremely controversial and idealistic view that practice mirrors theory.

MacIntyre has since backed away from the nominalist moral position to which his earlier claims seemed to commit him. He is now quite willing to use language drawn from outside contemporary descriptions to evaluate contemporary practices. But in interpreting, as opposed to criticizing, contemporary practices, he still uses the modern "stock of descriptions" to identify "the limits of social action" in the modern world. Since "there is no way to give us an understanding of any society except through the stock of stories which constitute its initial dramatic resources" (1984, 216), and modern theories provide us with no understanding of storytelling and the value of particular communities, he concludes that moral activity must be beyond "the limits of social action" in the modern world. MacIntyre's conclusion follows from his analysis of the limitations of modern theories rather than from an analysis of modern practices and institutions.

But if man is, as MacIntyre insists, "in his actions and practice as well as his fiction, a story-telling being" (ibid.), then we should expect men and women to turn theories, even liberal theories which insist on impersonal and antitraditional criteria, into the basis for new stories. This is precisely what has happened. The French turned liberty from tradition into a female figure, symbolic of the Republic's virtues and energy. American colonists turned Lockean liberal principles into didactic stories with which to educate their children. Modern intellectuals admire and seek to imitate the virtues manifested in the story they tell about Copernicus's rejection of the anthropocentric universe.[3] Similarly, the Kantian categorical imperative has generated stories that celebrate moral courage, while social contract theories have encouraged stories that celebrate the virtues associated with self-reliance. According to MacIntyre's own conception of human behavior, we must assume that it is only to the extent that liberal theories have generated such stories that they have shaped our character and practices. The Enlightenment attack on tradition could never have succeeded without itself "becoming tradition" (see Shils [1981, 21–23]).

Nothing disproves MacIntyre's contention that liberal theories have destroyed modern individuals' capacity to tell character-forming stories better than the very story he tells in *After Virtue*. This story, about the moral-political catastrophe that has overtaken us unawares in the transition to "modernity," has its own tradition, stretching back through German philosophers and Romantic social critics, at least to Rousseau. The tale of the social world we unwittingly lost through the triumph of modernity over some form of premodern—most often ancient Greek— thought is one of the most characteristic stories told by disaffected modern intellectuals.

But it is a story designed to counter an even more familiar and characteristic modern story, a story with which its tellers assume their audience is familiar: the Enlightenment story about the rescue of man's freedom and reason from the premodern dark ages of irrationality and dogmatism.[4] This story figures prominently in most liberal theories. MacIntyre is able to tell the tale he does only because modern individuals, to a certain extent, share in a community constituted by a story about the Renaissance and Enlightenment. The Enlightenment story serves to celebrate and promote the emulation of particular virtues: self-reliance, curiosity, intellectual courage, honesty, and so on. Perhaps these are not the best virtues to celebrate. Perhaps they hide terrible vices. But we must remember that it is to counter these stories and the characteristics they celebrate, rather than to rescue the storyless, virtueless modern individual, that MacIntyre and others like him tell their own stories.

To sustain his criticism of liberal practices, MacIntyre would have to go beyond his description of man as a storytelling being and demonstrate that a particular form of community, rather than community per se, is necessary for a desirable life and a healthy social order, and that liberal communities lack this form of communal life. MacIntyre does, at times, distinguish between a "genuine" moral community and other less genuine or nonmoral forms of community. But in many of his arguments he blurs this distinction.

MacIntyre admits that small pockets of storytelling and moral community persist in the modern world, but distinguishes a "well-ordered tradition" from fragmentary traditions like our own (see 1984, 146, 222, 110–11). The distinguishing feature of a "well-ordered tradition,"

MacIntyre seems to suggest, is that it is founded on a "genuine moral consensus," though he is quick to point out that genuine consensus is not the same as universal agreement. "Traditions, when vital, embody continuities of conflict. Indeed when a tradition becomes Burkean, it is always dying or dead" (222). Periclean Athens, his major example of a genuine moral community, he notes, is hardly a model of moral and cultural homogeneity. The Athenian moral tradition, he insists, is made up of a number of conflicting strands, strands never mediated by unanimity at some higher level (134–36).

But if "genuine moral consensus" is not distinguished by universal agreement on fundamental issues, what does distinguish it from our fragmentary moral traditions? MacIntyre does not answer this question very well. He insists that "we have all too many disparate and rival moral concepts . . . and that the moral resources of the culture allow us no way of settling between them rationally" (252). But how does that substantially distinguish our situation from that of Periclean Athens? If settling between rival moral concepts "rationally" means appealing to universally held standards of judgment, then the "healthy" moral tradition of Athens suffers from the same problems we do. If it means appealing to recognizable stories about admired characteristics and virtues, some of which oppose each other in commanding our allegiance, then we have a genuine moral community as well.

MacIntyre rightly denies the homogeneity of premodern moral communities. But he has no other means of distinguishing "genuine" from fragmentary moral traditions. In the end, it is *modern theory's* hostility to tradition that leads him to insist that genuine moral practice has broken down in the modern world. His suggestion that "the individualism of modernity could find no use for the notion of tradition" (222) is acceptable only if we are speaking of modern theory—and one aspect of modern theory at that. MacIntyre does not show that modern moral practices share that hostility to tradition. One may or may not like the particular mix of traditions that constitute modern individuals. MacIntyre clearly does not like them. But in order to sustain his criticism of them, he cannot rest content with denying that they are genuine moral traditions. Indeed, everything he says about human reasoning and practice leads us to expect that we will *not* find modern theory's hostility to tradition in modern practice, and that modern theory would not have exerted any influence on modern practice if it had not itself become "overgrown by tradition" (see Shils 1981, 21ff.).

The move from the critique of liberal theory to the critique of liberal practice is even more striking in Michael Sandel's recent indictment of John Rawls and "deontological liberalism." Sandel not only portrays Rawls's *A Theory of Justice* (1971) as the most representative and revealing example of liberal theory, a questionable enough assumption;[5] he goes on to use it as a guide to liberal practice in America. Rawls's theory, indeed all liberal theory according to Sandel, fails because it depends for its justification on an untenable view of the self as unencumbered by determinate characteristics and values. Only on the basis of such an untenable view, Sandel argues, can liberals justify putting the right before the good. Moreover, corresponding to the "unencumbered self" of liberal theory is a set of institutions and practices that Sandel calls the "procedural republic." The procedural republic represents the institutions and practices that embody the unencumbered self's insistence on the priority of right and the primacy of justice (Sandel 1982, 15–65; 1984).

Sandel seems to recognize a possible contradiction between his critique of Rawls and the assertion that contemporary American practices turn individuals into unencumbered selves. In his analysis of our "present predicament," he states that "in our public life we are more entangled, but less attached, than ever before. It is *as though* the unencumbered self presupposed by the liberal ethic had begun to come true." Given his critique of liberal theory, the unencumbered self *cannot* "come true"; so Sandel suggests that it is only "as though" it had come true. Nevertheless, he proceeds to insist that "our practices and institutions are themselves embodiments of theory" (1984, 94–95). Instead of seeking, like most social theorists, to explain the appearance of dissociation and detachment created by new forms of association and attachment, he seeks to identify and explain the actual dissociation of the liberal individual in the procedural republic.

Sandel's justification for treating contemporary practices as "embodiments of theory" follows MacIntyre's. He begins with the uncontroversial assumption that "to engage in a political practice is already to stand in relation to theory" (1984, 81). And, like MacIntyre, he then moves from this uncontroversial assumption to the extremely controversial and idealistic "view about politics and philosophy and the relation between them—that our practices and institutions are themselves embodiments of theory" (1984, 95).[6] Such a view considerably simplifies the task of understanding and criticizing liberal practices and institutions, since the limitations of liberal theory will then clearly mark out the limitations of liberal practice. But it does so only by treating liberal theory as an adequate tool for the interpretation of liberal practice, something that Sandel's own understanding of the limitations of liberal theory rules out. Thus Sandel finds it necessary to hedge about the actualization of the unencumbered self. To maintain his critique of liberal practice, the unencumbered self must be realizable; to maintain his critique of liberal theory, it cannot be realizable. Consequently, he describes our "present predicament" as one in which it is "as though the unencumbered self . . . had begun to come true."

Liberalism, Sandel suggests, fails as a theory. But,

despite its philosophic failure, the liberal vision is the one by which we live. For us in late twentieth-century America, it is our vision, the theory most thoroughly embodied in the practices and institutions most central to our public life. And seeing how it goes wrong as philosophy may help us diagnose our present political condition. (1984, 82)

If individuals, as Sandel insists, cannot live as unencumbered selves, and the "liberal vision is the one by which we live" and is "most thoroughly embodied in our practices and institutions," then the citizens of liberal regimes would seem to be deeply encumbered members of a community constituted by the "liberal vision" they share. Sharing a vision, they share determinate characteristic and values. Those values may emphasize self-reliance, individual responsibility, and respect for constitutional authority and legal agreements. One may prefer other virtues and characteristics in one's fellow citizens (as Sandel [1982, 175–83] clearly does). But, no matter how liberal theorists may describe and justify them, liberal regimes do inculcate shared standards and inclinations among their participants.

The "philosophic failure" of liberal theory necessarily invalidates the "liberal vision" by which many modern individuals live only if one assumes, as Sandel does, that the stock of concepts and descriptions provided by the dominant theories of an age provide the best characterization of that age's practices and institutions. Sandel's assumption that liberal theory, with all of its limitations, is "most thoroughly embodied in the practices and institutions most central to our public life" leads him to ignore the possibility that liberal practices and institutions may be desirable in spite of the limitations of the theories most commonly used to justify them. That liberal practices "live down" to liberal theory is something that he assumes rather than demonstrates.

But this assumption is unjustifiable alongside Sandel's characterization and critique of liberal theory. If liberal theory fails because it ignores the social constitution of individuals, then it is likely to mislead us in analyzing a political condition in which we are constituted by a shared "liberal vision." For whatever may be lacking in that shared vision, the practices that it informs cannot, by their very nature, "live down" to the dissociation of individuals that Sandel finds in liberal theory. Sociological dissociation—that is, dissociation among individuals constituted by a liberal vision—is not the same thing as theoretical dissociation, the dissociation among the self-constituted individuals assumed by some liberal theorists. Thus it seems unlikely, according to Sandel's own critique of liberal theory, that the way in which Sandel believes liberalism "goes wrong as philosophy will help us diagnose our present political condition." We may, of course, gain much insight into contemporary practices by examining their background theories. But there is a great distance between the weak and uncontroversial assumption that theory and practice condition and interpenetrate each other in a variety of unpredictable ways and the strong and controversial assumption that they mirror each other. Sandel, like MacIntyre, must make the latter assumption in order to justify his claim that the limitations of liberal theory will adequately account for the limitations of liberal practice.

II

Since dissociation is the focus of communitarian critiques of both liberal theory and practice, the communitarian critique of liberal theory seems to support and enhance a critique of liberal practice. For some time, observers of modern society have been presenting evidence of dissociation and alienation among citizens of liberal regimes. *Habits of the Heart* is the latest in a line of such presentations, a line that goes back to the work of Durkheim and Tocqueville. Given the evidence presented, liberal practice might appear to embody the fundamental limitation of liberal theory: a theoretical abstraction from the social constitution of individual reasoning and action.

But communitarians can draw this conclusion only by blurring the distinction between the two different conceptions of dissociation that support their critique of liberal theory, on the one hand, and their critique of liberal practice, on the other. In the first critique, the assumed dissociation of individuals should be absolute; in the second, it should be relative to other forms of association. Most communitarians, like MacIntyre and Sandel, reject liberal theory because it treats individuals as if they could reason and act apart from the various forms of social interaction that actually constitute them. Dissociation in this context means lack of association. At the same time, communitarians reject liberal practices and institutions because they promote a particular form of communal life that dissociates individuals more than many other forms. Dissociation here does not mean lack of association. Instead, it means a form of association that promotes far less of a *sense* of association among individuals than other forms. These two different conceptions of dissociation are the theoretical and the sociological conceptions identified above.

In criticizing the theoretical dissociation present in liberal theory, communitarians can rest their arguments on the relatively uncontroversial premise that individuals are constituted by the communities in which they live. In criticizing the sociological dissociation they claim to find in liberal practice, however, they must rest their arguments upon the far more complex and controversial premises that would prove that *particular forms* of communal life are necessary for a desirable human life or a healthy social order. It is not surprising, then, that they often try to use their critiques of liberal theory to enhance and support their critique of liberal practice. But once we distinguish between the two conceptions of dissociation used in communitarian critiques of liberalism, we see that they cannot sustain their argument without contradicting themselves.[7]

If individual character and rationality are socially constituted, then the theoretical form of dissociation is unrealizable in practice. To suggest that liberal practices and institutions turn individuals into dissociated, self-constituting atoms would bring into question the premise that individuals are constituted by the communities in which they live. To save that premise, communitarians would have to admit that liberal behavior and institutions grow out of a particular kind of community, a kind of community that liberal theory is blind to, or at least cannot explain. Once we distinguish liberal practices from the theories usually invoked to justify them, we see that the former enmesh individuals in "an elaborate social network of rules and the shared beliefs, values, assumptions, and so on that an accepted set of rules involves" (Flathman 1976, 185). Liberal practices and institutions may be "individualistic and individualizing" in character; but, as social practices, they "cannot be fairly described as atomistic and atomizing" (ibid.).

If liberal practice actually *succeeded* in dissociating individuals, liberal theory could not be criticized for ignoring the social constitution of individuals; for it could then be shown that the dissociated individual of liberal justification arguments is no mere abstraction. Whatever else it might lack, liberal theory would then adequately capture and explain an especially significant aspect of contemporary behavior and institutions. Either individuals are essentially social and consequently create liberal forms of communal life, or liberal institutions succeed in dissociating individuals, in which case liberal theory could explain individual behavior under liberal regimes.[8]

Communitarians, such as MacIntyre and Sandel, who draw their critique of liberal practice from their critique of liberal theory, avoid this self-contradiction only by blurring the distinction between the two conceptions of dissociation. The completely dissociated individual, Sandel's "unencumbered self," is an abstraction of theory. The unencumbered self's real-world analogues are as much socially constituted—fully encumbered—individuals as all others. Their limitations are not those of the self-constituting individual often assumed by liberal theorists, even if they often behave "as though" they were unencumbered selves. They draw their characteristic virtues and vices from their participation in a variety of distinctive forms of social interactions.

The theoretical dissociation assumed by liberal theorists to justify liberal practices tells us little about the sociological dissociation experienced by individuals. Indeed, the former is likely to mislead us about the latter, since the latter describes a form of association rather than the result of abstraction from forms of association. Even alienated individuals are deeply encumbered selves. We must be careful not to confuse a diminished sociological *sense of association* with a theoretical state of complete dissociation. Evidence of alienation among individuals is not necessarily evidence of the dissolution of social bonds.

A particularly striking example of the misleading use of liberal theory's conceptions to describe liberal practice occurs at the beginning of *Habits*. The authors comment on Brian Palmer, who seems to represent the model of the good life for many Americans. Successful and self-reliant, Brian Palmer has recognized the harmful consequences of his earlier single-minded pursuit of career and now pays much more attention to his family. The authors insist, however, that "despite the combination of tenderness and admiration he expresses for his wife, the genuine devotion he seems to feel for his children, and his own resilient self-confidence" (*H*, 8) his life rests on a "fragile foundation." His individualist values cannot justify the commitment to others, especially his family, which gives meaning to his life. Those values "leave the individual suspended in a glorious, but terrifying, isolation" (*H*, 6).

The authors of *Habits* come to this conclusion despite the fact that Brian Palmer never says he feels either terrified or isolated. They describe him as living in isolation because they assume that individualist values cannot provide the means of establishing affective bonds among individuals. In making this assumption, though, they ignore the communal form established by the *sharing* of liberal individualist values. Far from being isolated, Brian Palmer most likely receives great support from others who share his values, not least of all from his family, who probably respect and identify with him as someone who exemplifies qualities they admire. In a society that shares individualist values it is more likely the anti-individualist who experiences an *in*glorious, but terrifying, isolation. Those, for example, who deny the value of self-reliance in American society often experience a painful ostracism precisely because of their more communitarian values.

By treating conceptions provided by liberal theory as adequate descriptions of liberal practice, communitarian critics of liberalism are able to import the dichotomy between dissociation and social constitution from their critique of liberal theory, where it sometimes is appropriate, into their critique of liberal practice, where it is not. According to their own premises, however, communitarians should only offer us choices between different kinds of communities and socially constituted individuals. Socially constituted individuals with little sense of community are a distinct possibility; "unencumbered selves" are not. If all selves are socially constituted, the real choice is between kinds of community, not between unencumbered individuals and community. In criticizing liberal practice, communitarians are actually rejecting one form of community for another, rather than recommending community per se over dissociated individualism.

The blurred distinction between theoretical and sociological dissociation often leads communitarians to blur another distinction as well: the distinction between the generic and the specific sense of terms like *community, society,* and *association.* So far, I have been using these three terms interchangeably as a means of describing the generic form of social interaction among human beings. Quite often, though, communitarian critics of liberalism use the generic sense of *community* or *society* while discussing liberal theory, and the specific sense while discussing liberal practice.[9] In effect, they suggest that because individuals are constituted by their social interactions, they should live in a specific form of society, usually designated as a political or moral community.

But as Michael Oakeshott notes, no particular species of society or community corresponds to the adjective *social* in the modern suggestions that man is a social being (1975, 98 and 88). The defense of *community* in its specific, as opposed to its generic, meaning requires an additional argument that would establish a case for a specific form of communal life. The commonest arguments of this sort suggest that human beings require, either for psychic and moral health or for social stability, the kind of fairly small, stable forms of communal life, usually described, following Tönnies, as "community," which liberal "society" destroys. The validity of the communitarian case against liberal practice rests largely on the validity of such arguments, for an insistence on the generic social constitution of individuals adds nothing to the case against liberal practices and institutions.

Once we isolate the requirement for arguments that would comparatively evaluate particular forms of communal life, the communitarian critique of liberal practice no longer rests on relatively uncontroversial premises. Instead, the force of that critique now depends upon the strength of claims that viable lives and social institutions require a particular form of communal life. Advocates of these claims usually point to sociohistorical evidence of the destructive effects that individualizing forms of association have on individuals and institutions. But in spite of the seeming wealth of such evidence, these claims are more questionable than they initially appear—especially when one keeps in mind the distinction between sociological and theoretical dissociation that often, as in *Habits,* gets lost in the presentation of evidence about social and individual instability.

The authors of *Habits* conclude from their extensive discussions with Americans that "modern individualism seems to be producing a way of life that is neither individually nor socially viable" (*H,* 144). Only the older, more communitarian civic republican and biblical traditions can

save Americans from the threat posed by their individualist values. It is
only the moral capital provided by these older traditions that has saved
American lives and institutions from bankruptcy. "We owe the meaning
of our lives to biblical and republican traditions of which we seldom consciously think":   ·

> If we are not entirely a mass of interchangeable fragments within an ag-
> gregate, if we are in part qualitatively distinct members of a whole, it is
> because there are still operating among us, with whatever difficulties, tra-
> ditions that tell us about the nature of the world, about the nature of so-
> ciety, and about who we are as people. Primarily biblical and republican,
> these traditions are, as we have seen, important for many Americans and
> significant for almost all. (*H*, 281–82)

The authors of *Habits* present this claim about American individuals
and institutions as a conclusion suggested by their extensive discussions
with contemporary Americans. It seems to me, however, that they do not
consider the possibility that shared individualist values might generate
the affective ties essential to individual and social health. Whenever they
find evidence of moral bonds among contemporary Americans they immediately ascribe those bonds to the lingering influence of older biblical
and republican traditions. They simply assume that individualist values,
unconstrained by older, more communal traditions, lead to the atomization of society, that is, to the theoretical rather than sociological dissociation of actual persons.

Given their use of the sociological tradition of Tocqueville and Durkheim, the authors of *Habits* must deny that liberal theory provides an
adequate language for the interpretation and evaluation of modern social practices:

> There are truths we do not see when we adopt the language of radical indi-
> vidualism. We find ourselves not independently of other people and in-
> stitutions but through them. We never get to the bottom of ourselves on
> our own. We discover who we are face to face and side by side with others
> in work, love, and learning. All of our activity goes on in relationships,
> groups, associations, and communities ordered by institutional structures
> and interpreted by cultural patterns of meaning. Our individualism is it-
> self one such pattern. (*H*, 84)

Nevertheless, the authors of *Habits of the Heart* are, as we have already
seen, quite willing to use "the language of radical individualism," when
they speak of the "glorious, but terrifying, isolation" promoted by liberal
individualism. Indeed, they describe modern individualist culture as a
"culture of separation." This description would be consistent with their
sociological premises if it designated a pattern of association that deem-
phasized, relative to other such patterns, a strong sense of association
among its members. But *Habits* insists instead that "the culture of separa-

tion, if it ever became completely dominant, would collapse of its own incoherence" into "a mass of interchangeable fragments within an aggregate" (*H*, 281). Here, then, they use the language of radical individualism that they declared inappropriate for the description of social phenomena.

No wonder they do not seriously consider whether liberal individualist values might contribute to the formation of "those habits of the heart that are the matrix of moral ecology, the connecting tissue of the body politic." Although they take notice, unlike many communitarians, of the "widespread and strong identification with the United States as a national community," they simply assume that we must ascribe this supra-individual identity to the influence of the civic republican tradition (*H*, 250–51). They never consider the obvious alternative explanation of the growth of patriotism in an increasingly individualist age: that liberal individualist values and identification with the national community are mutually reinforcing. The authors, like many social theorists before them, seem to assume that liberal individualism is a universal solvent of community. But they confuse the generic and specific meanings of *community* when they assume that liberal individualism's corrosive effect on older, more traditional, and localized forms of communal life makes it hostile to all forms of community.

In fact, there is strong evidence that the spread of liberal individualist values goes hand in hand with the strengthening of an identification with national community. The age of liberal individualism is, after all, also the age of nationalism.[10] That may rightly distress both liberals and communitarians. But it indicates that the growth of liberal individualism does not destroy the capacity to create new forms of communal life. Indeed, some social theorists have argued that the sense of alienation experienced by many modern individuals is a by-product of the "historically unique measure of community of culture" that constitutes modern liberal societies. The very universality of that community, its unprecedented degree of horizontal as opposed to vertical integration, tends to hide it from our notice. Precisely because what is common is so universally accepted, we readily observe the sources of division and disintegration among us. For example, we focus on the unprecedented degree of vocational differentiation in modern individualist societies without taking notice of its dependence on an unprecedented degree of common education for the members of the community (Shils 1982, 73, 76, 81; Gellner 1983, 27).

Whatever the merits of these alternative interpretations of modern individualist societies, the authors of *Habits* rule them out, prior to any observation of modern individuals and institutions, by assuming an antagonism between liberal individualism and communal identity. This assumption limits the value of the evidence about American society they present. Their claim, that modern individualism "is producing a way of life that is neither individually nor socially viable," hinges entirely upon it. For, in themselves, the words of the Americans they interview provide very little direct evidence that American lives or institutions rest on dangerously fragile foundations.

III

Communitarian critics of liberal practice often describe their aim as the "reconstitution" of moral and political community among modern individuals. Some, like Robert Nisbet (1975, 230ff.) and the authors of *Habits* (286ff.), think that we can successfully reconstitute community under current conditions; others, like MacIntyre (1984, 263), think it would require a complete and very unlikely transformation of modern individuals and institutions. But both groups seem to ignore an important implication of their own critiques of liberal theory. If individual reasoning and action is socially constituted, then any *reconstitution* of community will require first a *deconstitution* of contemporary forms of communal life. Communitarian critics of liberalism, as much as liberal theorists before them, need to justify disencumbering contemporary individuals of many of their shared standards.

Communitarians rarely recognize their need to justify the deconstitution of contemporary communities because they so frequently exaggerate the theoretical dissociation of actual individuals. If liberal society were really a kind of "civil war carried on by other means" (MacIntyre 1984, 253), "a war of all against all . . . we make for ourselves, not out of whole cloth but out of an intentional distortion of our social natures" (Barber 1984, 75), then there would be no shared standards for them to uproot. Interestingly, this exaggeration of theoretical dissociation serves much the same purpose for communitarians that hypotheses on state of nature and original position serve for many liberal theorists: it allows them to use a model of theoretical dissociation to abstract from the dominant standards that constitute actual forms of communal life when they argue for different political and social standards. The primary difference between the two groups is that classical liberals generally make their theoretical deconstituting arguments explicit, while communitarians do not.

In the first part of this paper, I assumed, for the purposes of argument, the accuracy of the communitarian characterization and critique of liberal theory. There I did not ask why intelligent individuals would deny or choose to ignore something so obvious as the social constitution of human life. Here we see, at least, a partial answer to that question: the need to justify the introduction of institutions and practices that run counter to the standards constituted by present forms of communal life.[11]

Early liberal theorists faced a situation in which the weight of tradition and political power in their societies resided in extremely hierarchical forms of social and religious community, forms of community whose influence they sought to counter. Given this situation it is little wonder that liberal theorists sought to establish the authority of impersonal criteria, criteria that abstract from the socially constituted standards of their community. The appeal to tradition—which many liberals still pursued, couching their arguments in terms of long-lost "ancient constitutions"— was often a losing hand, as J. G. A. Pocock has shown in his study of seventeenth-century English political rhetoric (1967, 235–36). As long as individuals remain encumbered by their attachments to hierarchical and other-worldly traditions, liberal theorists have a strong incentive to defend the authority of impersonal criteria for moral and political judgment. The social context within which early liberal theorists argued may have recommended this anticontextualist approach.[12]

State of nature and social contract arguments provided early liberals with a powerful means of challenging the authority of the most influential traditions within their societies. It is obvious, however, from their use of such arguments, that they were quite selective in their disencumbering of individuals, as their critics since Rousseau have repeatedly noted. The individuals whom they describe in a presocial state of nature are deeply encumbered by any number of characteristics that they could gain only through mutual association. Not the least of these, as Rousseau notes, is their ability to introduce and understand a social contract. But liberals' unconcern about their failure to get all the way back to the state of nature need not be read as a sign of their naiveté about reason and nature. It might instead suggest that they were interested in impersonal criteria mostly as a means of disencumbering individuals of *particular* socially acquired characteristics, those associated with religious and hereditary hierarchy.

The major problem with the contractarian form of argument, as any number of critics have pointed out, is that it is only the particular meanings given to rationality and interest, meanings constituted by particular forms of social interaction, that enable liberal theorists to justify some practices and discredit others. Communitarian critics of liberalism repeatedly emphasize this limitation of liberal theory, but without noting that it poses a problem that they too must face.

Communitarians usually avoid dealing with this problem by, implicitly or explicitly, taking generic human sociability as a term of distinction. They can then ignore shared standards and forms of communal life that fall short of their vision of true sociability. As I suggested above, they often establish this critical standard simply by blurring the generic and specific senses of terms like community, sociability, and association. But in order to invoke consistently human sociability as a justification for deconstituting forms of communal life, they must supply a further argument that would justify the claim that the social character of human life establishes the need for a specific form of association.

Two arguments have traditionally been advanced to support such a claim. The first, Aristotelian teleology, suggests that sociability expresses an inner motion toward a particular form of life. The second, analogies to the natural or divine order of the universe, provides models, usually organic and hierarchical in character, for human beings to follow in the construction of their institutions. Contemporary communitarians, unlike many of their predecessors, rarely invoke these arguments, since they usually share with modern liberals a distaste for teleological argument and hierarchical communities. They thus tend to invoke a more recently constructed argument—Rousseau is the first to advocate it—about the distinct character of human sociability: the claim that the freedom and equal participation of individuals in shared practices is the defining feature of truly human communities. In the rest of this section I try to show that in defining human sociability in this way, contemporary communitarians implicitly rely on liberal arguments that they explicitly reject. I therefore conclude that communitarians have not escaped the challenge of justifying particular communal standards, the very problem they have identified as a failure in liberal theories.

I begin by considering Benjamin Barber's recent critique of liberal democracy, *Strong Democracy* (1984). Barber justifies his critique, in part, through his rejection of the "radically individual and solitary" "liberal portrait of human nature" (1984, 213). In its place "strong democratic theory posits the social nature of human beings and the dialectical interdependence of man and his government" (1984, 215), a position set out in the penultimate chapter of the book: "Citizenship and Community: Politics as Social Being."

Barber goes on to suggest that our need for a particular kind of political community follows as a consequence of this assumption:

> Strong democratic theory posits the social nature of human beings in the world and the dialectical interdependence of man and his government. *As a consequence,* it places human self-realization through mutual transformation at the center of the democratic process. (1984, 215, my emphasis)

Why does "human self-realization through mutual transformation" follow as a consequence of the "social nature of human beings"? And why is the shaping of individuals by liberal practices and institutions not an example of "human self-realization through mutual transformation"? Apparently some forms of society do not reflect man's social nature. "Social" and "human" are, for Barber, terms of distinction among the many forms of society and human life. Barber's critique of liberal theory explicitly rests on a relatively uncontroversial assumption about "the social nature of human being." But in order to build a critique of liberal practice from that assumption, he has to accept additional assumptions that allow him to use "social" and "human" as terms of distinction, assumptions that are not explicitly acknowledged. These assumptions are implicit in Barber's defense of a "strong democratic" definition of citizenship:

> If we accept the postulate that humans are social by nature, then we cannot regard citizenship as merely one among many artificial social roles that can be grafted onto man's natural solitariness. It is rather the only legitimate form that man's natural dependency can take. The civic bond is the sole legitimator of the indissoluble natural bond: it makes *voluntary* those ties that cannot in any case be undone, and it makes *common* and susceptible to mutuality the fate that is in any case shared by all men. (1984, 217)

Barber insists here that if we admit that "humans are social by nature," then we must accept citizenship, and a Rousseauian version of citizenship at that, as "the only legitimate form that man's natural dependency can take." He thus suggests that since human beings have a social nature, they must choose to live in a particular form of community. This conclusion follows from his premise only because he has written particular definitions of humanity and sociality into his key terms "human" and "social." Most social roles are "artificial"; they are "grafted onto man's natural solitariness." Rousseauian citizenship, however, is not artificial because it realizes something essential about human nature: it makes our social dependence "voluntary" and "common," and in doing so, becomes "the sole legitimator of the indissoluble natural bond." Though we are social by nature, the only legitimate social bonds are those we make voluntary and common. Only such bonds represent "human self-realization." Something about voluntariness and commonality defines humanity for Barber.

Barber's additional assumptions define human sociability in terms of capacities for self-imposed and generalized dependence. They support a philosophy of freedom, which, not surprisingly, resembles Rousseau's. But Rousseau justifies his claim that self-imposed generalized dependence characterizes a truly human community by means of a social contract argument. He argues that these forms of dependence are the only legitimate ones because no rational human being, disencumbered of certain socially acquired characteristics and interests, would exchange his independence for any other form of social dependence (Rousseau [1762] 1978, 52–56).

Barber offers nothing comparable to Rousseau's argument to justify his assumptions about human sociability. Instead, he writes his Rousseauian assumptions into his description of man's social nature. Since Rousseau's justification of these assumptions shares liberal theory's reliance on an impersonal and minimal social construction of rationality,

Barber cannot explicitly accept it. Nevertheless, he still uses the capacity of human beings to disencumber themselves of socially acquired characteristics and impose on themselves generalized and equalized forms of dependence to define man's humanity. In speaking of such relations as "the only legitimate form that man's natural dependency can take," Barber implicitly relies on liberal theory's deconstituting strategy. His particular characterization of man's social nature supports his critique of liberal theory, but not his critique of liberal practice. The social being of man, which Barber uses to do all the work in his critique of liberal practice, is itself defined in terms of impersonal a priori criteria, rather than by the sum of man's socially acquired characteristics.

Robert Unger's communitarian critique of liberalism in *Knowledge and Politics* (1975) ultimately shares the same problem as Barber's critique. Unger, like Barber, draws his critique of liberal practice from a "total criticism" of liberal theory, a criticism grounded in his assumption that human nature is essentially social. But, more consistently than Barber, Unger rules out an a priori definition of the substantive character of human nature apart from its socially acquired characteristics. Instead, building on left Hegelian arguments, he insists that the nature of the individual and the human species unfold historically in the practices and institutions created by our actions, that human nature has no unchanging core or essence. Unger thus rejects the assumption that

> there exists a human nature and then, separately from it, a variety of social experiences that might be responsible for agreement. But once we conceive of human nature as something that resides in the totality of relations men have with nature, with others, and with themselves, this image becomes irrelevant. It has to be dismissed together with the notion of a static kernel of humanity that stands apart from thoughts, feelings, and behavior, or with the belief that all participation in social life involves a turning away from what one truly is. (1975, 247)

But although human nature is not an unchanging standard apart from its social manifestations, it remains a *critical* standard for Unger. Not all social relations realize human nature. Unger concludes the paragraph just cited with the following assertion: "Whatever does not arise from domination is human nature; domination is the one form of social relation in which men's conduct fails to express their being" (ibid.). All social relations in which some form of domination persists do not count as expressions of man's "true" social nature. Communal standards provide an accurate picture of human nature, according to Unger, but only after domination has been eliminated from the social relations that support them. "Until the problem of domination is resolved, the search for community is condemned to be idolatrous, or utopian, or both at once" (1975, 252). Liberal theory, Unger admits, also seeks to confront the problem of domination, but in doing so it assumes the problem unsolvable and thus denies us the possibility of achieving a good life according to our nature (1975, 252–53). Man's social nature, as Unger conceives it, thus supports a critique of liberal practice, as well as of liberal theory.

But it supports such a critique only because Unger has slipped a strong additional assumption about human nature into his argument. By insisting that only "whatever does not arise from domination" expresses man's social nature, Unger suggests that virtually all social relations known over the course of history have failed to express man's true being. In itself, there is nothing absurd or self-contradictory about such a view of human history. But stated as the conclusion to an argument that begins with the assertion that human nature "resides in the totality of relations men have with nature, with others, and with themselves" (1975, 247), it seems questionable, to say the least. Either the "totality" of social interaction or that portion of social interaction that escapes relations of domination expresses human nature. If the former, then human nature provides no critical standpoint. Unger's argument amounts to the claim that the totality of social relations in *domination-free conditions* defines human nature. But to state the argument in this way makes clear Unger's need to justify the overcoming of domination as a precondition of the realization of human nature, that is, his need to justify theoretically disencumbering individuals of the standards constituted by the totality of their present social practices. Unger never provides such a justification. But without that theoretical justification his critical standpoint on liberal practice remains unsupported.

Once again, it is an assumption about human freedom and the illegitimacy of personal dependence, an assumption that Unger, like many other egalitarian communitarians, shares with liberal theory, which supports a communitarian critique of liberal practice. Unger can justify disencumbering individuals of all their present socially acquired characteristics, tainted as they are by domination, only because the tradition of argumentation established by contractarian political theory and Kantian moral philosophy, the very tradition that he criticizes so harshly, has accustomed us to identify human nature with the behavior of individuals unencumbered by the domination implicit in their ordinary social relationships. In order to maintain his critique of liberal practice, Unger would have to modify his critique of liberal theory.[13]

Robert Paul Wolff is one of the few recent communitarian critics of liberalism to face up to these problems of justification. His critique of liberal theory in *The Poverty of Liberalism* (1968) is designed to demonstrate the *possibility* of certain forms of community that, he argues, liberal theory rules out. These "modes of community are possible objects of social interest . . . of social neglect or even of social aversion" (1968, 194). Reflecting liberal theory's denial of their possibility, liberal societies place little value on these particular forms of community.

Wolff hopes that "once men are persuaded of the *possibility* of aspiring beyond the liberal goals of distributive justice and the satisfaction of private interests, they will find themselves drawn to the ideals of community." But he admits that his argument against the narrowness of liberal theory can in no way "be construed as an *argument* for affective, productive, and rational community," the three forms of community he discusses in his essay. Moreover, he notes that an argument for "rational community," which for Wolff corresponds to the political community of "morally and politically equal rational agents" that both Unger and Barber advocate, requires "an a priori demonstration . . . of our absolute obligation to see its actualization" (1968, 192–94).

To justify the rejection of all social practices and institutions that fail to treat individuals as morally and politically equal rational agents, one needs an argument that legitimizes the disencumbering of individuals of those standards and characteristics constituted by their present forms of communal life. The uncontroversial assumption that man is a social being cannot provide such a justification. Barber and Unger can treat it as if it does only because they smuggle into their definitions of "social being" and "human nature" a characterization of man as a free and equal being capable of self-legislation, a characterization supported by much more controversial premises than the assertion of man's social being. Such a characterization is, as we have seen, most often Rousseauian or Kantian. As a result, their critiques of liberal practice depend on the same assumptions that support the most important and influential justifications of liberal practice: social contract theory and Kantian deontology. Egalitarian communitarians thus share, as Robert Paul Wolff makes clear, the same problem of justification that faces liberal theorists: to find theoretical ways of justifying the deconstitution of present communal forms of life when only socially constituted criteria allow us to evaluate our practices.

IV

I have argued that liberal practices and institutions do not, indeed cannot, "live down" to the limitations that many contemporary communitarians have found in liberal theory. In doing so, I have not justified a preference for such practices and institutions. I have merely tried to demonstrate that recent communitarian critiques of liberal theory in no way justify a parallel critique of liberal practice.

I have also pointed out some problems in justifying particular forms of communal life that many communitarians share with the liberal theorists they so often criticize. The liberal emphasis on justification and the communitarian emphasis on explanation have tended to obscure the real disagreement between liberals and communitarians. The success of liberal theory's justification strategy has obscured, both for many liberals and their critics, the commitment of liberal theory to promote and defend particular ways of life and forms of community.[14] Communitarian critics of liberal theory, past and present, make an important contribution to political argument by reminding us that whatever liberal theorists may say, liberal practice promotes particular forms of community among individuals. But communitarians often do the same thing that they criticize liberals for doing: they recommend particular forms of community as if those forms exclusively embodied universal human characteristics. Liberal theorists do so by portraying particular socially constituted understandings of reason as *the* embodiment of *human reason*. Communitarians do so by portraying particular forms of communal life as *the* embodiment of *human sociality*.

Interestingly enough, it may be liberals who today are in the best position to base their justification on strictly communitarian assumptions and communitarians whose arguments require a theoretical justification for the deconstitution of actual communities. If modern Western individuals are typically constituted by liberal practices and institutions, then social theorists are likely to invoke liberal standards when explaining and justifying their communal standards.[15] To justify their rejection of liberal practices and institutions, communitarian theorists therefore need arguments to justify the deconstitution of these shared standards. The challenge to communitarians is to devise these arguments in a way that will not contradict their own premises.

PART THREE

Civic Practice

TEN

The Communitarian Critique
of Liberalism

Christopher Lasch

In the last ten or fifteen years, liberalism has come under criticism not only from so-called conservatives, who have more in common with liberals than they care to admit, but from those who appeal from liberalism not to individualism but to the ideal of community. The emergence of this communitarian criticism of liberalism, which cuts more deeply than the standard right-wing criticism, is one of the most hopeful developments in our recent history, not least because it promises to break the political deadlock between welfare liberalism and economic individualism, the opposition of which has informed so much of our politics in the past. The promise of communitarian thought is already suggested by the difficulty of situating it on the conventional political spectrum ranging from left to right. Without claiming to occupy any sort of vital center, and certainly without presenting itself as a compromise between two extremes, it is equally critical of left and right, and part of its value, as I shall try to show, lies in its ability to uncover the common assumptions and premises underlying these apparently antagonistic positions.

Because the communitarian point of view has yet to make a decisive imprint on our social and political thought, its exponents are not exactly household names. In many ways the most important thinker among them is Alasdair MacIntyre, whose masterpiece, *After Virtue* (1981), has provoked a great deal of commentary and criticism. Michael Sandel's *Liberalism and the Limits of Justice* (1982) is another indispensable book. The interested reader should also consult Thomas Spragens's *Irony of Liberal Reason* (1981), Jeffrey Stout's *Flight from Authority* (1981), and Michael Walzer's *Spheres of Justice* (1983), not to mention the exhaustive historical scholarship on civic humanism and republicanism, much of it inspired by J. G. A. Pocock's *The Machiavellian Movement* (1975). Finally there is the wide-ranging study of individualism by Robert Bellah,

Richard Madsen, William Sullivan, Ann Swidler, and Steven Tipton, recently published under the title *Habits of the Heart* (1985). No other book
has done so much to bring the communitarian critique of liberalism to
general attention.

It would be misleading to treat these writers as a school. What follows
will minimize the differences among them in the hope of identifying the
general trend of this type of thought. I shall elaborate these ideas in ways
that some of their authors might not endorse. Nevertheless, I shall try
to remain faithful to the spirit and basic principles of communitarian
thought, as I understand them.

Communitarians share with the right an opposition to bureaucracy,
but they do not stop with an attack on governmental bureaucracy; they
are equally sensitive to the dangers of corporate bureaucracy in the mis-
named private sector. Indeed they tend to reject the conventional distinction between the public and the private realms, which figures so
prominently both in the liberal tradition and in the tradition of economic individualism that has grown up side by side with it. The rise of
corporate bureaucracy is only one of a number of developments that
have undermined the usefulness of this distinction. Another such development is the infiltration of personal life by the market, as when modes
of personnel management and conflict resolution derived from labor relations come to be applied to familial relations, or again, when family life
comes to be considered as a set of contractual obligations. The recognition that an institution like the family can no longer serve, if it ever did,
as a haven in a heartless world prompts a search for a better way of describing its importance and value. The fact that the history of the family,
moreover—and of modern life in general—can be characterized with
equal plausibility as the privatization of experience (the "fall of public
man") and the invasion of privacy by the "social ethic" that allegedly pre-
vails in a society of "organization men" further weakens the explanatory
power of the public and the private as organizing categories. Communitarian thought tries to find a way out of this conceptual stalemate, just
as it hopes to end the political stalemate between left and right.

Communitarianism, then, rejects the kind of liberalism that seeks to
"empower" exploited groups by conquering the state and by extending
its powers on their behalf; but it does not propose to leave them at the
mercy of the corporations. It proposes a general strategy of devolution
or decentralization, designed to end the dominance of large organizations and to remodel our institutions on a human scale. It attacks bureaucracy and large-scale organization, however, not in the name of individual freedom or the free market but in the name of continuity and
tradition.

The dispute between communitarians and liberals hinges on opposing conceptions of the self. Where liberals conceive of the self as essen-

tially unencumbered and free to choose among a wide range of alternatives, communitarians insist that the self is situated in and constituted by tradition, membership in a historically rooted community. Liberals regard tradition as a collection of prejudices that prevent the individual not only from understanding his own needs but also from sympathetic understanding of others. They exalt cosmopolitanism over provincialism, which in their eyes encourages conformity and intolerance. Communitarians, on the other hand, reply that "intolerance flourishes most," in Sandel's words, "where forms of life are dislocated, roots unsettled, traditions undone" (1982, 17).

I said a moment ago that the crystallization of this communitarian critique of liberalism is one of the most hopeful signs of the times. I did not mean to imply, however, that it is something altogether new. On the contrary, it has a long history, which can be traced all the way back to the civic republicanism of the Renaissance, which historians are so eager to recover. Its historical career parallels that of liberalism itself, and it makes itself heard, however faintly at times, as a counterpoint to liberalism, sometimes, indeed, becoming almost indistinguishable from it. In the twentieth century, the communitarian tradition was present as an undercurrent in prewar progressivism, as interpreted by writers like Josiah Royce, Jane Addams, Mary Parker Follett, and Randolph Bourne; and it was carried on in late years by John Collier, Waldo Frank, Lewis Mumford, and Paul Goodman, among others. It was an important ingredient in the new left, and the recent revival of communitarian thought derives most immediately from the side of the new left that condemned bureaucracy and the "technological society" and favored decentralization, environmentalism, and "appropriate technologies."

Communitarianism has had its most important influence, perhaps, not so much on twentieth-century social and cultural criticism as on twentieth-century sociology, though even here it represents a minor, often discordant note. One can distinguish two traditions in American sociology. The first seeks to replace spontaneous cooperation, thought to characterize small-scale communities, with a new science of social control administered by experts. The second seeks to revive and preserve community values in complex industrial nation-states. How to accomplish this second objective was the problem bequeathed to sociology by the classical theorists who invented the modern science of society, especially by Tönnies, Weber, and Durkheim. Modern social theory had its very foundation in the distinction between *Gemeinschaft* and *Gesellschaft*, community and society; and much of its appeal to a broader audience lay in its claim to show how the two might be reconciled—how the advantages of the small group might be restored, as a countervailing influence, in societies based on the principle of bureaucratic anonymity. The decline of the extended family, the widening gap between generations, the weakening of traditions, the uprooting of individuals from the land, and the commercialization of leisure—all seemed to disrupt the transmission of social norms from one generation to the next. Mass society, it appeared, left people without firm moral guidelines. It gave rise to a condition of *anomie*, as Durkheim called it; and the only way to counter this tendency, according to a view that came to be widely held by many students of these developments, was to revive the culture of small face-to-face communities in a new form. The alternative both to the "individual and the crowd," as Follett put it, was the "neglected group," which provided a middle ground "between particularism with all its separatist tendencies, and the crowd with its levelling, its mediocrity, its sameness, perhaps even its hysteria" (1918, 152).

This kind of thinking has now become so familiar that it is difficult to recognize the assumptions behind it. Yet these assumptions must become explicit, and some of them explicitly repudiated, if the communitarian tradition is to free itself from some of the misunderstandings and confusion that have limited its effectiveness in the past. The most important of these assumptions—that shared values, not political institutions or a common political language, provide the only source of social cohesion—strikes us now as the essence of sociological common sense. In fact, however, it represents a radical break from many of the republican principles on which this country was founded. "The chief difficulty of our time," wrote Elton Mayo, "is the breakdown of the social codes that formerly disciplined us to effective working together" (1933, 88). All the social controls based on a "vigorous social code," he explained, "have weakened or disappeared" (1933, 172). The famous Hawthorne studies conducted by Mayo and his colleagues at the Harvard Business School tried to show how enlightened administration could recreate small groups in industry and provide workers with a sense of belonging. The Hawthorne studies influenced managerial practice and sociological theory alike, encouraging more and more intensive analysis of small groups and their internal dynamics. In his book *The Human Group,* a work that summarized much of this thinking, George Homans raised once again the familiar question: "How can the values of the small group be maintained on the scale of civilization?" (1950, 466). Like his predecessors and fellow students of group dynamics, Homans found it impossible to imagine any mechanism of social cohesion except the "spontaneous self-control" of small groups and "imposed control," as he called it—the coercive powers exercised by a highly centralized state (1950, 464). "If civilization is to stand, it must maintain, in the relation between the groups that make up society and the central direction of society, some of the features of the small group itself" (1950, 468). The most revealing and symptomatic feature of Homan's study is his inability to understand republican institutions except as another attempt to institutionalize patterns of cooperation that arise spontaneously in small groups. "All of these devices," he says, speaking of the Bill of Rights, universal suffrage, and the whole machinery of representative government, "are addressed to the problem of maintaining, at the level of a nation if not of a civilization, the values of the small group" (1950, 464).

The cult of the "little community," as Robert Redfield called it, has sunk so deeply into our thinking about these matters that we find it more and more difficult to conceive of any form of social solidarity that does not rest on shared values and spontaneous cooperation, on the one hand, or on engineered consent, manipulation, or outright coercion on the other. I will try to show that there is a better way of thinking about the problem of solidarity. Before entering that part of my argument, however, I would like to point out that the myth of the organic community, which is so often associated with criticism of acquisitive individualism, is an important source of the fruitless debate about nostalgia that seems to have become inescapable in discussions of social change and modern life. Because our conception of community life is so highly colored by feelings of nostalgia, the defense of community prompts the rejoinder that it grows out of a flight from modern complexity, a failure of nerve, a refusal to accept the ambiguities and uncertainty that go along with freedom itself. Thus the sociologist L. Digby Baltzell, in the introduction to a collection of essays entitled *The Search for Community in Modern America* (1968, 2–4), urges the reader to "ask himself whether or not he prefers our kind of voluntary society, which still emphasizes privacy and the minding of one's own business, to the more communal and cohesive, but perhaps more restrictive, societies" of the past. "All too many of us are more or less nostalgic about the good-old-days of spatial cohesion in the small, local community," according to Baltzell. As an example of this attitude, he quotes the definition of community offered by Robert Nisbet:

> "By community, I mean something that . . . encompasses all forms of relationships which are characterized by a high degree of personal intimacy, emotional depth, moral commitment, social cohesion, and continuity in time. Community is founded on man conceived in his wholeness rather than in one or another of the roles, taken separately, that he may hold in the social order. It draws its psychological strength from levels of motivation deeper than those of mere volition or interest. . . ."

The interesting thing about the debate concerning nostalgia is that defenders of modernity seldom challenge the sentimental conception of the community held by their opponents. Instead of objecting to Nisbet's identification of community with a "submergence of individual will," Baltzell argues merely that the "gradual erosion . . . of the traditional community ties which Professor Nisbet describes," while it has deprived men and women of the security of unquestioned habits and inherited dogmas, has created a society "based on free choice and common interests." Nostalgia for the little community serves not so much to preserve the past or to understand the ways in which the past unavoidably influences our lives as to idealize lost innocence. The atmosphere of sentimental regret with which it surrounds the past has the effect of denying the past's inescapable influence over the present. Those who deplore the death of the past and those who celebrate it both take it for granted that our age has outgrown its childhood. Both find it difficult to believe that history still haunts our enlightened, disillusioned maturity. Both are governed, in their attitudes toward the past, by the prevailing disbelief in ghosts.

"Our historical consciousness," writes Hans-Georg Gadamer, "is always filled with a variety of voices in which the echo of the past is heard" ([1960] 1975, 252). What is missing from the debate about individualism and community, as carried on up until now, is the possibility of a conversational relationship with the past, one that seeks neither to deny the past nor to achieve an imaginative restoration of the past but to enter into a dialogue with the traditions that still shape our view of the world, often in ways in which we are not even aware. Instead of merely addressing the historical record, we need to grasp the ways in which it addresses us. This does not imply a slavish, unquestioning attitude toward authority. Nor does it imply universal agreement. Traditions embody conflict as well as consensus; in many ways this is their most important aspect. As MacIntyre points out, "Traditions, when vital, embody continuities of conflict" (1981, 254, 222, 134–36). But if we conceive traditions in this way, instead of emphasizing the uncritical acceptance of authority and the uniformity of opinion that allegedly distinguish so-called traditional societies from the modern societies that rest on a "culture of critical discourse," we have to modify many of our received ideas about the problem of individualism and "community." Social solidarity does not rest on shared values or ideological consensus, let alone on an identity of interests; it rests on public conversation. It rests on social and political arrangements that serve to encourage debate instead of foreclosing it; and to encourage debate, moreover, not just about conflicting economic interests but about morality and religion, the ultimate human concerns. Public conversation means the systematic cultivation of the rhetorical arts and of the virtues classically associated with eloquence. It means respect for the power of persuasion, which is quite different, as Gadamer reminds us, from the ability to win every argument. The art of dialectics, he writes, "requires that one does not try to out-argue the other person, but that one really considers the weight of the other's opinion" ([1960] 1975, 330). Nothing testifies more clearly to the debasement of contemporary politics than the equation of "rhetoric" with ideological manipulation, electioneering, and hot air. The devaluation of public discourse is

a much more alarming development than the decline of ideological consensus. In order to counter it, we need to develop a political conception
of the community, in place of the organic and sentimental conception
that now tends to prevail.

A better understanding of tradition, then, sums up the first line of
revision to which communitarian theory needs to be exposed. By overemphasizing the importance of shared values, defenders of a communitarian politics expose themselves to the familiar charge that *community*
is simply a euphemism for *conformity*. The answer to this charge is that
tradition, and tradition alone, is precisely what makes it possible for men
and women to disagree without trying to resolve their disagreements by
the sword.

A second line of revision begins with an analysis of the character-
forming discipline of social practices.[1] It is specific practices, not civic life
in general, that nourish virtue. We can define practices, following
MacIntyre, as common projects in which the participants seek to conform to established standards of excellence. Practices in this sense have
nothing to do, as such, with the production of useful objects or with the
satisfaction of material needs. They have more in common with play
than with activities defined as practical in the conventional sense. Judgment or practical reason, as Aristotle understood it, is a mode of thinking not to be confused either with the "expression of private feelings" or
aesthetic preferences, with the goal-directed thinking known to the an-
cients as technical reason, or with the "type of universality characteristic
of cognitive reason," science, and speculative philosophy. Aristotle distinguished judgment or *phronesis* both from pure contemplation, which
seeks universal truths, and from technique, which seeks merely to solve
problems and to arrive at a given goal by the most efficient means. Judgment is the kind of skill one learns in the course of training for a practice
(like architecture, medicine, baseball, the performing arts, or the art of
political oratory), but it pursues goods internal to that practice, not the
external goods that seem so important to us. Considered from this point
of view, the choice of means has to be governed by their conformity to
standards of excellence designed to extend human capacities for self-
understanding and self-mastery.

Every practice requires its own virtues. Manual dexterity obviously
counts for more in surgery or piano playing than it does in most branches
of warfare, while certain kinds of physical courage count for less. There
is good warrant, however, for singling out judgment as the virtue that is
common to all, especially if we distinguish the mere "technique" of
piano—playing, say—from musicianship in the larger sense. Whether
the frame of reference is music, sports, medicine, or warfare, judgment
implies a sense of timing and proportion, a feeling for the relations between the parts and the whole, a painstaking attention to detail that is

nevertheless careful not to let details obscure the larger outlines of a performance, a willingness to improvise if necessary, an ability to combine spontaneous feeling with disciplined forethought, a kind of controlled exuberance, and most important and elusive of all, an ability to communicate the inner meaning of an activity to others so that they become vicarious participants. Judgment also implies an understanding of limits—of one's own capacities, of what the occasion will bear, of the narrowness of one's victory over competitors, of the fine line between success and failure, victory and defeat—and it is this recognition of limits, I think, that invests judgment with a moral quality and entitles us to discuss it under the heading not of prudence, with which it clearly has a lot in common, but of virtue. Perhaps the point can be stated most simply by saying that while excellence in a practice comes only after exacting technical training and discipline, it rests, at bottom, on qualities appropriately regarded as gifts, which it is the essence of virtue to acknowledge in a spirit of humility and thanksgiving. The consummately gifted practitioner, no less than the religious virtuoso, personifies, if only for a short moment, the state of grace or gratitude.

If it is important to understand why practices are so important to the moral life, it is equally important to understand how easily they are corrupted by ends extrinsic to themselves. Since excellence in a practice often brings an abundance of social rewards, it is notoriously tempting for people to pursue a practice for the wrong reasons—for the sake of money, say, or social status, or simply for the sake of besting their opponents, in which case it becomes perfectly acceptable to cheat. If they have no talent for the practice in question, the results are deplorable, as patients exposed to routine medical practice can readily testify; but if they do have a calling, as we say, the result is even worse, since faithless practitioners betray not only their clients and competitors but their own gifts as well. The point is not just that money and status tempt practitioners to lose sight of the intrinsic goods they ought to pursue. A more important point is that practices have to be sustained by institutions, which in the very nature of things tend to corrupt the practices they sustain. It isn't just that individuals are tempted by unworthy ambitions but that the institutional structures in which practices are carried out almost unavoidably underwrite and legitimize these ambitions. Thus the university provides a home for scholarship, but it also corrupts scholarship by subjecting it to standards of productivity derived from the marketplace, just as it corrupts instruction by reducing it to the standard units used to measure academic progress and achievement—courses, credits, grades, and cumulative grade-point averages.

Those who see professionalism as a purely disinterested pursuit of excellence ignore the institutional influences that often subvert this ideal. "Membership in a truly professional community," writes Thomas I.

Haskell, echoing Paul Goodman, "[cannot] be based on charm, social standing, personal connection, good character, or perhaps even decency, but on demonstrated intellectual merit alone" (1977, 33). Even if we shared Haskell's high opinion of "intellectual merit alone," we would still have to enter the reservation that it can easily be confused, in the academic marketplace, with the acquisition of professional credentials or, worse, with loyalty to an unspoken consensus. Haskell does not appreciate how easily the ideal of professional disinterestedness can be distorted by the social and political context in which it has grown up.

In any case, "merit," intellectual or otherwise, is a pallid way to refer to the virtues nurtured by the practice of a profession or calling. Part of the usefulness of the concept of practices lies exactly here, in its challenge to the academic shortsightedness that tends to see the professions, the intellectual professions in particular, as the highest (almost the only) form of disinterested activity. The range of practices is much broader, embracing activities having nothing in common except the exercise of judgment in the conquest of gratuitous difficulties. Once we identify what all practices do have in common, we can begin not only to understand the value of pursuits often undervalued by academics but to understand the value of professions themselves, which consists of their capacity to educate judgment, not the encouragement they give to "intellectual merit." The idea of merit, inescapably linked to the idea of deserts, confuses the issue by associating excellence too closely with its social rewards and by implying, moreover, that excellence is largely the product of strenuous effort (which deserves to be recognized and rewarded) instead of an expression of a "gift," the appropriate celebration of which is gratitude rather than the bestowal of prizes, awards, and other tokens of merit.

The virtues have their proper reward, if we insist on using this term at all, in the myths and stories that celebrate successful practice—stories best regarded, it seems to me, as an expression of collective gratitude. Every practice generates traditions, and these are handed down in the form of narratives, which provide the context that makes actions intelligible. Practices depend on and foster a conception of the self, as MacIntyre puts it, that "links birth to life to death as narrative beginning to middle to end" (1981, 191). By giving an account of our actions, narratives make us accountable—a circumstance, incidentally, that explains why stories must always bear the burden of moral education. An account of the virtues is incomplete, then, if it omits the importance of tradition, narrative traditions in particular, in commemorating admirable practice and in refining the standards by which it is judged. This brings us back to the first part of our discussion and links it to the second part, the analysis of judgment and practice. Part of the value of tradition, we can now see, is that it commemorates past achievements (by no means un-critically) and makes us all parties to those achievements—not that it enforces conformity to a common set of values.

Having examined tradition and practice and the links between them, we are now in a better position, I hope, to say just what a community consists of and what a communitarian politics ought to look like. A community consists of a diversity of practices, and its public life ought to nurture these practices, to encourage the widest possible diversity of practices, and to check the influences that tend to corrupt them. This is a more modest conception of politics than the nostalgic, utopian conceptions that have helped to bring communitarianism into disrepute. In the past, the community ideal has usually expressed itself either in a longing for some hypothetical state of nature, a state of primeval innocence antecedent to the invention of politics, or in the grandiose vision of a "great community" based on universal brotherhood and universal agreement. In either version, communitarianism looks forward—or backward—to a form of solidarity in which individuals lose themselves in the mass, in which the competitive spirit has been completely extinguished, and in which people find themselves in such entire agreement that political life becomes unnecessary and withers away.

The communitarian ideal, as elaborated in the past, has usually been antipolitical—either prepolitical or postpolitical. In the latter form, communitarianism looks forward to a social order in which politics has given way to administration, divisive conflicts having been resolved in such a way that only the technical details of production and distribution remain to be decided in public. It is no wonder that the communitarian tradition, even though it appeals so powerfully to the sociable impulses destined to be frustrated in a competitive, individualistic society, remains suspect. From the time of Plato onward, its social ideal contains unmistakably authoritarian implications. Experience indicates, moreover, that the republic of virtue in practice issues in a reign of terror. Even if a virtuous republic in the future somehow managed not to repeat that all too familiar experiences, it would still be open to the objection that life in such a state, like the afterlife imagined in the conventional Sunday-school heaven, would be intolerably boring. As William James once said:

> Such pictures of light upon light are vacuous and expressionless. . . . If this be the whole fruit of victory, we say, . . . better lose than win the battle, or at all events better ring down the curtain before the last act of the play, so that a business that began so importantly may be saved from so singularly flat a winding-up. (*The Dilemma of Determinism*)

Our formulation of the communitarian ideal avoids an outcome so "singularly flat." It does not aim at a republic of virtue in which all differences and distinctions have been forcibly suppressed or flattened out. It conceives of politics not as a way of compelling men to become virtuous but merely as a way of keeping alive the possibility that they may learn virtue by fitting themselves for a congenial practice. It insists, moreover, on the need for a plurality of practices, representative of the full range of human talents and inclinations. No single practice must be allowed to monopolize the definition of virtue—as the practice of war monopolizes it in the Spartan version of the republican tradition that has provided such a constant source of inspiration for communitarian theorists.

The attempt to answer liberal objections to the communitarian ideal, unfortunately, opens it to another objection: that in this revised form it becomes indistinguishable from liberalism itself. Isn't this pluralism exactly what liberals have always advocated? Isn't it precisely the essence of liberalism that the state should remain neutral in the struggle between rival values, rival religions, and rival definitions of virtue, providing only the public order that makes it possible for individuals to work out their salvation in private? What keeps our analysis from coming full circle, since it was the impoverishment of public life under liberalism, the relegation of all the important questions to the obscurity of private life, that gave rise in the first place to a communitarian critique of liberalism? In ridding itself of its objectionable features, hasn't this communitarian critique, in our hands, come to resemble what it criticizes?

These are important and difficult questions, but I cannot hope to do justice to them here. All I can do is to indicate what seems to me the heart of the matter, namely, the difference between a state that protects privacy and one that protects practice. Liberalism assumes that men and women wish only to pursue their private purposes and that they form associations only in order to advance these purposes more effectively. Its solicitude for individual rights extends to the right of association, but it finds it hard to conceive of voluntary associations except as pressure groups seeking to influence public policy in their own favor. This blindness deprives liberals of any perspective from which to criticize the corruption of practice by external goods. Pressure groups are by definition interested in external goods alone—quite appropriately, from a liberal point of view—and the task of politics, accordingly, is merely to decide among their competing claims. Internal goods, on the other hand, are no business of the state, in the liberal view. The state obviously has no authority to tell doctors how to practice medicine or baseball players how to field their positions. It steps in only when these practices acquire a public interest, when they affect the distribution of external rewards, in other words, or—not to put too fine a point on it—when there is money involved.

My objection to the liberal view of things can be simply summarized by saying that this is too narrow a conception of the public interest. The public also has an interest—one that should not be thought of principally as a material interest, but rather as a moral interest—in medicine or sports that are practiced with devotion, with primary attention to internal goods. This interest will not be satisfied, of course, by direct state interference in those practices, but it demands a policy, a far more effective policy than anything that now exists, designed to limit the degree to which they are compromised and corrupted by the pursuit of external goods.

The distinction between public and private, so dear to liberals, doesn't catch the important concerns, the ones that really matter. On the one hand, it takes too narrow a view of the public interest. On the other hand, it trivializes the activities that need to be protected and nourished. Liberalism is at its best when it condemns invasions of privacy; but this best is still not good enough. The concept of privacy has no moral content. It equates freedom not with submission to an exacting discipline but with the absence of constraint, the right to do as one pleases, the right to change one's mind every day. Both liberals and our so-called conservatives adhere to this empty ideal of freedom and privacy; they disagree only about what is truly private. For liberals, it is freedom of religion, freedom of speech, and freedom of sexual preference that need to be protected, whereas those who call themselves conservatives value economic freedom more highly. The left understands private life as primarily cultural, the right as primarily economic. When the left attacks individualism, it is "acquisitive individualism" that is referred to, whereas the right specializes in condemnation of ethical individualism and cultural anarchy. A more comprehensive indictment of individualism is called for; and the best way to bring it into focus is to organize political discourse not around the "invasion of privacy" but around the corruption of internal goods by external goods, the corruption of practices by institutions. Thus the objection to intrusive journalism is not so much that it violates the individual's privacy (the legal status of which has never been terribly clear) as that it trivializes the lives of those who might otherwise serve as models of character, discipline, and virtue. This example, if you will consider its implications, ought to indicate how a wide variety of familiar issues—including the separation of church and state, say, or the regulation of big-time athletics—can be recast in a new and much richer form once we set aside the distinction between private and public life and talk instead about practices and institutions. I apologize for the underdevelopment of such specific illustrations in this essay, but it was first necessary to clear the ground and to let in a little light, a little fresh air, in the hope that freshly planted seeds could then take root and begin to grow.

ELEVEN

Adversarialism in America and the Professions

William F. May

In a haunting, Dostoevski-like novel, *The Temple of the Golden Pavilion*, Yukio Mishima describes a Buddhist acolyte's obsession with the temple he serves. The beautiful building stands for the entire realm of outer forms—those made by men and the gods—seemingly obdurate and indifferent to the pitiful impotence of the acolyte himself.

Mishima uses a fine image to convey the split the acolyte feels between his own inner life and the outer world. He is a stutterer. Other men pass easily, effortlessly, through the doorway between the inner and the outer, but every time the hero of the story attempts to pass through the door, he turns the key only to discover rust in the lock.

The young acolyte feels both love and hatred for the beautiful temple; he resents it and yet its cold beauty holds him rapt in its service. Eventually he sets fire to the sanctuary in an ecstasy of destruction. Once again, Mishima uses a fine image to describe the deed. He tells us that the young incendiary does not think of himself as starting a fire; rather, he *releases* those fires already latent in the universe. This view of his deed reminds one of those modern militants and terrorists who reject the charge that they have introduced violence into the world through their deeds; they claim only to have released the violence that lurks beneath all things.

My essay on *Habits of the Heart* bears on the first of Mishima's themes. Toward the whole world of outer forms, institutions, and ceremonies, we sometimes feel like Mishima's stutterer. We have difficulty connecting our own interior life to those external forms that dominate the public scene. Our private happiness seems to have little to do with the public realm. This divorce between the public and private is the Ur-problem that precedes and helps create many others—the specific problems of poverty, unemployment, environmental issues, racial injustice, deficit spending, and the like.

Habits reflects this separation between the public and the private in its very structure: Part One, Private Life; Part Two, Public Life. The authors, however, do not altogether despair of our capacity to bridge the gulf between the two arenas; they cite resources at our disposal, both psychological and historical-cultural. Admittedly, the American people are highly individualistic. But the extensive interviews that the authors conducted with a wide range of middle-class and professional people also reveal a communitarian streak in the American character. As fragmentary, contradictory, and one-sided as their personal perceptions may be, even the most egoistic of citizens interviewed did not altogether lack some dim sense of the public arena in which their goals must be realized, and apart from which the purely private life is privative.

Further, the authors, borrowing from the historical analysis that Robert Bellah supplied in *The Broken Covenant* (1975), identify three layers in the American cultural tradition which provide the languages by which the American people interpret themselves. First and foremost, Lockean individualism shapes the convictions of the American people. The authors of *Habits* distinguish two different streams of individualism: the older self-assertive Lockean individualism and a more recent therapeutic, self-expressive individualism. While individualism supplies the "first language" of Americans, earlier layers of American culture, both religious and secular, offer a substantially communitarian vocabulary. Admittedly, Protestants, Catholics, and Jews differ from one another in the source of their appeals, and late Protestantism lapses into individualism. But historically, the three religious traditions in America provided a communitarian vision that contrasts with a later aggressive individualism. A secular version of that communitarian religious impulse appears in the republican-revolutionary tradition of eighteenth century America. This tradition emphasized not simply personal liberty but *civil* liberties and the necessity of a "public virtue" upon which the flourishing of those liberties depends. The authors thus discern some grounds, both psychological and historical, for reconnecting private energies with commitment to the public good in American life.

I do not propose to offer in this essay a critique of either the diagnosis or the therapies that the authors of *Habits* recommend, but to explore instead the Lockean myth—one of the cultural traditions they identify—as it shapes the American consciousness and, most particularly, the professional class. Specifically, the Lockean myth helps shape and express the basic relationship of modern professionals to their clients.

It would be bookish, of course, to claim that Locke's *Treatises on Civil Government* singly causes Americans to be what they are. Gary Wills is right: Locke did not invent America. A wide variety of forces—intellectual and otherwise—contribute in varying degrees to the power of adversarialism in America: religious pluralism, ethnic diversity, the open frontier, social mobility, the harshness of the climate, and the even harsher intellectual climate of Social Darwinism. Still, Locke's *Second Treatise* helps generally to give an adversarial cast to the American civic consciousness and, even more particularly, helps define adversarially the professional relationship.

This paper divides into two parts: first, I offer an exploded diagram of the Lockean political myth; then, I apply this political myth to the prevailing interpretation of the professional relationship. An appeal to the term "myth" does not dismiss a story as untrue. On the contrary, a story acquires mythic proportions precisely because it offers an important way of ordering the experience of a people. Flannery O'Connor once wrote, "You know a people by the stories they tell." John Locke, in effect, tells a story to give an account of the relative place of the state and civic order in human life. His story has nothing to do with the deeds of heroes, a Romulus or a Remus, a Nelson, a Mazzini, a Garibaldi, or a Cavour, a Washington—the American Cincinnatus—or a Lincoln. Rather this account of the origins and aims of a government centers on the cutting of a deal.

The political vision that justifies cutting the deal includes at least the following five elements: First, it postulates an original condition of humankind characterized by individual autonomy. Second, it orients any subsequent society to the satisfaction of interests and wants rather than to the attainment of moral ideals. Third, it traces the origin of the state to supreme evil rather than supreme good. Fourth, it encourages a passive rather than an active notion of citizenship. And, finally, it holds to a transactional rather than a transformational understanding of leadership.

These five elements reappear, in turn, in the interpretation of the professional relationship. The professional, as well as the state, derives original power from the threat of a negative. This negative threat defines the aims of the professional adversarially. The client correspondingly thinks of himself as the relatively passive beneficiary of the power that the professional wields on his behalf. Like the basic political contract, the professional contract exists chiefly to protect negative liberty; it satisfies wants rather than pursues ideals; and it encourages a transactional rather than a transformational understanding of the professional relationship. This Lockean vision, in summary, offers what I have elsewhere called a contractualist (or transactional) rather than a covenantal (or transformational) understanding of both the political and the professional relationship. This contractarian and adversarial outlook dominates the American scene. Whether it defines American culture more than other comparable societies in the West, I leave for others to decide.

THE POLITICAL MYTH

The very notion of a social contract—the central idea in Locke's political philosophy—assumes that current social arrangements can be properly assessed only if measured against a time and state of affairs that precede the social contract. Locke called this prepolitical time the state of nature. Therewith Locke was not simply describing an actual state of affairs, but a natural, undistorted ideal condition, in which each individual enjoys a full measure of autonomy, a kind of executive and legislative power over his or her own life. Each is born "absolute lord of his own person and possessions; equal to the greatest and subject to nobody." This postulate of autonomy associates freedom with a kind of negative liberty—that is, a freedom from interference at the hands of others, a right to do, not absolutely but largely, as one pleases as long as one's actions do not interfere with the similar autonomy and authority of others, and as long as they do not undercut, as in the case of suicide, which Locke opposed, the very possibility of the self's own further action.

Further, the society orients to interests rather than ideals. In effect, the *ideal* state of affairs is one in which people act freely according to their own wants and interests rather than bend to moral ideals—either the ideals of others or those espoused by organized society.

The very concept of a social contract implies that self-interest supplies the *Arche,* the ruling principle, that establishes and preserves civil society. Like any marketplace contract between merchants, the comprehensive social contract justifies itself as serving the interests of all parties to an agreement. All share in common the rational desire for a government that maximally protects the wants and interests of each. Whatever one gives up in joining the society, one does not give up one's basic self-interest. Locke hardly envisages a state that heroes found and sustain through their sacrifices.

To what degree have autonomy and self-interest dominated the American social vision? Earlier historians (such as Carl Becker and Louis Hartz) have seen the spirit of Locke everywhere, including the revolutionary period. Other historians, upon whom Bellah relies, have emphasized two earlier layers in the American experience that differ in their account of the relative importance of negative liberty and self-interest in human affairs.

The pessimistic Puritans recognized the power of self-interest in human beings, but they were also communitarian; they envisaged, at least ideally, a social covenant that subordinated the will of each to the common good. The republicans of the eighteenth-century revolutionary period broke with the religious language of the Puritans, but they insisted no less on the notion of the common good. A republic required from its citizens a readiness to sacrifice private want and interest to public good. Such public virtue constituted the very soul of a republic. Self-interest alone would not create a nation, or, at least, not the nation they envisaged. The republic required public virtue of its citizens not only instrumentally to win a war of independence—in time of war, one always asks citizens to sacrifice self-interest to the common good—but also to sustain the kind of public realm to which its citizens were committed.

The revolutionaries followed Montesquieu in these matters. Every form of government depends upon an *Arche,* that is, a beginning principle or primordial energy, that informs and unifies the country. A despotic government relies on fear, while a monarchal government depends upon the aristocratic aspiration to honor and excellence. But a popular government, argued Montesquieu, lacking the glue of fear or an aristocratic code of honor, would fall apart unless it cultivated public virtue in its citizens. To survive as a public entity, a republic requires of its citizens a willingness to sacrifice private want and interest to public good. That is why the phrase "public virtue" ranked immediately after "liberty" as the term most often invoked in the revolutionary literature, and why, the "pursuit of happiness" meant first and foremost, according to many commentators, not the pursuit of private gratification but the location of happiness in public pursuits. For the revolutionaries the role of the citizen designated a kind of indelible public office compared with which the magistrate was but a temporary post. The notion of a "private citizen" was a kind of contradiction in terms. Public virtue rather than self-interest was the beginning principle of republican government. So goes the argument.

But by 1787 the revolutionary vision of a republic based on public virtue did not seem to correspond to the political reality. The spirit of 1776 lost its cohesive power. Getting rid of the British, surprisingly enough, did not get rid of self-interest or what some called "sin." The country factionalized. People seemed to center their lives on self-interest, removing public service to the margins. But to eliminate self-interest and factionalism from human affairs, one would also have to eradicate that liberty which is at their root. Thus the federalists sought a device for restraining self-interest rather than eliminating it. Better yet, they wanted mechanisms that, far from curtailing self-interest, would actively rely on its omnipresent power to keep its negative effects within limits. Their solution to the problem of governance that human nature posed (what Madison called the "defect of better motives") was the invention of 1787, the Constitution of the United States.

Indeed, America has relied on four basic mechanisms to allow it to function as a country without demanding too much public virtue of its citizens. First among these mechanisms is the Constitution itself.

The framers of the Constitution saw it as responding to the adversarialism that one already finds in nature—force pitted against counterforce—a conflict that could also be seen reflected in human society, faction pitted against faction. The device they adopted is familiar: a governmental design that relies on the separation of powers—legislative, executive, and judicial—and that distinguishes local, state, and national centers of power. They sought not to eliminate ambition from human affairs, but to pit ambition against ambition in order to keep ambition within limits. No person, faction, or majority can dominate all others. Through this device of countervailing powers, the framers sought to compensate for the "defect of better motives."[1]

The second basic mechanism upon which Americans rely is the free marketplace. Adam Smith assumed that people act out of self-interest. One need not exhort the butcher to act according to public virtue; one simply wants him to be a good butcher. His rigorous pursuit of his own self-interest will eventually redound, through the mechanism of complex market-exchange, into the commonwealth of nations. The marketplace assumes some virtue in those who participate in its exchanges, but not public virtue. The aggressive pursuit of one's own wants and interests requires the personal virtues of industry, honesty, and integrity; but otherwise, one can pursue one's own career without a wandering eye on the common good. The latter will result automatically from the essentially individual pursuits of each.

A third mechanism, to which the free market leads, is the large-scale economic organization, the corporation. Corporations contribute to social life by mobilizing professional skills more efficiently and productively than small-scale mom-and-pop stores. The corporation's superior productivity depends, to be sure, upon virtue in its personnel—cooperativeness, orderliness, and the personal qualities required to develop specialized skills; but on the whole, it places no extraordinary demands upon its workers. It offers people the opportunity to do great things without themselves being great. Rather than heroism, it requires only a self-interested careerism that will enable employees to develop those skills that, in a complex division of labor within the organization, allow them to perform assigned tasks within a larger whole. The large-scale organization encourages managers to develop the art of politics—the ability to act in concert with others—but an art of politics shorn of its object: the *common* good. It is enough to serve the primary mission of the organization from which the private advantage of its members can be immediately derived.

Finally, the mechanisms of the university and those of the marketplace and the corporation require yet a fourth—the modern, positivist university. Unlike ancient schools that prepared people for citizenship or cultivated virtue in citizens, the modern university aims to develop its students' skills. The marketplace, and especially the large-scale organization that flourishes within it, needs trained people and looks to the university to supply them. Meanwhile, the university has taken as its primary task the production and transmission of objective knowledge, an aim that by definition excludes moral questions from the classroom. For the positivist position holds that moral judgments reflect merely private, subjective, emotional preferences and therefore are not fit subjects for discussion, debate, and resolution in the university. Thus the university can furnish objective information useful to technical intelligence in determining how to get from here to there, but it cannot appropriately raise the moral question as to whether the "there" is worth getting to.

In consequence, university students are free to acquire a private stock of knowledge and operational skills to be sold on the open market to the highest bidder. Who is to say otherwise? If moral choices are a matter of private want and preference, each student can do as he pleases with the knowledge and skills acquired for his own private and intellectually unassailable reasons. And so careerists graduating from the professional schools flock to the large corporations, which the largest universities increasingly come to resemble. In some such way, the four mechanisms reinforce one another in American life. The universities train people for the corporations that compete in the marketplace within a constitutional framework, and none of these mechanisms demands much more than prudent self-interest from individual citizens. So goes the theory in each of its contributing parts.

Now we must return to our third baseline in Lockean thought, the question of the origin of the state. In classical Greek and several strands of Christian thought, the state had its origins in a *Summum Bonum:* either in the beneficent work of the gods, the sacrifice of heroes, the natural sociality of man, the philosopher's approximation of eternal ideas, or the supervening activity of providence. Correspondingly, the state had a positive mission above and beyond public safety—to enhance the common good and to promote the achievement of levels of personal excellence that would not be possible apart from communal life. The biblical tradition more complexly derived the state both from the positive intentions of God and from God's somewhat reluctant accommodation to the sinfulness of humankind. But it never so traced the origins of the state to sin as to place its derivation beyond God's purposes (see 1 Samuel).

Social contract theory, however, traced the origin of the state not to a supreme good, but to a supreme evil. Thomas Hobbes stands at the head of this tradition, positing an original state of nature that is one of relentless war. The natural condition of man (if imagined apart from the existence of the state) is subject to "continual fear and danger of violent death." This miserable condition results less from man's helplessness before a harsh and inclement natural environment than from the predatory assaults of human nature itself. Man is born with a limitless appetite for goods and glory that creates enmity between man and man. Men enter into the social contract to protect themselves from themselves. They create and hand over to the state a monopoly over the power of death (the power to enforce contracts, to jail, to execute, and to make war) in order to shield themselves from the violent death that would surely be theirs without the protection of the state. Thus, the state is founded in a negative—what Gerald Strauss in his studies of Hobbes called a *Summum Malum*. The fear of death crowds us together in the Hobbesian account of origins.[2]

Although Locke paints the human scene in somewhat lighter colors, he hardly works in pastels. Like Hobbes, he still founds the state in the provocation of a negative. Men compact together not because they are drawn to a common good, but because a common evil threatens them. What, after all, could prompt a self-interested man in the state of nature to "give up his empire" as "absolute lord of his own person and possessions" except that he experiences a severe threat to the enjoyment of his goods and stands to gain some protection through the exchange? In his crucial discussion of the "ends of political society and government," Locke describes the original condition of man as lordly and autonomous, but he concedes immediately that the security of man's status is "very uncertain and constantly exposed to the invasion of others." The enjoyment of his property is equally "unsafe and very insecure." His freedom is "full of fears and continual dangers." Thus he surrenders a portion of his powers, legislative and executive, to escape the "inconveniences of nature."

Clearly, for Locke, the state derives not from a positive, either divine or human, but from negative threats. Indeed, the state would overstep its negative functions if it appropriated to itself more positive goals. The state must chiefly aim to negate the negative in human life (to protect persons and property against the threat of enemies without and thieves and murderers within) and not to appropriate to itself positive tasks, whether to enhance the common good or to assist its citizens in the attainment of personal excellence. Moreover, since self-interest establishes the social contract, citizens have the right to dissolve the contract or withdraw from it, if the sovereign should fail to keep his side of the bargain by failing to provide basic protection or by exercising additional, arbitrary powers.

Apologists for this classical liberal understanding of the state believe that a merely negative justification for the state keeps it limited. But the emphasis on negative threats can, in fact, lead to an enlargement of the state's powers. The fear of the negative so dominates the modern psyche that it tends to justify any and all offensive measures. The defense department in a government usually finds it easier than any other unit to justify its budget, even in times of financial stringency. Advocates for other items in the budget usually like to cast their arguments in the negative rhetoric of battle: the war on disease, the war on poverty, or the war on energy dependence. Most dictators have usually enlarged their power not through the good that they would promote, but through the evils from which they would protect their nations. Hitler needed his

Jews; Stalin, his kulaks; and Senator Joe McCarthy, his communists, to enhance themselves in the eyes of their followers.

Further, the negative myth about origins contributes to and reflects the power of the essentially private emotion of resentment in modern politics. In a sense, humiliation gives birth to the Lockean state. The original condition of man, at least ideally, is free, autonomous, propertied, and equal. But the individual cannot protect his own life, liberty, and property, hence he has to surrender (Locke's terms are "give up" and "part with") a portion of his sovereignty. It would be better if it were otherwise, but man's weakness necessitates the surrender. The individual's first act as a citizen is a kind of capitulation (consented to in a sense, but also compelled by threat). Man diminishes, as it were, his manhood to secure protection.

What one gets in exchange has meaning only for one's private life—the protection that one obtains for one's person and property. It promises no amplification of one's public life. Therefore all the natural suspicion that obtains in commercial transactions applies to the social contract. One looks at the political product as one would look at any other product one has purchased to see whether one gets fair value or whether one has been cheated. Governing is not what one *does,* but what one consents to and continues to purchase through taxes, and what one quickly resents should it fail to support the pursuit of private goals.

The liberal myth tends to encourage a notion of the citizen as passive beneficiary rather than active participant in the political order. Michael Walzer (1983) has observed that the Lockean citizen is fully active at but two points: at a prepolitical moment in the creation of the state, and at a postpolitical moment in its revolutionary dissolution. In the interim period, one assumes that the state will provide protection so that one may pursue his own private wants and interests. In that context, when happiness gets defined as private happiness, the dangerously private and volatile emotion of resentment alone energizes politics in protection of that happiness.

Finally, to borrow a term from James MacGregor Burns, the Lockean vision entails a transactional, rather than a transformational, understanding of political leadership. The transactional leader takes at face value the preferences and interests of people and strikes off the best bargain he can in satisfying their aspirations for prosperity and protection. Transactional leadership is a kind of marketplace leadership. Citizens in the Lockean state give the government power in exchange for protection, thereby freeing citizens to pursue and gratify their own private interests and wants. In the transaction, one's minimal interests are satisfied, but one's character is unaltered, untransformed. This fits in with a libertarianism for which only autonomy is unconditional—all else is optional—and it matches philosophically that brand of consumerism that equates values with preferences and provides no independent ground for their criticism or transformation.

This vision of the political order allows for no concept of the common good other than the aggregate of overlapping private interests of those individuals who are members of the society. The politician is broker, negotiator, bargainer, and compromiser—pure and simple. Appeals to the public interest are empty rhetoric, and action on behalf of the leader's own notion of the common good, a dangerous display of pride.

THE POLITICAL MYTH AS IT SHAPES
THE PROFESSIONAL TRANSACTION

Structurally, the professional's relationship to the client resembles the relationship of the Lockean state to the citizen. Both the state and the professional owe their original authority to the threat of a negative. Both the citizen and the client are relatively passive beneficiaries of powers exercised by others. Both the citizen and the client are largely active at only two moments: the points of entry and exit when ties are established and dissolved. These structural similarities frame the other resemblances between the Lockean social contract and the contract that largely pertains today between the client and the professional. The latter relationship orients to negative liberty, it satisfies wants rather than pursues ideals, and it encourages a transactional, rather than a transformational, understanding of the professional exchange.

Just as the state derives its authority from its capacity to protect the citizen from a negative—from the threat of murder, injustice, and theft—so the professional largely draws authority from the power to protect clients from threats to their well-being. Men and women would be better off if they could function in a state of nature, that is, if they could do without the interventions of the professional and the state. Unimpaired sovereignty is the ideal state of things. The professional and the state are born of exigency. The Lockean state came into being to handle threats that mere aggregates of isolated individuals cannot master. Similarly, the client needs the professional to handle problems that exceed his competence and power. "You need a doctor," or "get a good lawyer," is advice we receive when we need someone to battle for us against sickness, disease, death, loss of fortune, or threat of jail.

This negative derivation of professional authority leads to a more adversarial understanding of the professional task. The modern physician largely defines himself or herself as a fighter in the battle against disease, suffering, and death. Medicine has generalized from the germ-theory of disease and interpreted all disease, along with the underlying professional task, in military terms. The patient understands himself to be in the grip of an alien, destructive power, so he resorts to the fighter-physician whose tactical skill and store of armaments will rescue him from destruction. (Even when the patient distrusts the physician and relies on lay medicine, a somewhat grim military dedication sets in.)

Adversarialism dominates the practice of law in this country with its central provision for courtly battle. The lawyer defends clients against the encroachment of others, both private parties and the state. Adversarialism in the law differs from medicine in two ways: first, the client has a human rather than a metaphysical adversary; and second, the proceeding pits professionals against one another, often in the public arena, a spectacle not often seen in other of the learned professions except for the academic.

Apologists for the adversary system in the law usually invoke the picture of the powerless, resourceless individual pitted against the majesty of the state. But, more often than not, the talented lawyer, given the distribution system of the marketplace, works for a huge corporation. The poor and the middle class often cannot pursue their grievances in court. Inequities in the distribution system and delaying tactics often stack the deck in favor of the powerful.

The adversarial game, moreover, encourages a kind of antinomianism in the client. The law no longer functions as a minimal statement of obligations to the neighbor that points beyond itself to a higher righteousness; rather, the law functions as a convenient collaborator in unrighteousness. It lets the client know what he can maximally get away with.

The accounting profession, more than any other, built into its titles the concept of *public* responsibility. A certified *public* accountant vouches for the accuracy of all records pertaining to the financial condition of an institution; but increasingly over the years, the accountant has interpreted his or her primary task as that of private lieutenant in the client's battles against competitors and taxes.

The press, of course, has largely defined itself in adversarial terms. It behaves as though it has not done well until it draws blood from those interviewed. Why rest content with reporting conflict if the sly photograph or the intrusive question can help to create it? And the professional manager of the large-scale organization, of course, champions the cause of the company in an environment perceived in often hostile terms, pressing for advantage against competitors, unions, markets, and the government. The spirit of Social Darwinism lives on in the psyche of company careerists long after the dress-parade version of that philosophy has passed. Even the engineer slips into an adversarial mode as he designs the technology for the "conquest" of space, time, and the inconveniences of a hostile nature. Advances in American technology were the key to conquering a harsh natural environment and converting it into the source of great wealth. Compared with the more domesticated and clement environment of Europe, America offered extremes in weather and huge unoccupied spaces. The scientists and engineers had the job of providing the weapons to subdue the environment—central heating to fight the cold; air conditioning to fight the heat and humidity; trains, telephones, cars, and planes to conquer space; bulldozers to carve up the terrain; shafts to mine it; test tubes to manipulate materials into prodigal new forms; and reactors to unleash their even more prodigal energies.

W. H. Auden once observed that in traditional Europe, nature was an animal to be trained, but in America, a dragon to be slain. The metaphor suggests hostility between man and his environment but also promises, according to ancient myth, fabulous reward to the hero who can conquer the dragon. Once the dragon is slain, riches pour out of its open belly. Never mind the ugly carcass that remains. Thus, Americans have been prone in the past to accept cities in disarray, a landscape slashed, and the befouling of the water and air as part of the price of the battle. For environmentalists, increasingly, the price of conquest seems too great and in the long run irreversibly unpayable. Thus they look for ways to call back the dragons unloosed to fight the dragon. Others—now in political power—believe that the battle, more than ever, must be fought. The real dragon, therefore, is the federal government that stays the hands of those who would extract riches from the environment. The enemy has become the federal government itself. Get the government off our backs.

The negative derivation of professional authority has three adverse consequences that should provoke some readiness for alternatives, or, at least, for some shifts in balance and emphasis. Professional authority derived from fear is difficult to limit; it is expensive, and it eventually provokes a backlash.

First, on the whole, it is more difficult to set limits upon the action of an agent or an agency that acquires its authority in the reflexive struggle against the threat of evil. I have already tried to press this point with respect to the state's power. Similarly, a professional authority based on a negativity alone has difficulty staying within limits because patients and clients do not have their fears under control.

The dynamics are most obvious in the case of medicine, since the fear of death is the deepest and most pervasive fear of all. "Whatever you say, doctor" may be the prudent compliance of a man or woman who has experienced a brush with death. But it soon translates into "whatever tests you order," and "whatever paces you put me through in the hospital, because I obviously need your help in fighting this battle."

Similarly, the lawyer who fights for a client against a threatened loss of liberty and property tends to feed upon the seriousness of the crisis. The right of appeal, the rules of evidence, the threat of equally or more adept lawyers on the other side of the case—all serve to generate a momentum in which the necessities of battle take precedence over other considerations. Litigation soon becomes a way of life for the stricken client, and the lawyer's power, control, and fees expand accordingly.

Even the academic profession in this country has depended mostly on a negative justification for its authority. It has largely sold education not as the pathway to truth, but as the escape route from poverty and insecurity. It has promised all takers an expansion of power, control, and opportunity. Universities become the carriers that would transport the young to better neighborhoods and more secure jobs, just as the great ships once bore their parents from Europe to the land of opportunity. Sold on these terms, the educational system oversold itself, expanding to the point that it became the overinflated enterprise that it is today, no longer able to deliver on the promise of job security; indeed, its own future looks somewhat precarious.

However, even the effort to combat the negative effects of professional action contributes to the growth of professional power and increases the cost of services. One needs, in the first instance, professional expertise to fight against threats of life, limb, and property, but then one needs the professional to protect the layman from those tricky powers mobilized to wage the fight. The professional must devise the technology to subdue a hostile environment and then devise further technologies to tame the technology conjured in the first instance. One needs a surgeon to perform an operation, but also an anesthesiologist to make it a safe one and the opinion of a second surgeon to determine whether it is justified. If it proves unwarranted, then one needs a lawyer to pursue the case in court, and accountants to monitor costs. The negative derivation of authority imposes high costs, even in the effort to contain costs, and inevitably leads to a resentment directed against the professional. The authority and prestige of the professional are great but precarious. Physicians and lawyers are the object of great anger. They are subject to retaliatory action if through incompetence or greed they impose on the patient-client what they are commissioned to resist. Since the stakes are so high and since institutions can suffer from the publicized incompetence of a single practitioner, professionals quickly draw around the endangered colleague like a herd around a wounded elephant.

Public resentment is reinforced by the interim passivity of the patient-client in the contractual model. For the patient-client tends to be active at but two points—in the choice of the professional and in the dissolution of the tie. He experiences the relationship as a forfeit and loss of autonomy; he both obeys his doctor and feels uneasy about his obedience. Moreover, to the degree that the patient is passive—triply passive to the ravages of disease, the ministrations of the professional, and the medical technologies employed—the patient seems to make no contribution to the ends pursued. What the professional offers is a product, perhaps gratefully received at the outset, but with a gratitude that slides only too easily into disappointment and resentment. So the patient becomes active again only in dissolving the professional tie or retaliating with a malpractice suit.

I doubt whether adversarialism can be wholly excised from American life. One cannot expect self-surgery on the American character. Nor would such a result be altogether desirable. Adversarialism is not purely destructive. The modern conviction that the journalist must challenge the high and mighty or that the lawyer should speak for the resourceless traces back to the earliest religious and cultural traditions of the West. The Hebrew prophets upbraided the powerful and took up the cause of the widow, the orphan, and the stranger as God's own. Sophocles gave us Antigone, probably the most impressive lawyer in all literature.

A democracy reflects these earliest convictions when it construes loyalty to the client to be a public duty. A democracy would extend its protection and services to those who are at odds with the society or whose experience of distress pitches beyond the ordinary goods of life. In effect, in a democracy, some dignity attaches to being wrong, and the professional functions, in part, to honor that dignity. While adversarialism has its difficulties, a totalitarian fusion of political powers, the reduction of the press to a mouthpiece of the state, and the collapse of the distinction between defense, prosecutorial, and judicial functions in the legal system would be objectionable.

Although wholly supplanting adversarialism may be impossible and undesirable, counterbalancing its weaknesses is imperative. There are signs, moreover, that a more collaborative, less adversarial model, and a more critical, less prosecutorial style can take hold.

It should be noted at the outset that one cannot altogether dispense with an adversarial element in the social structure. All positive derivations of authority contain a negative aspect. The state that derives from a Supreme Good cannot do without some provision for military or police power. The physician who aims for the health of the patient must ordinarily relieve suffering and prevent death. The positive aim of an educational system must include, as well, the negative activities of discipline and censorship; no educational system gets along without them.

A society, however, differs mightily in spirit and atmosphere, depending upon whether the positive or negative aim has priority. The schoolroom varies immensely depending on whether discipline subordinates to education or itself becomes the secret purpose of the facility. The medical task changes substantially when the relief of suffering and the prevention of death, rather than the pursuit of health, dominate the enterprise. The agenda looks different when the attraction of a good rather than the repulsion of an evil primarily provokes the emergence of the state or the professional relationship.

Further, there are some signs of movement in a more positive direction. In the modern world, to be sure, the germ theory of disease has tended to conform all disease to the military model. But it has become clear today that health depends upon much more than the successful outcome of transcendental battle. It requires the positive reconstruction of habits and regular access to those goods on which health depends. It requires emphasis on preventive, rehabilitative, and chronic care—not just acute-care medicine.

Not even the law is without its reformers from within. Judge Marvin Frankel, in his essay "The Search for Truth—An Umpireal View," does not opt for the European inquisitorial legal system, yet urges that judges be furnished with their own independent investigatory staffs to enable them better to arrive at the truth and a just judgment. So conceived, the courtroom is the scene of an inquiry and not just a contest. The lawyers are independent agents in that inquiry and not just hired mercenaries. Judges have responsibilities to the truth and a just verdict, not the minimal functions of umpires who merely assure that a contest has been fought according to mutually agreed upon rules.

Further, the *New Model Rules for Professional Conduct,* which the Kutak Commission submitted to the American Bar Association for discussion and eventual approval, attempted to redress the balance. The commission drew back from the extreme of the adversarial model in substituting "diligence" for the religious term "zeal" as the measure of devotion the lawyer owes to his or her client. More important, the *New Model Rules* no longer assume (in the fashion of the older code) that litigating in the courtroom is the lawyer's central function. In the ordering of the lawyer's tasks, the new code places the lawyer's role as advisor and counselor ahead of responsibilities as courtroom advocate, and the list of legal functions is expanded to include counselor, advocate, negotiator, evaluator, and arbitrator. (This change in emphasis corresponds roughly to the proposed shift in medicine away from acute care to preventive, rehabilitative, and chronic-care medicine.) While subsequent revisions by the bar association of the commission's proposals amply demonstrate the leadership's continuing commitment to the power of adversarialism, the event, as a whole, exhibits the existence of other voices.

Inevitably, a more positive understanding of the professional's task requires a more transformational understanding of the relationship of professionals to their patients, clients, and consumers. If physicians are to aim not merely at the prevention of death but at the pursuit of health, then they must seek a more active collaboration with patients in health maintenance. The medical transaction entails the transformation of habits, not just the purchase of strategic services.

Similarly, the lawyer must understand the roles of counselor and negotiator as something more than the pursuit of courtroom advantage by other means. The Kutak Commission, in fact, held that the lawyer as counselor and negotiator owes clients moral advice and not just technical legal skills. In the political arena, the long-range solution to the energy needs of the country will not occur simply through ever more intense efforts to plunder nature, but through a collective effort upon the part of political leaders and citizens to transform national habits.

The term *transformation,* of course, awakens fears of paternalism. As soon as one speaks of the physician, the lawyer, the manager, and the political leaders as engaged in the transformation of habits (rather than merely the gratification of wants), one fears the overbearing authority figure that haunts the American past. We recall the moral officiousness and cramping paternalism of the Puritans; we have known only too many professionals who have assumed that "father knows best." All of us have suffered professionals who ignorantly preached their politics when we would have preferred to pay them for their services and be on our way.

Efforts to transform, moreover, founder on the fact of pluralism. A society with diverse constituencies can ill afford too many efforts to transform. Are we not better off embracing the libertarian alternative that would restrict institutions and professional groups largely to instrumental goals? Why not assume that all community among us is merely useful rather than moral, that its function is to gratify our wants rather than to foster in us the aspiration to excellence? Why not rely on mechanisms rather than insight to cope with conflicting interests?

Transformational leadership falls prey to the aforementioned difficulties unless one reckons with teaching as its essential ingredient in a pluralistic society. I close, therefore, with a word about the professional as a teacher. No physician can engage in preventive, rehabilitative, and chronic-care medicine without teaching his or her patients. Words are to a prescription what a preamble is to a constitution. They help us interpret the meaning of the entire process. Teaching helps to heal the patient, to "make whole" the distressed and distracted subject.

Other professions must also teach. The nurse and the social worker must engage in teaching their patients and clients if they would work well. The lawyer, to be sure, offers technical services in drawing up contracts and appearing before the bar, but must also teach clients. Counseling is the functional equivalent of preventive medicine in the practice of the law. The constitutional powers of the president of the United States founder if the president fails in that office of which the Constitution never speaks: as teacher to the nation. The president's office may no longer be a bully pulpit, but Jimmy Carter's presidency demonstrated the difficulties we face without a leader who knows how to use his office as a bully blackboard for the nation.

If the professional finally must be a good teacher and not just a technician-fighter, then we need to rethink those aspects of the liberal arts component in both undergraduate and professional education that cultivate the qualities of a good teacher—a capacity for critical inquiry, a direct grasp of one's subject, a desire to share it, verbal facility, and sensitivity to one's audience. Theoretically at least, requiring a liberal arts background for professionals should produce people who are pedagogically skilled. Unfortunately, however, academicians have assumed that only *some* of their graduates become teachers. Therefore, they have treated teaching as a segregated profession. Teaching is, of course, a special profession; but at the same time it ought to be the aim and purpose of a liberal arts education to turn out good teachers whether students go into the teaching profession or not. Nonacademic professionals must teach, even as they dispense esoteric services. How else will they be bearers and transmitters of their heritage and fit practitioners and interpreters of their art?

TWELVE

A Constructive Freudian Alternative to Psychotherapeutic Egoism

Ernest Wallwork

The authors of *Habits of the Heart* associate the pervasiveness of American psychotherapeutic ideas with the contemporary eclipse of the public virtues they champion. Psychotherapy is displayed as having a role in legitimating an extreme form of egoistic individualism that subverts all values other than satisfaction of the isolated individual's purely arbitrary preferences.[1] As the authors would have it:

> The therapeutic ideal posits an individual who is able to be the source of his own standards, to love himself before he asks for love from others. . . . The therapeutic attitude denies all forms of obligation and commitment in relationships. . . . [It] liberates individuals by helping them get in touch with their own wants and interests, freed from the artificial constraints of social roles, the guilt-inducing demands of parents and other authorities, and the false promises of illusory ideals such as love. (*H*, 99–102)

This depiction of psychotherapeutic culture is a familiar one. It concurs in the main with Philip Rieff's description of "psychological man" in *Freud: Mind of the Moralist* (1961) and *The Triumph of the Therapeutic* (1968) and with Christopher Lasch's portrayal of *The Culture of Narcissism* (1979).[2]

There are several difficulties with this familiar thesis, however. The various schools of psychotherapy, like the larger culture they mirror, do not monolithically embrace radical individualism.[3] Indeed, as I shall demonstrate, even classical psychoanalysis, despite its affinity with radical individualism, takes seriously the sociability of persons. The importance of other-regarding and societal relations is even more explicit in the writings of psychotherapists Harry Stack Sullivan, Carl Rogers, Erich Fromm, Erik H. Erikson, W. Ronald Fairbairn, Donald Winnicott, and Harry Guntrip. Even if we admit that the notions of interdependence and commitment which psychotherapy offers are not as influential on the *cultural* level as its language of radical individualism, they are extremely significant in *clinical* practice, where psychotherapy represents a major resource for helping persons to assume moral responsibilities, including public ones, that they have shunned out of neurotic anxieties. On the levels of both theory and praxis, then, *Habits* is wrong to view psychotherapy as necessarily antagonistic to the biblical and republican traditions.

Similarly, an attribution of egoistic individualism to the psychotherapeutic view of human nature fails to do justice to the richness of the mixed-motivational interpretation of behavior that informs most depth psychological perspectives. And significantly, this attribution raises doubts about the adequacy of the book's own view of human nature. The authors view the self as essentially a social self, malleable by culture and social experience. They do not grapple with how unconscious motives may subvert or compromise conscious intentions to be moral. Yet such unconscious motives as narcissism and aggression unquestionably exist and cast suspicion on both the diagnostic and prescriptive claims of *Habits*. When unconscious dynamics are considered, as indeed they must be, the realism of the book's somewhat romanticized description of the golden ages of America's communal past must be questioned and its hopes for a moral revival must be seriously qualified. The problem with the view of human nature in *Habits* may be illustrated with respect to particular issues. For example, the book's discussion of marriage strikes one as dissatisfyingly naive and unhelpful. Taking the statements of interviewees at face value, the authors contrast the evangelical Christian ideal of selfless marital love with the seemingly selfish concerns expressed by therapeutically informed secular couples and criticize the therapeutic ideal as falling short on commitment and duty. In the context of their overarching praise of commitment, they leave the clear impression that the evangelical ideal is superior.

Depth psychology reminds us, however, that things are seldom what they seem in human affairs, especially in intimate relations, and this possibility calls for deeper analysis of the strengths and weaknesses of these rival views of marriage. It is possible that the marital ideals of therapeutically informed couples are much stronger than their words might suggest, precisely because they are able to attend to concerns for mutual enrichment without papering over problems; whereas the evangelicals' reverence for paternalistic authority may demand ongoing observance of the forms of marriage that allow deep psychopathologies to fester and unexpectedly (and, in the eyes of the evangelicals themselves, inexplicably) erupt in verbal and physical abuse. And as an ethical position, perhaps it is better to terminate marriages that have gone irretrievably awry than to perpetuate mutual unhappiness in the name of obligations that transcend human interests.[4]

Habits' unqualified endorsement of the moral virtues of social commitment and concern for the common good is similarly highly problematic. A psychotherapeutically informed view of human nature makes one
suspicious of the book's neglect of the potential for the pathological mis-
firing of social commitment. The writings of Freud and Erikson, for example, point out that the deepening of communal ties runs the very real
risk of fanning the flames of group narcissism and often has the effect of
turning outsiders into enemies to be cruelly repudiated (see Freud, *Standard Edition* [*SE*], 18:69–143; Erikson 1968, 41–42, 298–99). The human being's propensity for hypocrisy, and especially for using the highest communal ideals destructively against outsiders and minorities, is
something that reformist prescriptions cannot afford to disregard.

Finally, I would point out that even taken on its own terms, *Habits'*
critique of psychotherapy fails to cohere. If one accepts the authors' insistence on the radical individualism of the psychotherapeutic tradition
and also accepts that psychotherapy commands as much legitimating
power in contemporary culture as the book contends, then the authors'
practical aim of fostering a revival of the biblical and republican traditions appears to be seriously subverted and perhaps even empty. If the
authors' call for a nourishing of communitarian values is to have any im-
mediacy, which seems to be their intent, either it must be possible for
such concepts as interdependence, commitment, and the value of the
common good to find legitimation in the reigning psychotherapeutic
ideology (which requires psychotherapy to be in reality less narrowly individualistic and destructive of community than is portrayed in *Habits*)
or the psychotherapeutic tradition does not have a lock on contemporary culture and cannot be blamed as strongly for moral malaise.

My aim in this essay is to respond to these problems by looking at what
Freud has to say about narcissism, love, and public spiritedness. I hope
to show that even psychoanalysis—the school of psychotherapy most
aligned with psychological egoism—emphasizes the importance of nonegoistic behavior. I also intend to identify some important ethical resources in psychoanalysis that may help to offer a way out of the isolated
individualism and exclusive privatism of contemporary American culture and that might also help link the reigning psychotherapeutic culture to the biblical and republican traditions. This is not to say that the
psychoanalytic view of human nature is particularly sanguine. One of
the primary contributions of Freud's work is the recognition of the pervasiveness and depth of aggressive instincts and egoism in human beings. While the hard truths about human nature revealed by psychoanalysis are not the focus of the present essay, I do wish to emphasize
that they call for adopting a "hermeneutics of suspicion" (Ricoeur 1970)
toward even our highest moral ideals and values, lest they represent sur-
reptitious rationalizations of patent immorality.

This essay focuses on Freud's writings not only because he enjoys commanding cultural authority but also, and primarily, because more than any other depth psychology theorist, he addresses the issues of self-other relations—including egoistic individualism, love, and privatism—that *Habits* seeks to place on the forefront of the contemporary cultural agenda. What Freud says about these issues is not well known, in large part because he has been misread through the distorting glasses of American individualism, the historical and structural origins of which *Habits* brings out so well.

UTILITARIAN INDIVIDUALISM

Habits of the Heart is interested in psychotherapy chiefly as a cultural form, as a language for thinking about self and society. The book's authors are expressly not interested in psychological theory on its own terms, as a body of knowledge and a technique of investigation and cure (*H*, 317 n.1). And yet, the book cannot avoid discussing the theoretical supports for what it calls "utilitarian individualism," namely, that form of individualism that "sees human life as an effort by individuals to maximize their self-interest" (*H*, 336).[5] For example, the authors trace the contemporary cultural distrust of "morality" to the psychoanalytic explanation of how we come to be moral through the introjection of parental values. Acceptance of this explanation by patients in therapy is said to engender a moral relativism that is responsible, in turn, for today's pervasive egoistic utilitarianism:

> At that point [after discovering the infantile foundations of morality] they [patients] begin to develop values on the basis of wishes and wants. . . . The question "Is this right or wrong?" becomes "Is this going to work for me now?" Individuals must answer it in light of their own wants. The workings of the world are best seen in terms of the costs it exacts and the satisfactions it yields. Each of us faces cost-benefit "tradeoffs" in satisfying some wants at the expense of others. (*H*, 129)

Freudian theory, which is the seedbed of virtually all contemporary schools of psychotherapy, is the source of the ideas that are being interpreted in this passage. It was, of course, Freud who first proposed the infantile origins of superego morality. In addition, his work also appears to dignify the belief that we are all egoistic utilitarians by its insistence on the ubiquity of unconscious "narcissistic" and "hedonistic" motives. These concepts have given currency to the view that Freud—and, through him, the psychotherapeutic tradition as a whole—represents a sophisticated form of psychological egoism. Ian Gregory (1975, 102) succinctly articulates this familiar interpretation: In Freudian theory, man "may achieve a certain guile in pursuing his satisfaction, i.e., he becomes subject to the reality principle, but his end is always the same, his own gratification. He is, in short, wholly self-absorbed, utterly selfish, not capable of forswearing instinctual satisfaction." (See also Fromm 1955, 74–75; Asch 1952, 19; Rieff 1961, 174.)

Under this conventional reading, psychoanalysis is understood to hold that there is nothing surprising or morally condemnatory in radical individualists devoting themselves exclusively to the satisfaction of their own interests and wants. Man can do no other; he can only act for his self-interest well or poorly, openly or covertly. In this case, a premium will be placed on knowing what one's interests and desires are. Thus utilitarian individualists would scan their feelings "while making moment-by-moment calculations of the shifting cost/benefit balances" (H, 139).

And yet, there is at least this puzzle about attributing psychological egoism to psychoanalysis: Freud himself seems to draw quite different conclusions about the moral significance of his therapeutic findings. He writes:

> Finally, one can only characterize as simple-minded the fear which is sometimes expressed that all the highest goods of humanity, as they are called— research, art, love, ethical and social sense—will lose their value or their dignity because psycho-analysis is in a position to demonstrate their origin in elementary and animal instinctual impulses. (*Collected Papers* [*CP*], 5 : 128)

> It is not our intention to dispute the noble endeavours of human nature, nor have we ever done anything to detract from their value. On the contrary, . . . we lay a stronger emphasis on what is evil in men only because other people disavow it and thereby make the human mind, not better, but incomprehensible. If now we give up this one-sided ethical valuation, we shall undoubtedly find a more correct formula for the relation between good and evil in human nature. (*SE*, 15 : 146–47)

Again, and in contrast to *Habits*, Freud declares: "I quite agree . . . that PA [Psychoanalytic] treatment should find a place among the methods whose aim is to bring about the highest ethical and intellectual development of the individual" (cited in Hale 1971, 170).

Freud does not say exactly what he means by the expressions "the noble endeavors of human nature" and "the highest ethical . . . development of the individual," but he indicates throughout his writings that human beings at their noblest pursue such intrinsic goods as knowledge, art, creative work, love, and community (see *SE*, 21 : 74–85).

Furthermore, Freud makes it plain in discussing the nature of mature love that it involves a nonegoistic dimension. Eros, in the "wide" sense of Freud's mature writings, fans out beyond self-love to include love of others for their own sake (*SE*, 18 : 90–92; for further discussion, see Wallwork 1982). He states: "Love for oneself knows only one barrier—

love for others, love for objects" (*SE*, 18:102). Indeed, the absence of truly other-regarding love is viewed by Freud as a pathological degradation of normal love: "To ensure a fully normal attitude in love, two currents of feeling have to unite—we may describe them as the tender, affectionate feelings and the sensuous feelings" (*CP*, 4:204). Because "tender" and "affectionate" feelings are evoked by "the highest mental estimation of the object," acts motivated by such feelings are done "ihnen zu Liebe"—literally, "for love of them" as separate persons independent of oneself (*SE*, 18:92).

The crucial question, then, is this: How are these two seemingly incompatible positions—psychological egoism and acknowledgment of nonegoistic motives—compatible? The answer is partly to be found in Freud's opposition to reductionism and partly in his appreciation of mixed motivations.

Contrary to Freudianism vulgarized, the founder of psychoanalysis himself vigorously opposed the systematic reduction of all conscious motives to unconscious, infantile roots. That mature affection is genetically rooted in infantile egoism did not mean for Freud that the nonegoistic aspects of love could be negated by reducing them to their origins. The concept of sublimation holds that normal psychological development involves a genuine "transformation" of infantile motivations (*SE*, 14:61). Freud states that the goal of a sublimated motive is related genetically to the abandoned one but is "itself no longer sexual and must be described as social. We call this process 'sublimation,' in accordance with the general estimate that places social aims higher than the sexual ones, which are at bottom self-interested" (*SE*, 16:345).

On the grounds that a sublimated activity is not simply a disguised form of a more primitive motivation, Freud warns against confusing mature, "affectionate" love of others for their own sake with earlier, egoistically motivated sensual ties. Unconscious narcissism may explain overly demonstrative, "needy" love (see *SE*, 14:67–102), but in many cases unconscious narcissism remains no more than a potentiality within the complex motivational system of the mature adult.

Freud certainly believed that psychoanalysis showed "that the sexual ties of the earliest years of childhood also persist, though repressed and unconscious" and that wherever there is an affectionate feeling, "it is successor to a completely 'sensual' object-tie with the person in question or rather with that person's prototype (or *imago*)" (*SE*, 18:138). But Freud also declared that it was a different issue "whether in a given case this former complete sexual current still exists under repression or whether it has already been exhausted":

It is quite certain that this current is still there as a form and possibility, and can always be cathected and put into activity again by means of regres-

sion; the only question is . . . what degree of cathexis and operative force it
still has at the present moment. Equal care must be taken in this connection to avoid two sources of error—the Scylla of underestimating the importance of the repressed unconscious, and the Charybdis of judging the
normal entirely by the standards of the pathological. (Ibid.)

Freud's doctrine of mixed motivations also helps him avoid inconsistency when he stresses humankind's propensity for both egoism and the
so-called higher motivations. While the cultural reception of his work
has neglected the mixed-motive doctrine (at considerable cost), it is one
of Freud's most important discoveries that our actions are overdeter-
mined, that is, they are the product of multiple motivations, some conscious, some unconscious, some good, some bad. Freud writes: "It is very
rarely that an action is the work of a *single* . . . impulse. . . . In order to
make an action possible there must be as a rule a combination of such
compounded motives" (*SE*, 22 : 210).[6]

Unconscious motivations are predominantly egoistic or aggressive,
but these may be trumped by more powerful other-regarding motivations, though self-interested motives manage more frequently than we
realize to enter into compromise formations with our conscious nonegoistic intentions.

Freud's mixed-motive doctrine makes it possible to recognize the
significance for behavior of unconscious egoistic motivations, as most
schools of psychotherapy do, without supporting the conclusion pur-
portedly drawn by some of the therapeutically informed interviewees in
Habits that there is no basis for morality other than enlightened self-
interest. Freud's point is the comparatively more modest one, consistent
with acknowledging traditional moral principles, that our moral actions
tend to be mixed with selfish and aggressive inclinations.

TOWARD A THERAPEUTICALLY INFORMED SOCIAL ETHIC

The ethical views attributed to psychotherapy in *Habits* revolve around a
radically antinomian and antisocial concept of freedom. Psychotherapy,
in the book's view, aims at freeing the self from the inhibiting constraints
of obligations and commitments. It is said to leave the individual fundamentally alone, inwardly isolated even among friends and family, with
little, if any, sense of commitment to groups and larger communities beyond what these are believed to contribute to the individual's personal
benefit.

The purported psychotherapeutic emphasis on freedom to the exclusion of other values is attributed partly to the predominantly negative
view of moral obligations that is said to prevail in psychotherapy, but it
is also attributed to the celebrated value-neutrality of the therapist.
Therapy, in removing inhibitions, undoing repressions, correcting dis-

tortions, and reducing anxieties, places negative freedom at the patient's disposal. But it does not dictate to the patient how to use this newly won freedom, lest in doing so it shackle the patient once again with debilitating dependencies. The therapist does not encourage the patient to fall in love or otherwise tell the patient what one must do to live a full life, but simply offers the patient an opportunity to determine what he or she wants to do.

From the fact that psychotherapists find it morally desirable (in terms of the values of nonmaleficence, autonomy, and beneficence) to eschew moral *coercion* in the clinical setting, it does not follow that psychotherapists need draw the conclusion, enunciated by some interviewees in *Habits,* that value preferences other than freedom and truthfulness are totally arbitrary. Indeed, it is awkward for the psychotherapist to embrace the concept of completely arbitrary preferences and at the same time distinguish between psychopathology and normal behavior, since this distinction presupposes that some preferences are better than others.[7] In classical psychoanalytic theory, for example, sadism, masochism, and narcissism are clearly undesirable motives that Freud does not hesitate to describe as "pathological" and even as "evil," while love and creative work are unquestionably good (see *SE*, 21:74–85).

These normative distinctions embedded in psychotherapy are made partly by appealing to the sociality of persons; that is, it is tacitly assumed that persons are made for life with others. Over against the liberal ideal of the radical separateness and distancing of selves, Freud's account of psychological development stresses the deep attachments—for example, of mothers and infants—that bind the self to others. In fact, the self does not exist for Freud except as it is constituted through the long process of psychosocial development in which the growing person comes to understand himself through such processes as identification, object-love, introjection, internalization, and transference.[8] These processes require both that the self direct itself outwardly toward the world of persons and things and that it receive back the approbation of other persons (see, e.g., *SE*, 14:67–102, 237–58; 18:88–143).[9]

Of course, Freud often stresses the importance of liberating ourselves from childhood dependencies. But the liberating process in psychotherapy occurs by making use of the self's primordial capacity for both transference love and a therapeutic alliance. If this capacity is absent as a consequence of severe narcissistic fixations, therapy is either impossible or extremely difficult. The ideal of liberty in psychotherapy is not defiantly to proclaim one's sovereign, "narcissistic" independence of others. Rather, it allows for acknowledgment of the manifold ways in which one is interdependent with others. If some of these interdependencies are undesirable, others, such as loving and being loved, are among the highest values known to human beings. That such love can be understood as entailing an enduring and deep commitment that confers moral obligations is indicated by Freud's comment that love "imposes duties on me for whose fulfilment I must be ready to make sacrifices" (*SE*, 21: 109). Such sacrifices are not equated with the infantile dependencies from which the patient needs liberation.

Habits would have us believe that psychotherapy—insofar as it acknowledges the worth of mutual love—promotes privatism. Indeed, psychotherapy is evaluated negatively in the book precisely because it so deeply threatens the republican tradition that identifies freedom with public solidarity and the activities of citizenship.

It is therefore significant that Freud was also aware of the dangers of privatism, which he refers to as the "exclusiveness" of love. He gives as examples a pair of lovers who believe themselves "sufficient to themselves": "The more closely the members of a family are attached to one another, the more often do they tend to cut themselves off from others, and the more difficult is it for them to enter into the wider circle of life" (*SE*, 21 : 103). Civilization with all its myriad benefits requires that the centrifugal forces of exclusiveness be effectively countered by bonds joining individuals "together into larger unities," Freud argues.

It is commonly believed that Freud presents a basically Hobbesian account of social bonds, whereby social obligations are justified ultimately by their success in securing the self-interests of individuals. But Freud explicitly rejects the notion that mutual self-interest provides a sufficient foundation for social solidarity. Freud is actually a rather severe critic of the liberal theory of society as nothing more than a contract among atomistic, egoistic individuals. Most people would probably be surprised to know that he declared that love operates in civilization to "[bind] together considerable numbers of people . . . in a more intensive fashion than can be effected through the interest of work in common" (*SE*, 21 : 102).

In a like vein, he notes that "civilization is not content with [the] bonds of common work and common interests." Rather,

> it aims at binding the members of the community together in a libidinal way as well and employs every means to that end. It favours every path by which strong identifications can be established between the members of the community, and it summons up aim-inhibited libido on the largest scale so as to strengthen the communal bond by relations of friendship. (*SE*, 21 : 108–9)

It is noteworthy that the concept of communal solidarity here is rooted instinctually in Freud's mature concept of Eros, which is defined broadly as that "which holds all living things together" (*SE*, 18 : 50). This represents a change in psychoanalytic theory, introducing Eros as a substitute for purely sexual libido. The meaning of the sexual instincts for human relations is thereby expanded beyond its usual connotations of genital sexuality (as well as beyond Freud's earlier definition of sexuality in terms of the sensual modalities associated with the erogenous zones) to encompass all forms of interpersonal sympathy and altruism, which become expressions of the instinctual equipment of Homo sapiens. The wider concept of Eros may not coincide exactly in meaning with Plato's use of the word or with St. Paul's understanding of *agape*, as Freud (*SE*, 18:91) erroneously contends. But Eros nonetheless plays much the same function in Freud's social thought as it does in the republican and biblical traditions to which he compares it. For Freud holds that "civilization is a process in the service of Eros, whose purpose is to combine single human individuals, and after that families, then races, peoples and nations, into one great unity, the unity of mankind" (*SE*, 21:122).

Freud, of course, is also aware of the many ways in which civilization opposes and frustrates the individual's search for happiness. Individuals seek direct sensual pleasure in whatever ways they can get it, whereas societies try to confine pleasure seeking within narrow boundaries. And although individuals could be content in the isolation of a couple or a small family, civilization forces people to participate in wider forms. Too, civilization's moral obligations often conflict with the self's interests. These and other tensions between the individual and society have convinced Freud's therapeutic descendants that there is an irreconcilable conflict between the individual's desire for happiness and the requirements of civilization. And it is this notion of an irresolvable conflict that *Habits* critiques on the grounds that private life and public life are "so deeply involved with each other" that the impoverishment of public life entails the impoverishment of the private domain (*H*, 163).

But Freud takes the more realistic tack of preserving the tension without presenting it as irreconcilable. Unlike the conflict between the life instinct and the death instinct, the conflict between the good of the individual and that of society can in principle be harmonized, but only under cultural conditions far less repressive than those prevailing in Western civilization:

> [The] struggle between the individual and society is not a derivative of the contradiction—probably an irreconcilable one—between the primal instincts of Eros and death. It is a dispute within the economics of the libido, comparable to the contest concerning the distribution of libido between ego and objects; and it does admit of an eventual accommodation in the individual, as, it may be hoped, it will also do in the future of civilization, however much that civilization may oppress the life of the individual today. (*SE*, 21:141)

The reason such an accommodation is possible is that both the urge "towards personal happiness" and the urge "towards union with others" express deeply rooted desires of individuals: "The development of the individual seems to us to be a product of the interaction between . . . the urge . . . which we usually call 'egoistic,' and the urge towards union with others in the community which we call 'altruistic'" (*SE*, 21 : 140). Reconciliation is possible through an expanded understanding of happiness that includes the pleasures of social participation alongside those of egoistic satisfaction. As Freud observes, "Integration in, or adaptation to, a human community appears as a scarcely avoidable condition which must be fulfilled before the aim of happiness can be achieved" (*SE*, 21 : 140). Rejecting the notion that happiness can be found by a strategy of isolating oneself from others, Freud advises that, "There is, indeed, another and better path: that of becoming a member of the human community. . . . Then one is working with all for the good of all" (*SE*, 21 : 77–78). Here are important grounds for linking the psychotherapeutic tradition with the classical republican and biblical traditions. All three identify the individual's well-being with public solidarity and the activities of citizenship.

But Freud's mixed-motive theory also warns, as *Habits* does not, against deceiving ourselves with high-minded language about devotion to the public or common good. If a politics of commitment is desirable as an antidote to the antipolitics of radical individualism, nevertheless, as Freud's work reminds us, inflated ideals often end in harm. They do so partly because they tend to be used to deny and repress egoistic and aggressive motives that become all the more powerful for being denied legitimate expression. But in addition, when high moral ideals are shared by a community, the very ideals that inspire intragroup solidarity simultaneously tend to trigger derogatory attitudes and aggressiveness toward outsiders, who easily become the butt of projections based upon the projectors' worst fears about themselves. Freud writes soberingly of the ways even the biblical tradition's ideal of universal love has served to divert aggression onto outsiders:

> It is always possible to bind together a considerable number of people in love, so long as there are other people left over to receive the manifestations of their aggressiveness. . . . In this respect the Jewish people, scattered everywhere, have rendered most useful services to the civilizations of the countries that have been their hosts: but unfortunately all the massacres of the Jews in the Middle Ages did not suffice to make that period more peaceful and secure for their Christian fellows. (*SE*, 21 : 114)

Given that we have no reason to believe that these constraints on morality have evaporated, there is cause to worry about what a moral revival centered upon the biblical and republican traditions in this country would mean for the treatment of those who are not part of the perceived in-group. *Habits'* own language is sometimes troubling in this respect, in-

sofar as it identifies the American tradition with the white, Western heritage to the neglect of those many other traditions that stand in tension
with it. One wonders who is included and who is excluded when "we" is
used in the book, and what this means for those who are excluded because they have difficulty identifying with the biblical and republican traditions. In all fairness, the authors themselves value inclusiveness, but
the traditions on which their practical proposals rely have been historically highly prejudiced and destructive in their treatments of anyone
who is really different.

CONCLUSION

The authors of *Habits* fail to search for resources in the psychotherapeutic tradition that might offer a way out of the alleged contemporary
cultural malaise. In part this oversight results from the book's focus on
popular culture—and popularized psychotherapy is radically individualistic. But the authors view psychotherapeutic *practice* as generally corrosive of the values of social solidarity, public responsibility, and concern
for the common good. By their account, psychotherapy cures by detach-
ing persons from society and human relationships, whereas traditional
therapies—shamanism, faith healing, common worship—bring "'the
community into the healing process'" (*H*, 121).

If I am correct that Freud, and, by implication, the tradition indebted
to him, contains a perspective on self-other relations that indeed comple-
ments that advanced by the authors of *Habits*, there are potential correc-
tives in psychoanalytic theory itself to a radical individualism that is fed
by popular misconceptions of psychotherapy. For Freud, the self is not
an island, but part of a wider social ecology. Nor are values completely
arbitrary. In the search for happiness in life, each of us is constrained by
instincts that direct the self toward others such that happiness cannot be
achieved in isolation from our fellows. The narrative that the individual
reworks in therapy is not the only historical story the individual needs.
We each also need narratives of particular communities in relation to
which our unique life history makes sense. Freud himself indicated the
importance of these larger historical narratives when, addressing the Society of B'nai B'rith in Vienna in 1926, he spoke eloquently of the "inner
identity" and "obscure emotional forces" that made "the attraction of
Jewry and Jews irresistible" to him (*SE*, 20:273).

Psychotherapy as a practice does not set out to articulate and make
meaningful these larger historical narratives, any more than communities of memory have as their primary purpose the healing of individual
psychopathologies. The myths and rituals in psychotherapy are private
rather than public. But psychotherapy can help individuals understand
the special meaning that historical traditions and communities assume in

their own lives, thereby enabling each patient to work out his or her own
solution to the ultimate questions of human existence. Psychotherapy is
also in a position to counter the idea that we Americans are self-made
individuals who have made it all on our own and consequently deserve
the privileges we enjoy free of responsibility for others. In place of self-
reliance, psychotherapy teaches that we have always been and always will
be vulnerable to, and in varying degrees dependent upon, others, especially in the area of self-esteem. To the extent that therapy enables us
better to understand our unconscious needs, it is capable of helping to
create more open, more intense, more sensitive, more loving relationships. The uncovering of unconscious motives is also invaluable for de-
fusing prejudices and projections that hinder us from acknowledging
the rights of others, especially of those people who seem very different
from us.

Psychotherapeutic beliefs and practices are not implacably hostile to
cooperative participation in the public realm. Rather, they just may help
to transform radical individualism by reconnecting persons to communities of memory, albeit on somewhat different terms than those that
prevailed in simpler times when individuals identified themselves un-
questioningly with public myths and rituals. Psychotherapy does help
one to develop a critical distance from the public realm, just as it encourages a sense of the separateness of persons, but it does so in a way that
calls for a transformed understanding of our interdependence. Unfortunately, the negative attitude adopted toward psychotherapy in *Habits*
prevents the authors from utilizing psychological insights in developing
a more sophisticated understanding of the delicate and dynamic balance
of our independence and interdependence. What is needed is a social
theory, compatible with contemporary psychosocial experience, that
goes considerably beyond anything the biblical or the republican tradition has yet envisioned. This is a matter that awaits the continuation of
the dialogue that the authors of *Habits* have begun.[10]

PART FOUR

Religious Practice

THIRTEEN

Justice As Participation: Public Moral Discourse and the U.S. Economy

David Hollenbach, S. J.

When the church ventures to preach or teach about the relevance of the Gospel to the public life of a pluralistic society, it can expect to become involved in a certain measure of controversy.[1] This controversy is likely to be particularly lively when the preaching or teaching touches people's pocketbooks. And the potential for quite nasty disputes is perhaps greatest when the discussion moves beyond questions of how people should voluntarily use their money, talent, and other economic resources, to questions of public policy—for these policies affect people's freedom, inevitably broadening freedom of choice for some, and limiting it for others.

In November 1986, the National Conference of Catholic Bishops (NCCB) issued a pastoral letter, *Economic Justice for All: Catholic Social Teaching and the U.S. Economy.* The drafting process involved broad consultation and wide public debate. It is hoped that dialogue will continue in both the church and the larger society. All this has reinforced my conviction that the church has the capacity to be what James Gustafson (1970, 83–95) has called "a community of moral discourse," as well as the ability to stimulate such discourse in the broader society. Serious and sustained discussion of the moral dimensions of American economic life can be very productive.

At the same time, the bishops' project has revealed deep fissures in the moral content of American culture. The fissures are also evident in the research summarized and interpreted in *Habits of the Heart.* The fault lines that lie just beneath the surface of our national life are the result of competing convictions about the meaning of the central moral and political norms of social life. Should these fault lines give way, the social earthquake could be great indeed.

In particular, the debate has vividly revealed the conflicting notions of justice held by Americans. The purpose of this essay is to analyze what the bishops' letter says about the meaning of justice and to relate the moral argument of the letter to several other contemporary interpretations of the meaning of justice. Like *Habits*, this essay argues that a renewal of the biblical and civic republican strands of American culture would contribute greatly toward achieving a more just society. The biblical and republican traditions converge in understanding justice as a form of active participation in social life, while injustice is, at root, a kind of exclusion from human community. The notion of justice as participation will be proposed as the possible basis for the new cultural consensus that can help the nation address the urgent problems that face it.

Disagreements about moral and religious questions will, by definition, be present in every pluralistic society. But when the disagreements concern the most fundamental norms of social and political life, the situation begins to look ominous. Over twenty-five years ago, John Courtney Murray observed that discourse on public affairs must inevitably move from debate on specific decisions or policies upward "into realms of some theoretical generality—into metaphysics, ethics, theology." Unfortunately, he added, "this movement does not carry us into disagreement; for disagreement is not an easy thing to reach. Rather, we move into confusion," a situation in which "soliloquy succeeds to argument" and prejudice and suspicion replace civil discourse and reasoned debate (Murray 1960, 15–16).

The fury with which some critics have publicly denounced the drafts of the bishops' letter as Marxist in fact and totalitarian in implication is evidence, I think, of the confusion present in the debate. For example, one of the more vociferous of these critics has suggested that the letter "is secretly smuggling an egalitarian, socialist concept into Catholic thought" and has adopted "an un-American concept of justice" (Novak 1985). This kind of language is a symptom of a very real disease in our society. Murray named this disease "barbarism," a condition in which public debate about justice "[either] dies from disinterest, or subsides into the angry mutterings of polemic, or rises to the shrillness of hysteria." When such things happen, Murray said, "you may be sure that the barbarian is at the gates of the city" (1960, 12).

More recently, Alasdair MacIntyre has offered a somewhat similar diagnosis of the state of our public moral discourse. In MacIntyre's view, post-Enlightenment ideas and social institutions have destroyed the possibility of giving any universally plausible and rational account of the foundation of morality. He describes our situation as one in which moral language is frequently used, but most often to express disagreement. There seems to be "no rational way of securing moral agreement in our culture" (MacIntyre 1981, 6). As a result of the culturally fragmenting effects of modern individualism, we have lost a coherent moral vision as well as the kind of coherent institutions of communal life needed to sustain such a vision:

> Modern moral utterance and practice can only be understood as a series of fragmented survivals from an older past and . . . the insoluble problems . . . generated for modern moral theorists [will] remain insoluble until this is well understood. (MacIntyre 1981, 104–5)

For MacIntyre, this moral breakdown is both most evident and most dangerous in our inability to achieve agreement about the meaning of justice—the central virtue of political life. We lack the fundamental prerequisite for being a political community at all, and raw Nietzschean power threatens to replace reason and justice as the guiding force in social life. In short, our situation is that of a new "dark ages." MacIntyre's diagnosis is considerably more pessimistic than Murray's, for he concludes that "the barbarians are not waiting beyond the frontiers; they have already been governing us for quite some time" (1981, 245).

The prescription MacIntyre offers for this disease is the cultivation of the virtues of social life in small local communities, a kind of modern equivalent of the monasticism of Saint Benedict. Only in more intimate communities of this sort can we hope to recoup the intellectual and moral resources needed for genuinely civil existence. Before attempting to discern the meaning of justice writ large—that is, justice in the life of society as a whole—the meaning and reality of justice writ small must be cultivated, that is, justice as a virtue of persons and small groups.

This appeal for the retrieval of the primacy of virtue and character strikes a sympathetic chord in the Christian understanding of the moral life. Indeed, the bishops' pastoral letter stresses the importance of personal virtue in any just society. Thomas Aquinas's Christian appropriation of the Aristotelian discussion of the virtues shows that this is a typically Roman Catholic emphasis. In addition, the letter borrows from the Lutheran and Calvinist understandings of personal vocation to ground the economic responsibilities of all members of the Christian community—workers, homemakers, managers, financiers, and government officials. The church itself, moreover, must be a community that nurtures and sustains both the virtues of each of its members and their vocations to be disciples of Christ in the midst of daily life.

Nevertheless, renewal of the sense of vocation and of personal virtue is not the whole of what the bishops have set out to do. Their purpose is not only to encourage the personal moral and religious development of Christians but also to address the larger economic institutions and policies of the nation (NCCB 1986, no. 27). In order to do this successfully in a pluralistic society, the bishops need a moral language that is intelligible and plausible to those who do not share their tradition. If one accepts MacIntyre's analysis of contemporary Western culture, no such language exists, and the bishops' second goal is unrealizable.

Stanley Hauerwas, a theologian strongly influenced by MacIntyre, has argued that the effort by Christians to shape public policy within the presuppositions of a liberal, pluralist society is not only futile but theologically illegitimate. In Hauerwas's theology, the church's social task is to bear faithful witness to the story of Jesus, not to cast about trying to find moral arguments that will be persuasive to non-Christians. Hauerwas fears that if the church seeks too much influence in shaping the policies of a pluralist society, its commitment to Jesus Christ will inevitably be contaminated and co-opted by the falsehood and violence that are evident in "the world." In his words, "Once 'justice' is made a criterion of Christian social strategy, it can too easily take on a meaning and life of its own that is not informed by the Christian's fundamental convictions. It can, for example, be used to justify the Christian's resort to violence to secure a more 'relative justice.' But then we must ask if this is in fact the justice we are to seek as Christians" (1983, 112–13).

Hauerwas concludes that the church should cease and desist from the attempt to articulate universal moral norms persuasive to all members of a pluralistic society. It should return to its proper task of building up the Christian community of faith, love, and peace. The church does not "have" a social ethic to guide the life of society as a whole. It should "be" a social ethic; its own life of faithfulness should bear witness to what the world should be but unfortunately is not (Hauerwas 1983, 99–102).

Hauerwas's affirmations about the importance of faithfulness to the story of Jesus, about costly discipleship, and about strong bonds of mutual service within the Christian community are fully affirmed in the bishops' letter. The letter makes a major effort to ground a discussion of economic ethics in the Scriptures, in the liturgical life of the community of faith, and in the call to conversion and discipleship. It also goes quite far in confessing the sinfulness of the institutional church's own internal economic life in areas such as fair wages, responsible stewardship of resources, and the like. Its disagreement with Hauerwas is with his *exclusive* concern with the quality of the witness of the Christian community's own life. In the traditional categories of Ernst Troeltsch, the bishops refuse to take the "sectarian" option of exclusive reliance on the witness of the Christian community that Hauerwas recommends. They continue to rely on a "church-type" ecclesiology. They believe that the church has a responsibility to help shape the life of society as a whole. And the fulfillment of this responsibility calls for dialogue and argument about the norms of justice that should govern the life of our pluralistic society.

The theological argument between sect-type and church-type versions of the relation between the Christian community and the larger society is an ancient one. I will not attempt to deal with it here. One brief statement will suffice. The bishops succinctly summarize the reasons for their conviction that a fruitful relationship can exist between the Christian community and our pluralist culture:

> Biblical and theological themes shape the overall Christian perspective on economic ethics. This perspective is also subscribed to by those who do not share Christian religious convictions. *Human understanding and religious belief are complementary, not contradictory.* For human beings are created in God's image, and their dignity is manifest in the ability to reason and understand, in their freedom to shape their own lives and the life of their communities, and in the capacity for love and friendship. (NCCB 1986, no. 61)

Note well: they do not say that human understanding and religious belief are *identical,* but rather that they are not in opposition to each other. Furthermore, a relationship of complementarity means that human wisdom and Christian belief must be mutually enriching and mutually corrective of each other. The church can and should learn from the world; the world can and should learn from the Gospel and the whole Christian tradition.

This methodological presupposition, however, does not solve the substantive question, raised by Murray and MacIntyre, concerning the fundamental norm for public life and public policy. If our pluralistic society is fundamentally "confused" about the meaning of justice, and if it has lost the ability to reach an agreement on such meaning, then one wonders what it means to say that the human understanding of justice and the Christian vision are complementary. If the meaning of justice has been fractured into incompatible fragments, each being advocated by a particular ideological camp, then the nice synthesis of faith and culture suggested in church-type ecclesiologies is an illusion. We would be forced back to the sectarian option of a community of faithful witness, not because of Hauerwas's theological objections, but because our society lacks a shared culture to which faith can relate. We would face what George Lindbeck (1971), with a good Lutheran sense of irony, has called the "sectarian future of the church." Is this the case? My answer depends on a distinction between a judgment about the quality of the present popular debate on the meaning of justice in our society, and a conclusion about the future possibilities for this debate that are being opened up by several moral and political philosophers.

First, the current popular debate. If one looks at popular opinion about the meaning of economic justice in our society, the lack of consensus is evident. There are deep disputes about the merits of the free market, about the desirability or effectiveness of programs designed to aid the poor and the unemployed, about the level of inequality that is tolerable or desirable, about the legitimacy of affirmative action programs, about the relation between equality of opportunity and equality of outcomes, and about the relation between our responsibilities to vulnerable U.S. workers and to those who work in industries abroad that compete for the jobs of U.S. workers. The economic debates in Congress are so often stymied because they are riddled with conflicting claims. And there is no agreement about which of these claims take priority.

A certain amount of this is, of course, an inevitable part of the democratic political process. It would be dangerous to think that a single set of moral insights could be invoked to settle all these disputes. The wish for a fully rational political process can easily become a wish for a single intelligence to direct it. That way lies tyranny.

Tyranny, however, is not the only way to avoid paralysis and the breakdown of debate into pure interest-group, single-issue politics. The alternative is the development of a fundamental consensus about the *premises* of public debate, shared convictions that enable us to replace confusion and prejudice with real arguments. In Murray's words:

> The whole premise of the public argument, if it is to be civilized and civilizing, is that the consensus is real, that among the people everything is not in doubt, but that there is a core of agreement, accord, concurrence, acquiescence. We *hold* certain truths; therefore we can *argue* about them. It seems to have been one of the corruptions of intelligence . . . to assume that argument ends when agreement is reached. In a basic sense the reverse is true. There can be no argument except on the premise, and within the context of agreement. (1960, 10, emphasis added)

Murray called this consensus the "public philosophy," a phrase borrowed from Walter Lippmann. The authors of *Habits* see their work as a venture in public philosophy, which William Sullivan has described as "a tradition of interpreting and delineating the common understandings of what the political association is about and what it aims to achieve" (1982, 9). Murray argued that the core of public philosophy is a passionate conviction, rooted in clear understanding, about what is "due to the equal citizen from the City and to the City from the citizenry according to their mode of equality." In other words, the central conviction in the consensus that should shape public argument is an understanding of and devotion to justice, the "ground of civic amity . . . the ground of that unity which is called peace. This unity, qualified by amity, is the highest good of the civil multitude and the perfection of its civility" (Murray 1960, 8).

In 1960 Murray acknowledged somewhat ruefully that such a public philosophy was at least precarious and quite probably nonexistent in modern America. Nevertheless, he refused to give up so easily, for no constitutional commonwealth can succeed in the absence of this kind of consensus. If we lack the public philosophy we need, we must recreate and regain one:

> The further conclusion will be that there is today a need for a new moral act of purpose and a new act of intellectual affirmation, comparable to those which launched the American constitutional commonwealth, that will newly put us in possession of the public philosophy, the consensus we need. (Murray 1960, 87)

We need, in the words of the bishops, a "new American experiment," a new way of thinking about justice and new institutions to secure it for all. The bishops state that by drawing on the resources of the Catholic Christian tradition they hope to make a contribution to this new consensus about the meaning of justice and a new experiment in achieving it. Like the authors of *Habits*, the bishops are seeking to retrieve the central values of biblical faith and civil virtue in order to contribute new moral purpose to American economic and cultural life.

The bishops and the authors of *Habits* are not alone in sensing the need for a renewal of public philosophy at this critical juncture in the history of the United States. Since John Rawls published *A Theory of Justice* in 1971, dozens of moral and political philosophers have offered serious analyses of the meaning of justice in our nation. Their theoretical approaches cover a wide spectrum, perhaps as broad as the diversity of public opinion on this subject. For example, the libertarianism of Robert Nozick stresses the primacy of the right of private property and freedom of exchange in the marketplace. Rawls's liberal democratic theory is committed first to the right of equal freedom for all and, within the framework of such equal freedom, to assisting those most in need. Michael Sandel argues that any adequate moral theory must be built on convictions about the fullness of the human good, convictions that are formed and sustained only in communities shaped by friendship, tradition, and shared vision. For Sandel, therefore, any notion of justice that seeks to circumvent the differences of tradition and vision of the good among historical communities is necessarily limited and even flawed. Michael Walzer contends that equality is at the root of the meaning of justice. But for Walzer, equality is a complex concept, with a meaning that is partly the same and partly different in different spheres of life, such as the polity, the workplace, the system of merit and status, and the family.[2]

This welter of competing presuppositions for a theory of justice could easily be seen as a vindication of MacIntyre and Hauerwas. On the contrary, I interpret it as a source of hope. We may well be witnessing a movement from sheer confusion about the meaning of justice to genuine argument about it. The basic consensus of a public philosophy is far from achieved, but the outlines of a framework for real debate are taking shape. And if we could agree on this framework, a lot of the fog would lift. It would not move us into the light of noonday, or raise us totally out of Plato's cave into the blinding brightness of the pure good, but it would surely help us figure out a better way to understand the complementarity of all the fragments of human wisdom and Christian religious conviction.

I do not intend to offer some grand synthesis of Rawls, Nozick, Sandel, Walzer, and the other participants in the current American argument about the meaning of justice. In fact, one of my chief points is that there is not one meaning of justice in some univocal sense. All the interlocutors in the current disputation have got their hands on some part of the reality we are in search of. Socrates knew this phenomenon well: dialectic, that is, argument, is a process of sorting through a host of opinions to discern what is true in each, in search of that which is most true, most good. The argument about what justice means is as old as Western civilization. The quality of the argument today may well determine whether this civilization has a future, or whether its future will be in any sense civilized. In the face of these high stakes, I think that the sectarian retreat of MacIntyre and Hauerwas is ultimately, if unwittingly, a failure of nerve. It fails to appreciate new possibilities present today for expressing love of one's neighbor by engaging in the long march of cultural transformation.

So then, what do I propose? Let me start with two central theses, one from Rawls and one from Walzer. First, Rawls has proposed a theory of "justice as fairness." This theory is not based on any commitment about what is ultimately *good* in human life. Justice-as-fairness, Rawls states, has no metaphysical presuppositions about human purpose, human ends, or what finally makes people happy. On ultimate ends and the full human good we must be free to disagree. All we need to get the concept of justice off the ground, Rawls has argued, is a mutual desire to work out "a fair system of cooperation between free and equal persons" (1985, 231). He thinks that such a basis can be laid down without decreeing an end to pluralism among our various visions of the good. Nor does justice-as-fairness want to abolish the commitments people have to goods greater than fairness. In addition, justice-as-fairness does not depend on the belief that individual autonomy is an end in itself. But it does presuppose that free choice regarding ultimate ends and personal goals must be politically protected in a just political community. Further, within a context of a primary commitment to free choice, justice-as-fairness seeks to identify "the kernel of overlapping consensus" among the various ideas of the full human good that different persons and groups hold, a consensus which "when worked up into a political conception of justice turn[s] out to be sufficient to underwrite a just constitutional regime. This is the most we can expect, nor do we need more" (Rawls 1985, 246–47).

Justice-as-fairness turns out, then, to be a vision of a tolerant society that respects freedom and wants to aid those in need as long as this aid is compatible with the freedom of people to disagree about their personal definition of happiness.

Is this really enough? I think not. And the most cogent argument to express my disagreement comes from Michael Walzer's *Spheres of Justice* (1983). Walzer, too, wants to respect differences. But his definition of the differences that count is quite different from Rawls's. Walzer knows that people do not achieve happiness or full lives apart from friendship, kinship, and many other particular nonuniversal relationships. But note: for Walzer, *relationship* is key. Who is in positive relationship with me determines to whom I have certain obligations of justice. And the *kind* of obligation I have depends on the *kind* of relationship it is: political, familial, economic, ecclesial, and so on.

Thus, for Walzer, the diverse kinds of communities we belong to are the sources of diverse "spheres of justice." The big word *justice* is differentiated into smaller parts, but this does not mean that it is blown apart into utterly incompatible fragments. The key to Walzer's argument about the unity among the different spheres of justice is his concept of membership.

Let me outline his main thesis. In arguing about justice, we are arguing about who gets what, and on what basis they get it. We are also arguing about who gives what, and on what basis they give it. We are arguing about the criteria that should govern sharing in the creation and distribution of the goods of some kind of community, whether it be an economic, political, honorific, or familial community, or even a community of grace. Thus, the bottom-line question in arguments about justice is this, *Who counts* when we talk about sharing in the goods that come from being part of a particular kind of community?

Fairness is thus not simply a matter of the size of the slices of the pie being distributed. More basic than the arguments about the relative portions is the one about who should be at the table in the first place. The answer to this question differs in different spheres of human existence. An employer distributing wages has obligations to employees that he does not have to nonemployees. A community bestowing honor and praise will select honorable and praiseworthy people; Nobel prizes go to peacemakers and eminent scientists, not warmakers and charlatans. In family life, parents face the awesome task of loving each of their children equally while acknowledging and encouraging their different gifts. And though each of us has very important obligations to those outside the bonds of kinship, we do not have the same *kind* of obligations to people down the block or halfway around the world that we do to spouses, children, or parents.

A central question in disputes about justice, therefore, is that of specifying the set of relationships or particular kind of community we are talking about when urging a particular standard of justice. In short, who is a member of the club to which the standard of justice is to apply? In Walzer's words:

> The primary good we distribute to one another is membership in some human community. And what we do with regard to membership structures all our other distributive choices: it determines with whom we make choices, from whom we require obedience and collect taxes, to whom we allocate goods and services. (1983, 31)

The criteria of membership, of course, are different for different kinds of communities, and therefore the criteria of justice will vary from one zone of life to another. Justice has a plurality of meanings because we have many kinds of relationships in our lives. In some of them, such as the political community, a standard of strict equality applies: One person, one vote. In others, the criterion of merit is relevant; the grading of exams is a case in point. In still other areas, need is the relevant measure. Parents do not do justice to their children if they treat one who is physically disabled in an identical way with one who is not.

Respect for the richness of social life, therefore, calls for a nuanced and differentiated understanding of the meaning of justice. A single criterion, such as need or merit, administered by a single institution, such as the government or the market, betrays the rich and complex reality of social existence. On this key point, the tradition of Catholic social ethics is remarkably close to Walzer's thesis. In line with this tradition, the bishops' letter makes a distinction between the state and society. Society is the more inclusive reality, composed of many subcommunities of various types: families, neighborhoods, labor unions, small businesses, giant corporations, farm cooperatives, a host of voluntary associations, and the churches. Respect for this pluralism of communities rests on the fact that justice is not the concern of the political community alone, nor is it to be administered solely by the state. The freedom of these other forms of human community to exist and to operate according to the kinds of communities they are must be protected. This is the substance of what Catholic thought calls the principle of subsidiarity. Note, however, that these other communities are not purely *private* bodies. They are parts of *society*, ways in which persons come to participate in social life.

This way of formulating an approach to the meaning of justice is an important point of intersection between the bishops' letter and the contemporary philosophical argument. For example, in a statement not fully of a piece with his contractarian presuppositions, Rawls has recently stressed the notion of membership as key to his understanding of civic life:

> Since Greek times, both in philosophy and law, the concept of the person has been understood as the concept of someone who can take part in, or who can play a role in, social life, and hence exercise and respect its various rights and duties. Thus we say that a person is someone who can be a citizen, that is *a fully cooperating member of society over a complete life*. We add the phrase "over a complete life" because a society is viewed as a more or less complete and self-sufficient scheme of cooperation, making room within itself for all the necessities and activities of life, from birth to death. A society is not an association for more limited purposes; citizens do not join society voluntarily but are born into it, where, for our aims here, we assume they are to lead their lives. (1985, 233)

To be a person is to be a *member* of society, active within it in many ways through diverse sets of relationships. The key question that the bishops would place on the national agenda rests on the premise that the meaning of justice rises from this link between personhood and social participation.

It is in this framework that the bishops' letter most directly challenges American economic and cultural life today. They state the challenge this way:

> *Basic justice demands the establishment of minimum levels of participation in the life of the human commuity for all persons.* The ultimate injustice is for a person or group to be actively treated or passively abandoned as if they were nonmembers of the human race. (NCCB 1986, no. 77)

The antithesis of such participation can be called marginalization—exclusion from active membership in the human community.

Unjust exclusion can take many forms, as justice can take many forms. There is political marginalization: the denial of the vote, restriction of free speech, the tyrannical concentration of power in the hands of a ruling elite, or straightforward totalitarianism. Exclusion can also be economic in nature. When persons are unable to find work, even after searching for many months, or when they are thrown out of work by decisions they are powerless to influence, they are effectively marginalized. They are implicitly told by the community: "we don't need your talent, we don't need your initiative, we don't need *you*" (NCCB 1986, no. 141). If society chooses to acquiesce rather than mitigate this situation, injustice is being done. One can hardly think of a more effective way to deny people any active participation in the economic life of society than to cause or allow them to remain unemployed. Similarly, when persons face hunger, homelessness, and the extremes of poverty and society fails to allocate its resources to meet their needs, in effect the poor are being treated as nonmembers. As Walzer puts it:

> Men and women who appropriate vast sums of money for themselves,
> while needs are unmet, act like tyrants, dominating and distorting the dis-
> tribution of security and welfare. . . . The indifference of Britain's rulers
> during the Irish potato famine of the 1840s is a sure sign that Ireland was a
> colony, a conquered land, no real part of Great Britain. (1983, 76 and 79)

In the same way, the hungry and homeless people in this nation today
are no part of anything worthy of being called a commonwealth. The
extent of their suffering shows how far we are from being a community
of persons.

The bishops' general normative perspective is made concrete by their
survey of the extent to which people are excluded or left behind in the
economic life of the nation and throughout the world today. Over eight
million Americans are looking for work but are unable to find it, and
thirty-three million Americans are below the official poverty line. One of
every four children under six and one of every two black children live
in poverty. One-third of all female-headed families are poor. Between
1968 and 1978, one-fourth of all Americans fell into poverty during at
least one year. Beyond our borders, at least 800 million persons live in
absolute poverty and nearly 500 million persons are chronically hungry.
This, despite fruitful harvests worldwide and a food surplus in the U.S.
that is driving down prices and sending thousands of American farmers
into bankruptcy.

In the face of these realities we have to ask whether being born into
the human race is any guarantee that one will be treated as a person in
Rawls's terms: "a fully cooperating member of society over a complete
life"? Even raising the question is an invitation to cynicism. The chief
problem in explicating an adequate concept of justice in our society today is not the different conceptions Americans have of what makes for
full happiness or what private "life-plans" are worth pursuing. The
problem is that many would prefer not to reflect on what it means to say
that these marginalized people are members of the human community
and we have a duty to treat them as such.

On the basis of their biblical faith and their tradition's emphasis on
civic obligations to the common good, the bishops are unable to ignore
economic injustice—though our culture seems tempted to do so. On the
basis of their conviction about the complementarity of Christian faith
and human understanding, the bishops are seeking to engage the debate
about the meaning of justice through arguments parallel to those I have
made here. They state that "no one may claim the name Christian and be
comfortable in the face of the hunger, homelessness, insecurity, and injustice found in this country and the world" (NCCB 1986, no. 27). I
would add, no one may claim to be genuinely human and remain at ease
with these problems. That, I believe, is the beginning of a consensus or

public philosophy, a consensus the authors of *Habits of the Heart* are also seeking to build. Within the framework of such a public philosophy we can argue about how to overcome these injustices. But there can be no legitimate debate in a truly civilized society on whether we have a duty to overcome them.

FOURTEEN

Are We Preaching a "Subversive" Lectionary?

J. Irwin Trotter

I want to consider why there has been such ready acceptance of the new Common Lectionary among free-church preachers. Equally important, why is this happening primarily in North America? The Lectionary has not found such universal acceptance in Protestant Europe or in other places. This reliance on the Lectionary by the free churches is primarily a North American phenomenon.

It is curious that after 350 years of resisting preaching from a lectionary, free-church preachers seem to be turning to the use of this Lectionary. Two hundred years ago, John Wesley sent a revised Book of Common Prayer, which included a lectionary, to be used by the Methodist Episcopal church. North American Methodists promptly ignored it for the next 200 years. But now, what we Protestants would not accept from John Wesley, we are accepting from the Holy Father! The Lectionary that is winning much acceptance is the Roman Catholic lectionary, out of Vatican II. Does it not seem curious that this is happening in the free churches in North America?

Although I have not taken a poll (nor have I seen one) to determine how widely the Lectionary is being used, my guess is that well over half of the preachers in the free churches are currently using the Lectionary to supply their texts for preaching. So I raise this question, Why has this Lectionary found such favor in the North American free churches after 350 years of preachers' finding texts on their own?

PRINCIPLES OF THE COMMON LECTIONARY

This widespread use is even more puzzling in that the common Lectionary reflects an ecclesiology that is communal, organic, and sacramental.

This is not surprising in a Roman Catholic lectionary, for the Roman Catholic church is certainly communal, organic, and sacramental.

In a way, this communal liturgy was a recovery for the Catholic church, which had slipped into very personalist and solitary ways of worshipping—"telling your beads" alone in a corner, while the priest was whispering the Mass in Latin. The Liturgical Movement in the Catholic church had been trying to renew and revitalize worship for 150 years, and a liturgy growing out of a communal ecclesiology was really a recovery for Catholics of a fundamental tradition (Sacerdotal Communities, 1964). The Liturgical Movement was so widely accepted at the time of Vatican II that the adoption of *The Constitution on the Sacred Liturgy* (1964), which included the directives for revising the lectionary, was the very first act of the council.

A lectionary is "a canon within the Canon." The passages included in a lectionary are more influential than any of the rest of the Canon because we hear these particular passages in Sunday worship. So it is fair to ask, what principles did the Concilium follow in selecting texts for the Common Lectionary? I will focus on two determinative principles from among several.

One principle is a strong Christo-centric bias (Bailey 1977). The reason for this is obvious—the Lectionary is chosen to be used with the Sunday observance of the Mass. Therefore, one of the principles the Concilium worked from is that the texts must be Christological in focus. At first glance that seems appropriate for Protestants as well, but let us examine some of the results.

The first consequence of this Christo-centric bias is a subordination of the Old Testament to the Gospel lesson, that is, the Old Testament is used mainly in its Christological passages. (Isaiah gets a big play.) As Sanders (1983) and many others have pointed out, this criterion of selection undermines the integrity of the Old Testament. One of the most dangerous implications here is the opening this makes for the possible revival of anti-Semitism in the church's life. Unless the Old Testament is seen as having an integrity of its own, there is always the danger that Christians will slip back into that feeling that somehow they are superior to Jews. Moreover, and equally important to many Protestants, the subordination of the Old Testament to Christology means that the "social prophets" will not be widely read and the social critique in these books will be slighted.

The second consequence of this Christo-centric bias is that the Lectionary is organized around two great festivals, Easter and Christmas, and their doctrinal emphases—Resurrection and Incarnation. One practical result of this is that for half the year the continuous reading of scripture (a free-church tradition) is repeatedly interrupted by festival occasions. More importantly, the whole Lectionary is subservient to the liturgical function (Bouyer 1964). As a result of a North American consultation on liturgy that began in 1978, these liturgical features were somewhat modified in the Common Lectionary. (This consultation joined together Roman Catholics and many free churches and liturgical Protestants.) But while modified, the liturgical functions remain primary for the Lectionary.

The second, and more important, determinative principle of the Lectionary is only implicit. At first, Protestants rejoiced when this new Lectionary came out because we thought (quite rightly) it represented a renewed Catholic interest in the Bible. *The Constitution on the Sacred Liturgy* (1964) says "the treasures of the Bible are to be opened up more lavishly." And it declared that there should be no Eucharist without preaching. Protestants, on reading that, immediately welcomed Catholics into the Reformation. But they failed to realize that the phrase "no Eucharist without preaching" can also be turned the other way—"No preaching without a Eucharist!"

Thus, the organizing principle of the Lectionary is the central importance of the Eucharist in the worship of the church. Salvation is not something that happens individually; it is incorporation into the whole (Wegman 1983). As John Henry Cardinal Newman (1864) said: "From the time that I became a Roman Catholic, of course I have no further history of my religious opinions to narrate." What he meant, in part, is that salvation for Roman Catholics is communal, sharing the faith of the community, the body of Christ. Preaching has the function of drawing persons into this Eucharistic fellowship (Congar 1968). This is the basic organizing principle behind the Lectionary.

Now some Protestants will rush to say that these same texts can be preached in a Protestant way. This is true. But I would suggest that to use a lectionary *at all* is to have a new and more communal understanding of worship and the church. It means that I am no longer going to choose my own text, but I am under some kind of communal authority as to what the text should be. We all use the same text on the same Sunday. There is a communal sense, and a communal authority, in the very use of a lectionary. Clearly, this does not sound very "free church."

NORTH AMERICAN FREE-CHURCH PREACHING

Traditional Protestant preaching in North America is based on an ecclesiology that is individualistic, atomistic, and voluntaristic. Just the opposite of the ecclesiology that produced the Common Lectionary! Let me illustrate the conundrum by mentioning three great free-church preaching traditions in North America. I have classified them by their function, that is, by what preaching is supposed to produce.

The first is didactic or guidance preaching. Here the function of preaching is to instruct and guide, with the appeal primarily to the intellect. The goal is enlightenment. With its origins in Puritan preaching (Elliott 1974), this is perhaps the oldest preaching tradition in North America. It is also the tradition from which most of our famous preachers come: Horace Bushnell, Theodore Parker, Henry Ward Beecher, Phillips Brooks, Washington Gladden, Henry van Dyke, Frances Willard, Harry Emerson Fosdick, Norman Vincent Peale, Georgia Harkness, and Gerald H. Kennedy. This tradition includes both the social gospel and positive thinking movements, since the function of both is to educate, and it is the mainstream of preaching in North America. In the introduction to one of his books of sermons, Bishop Gerald Kennedy (1948) wrote: "A young man said to me one night after a lecture, 'If Christians work so slowly and we have so little time, what hope is there?'" And Kennedy's reply was: "Only an *awakening* to the need for the heroic acceptance of Christ's way can save us." This preaching means to get people's individual minds straight, to "awaken" them one by one.

The second tradition, evangelical preaching, has been in some ways even more influential than guidance preaching. Here the function is to convict of sin and to bring to repentance. The appeal is not so much to the intellect as to the will, and the goal is the submission of the individual will to God's will. A combination of Puritan Calvinist theology and German voluntaristic pietism first forged in Britain, evangelical preaching struck a sympathetic note on the American frontier, and every denomination in the United States has been heavily influenced by it. All the best-known evangelists in North America have had Calvinist origins: Jonathan Edwards, George Whitefield, Charles Finney, Lyman Beecher, Dwight Moody, as well as the revivalists in Kentucky. Even the two Billies, Sunday and Graham, come from that tradition (Weisberger 1958). There have been strong evangelists in other traditions, too, but Calvinists dominate.

Finally, we have the Pentecostal tradition, in which the function of preaching is to evoke ecstatic praise, to bring people to an ecstatic experience of the Spirit. Pentecostal preaching appeals neither to the intellect nor to the will but to the spirit. Leaving the Calvinist tradition almost completely, Pentecostalism enters more exclusively into pietism, especially the Wesleyan brand. White Pentecostalism developed from the "holiness" movement (Synan 1971), led by Phoebe Palmer, John and Martha Inskips, and Robert and Hannah Smith. At the famous Azusa Street Revival in Los Angeles (1906–1909), organized by W. J. Seymour as a black revival, white holiness Pentecostalism and black Christianity found each other. What the black religious experience had always known, white Pentecostals struggled to discover—namely, a form of religion still in touch with the spirit, with the primeval ecstatic experience. Among well-known exponents of this style of preaching are Aimee Semple McPherson, Kathran Kuhlman, the younger Oral Roberts, and James Forbes. In the past twenty-five years this style of preaching has become increasingly important in the American church.

Despite their differences, all three of these preaching traditions assume that people will individually appropriate what is preached. Since North American Protestant ecclesiology is individualistic, atomistic, and voluntaristic, why are we preaching from a Lectionary based on an ecclesiology that is communal, organic, and sacramental? Is this a "subversive" Lectionary? Are we naively or unconsciously backing into another tradition? Or is there a cultural change that is moving Protestantism to a more communal ecclesiology?

INDIVIDUALISM OUT OF CONTROL

I think we find the Common Lectionary congenial because we are already moving toward a more communal ecclesiology, a more communal understanding of the church. My contention is that North American culture at this time reflects an individualism out of control, and that preachers are choosing to preach the Common Lectionary, in part, in response to that cultural reality.

North Americans have always been inclined to individualism. There combined on this continent the Enlightenment, Protestantism, and self-reliant frontier life—three forces impelling us toward individualism.

Habits of the Heart spells out the new revival of individualism in American life today. Following Tocqueville's analysis of American culture, made over a century ago, *Habits* describes the hallmarks of an extreme individualism in our culture: persons feel that they can rely only on themselves, that they must make a mark for themselves as individuals, that they must accumulate as much wealth as possible, and work essentially for self-centered ends. Describing Americans of 150 years ago, Tocqueville said:

> They owe nothing to any man, they expect nothing from any man; they acquire the habit of always considering themselves as standing alone, and they are apt to imagine that their whole destiny is in their own hands. . . . [This] threatens in the end to confine him entirely within the solitude of his own heart. ([1835–40] 1864, 121)

Tocqueville cited two institutions that ameliorate this narcissism and make it possible for Americans to be altruistic and live in community. One is what he called "republican politics," which I would translate as "participatory democracy," and the other is "biblical religion." Republican politics and biblical religion are the two institutions in American life, according to Tocqueville, that can draw people out of individualism into a more self-giving and interdependent stance.

When individualism in American culture gets out of control, it can become very destructive of personhood and society. Many analysts of our culture believe that this, in fact, has happened. In the 1970s, called the "me" decade, a movement began in reaction against the social involvement and caring of the sixties. This social reaction took the form of an individualistic pursuit of materialism with a vengeance. In the eighties, we have seen a new self-centeredness, described as a "new narcissism."

Our individualistic spirit is not only a danger to our own souls but also a danger to the world at large when it informs our nation's foreign policy. The U.S. response to the World Court's disapproval of our actions in Central America can be interpreted as a disavowal of our responsibility to the world community. Similarly, our unilateral invasion of Grenada seems to exemplify our impatience with the collaborative process for achieving international justice. Consider, too, the continuing arms race on which we insist, even in the face of the objections of our allies.

Yet, just as the culture seems to be going one way, the churches seem to be moving in another, with preachers turning to a more communal understanding of the Church. How are our two antidotes to individualism—"republican politics" and "biblical religion"—faring?

Politics seems to have surrendered to nostalgia and individualism. In Ronald Reagan's second inaugural address, one can hear a disavowal of the communal role of government in favor of individualism: "Every dollar the Federal Government does not take from us, every decision it does not make for us, will make our economy stronger, our lives more abundant, our future more free." Indeed, like other politicians, Reagan surrenders the altruistic social responsibilities to the churches, challenging the churches to pick up the social services that the government is dropping: "Of all the changes that have swept America the past four years, none brings greater promise than our rediscovery of the values of faith, freedom, family, work and neighborhood." Of course, no one is against faith, freedom, family, work, and neighborhood. But one hears a nostalgia for simpler times, for a less complex environment, in Reagan's appeal. To speak of family, work, and neighborhood in an era when the family is falling apart, unemployment is high, and most Americans live in great megalopolises is simply a call to nostalgia.

The unreality of such rhetoric makes political participation frustrating and unfulfilling. No wonder there are so many political dropouts in our time. Half of the population does not vote at all. We have little sense of participating in the process anymore. Whatever one thinks of Ronald Reagan, certainly the 1984 election showed that at least the voting part of the population does endorse his view of politics and reality. Politics seems to be surrendering its ability to call us to altruistic service.

In many quarters religion also seems to be going with the flow of individualism and narcissism. Consider the Reverend Terry Cole-Whittaker, or Reverend Ike, Robert Schuller, and others of their ilk. Cole-Whittaker distributes bumper stickers that reduce her theology to four words: "Prosperity, Your Divine Right!" No one is responsible for anyone else, she says, and one should not get caught up in other people's "guilt trips." "You are unlimited, you are valuable, you are worthwhile, you are abundant, you are the treasure," she declares.

Now, let me hasten to say that Cole-Whittaker is not an original. She typifies a long preaching tradition in America, a didactic school that began perhaps with Cotton Mather, who preached to enhance the self-esteem of people discouraged by "hellfire and damnation" preaching. Ralph Waldo Emerson certainly would have approved of Terry Cole-Whittaker: "Then again, do not tell me, as a good man did today, of my obligation to put all poor men in good situations. Are they my poor?" asked Emerson in the essay "Self-Reliance." And: "I tell thee, thou foolish philanthropist, that I grudge the dollar, the dime, the cent that I give to such men as do not belong to me, and to whom I do not belong." Henry Ward Beecher undoubtedly would have approved of Cole-Whittaker as well:

> The question is not what proportion of his wealth a Christian man may divert from benevolent channels for personal enjoyment through the elements of the beautiful. For, if rightly viewed and rightly used, his very elegances and luxuries will be a contribution to the public good. . . . [a] contribution to the education of society. (*Star Papers*, 1855)

And remember Russell Conwell and his famous sermon, "Acres of Diamonds": Everyone can and should get rich. "Opportunity lurks in everyone's backyard." Many other churches, along with Terry Cole-Whittaker's, have taught the gospel of political nostalgia and rampant individualism.

A NEW COMMUNAL PROTESTANTISM

However, at the same time, other churches are instinctively moving toward a communal emphasis, beginning to reclaim that part of our Christian heritage that makes us, as *Habits* puts it, "communities of memory and hope" in which we see ourselves engrafted into a larger whole wherein salvation is not simply individualistic. I think it is this perception of individualism gone berserk that has moved us, after resisting for 350 years, to be open to a lectionary and all that implies for ecclesiology. We are groping for a more corporate, communal, organic reality in the Church to balance the general culture's individualism, and to make openings for altruism and caring.[1]

Earlier, I asked if this is a "subversive" lectionary. The word *subversive* means "turning over," and this, I think, is precisely what is happening in the ecclesiology of mainline Protestantism in the United States. We are "turning over" our traditional emphasis on individualism to a more communal and corporate conception of the Church. Moreover, as Tocqueville and *Habits* help us understand, this is also a continuance of the Church's historic role, as the balance to the extreme individualism in our culture. The Church is one institution in which people can lose themselves, hear a call to a higher loyalty, and find the need to be of service to others. Canonical hermeneutics and the new understanding of biblical preaching have come just in time, and their popularity relates to this same cultural phenomenon. The importance of interpreting the Bible with concepts of "covenant identity," "memory," "anamnesis," and "dynamic analogy" are part of this new appreciation and respect for the role of community in the Church's life (Sanders 1979).

But this is disturbing as well. As we Protestants rediscover our true "catholic" heritage, are we, after 350 years of close identification between Protestantism and the culture, breaking with our culture? Are we doomed to be a peripheral minority in this culture in the future? We have had a taste of that already—the leaders of the mainline denominations and of the National Council of Churches have not been invited to the White House or consulted by national leaders during Reagan's term. We have reached the point where traditional Protestantism has so little influence in national policy-making that some churches have resorted to civil disobedience in the sanctuary movement. In another time, our church leaders would have been able to modify and redirect national foreign policy before it reached the point of civil disobedience.

Possibly we are now becoming the creative minority in this culture rather than "Volkkirche." But perhaps we may now be in a position to lead this culture out of its destructive individualism, away from the narcissism that seems to characterize the eighties, into avenues of public service and self-giving, into a world community where national self-interest is superseded by a common world responsibility. It is not clear what the future role of the Church in North America will be, but there can be little doubt that we are groping toward a new understanding of community in the Church and for the world.

FIFTEEN

The Liberal Ethic and the Spirit of Protestantism

Richard Wightman Fox

I

Max Weber's *Protestant Ethic and the Spirit of Capitalism* (1905) was not the first work to note the striking affinity between religion and worldly endeavor in Protestant America. Alexis de Tocqueville, as usual, anticipated in the 1830s what later observers like Weber spelled out: the United States was the most secular of nations, yet also the most religious. A century and a half after Tocqueville's *Democracy in America,* this paradox has again pressed itself into public consciousness.

No doubt America has become more secular since Tocqueville's time. But secularization has meant the transformation, not the elimination, of religion. Secularization contains within it, strangely enough, a certain kind of sacralization.

Today most people associate religion with conservatism. In fact there is a noticeable, though relatively unpublicized, resurgence of religious interest and commitment among liberals. Certainly it does not yet match the conservative revival of the last decade. But the liberal ethic is once again being shaped by the spirit of Protestantism.

To understand how liberalism and Protestantism are interacting today, we have to clarify how they have been linked in the past. Immediately, we confront a confusing conceptual morass, because contemporary liberalism and nineteenth-century liberalism are in a certain sense polar opposites. Nineteenth-century liberals resemble many twentieth-century conservatives. In twentieth-century America almost all conservatives have been liberals of the nineteenth-century, free-market variety. We have had very few true conservatives, very few T. S. Eliots, who embrace a hierarchical view of society and celebrate the richly textured density of a culture built upon clearly demarcated social classes.

Today's conservatives do not venerate the past, despite their sentimental appeals to tradition and authority. Like the bourgeois liberals of the nineteenth century, they bury the past in a dynamic rush to build and accumulate. The tradition they embrace is not that of Edmund Burke but that of William Graham Sumner, the late-nineteenth-century defender of laissez-faire economics. This "classical" liberalism is the movement of rational calculation, of abolishing inherited restraints, of extending the sway of an open marketplace. It is the ideology of the dynamic individual who bewails the fetters of traditional communities and relishes the risks and rewards of free exchange.

In the nineteenth century it was obvious that Protestant religion was a vital support for liberal bourgeois expansion. Weber merely offered a memorable expression of what Americans and many Europeans saw around them: the rationalized, systematized pursuit of material gain was plainly linked to the "worldly asceticism" promoted by Calvinist religion. A liberal economics seemed mandated by a religion that put the individual settling of accounts with God at the center of piety. The decontrolling of the religious market—thrusting the believer into an unmediated encounter with God—paralleled the deregulation of the economic market.

The believer resembled the buyer and seller in another respect. Contact with God might be unmediated, but it was still very mysterious; the Christian did not exercise control over the relationship. So too the individual's immersion in the ever-expanding market: he was called to participate in a web of activity whose source and logic always lay beyond his control. Survival in the market, like salvation in the heavenly city, was by faith, not just by works: faith in the willingness of distant traders to accept the obligations of rationalized, systematized exchange. Calvinist religion and liberal economics put intense pressure on the individual soul. There were no final guarantees of success. One could neither see God nor shake the invisible hand.

In the nineteenth century a split developed in liberal ranks. Not only did agnostics like John Stuart Mill decry the cultural devastation—the standardized mediocrity—produced by industrial "progress." Not only did secular reformers like Henry George condemn the displacement of hordes of workers whom the free market reduced to "wage slavery." Religious liberals in the Calvinist tradition also challenged the inequalities that the industrial world exacerbated. The Social Gospel of Washington Gladden, Richard Ely, and Walter Rauschenbusch was at the heart of the broader progressive movement that ultimately transformed the meaning of the term *liberal*.

By the early twentieth century the liberals were no longer the free-marketeers but the advocates of renewed state controls over the market. These controls were to be exercised in the interest of greater opportunity and justice for all; but in retrospect, it is plain that they were in the particular interest of the emerging professional classes, who offered their expertise as managers of the public and private spheres. An expanding state, linked to burgeoning bureaucracies in business, education, health, corrections, and other fields (including religion), may have helped the poor in some important ways, but they also helped the helpers of the poor.

It is hard to believe that as recently as the 1960s this liberal faith in expertise, in the helping professions, in the power of the state to discipline business and to promote justice, was still intact. It may appear to have been a purely secular vision, but it was not. Liberal religious leaders were key preachers of the secular faith in professional, scientific, social management. One sign of the power of that vision up until the middle of the twentieth century was its capacity to generate celebrated religious spokesmen, from Reinhold Niebuhr in the 1940s and 1950s to Martin Luther King, Jr., in the 1960s. The liberal ethic combined a potent moral sensibility—a commitment to justice and opportunity for the disadvantaged—with a faith in the power of public authority to embody that vision in law. Religious and secular perspectives overlapped and reinforced one another.

A telling indicator of the exhaustion of liberalism today is that it lacks an acknowledged theologian. In the 1980s we have liberal astronomers, liberal psychologists, liberal actors, and, in the churches, liberal activists aplenty. But there is no liberal theologian to link liberal politics to spiritual meaning or transcendent purpose. Today's liberalism lacks faith in itself and confidence in its historic mission. Liberals join conservatives in depreciating the capacity of the state to enact or guarantee justice. They increasingly tout the wonders of the entrepreneurial spirit. There is disarray in liberal ranks because the quest for justice and equality of opportunity has lost its faith in the power of public authority to discipline private authority. Even many liberals suspect that public authority is illegitimate and pernicious. President Reagan's campaign to privatize authority has met little resistance from liberals because so many of them silently share his view.

II

In the midst of this political and cultural confusion, a serious reexamination of liberalism is beginning to take place. The works of Lutheran pastor Richard John Neuhaus and Berkeley sociologist Robert Bellah are especially interesting because both try to rethink the relation between the liberal ethic and the Protestant spirit. And they attempt to reconceive the idea of public authority. Neuhaus is a significant figure in the church community: he is determined to seize the initiative from the fundamentalists and regenerate liberal politics and religion alike. Bellah is a leading academic who urges his fellow social scientists to transcend narrow professionalism and cultivate a new role as public philosophers. Neuhaus is less sure than Bellah that academics can supply moral leadership, but both writers sense that America needs a new public philosophy that is both liberal and religious. Both believe that spiritual perspectives are essential to prevent liberalism from degenerating into a manipulative program of social engineering.

To put their contributions in context, we need to look at Reinhold Niebuhr's work in the middle third of this century. The booming voice of this champion of liberal reform has not been replaced since it fell silent two decades ago. He is still the starting point for further thought about the liberal prospect. The best way to summarize what Niebuhr did for liberalism is, appropriately, to offer a paradox: he gave liberalism a new lease on life in the 1940s and 1950s by attacking the liberalism of the 1920s and 1930s. He helped liberals mobilize their forces at mid-century, but the irony is that he may also have helped in the long run to undermine liberal self-confidence. His work may have been a partial cause of the contemporay liberal confusion.

In his classic *Moral Man and Immoral Society* (1932), Niebuhr castigated the liberal progressive creed that had underlain American reform movements since the late nineteenth century. It was hopelessly naive, he thought, about the power of human beings to shape society through reason and good will. Liberals were utopians: whether religious or secular, pacifist or nonpacifist, they foolishly imagined that human community could come to resemble a Kingdom of God on earth.

Niebuhr's liberalism was still religiously based, but his religion no longer offered assurance of a future realm of love and fellowship. Instead, it offered assurance that no such community was possible. His God condemned the human hubris that sparked such a dream—yet paradoxically commanded men and women to struggle step by step to bring justice to bear in human relations. Niebuhr circumscribed the liberal quest for the just society but he did not abandon it. His liberalism was constrained by the tragic limits he detected in human nature itself: human creativity was constantly compromised by human pretensions. If Freud erased the sharp line between normality and abnormality, Niebuhr did the same for good and evil. Human beings could not help doing some evil in the course of doing good.

In the 1940s and 1950s, Niebuhr's liberalism-within-limits could still mobilize strong commitment: Adlai Stevenson, Hubert Humphrey, Arthur Schlesinger, Jr., George Kennan, and many others were buoyed by his vision. His personal charisma was a vital source of the liberal energy that persisted in the postwar world. But as Niebuhr himself retired from the social arena in the 1960s, the power and coherence of his "Christian realism" dissipated. It was less and less distinguishable from the secular realism of the forces of John F. Kennedy: moral men had to play hardball if they were going to outmaneuver the enemies of freedom around the world. This hard-bitten, worldly-wise interventionism bore a superficial resemblance to Niebuhr's tragic sense of limits. Actually it was much closer to the older liberal faith in the unbridled power of moral men to remake the world.

Niebuhr's political vision was determinedly paradoxical. On one level it was resolutely secular. There was for him no specifically Christian politics. He feared the fanaticism that all religions—including secular religions like Communism—tended to bring to the public sphere. He despised the religious zealots on the left or the right who sought to impose a particular moral program in the public realm. The quest for community, in his view, was a chimera. The social arena would always be marked by the conflict of interest groups. Discord, balance of power, a cacophony of opposing units: that was the fate of humankind in any era, but it was especially the fate of humankind in modern mass society.

Yet, Niebuhr's vision was also thoroughly religious. Not only in the sense that for him the secular world of push and pull was all one could expect in view of the biblical understanding of human nature: the fallen self inevitably sought to aggrandize itself and therefore generated a quest for power and a conflict of interest in society. Niebuhr's vision was also religious in the sense that the secular world needed always to be challenged by the biblical understanding of justice. A democratic policy had to be undergirded by the notion of a transcendent God who endowed all human beings with dignity and held them all accountable for their actions.

The point was to keep the secular realm free of religious domination and at the same time infuse it with religious perspective. Left to itself the secular world would descend into pure amorality: the warfare of all against all. A strictly secular culture might generate reform movements, but those movements would in all likelihood merely impose social peace through expert psychological management or the direct suppression of dissent.

Niebuhr wavered on the question of whether a moral consensus could be built in America. At times he implied that the secular realm would spin out of control if Americans did not come to share a collective biblical perspective. At other times he seemed satisfied that the secular society could be kept on course as long as it was subject to prophetic criticism from a minority of powerful voices like his own. On balance he seems to have felt that cultural fragmentation had progressed too far for Christians to dream again of a homogeneous world view. Rather, the Christian's job was to inject a tension into secular society, make it doubt itself, challenge its normal preference for efficiency and social peace over justice and social progress.

Niebuhr's paradoxical balancing act was an ingenious effort to reconcile the religious and the secular. The secular was to be protected from domination by the religious, and the religious was to challenge and discipline the secular. But serious questions remained. How could religious critique be embodied in society? Was it really enough to rely on prophets crying in the wilderness? He may have been led astray by the evident power and influence of his own individual voice. Prophets are not born in every generation. Could the church itself become a countervailing power? Could other kinds of fellowships emerge to challenge the assumptions of the secular? Niebuhr could avoid thinking about institutional supports for the liberal ethic because, like most progressives between the late-nineteenth and mid-twentieth centuries, he assumed that the state was the ultimate guarantor of justice.

Moreover, Niebuhr may have had too benign a view of secular society itself, too great a confidence that the conflict of interest groups—under the surveillance of government—would produce a rough approximation of justice. By banishing the quest for communal fellowship from the liberal Protestant political vision, Niebuhr may have settled for too little. He may have underestimated the individual's capacity to pursue more than his or her own self-interest. He was certainly right that few could aspire to the selflessness of the saints. But that truth may have kept him from appreciating the potential even of ordinary people to pursue a life of public virtue. If individuals do have the capacity to join together in community to debate their future, then the idea of public authority can be securely rooted.

III

Richard Neuhaus's *The Naked Public Square* (1984) and *Habits of the Heart* are essential documents in the current reassessment of liberalism, and both are forceful efforts to push beyond Niebuhr's work—though neither is explicitly framed in those terms. Neuhaus, while sharing Niebuhr's view that human society will never become an integral community, insists that America needs a new moral consensus based on biblical religion. The secular vision that Niebuhr implicitly endorsed is for Neuhaus a primary cause of the contemporary liberal impasse. The authors of *Habits* agree that America needs a new consensus, and they appear more sanguine than Neuhaus that community can actually be rebuilt. But both books insist that the key to liberal renewal is a new conception of public authority built upon a new sense of public participation. Both contend that the cultivation of public virtue informed by a religious commitment is the sine qua non of a rejuvenated liberalism.

The Naked Public Square is a potent polemic against both fundamentalism and secularism, ironic allies in a contemporary campaign to keep religious values out of the public sphere. Neuhaus rightly argues that fundamentalists—who make a great deal of religious noise in public—actually undermine the contribution religion can make to public discourse. They enter the political arena in search of power and influence, but they do so on the basis of a private vision that is not subject to public debate. They can win victories for that vision, but victories only for a particular interest group. Despite their intention, they, like the secularists, would banish religious values from public discussion, and so further weaken the moral and religious consensus that has historically buttressed American democracy.

That consensus, which Neuhaus wants to restore, did not mean agreement on particular policies, but on the fundamental principle that the nation stood under (the judgment of) God. This basic biblical perspective put the state in its proper, limited place. It insisted that public authority be dispersed among a variety of institutions, including the church. For Neuhaus this notion of plural authorities is our only protection against the modern state, which in America as elsewhere has "totalitarian" potential. We need a transcendent referent, "an agreed-upon authority that is higher than the community itself," to check the pretensions of the national authority. And to guarantee "the rights of persons, especially of the most vulnerable"—rights best protected when understood as bestowed not by the community but by a "divine" source beyond the community (1984, 76, 118).

Not only does the biblical perspective, in Neuhaus's view, offer the best kind of moral consensus for modern America. It is the only kind of moral consensus that Americans, given their "incorrigibly religious" character, could attain. Neuhaus vehemently dismisses the notion that America is a secular culture. He believes that idea was imposed on us by certain unnamed "elites who define what America is about" without bothering to "consult" anyone else. It is an idea contrary, he alleges, to "sociological fact" (1984, 103, 113).

But Neuhaus misses the boat here. He himself shows repeatedly that much religion in modern America has become a therapeutic service industry. Much fundamentalist religion, he notes, "disturbs none of the presuppositions of a secular culture, contenting itself with offering religiously coated pills for the promotion of health and happiness." And mainline churches have themselves turned increasingly into psychological and social agencies: "'meeting the needs' of individuals for spiritual and other satisfactions." Therapeutic religion is a basic component of a secularized society. The mere fact that most people practice a religion does not prove that they are religious in any strict sense or that their culture is nonsecular (1984, 45, 142).

By forgetting his own trenchant observations and insisting that America is in fact "incorrigibly religious," Neuhaus manages to avoid the key problem: how to develop a moral consensus based on biblical wisdom when American culture is so deeply infused with a therapeutic sensibility. How can the idea of a transcendent referent be made persuasive when even the churches have reduced salvation to "health and happiness" and God to a beaming, glad-handing spiritual consultant? Neuhaus imagines that the prime obstacles to liberal renewal are the state and the knowledge elites who supposedly conspire to label America a secular society. But his own book suggests that the problem lies much deeper: in an embedded ideology of self-absorption that has dominated American culture for several generations.

Astonishingly, Neuhaus never suspects that the business community in general and the advertising industry, in particular, have played any part in undermining the idea of transcendent authority. Yet those elites have plainly contributed over the last century to the creation of a secular-religious society in which the pursuit of the good life gradually displaced the pursuit of eternal life. Inherited ideals such as self-sacrifice, personal responsibility, and long-range commitment faded from consciousness as newer ideals took root: living for the moment, getting in touch with one's feelings, learning to be nonjudgmental about other people's "lifestyles."

It is an article of faith for Neuhaus that only religion can save us from certain disaster—the disaster of creeping totalitarianism, of an aggrandizing state that will conquer and occupy the public square if religion does not root itself there. For "there are no areligious moral traditions of public, or at least of democratic, force in American life" (1984, 154). But just as he conceives the problem too narrowly—how to defend a religious culture against the state and bring a religious notion of virtue back to the public sphere—he has too narrow a conception of the American cultural tradition.

As the authors of *Habits of the Heart* show, America possesses, in addition to the biblical legacy, a secular inheritance of public, democratic force: the republican tradition. In the republican vision, freedom is to be found not in the pursuit of self-interest, but in the collective activity of the polis. Liberty is conceived not as doing one's own thing in isolation, but as participation with others in a common task. Liberty means combining self-expression and self-limitation. Individual fulfillment is a function of group engagement. The republican view reinforces the modern liberal Protestant conviction that acquisitiveness needs to be disciplined, brought under communal control.

Habits of the Heart is a stirring plea for a new liberal ethic based on these two older traditions, religious and secular. The authors of *Habits*, unlike Neuhaus, concede that America is a secular society. It is secular with a vengeance: so thoroughly transformed by therapeutic ideals that it has forgotten not only its biblical heritage but its republican vision as well. When middle-class Americans speak in interviews about their deepest feelings or their ultimate goals, they invariably use the language either of utilitarian individualism (every person for himself in the battle to get ahead) or of expressive individualism (to each person his own "growth," "value system," or "lifestyle"). The dominant language of individualism rules out a conception of shared communal values.

Yet the authors of *Habits* do not despair, any more than Neuhaus. Neuhaus urges Americans to reject the erroneous dogma that theirs is a secular culture: Don't let the intellectuals or the media mislabel you, take back your true identity as a religious people. *Habits* calls on Americans to realize that their behavior is better than their rhetoric. Americans often do live communal lives, making long-term commitments to family and friends, subordinating self-interest to the needs of others, and working in groups for social justice or political change. The problem lies in language, not in action or in social or political institutions. There is no structural impediment to recovering the biblical and republican traditions. Communal discourse can readily displace the currently dominant rhetoric of individualism.

The problem here is whether one language can be substituted for another quite so easily. Just as Neuhaus shows us a degenerated Protestant religion and then assures us we are still a genuinely religious nation, the authors of *Habits* depict a deeply disordered culture and then tell us not to worry: inherited resources lie close at hand, reach out and put them to use. The implicit message resembles Neuhaus's: the American people are better than they think they are (or, in Neuhaus's version, than their self-appointed elites think they are). But in each case the initial diagnosis of cultural disarray seems more persuasive than the final act of reassurance.

The determined hopefulness of *Habits of the Heart* might have been less arbitrary had the authors directly confronted—and answered—the cultural pessimism of two of the book's significant precursors: Alasdair MacIntyre's *After Virtue* (1981), which is the immediate inspiration for much of the argument, and Robert Lynd and Helen Lynd's *Middletown* (1929) and *Middletown in Transition* (1937). The Lynds detected in Muncie an ominous prospect: new cultural forces, from national advertising and movies to religious and civic boosterism, had jeopardized and perhaps irreversibly undermined the locally based, democratic fellowship of nineteenth-century northern Protestant culture. The survival of "languages" may not matter a great deal if their cultural supports have crumbled.

In view of *Habits'* disdain for "narrowly professional social science," which exhibits "little or no sense of history" and fails to provide a "narrative" of our collective experience, it is odd that the authors do not say more about the prehistory of this kind of analysis. The Lynds, along with David Riesman's pivotal *The Lonely Crowd* (1950), are mentioned but receive only the most cursory attention. Much more attention goes to Tocqueville, but even here the treatment ought to have been pressed further. *Habits* emphasizes the Frenchman's attack on privacy—his concern for the survival of civic life—and minimizes his simultaneous concern for the survival of individual excellence and even eccentricity in the face of communal conformity.

Tocqueville was troubled, especially in his *Recollections* after the revolution of 1848, by the tragic possibility that individualism was fundamentally at odds with communalism. *Habits* implicitly follows Rousseau, Durkheim, and the American liberal Protestant tradition in the conviction that there is in principle no obstacle to individual fulfillment in community. That belief is certainly defensible, but it needs to be defended— against the dissenting judgment of much nineteenth- and twentieth-century thought, from Dostoevski and Nietzsche to Weber and Freud.

These criticisms of *Habits* cannot detract from the book's great achievement: its very telling analysis of the spread of the therapeutic mentality. It is the pointedness of that very analysis that undercuts the authors' desire to lead their readers out of the wasteland. They show that we make a mistake if we view America as President Carter did in his famous gloom-and-doom "narcissism" speech: a hedonistic culture devoted to things, to buying, to relaxation. The problem goes deeper; it cannot be solved by renouncing new possessions or making leisure more purposive.

A therapeutic society is not best understood in terms of pleasure seeking or mass buying. It is more basically a culture of self-absorption, of limitless "growth": growth in one's own experience of novel lifestyles, growth in one's tolerance for alternative lifestyles, growth in one's capacity to tap one's current feelings. The heart of the therapeutic ethic is nonjudgmental openness. Marriage and friendship, as *Habits* shows, have largely succumbed to therapeutic redefinition: they have become "communication," letting one's spouse or friend be his or her own "person."

This redefinition may have borne important fruit in freeing women from unreasonable constraints within the family. But the cost has been heavy: a loosening of bonds that used to protect individuals from the tyranny of momentary feelings. The older model of relationships assumed the possibility of conflict and guilt: conflict when one partner failed to adhere to inherited standards of value, guilt when one realized one had breached those standards. It is conflict and guilt that a therapeutic sensibility cannot stomach. Self-acceptance, acceptance of the other, no-fault relationships: these become the central moral norms.

A therapeutic culture cannot tolerate transcendent values because those values present artificial barriers to individual growth. Individual feelings become the measure of value. As *Habits* shows, following MacIntyre, that is a fragile foundation for morality. It undercuts not only long-range commitments—which traditionally one is obliged to maintain even when one doesn't feel like it—but also a stable sense of selfhood. The great strength of *Habits of the Heart* is its clear understanding that communal commitment and individual fulfillment rise or fall together. There is no private virtue that does not presuppose a public virtue, and vice versa. The key threat to individual freedom in modern society is not the state, as classical liberalism (and to a large degree Richard Neuhaus) supposes, but the atrophy of communal life. Rebuilding the liberal ethic requires drawing on both the biblical and republican conceptions of freedom—freedom as responsibility, as adherence to values that are grounded not just in the self but in communal tradition. A new liberal politics can emerge only when new communal bonds have been forged. Public authority has to be legitimated anew.

IV

The diagnosis of cultural disarray presented in *The Naked Public Square* and *Habits of the Heart* brings one back to the perspective of Reinhold Niebuhr. In the face of a deep-seated therapeutic culture, it seems utopian to dream of a new moral consensus—whether based on religion alone or on religious and secular traditions. It seems more reasonable to try to keep those traditions alive as critical tools with which to keep the culture (not just the state) under judgment. Neuhaus and the authors of *Habits* are themselves significant critical voices. They can certainly play a role in building local communities within which older values—the long-term pursuit of justice, the long-term pursuit of virtue—are cultivated. But Niebuhr's "realism" provides important protection against the disappointment liberals will inevitably experience in trying to replenish the reservoir of public morality.

Not only are individuals, in Niebuhr's view, prone to subvert communal bodies for selfish ends. Not only are groups prone to aggrandize themselves at the expense of other groups. Not only, that is, are even the most cooperative human activities always shot through with conflict and deceit. The assumption that there is a fundamental fit or affinity between individual and community—an assumption that informs *Habits* in particular, just as it informs the entire republican tradition—is difficult to sustain. No conceivable institutional changes can erase the will to power that individuals and communities seem inevitably to display.

But Niebuhr's view does not consign us to throwing up our hands. It asks us above all not to misread the signs of the times. It asks us not to ignore that there are powerful institutions—corporations, advertising, the media—which have a vested interest in keeping Americans in the vanguard of "experience," on the cutting edge of "lifestyle." Communal commitments are under constant attack: not by intellectuals or counter-cultures, as conservatives imagine, but by corporate capitalism itself. The

Niebuhr of *Moral Man and Immoral Society* managed to keep both the inveterate human will-to-power and the intractable (though in principle reformable) institutional sources of injustice firmly in view—without forgetting that citizens could still act responsibly to seek justice.

Niebuhr's position would have been stronger had he developed a theory of public virtue, a task that both Neuhaus and the authors of *Habits* agree is the first order of business for liberals today. After the 1930s, Niebuhr joined the other liberals of his generation in tending to reduce the ideal of justice to the ideal of equalizing incomes and standards of living. On the whole he did not address the more basic problem, which *Habits* in particular poses with force: how to equalize access to the means of knowledge, to the means of decision making, to the means of communally grounded fulfillment.

But the positions of *Habits* and Neuhaus would be stronger if they were to emphasize, with Niebuhr, that rooting traditional values securely in the modern era will require a very substantial social, cultural, and political transformation. There is no shortcut to such a transformation. Indeed, its starting point must be the same cultivation of public virtue that the authors of *Habits* and Neuhaus seek, and that is a very long-range prospect. But as Niebuhr himself liked to observe, "Nothing that is worth doing can be achieved in one generation." In this instance his counsel of patience is plainly on the mark.

SIXTEEN

A Christian Critique
of Christian America

Stanley Hauerwas

SETTING THE AGENDA: A REPORT ON A CONVERSATION

At a conference on narrative and virtue I had an encounter with a philosopher, which raised the problem with which I wish to deal. My philosophical counterpart is a Peircian and a committed Jew. In his paper he had argued that most of the rational paradigms accepted by contemporary philosophy cannot make sense of Judaism. We began by exchanging views about why current ethical theory seems so committed to foundationalist epistemological assumptions. We shared a sympathy with anti-foundationalist arguments, though neither of us wanted to give up the possibility of some modest realist epistemology. We were also equally critical of liberal political theory and in particular the ahistorical character of its methodology. Then our conversation took a turn for which I was unprepared. It went something like this:

Philosopher. Do you support prayer in the public schools?

Theologian. No, I do not because I do not want the state sponsoring my faith.

Philosopher. That is not the real reason. You are just afraid to be for anything that Jerry Falwell is for. You really are a liberal in spite of your doubts about liberalism's philosophical adequacy.

Theologian. That is not fair. I did not say I was against school prayer because I think such prayer is coercive, though I think such considerations are not unimportant, but because state-sponsored prayer cannot help but give the impression that the state is friendly toward religion. Moreover, prayers, insofar as they can pass muster in a religiously pluralistic context, are so anemic that they cannot help

250

but give a distorted view of God. So I am against school prayer not because it is against the tenets of liberalism but because it is a theological scandal.

Philosopher. That is not good enough. Christians typically do not give a damn about the Jews. You Christians want to create a civilization and society and then walk away from it when the going gets a little tough. Of course the prayers sponsored by public authorities are degraded but they still remind people that they are creatures. A vague god prayed to vaguely is better than no god or prayer at all. Otherwise we face the possibility of a neopagan culture for which liberal procedural rules of fair play will be no match.

Theologian. I am a bit surprised to hear you argue this way. After all, Christians have persecuted and killed Jews with as much enthusiasm as anyone. I would think you would feel safer in a secular culture than one that is quasi-Christian. Indeed has that not been the dominant social strategy of Jews since the Enlightenment? The way to secure protection from the Christians is to create and support liberal societies where religion is relegated to the private sphere and thus becomes unavailable for public policy directed against the Jews or those of any other religious faith.

Philosopher. I do not deny that is the strategy of many Jews, but I think this century has shown it to be a decisive failure. Pagan societies kill us with an abandon that Christians can never muster. Christianity, even in a degraded form, at least has material convictions that can make the persecution and killing of Jews problematic. Paganism has no such convictions, so I will take my chances with the Christians and their societies. After all, we Jews do not ask for much. We just do not want you to kill our children. Living in quasi-Christian societies means we have to put up with a lot of inconvenience and prejudice—Christmas as a school holiday—but we Jews have long known how to handle that. We flourish under a little prejudice. What we cannot stand is the false tolerance of liberalism that relegates us to the arena of being just one religion among others.

Theologian. So if I understand you rightly, you are suggesting that you want me as a Christian to support school prayer, even if such prayers are but forms of degraded Christian religiosity, because at least that continues to underwrite the assumption that we are a "religious" society. Such an

	assumption allows an appeal to a higher standard of jus-tice that makes the survival of the Jewish people more likely.
Philosopher.	That is about right. You Christians have to take responsi-bility for what you have done. You created a civilization based on belief in God and it is your responsibility to con-tinue to support that civilization.
Theologian.	But you know that such a social strategy cannot but lead to the continued degradation of Christianity. The more Christians try to make Christianity a philosophy sufficient to sustain a society, especially a liberal society, the more we must distort or explain away our fundamental beliefs. Therefore in the name of sustaining a civilization, Chris-tians increasingly undercut the ability of the church to take a critical stance toward this society. Even when the church acts as a critic in such a context, it cannot be more than a friendly critic since it has a stake in maintaining the basic structure of society.
Philosopher.	Why should that bother me? Christians have always been willing in the past to degrade their convictions to attain social and political power (of course, always in order that they might "do good"). Why should they start worrying about being degraded now? On that score it seems a little late. For the church to worry about being pure is about as realistic as for Madonna·to worry about being a virgin. It is just too late. So if you care about the Jews you ought to support school prayer.

Our conversation did not end at this point, but it is enough for my purposes. Even though most of what my philosopher friend has to say is right, for theological reasons I still cannot support school prayer. That I cannot puts me at odds with the social strategy of many Christians, both liberal and conservative, in America. In the next section I will try to ex-plain why this is the case. Then I will be prepared to suggest what a more radical Christian critique of America entails both in terms of its logic and as a political strategy.

LIBERAL CHRISTIANITY AND AMERICAN DEMOCRACY, OR WHY JERRY FALWELL IS SUCH A PAIN

Since the turn of the century, a dominant theme in Christian social ethics has been the Christian's responsibility for societal affairs. Time and time again it is argued that faith and action cannot be separated. Religious convictions cannot be relegated to one sphere of our lives and social and political activities to another. Since the faith of Christians is a faith that does justice, there is no way we can avoid political activity. Whether the political realm is viewed Lutheran-like as a realm of lesser evil or more Calvinistically as the arena of the mediocre good, Christians cannot avoid involvement in the political process. That is especially the case in a democratic society in which the actions of individual citizens can make a difference.

Armed with these presuppositions, Christians in the "mainstream" denominations attacked those Christians who maintained no particular social or political responsibilities. This position, they argued, pietistically relegates salvation to the individual's relation to God and thus betrays the essential Christian claim that God is Lord of all creation. It must be remembered that Jesus came preaching a Kingdom that makes it impossible for his followers to be indifferent to injustices in the world. On these grounds mainstream churches, such as those that constitute the National Council of Churches, urged Baptists and other pietistic Christians to join them in the political struggle to make this a more just society. As is often pointed out, not to take a political stand in the name of being Christian in fact is to take a political stand.

Pietists, in defense of their position, sometimes responded by appealing not to their theological convictions but instead to what they considered the normative commitments of American society—namely, that the Constitution has erected a "wall of separation between church and state." In the name of maintaining freedom of religion, the church claims no competency in matters political. The difficulty with this position, however, is that it attributes a perspective to the Constitution that simply is not there. Neither the free-exercise clause nor the nonestablishment clause prohibits Christians, either as organized in churches or as individuals, from seeking to influence their society or government. To the extent the free-church tradition allows itself to be so excluded from the public arena, moreover, it underwrites an individualistic account of Christianity that is antithetical to its very nature.

Such was the state of the debate among Christians until recently. Everything changed when the message finally got across to the pietistic Baptists. They have become politically active, seeking to influence our society and government to support causes in the name of making this a better society. Jerry Falwell is convinced, just like Martin Luther King, Jr., that Christians cannot abandon the political realm in their desire for justice. They must seek through constitutionally guaranteed means to influence our political representatives to prevent abortion, to support democratic regimes around the world, to support Israel, to provide support for the family, and so on.

This is a triumph for mainstream Christianity, but it is not a victory being celebrated. To the mainstream's dismay, the once politically inac-

tive pietists are supporting the "wrong" causes! The temptation is to try
to defeat this new political activism by using the slogans of the past—
religion and politics do not mix, or one should not try to force religious
views on anyone through public policy—but this is to go against the position the mainstream has been arguing for years.

In order to understand how American Protestantism has reached this
point, we need to review some aspects of the history of Christianity in
America. I am not going to rehearse the story of Puritan America or engage in the debate about how "Christian" America has been.[1] While such
studies and questions are interesting and may still have some normative
importance, they are not crucial for helping us understand why Falwell
presents such a challenge to mainstream Christianity. Rather, we need to
appreciate why Christian ethicists in America, especially since the nineteenth century, have assumed that Christianity and democracy are inte-
grally related.

They have done so because America stands as the great experiment in
what Max Stackhouse has identified as "constructive Protestantism."
Stackhouse notes that in *The Social Teaching of the Christian Churches* (1911),
Ernst Troeltsch argues that only two major Christian social philosophies
have ever been developed—the Catholic and the Calvinist. Yet each of
these as social philosophies no longer seems viable:

> The vision of an organic, hierarchical order sanctified by objectified means
> of grace, and that of an established theocracy of elect saints who are justi-
> fied by grace through faith, must both be judged as no longer live options
> for social reconstruction. This is not to suggest that these visions do not still
> hold power. . . . But this *is* to suggest that these two forms of "Christen-
> dom" have ended—or rather, have played their part and now must yield
> the stage after their immeasurable contribution to the drama of Christian-
> ity in modern culture. (Stackhouse 1968, 21)

According to Stackhouse, the crucial question is whether Christianity
can develop another social philosophy. If it cannot, it would seem that
the social ethical power of Christianity is at an end. Stackhouse argues
that American Christianity has in fact developed a third option: "conciliar denominationalism." He sees the character of this new form of social
philosophy prefigured in the work of Walter Rauschenbusch, who held
together two conflicting motifs, sectarianism and Christendom, that constitute the unique blend of conciliar denominationalism:

> On the one hand, Rauschenbusch came from an evangelical background,
> from which he gained a sense of intense and explicit faith that could only
> be held by fully committed members. On the other hand, Rauschenbusch
> lived in the age of lingering hope for a catholic "Christian culture" and in
> an age that, especially through the developing social sciences, saw the legiti-
> macy of secular realms. He, like the developing conciliar denominations,

saw the necessity of the select body of believers anticipating the Kingdom in word and deed in good sectarian fashion, and of taking the world seriously on its own terms, as did all visions of Christendom. These motifs conspire in his thought to produce a vision of a revolutionized responsible society for which a socially understood gospel is the catalyst. (Stackhouse 1968, 22–23)

As the champion of liberal Christianity, Rauschenbusch could speak straightforwardly of the need to "christianize" social orders. "It is not enough to christianize individuals; we must christianize societies, organizations, nations, for they too have a life of their own which may be made better or worse" (Rauschenbusch 1968, 102). On that basis he thought it quite possible to speak of saved and unsaved organizations:

> The one is under the law of Christ, the other under the law of mammon. The one is democratic and the other autocratic. Whenever capitalism has invaded a new country or industry, there has been a speeding up in labor and in the production of wealth, but always with a trail of human misery, discontent, bitterness, and demoralization. When cooperation has invaded a country there has been increased thrift, education, and neighborly feeling, and there has been no trail of concomitant evil and no cries of protest. (Rauschenbusch 1917, 112–13)

The difference between saved and unsaved social orders, from Rauschenbusch's perspective, is quite simple—saved social orders and institutions are democratic. As he says,

> the social sciences confirm the correctness of Christ's protest against the stratification of society in ranks and classes. What is the general tendency toward democracy and the gradual abolition of hereditary privileges but history's assent to the revolutionary dogmas of Christ? (Rauschenbusch 1968, 199)

The Kingdom of God is not a concept or ideal for Rauschenbusch; it is a historical force at work in humanity. The way it ultimately works out, moreover, is in the form of democracy. As he puts it, "Where religion and intellect combine, the foundation is laid for political democracy" (Rauschenbusch 1917, 165).

If, as Stackhouse suggests, America is the great experiment in "constructive Protestantism," it seems what is Christian about that construction is democracy.[2] For Rauschenbusch is hardly an isolated figure who claims a close interrelation between Christianity and democracy. As Jan Dawson has recently argued, at the turn of this century there developed a "faith in the spiritual oneness of Christianity and democracy, based on the democratic theology of Christianity and concerned primarily with the survival of Christianity in troubled modern democracies" (Dawson 1985, 47). To support democracy became a means of supporting Christianity, and vice versa.

Dawson quotes an article by Lyman Abbott, successor to Henry Ward Beecher, published in the liberal Christian paper *Outlook* in 1906, to the effect that: "Democracy is not merely a political theory, it is not merely a social opinion; it is a profound religious faith. . . . To him who holds it, this one fundamental faith in the Fatherhood of God and in the universal brotherhood of man is the essence of democracy" (1985, 48). If democracy was seen as the institutionalized form of Christianity, it was no less true that democracy was dependent on religion to survive. Thus in 1907 Robert Ashworth wrote in the *Chicago Divinity School Journal:* "the fate of the democratic movement rests ultimately upon religion. Religion is essential to democracy, and is, indeed, its foundation. It is based upon the New Testament principle of the equal value of every soul in the sight of the Divine Father" (cited in Dawson 1985, 48).

A direct theological appeal in support of democracy becomes more muted as Christian thinkers are increasingly aware of the religious and social pluralism of America, but that does not lessen their enthusiasm for democracy as that form of society and government that best institutionalizes Christian social philosophy. Reinhold Niebuhr is certainly a case in point. Vicious in his critique of the theological and social optimism of the "social gospels" in its defense of democracy, he never questioned the assumption that democracy was the most appropriate form of society and government for Christians. What was needed, according to Niebuhr, was a more adequate basis for democracy in a realistic account of human nature. Such an account was to be found primarily in:

> [the] Christian view of human nature [that] is more adequate for the development of a democratic society than either the optimism with which democracy has become historically associated or the moral cynicism which inclines human communities to tyrannical political strategies. (Niebuhr 1944, xiii)[3]

In effect, from Rauschenbusch to the present, Christian social ethics has had as its primary agenda to show why American democracy possesses distinctive religious status. The primary subject of Christian ethics in America has been America (see Hauerwas 1985, 23–50). As exemplified in the work of John Courtney Murray, this has even become the current project for Roman Catholic social ethics. Murray's task was to make America amenable to Catholic social theory by interpreting the separation of church and state as a confession by the state of its incompetence in matters of religion, and to make Catholics amenable to America by showing that Catholics can enthusiastically support democracy as an imaginative solution to the problem of religious pluralism (see Murray 1953a, 1953b, 1960). His even stronger argument was that American democracy, whose political substance consists in an order of rights antecedent to the state (1960, 308), can be sustained only by the kind of natural law theory carried by Catholicism in contrast to the individualism of Locke and Hobbes.[4]

It is against this background that one must understand and appreciate the work of Richard Neuhaus. In his much publicized book, *The Naked Public Square: Religion and Democracy in America* (1984), Neuhaus argues that we are facing a crisis in our society. Because religious discourse has increasingly been excluded from our public life, he fears a moral vacuum has been created. This vacuum threatens constantly to be filled by totalitarianism, as the isolation of the individual from mediating structures gives us little power to stand against the omnivorous appetite of the bureaucratic state.[5] The only way out of this predicament is to mend

> [the] rupture between public policy and moral sentiment. But the only moral sentiment of public effect is the sentiment that is embodied in and reinforced by living tradition. There are no a-religious moral traditions of public, or at least of democratic, force in American life. This is not to say that morality must be embodied in religion nor that the whole of religion is morality. It is to say that among the American people, religion and morality are conjoined. Religion in our popular life is the morality-bearing part of culture, and in that sense the heart of culture. (Neuhaus 1984, 154)

From this perspective Neuhaus is appreciative of the Moral Majority. For in spite of the crudeness with which they often put their position, they at least raise the issue of the public value of religion that at one time was the agenda of political liberals. Rather than condemning the Moral Majority, Neuhaus seeks to help them enter the public debate by basing their appeals on principles that are accessible to the public:

> Publicly assertive religious forces will have to learn that the remedy for the naked public square is not naked religion in public. They will have to develop a mediating language by which ultimate truths can be related to the penultimate and prepenultimate questions of political and legal content. In our several traditions there are rich conceptual resources for the development of such a mediating language—whether concepts be called natural law, common grace, general revelation, or the order of creation. Such a civil engagement of secular and religious forces could produce a new public philosophy to sustain this American experiment in liberal democracy. The result may not be that we would agree with one another. Indeed there may be more disagreement. But at least we would know what we are disagreeing about, namely, different accounts of the transcendent good by which we might order our life together. Contra Justice Blackmun and legions of others, democracy is not served by evading the question of the good. Democracy becomes a political community worthy of moral actors only when we engage the question of the good. (1985, 14–15)[6]

Neuhaus challenges mainline Protestant liberalism to live up to its commitment to sustain democracy as the socially specific form that Christianity should take. As he puts it, "the main line of the mainline story was confidence and hope regarding the Americanizing of Christianity and the Christianizing of America" (1984, 220).[7] Indeed, he argues that in spite of their fervor for disestablishing Christianity in America, most liberals remain committed to "Christianizing" the social order. Only the synonyms for *Christianize* today "include terms such as justice, equality, and sustainability" (Neuhaus 1984, 230).[8]

This helps explain the enthusiasm for the work of John Rawls among those working in Christian ethics. Harlan Beckley puts the matter well as he notes that the emergence of a politically powerful Christian right has made vivid a dilemma that Christian ethics has still to resolve:

> The dilemma is: How can an evaluation of the distribution of rights, duties, benefits, and burdens which society necessarily imposes upon all of its citizens be faithful to Christian beliefs without forcing others to accept the distinctive moral implications of beliefs they do not and should not be required to share? (1985, 210–11)

According to Beckley: "This dilemma can only be resolved if the justification for principles of justice is founded upon general beliefs and values that others hold, or can be reasonably expected to hold, and which Christians can affirm on the basis of their distinctive beliefs" (1985, 212). In order to accomplish this resolution Beckley argues "that the distinctively Christian moral ideal of love obligates those who adhere to it to embrace the beliefs which undergird John Rawls' idea of justice as fairness" (ibid.). Rawls thus becomes the language of common grace that continues the project of Christianizing America.

Of course there are disagreements among Christian ethicists on this score. Neuhaus, for example, thinks Rawls's theory threatens to destroy "the individual by depriving him of all those personal particularities that are the essence of being an individual" (1984, 258). As a result, Rawls's account is ahistorical in contradistinction to the "Judeo-Christian tradition" which is "premised upon the concept of real history, real change, happening in an incomplete universe that is still awaiting its promised fulfillment" (1984, 258).[9] What is needed, according to Neuhaus, is a recovery of some substantive account of the goods that make a good society possible through attending to the concrete desires of real people who are not required to leave their religious convictions behind when they participate in the public arena.

This same set of issues is at the center of *Habits of the Heart*. The critique of individualism that is the hallmark of this work is but part of a larger agenda that is in essential continuity with the hope to Christianize America. As the authors suggest, in spite of our individualism,

> we have never been, and still are not, a collection of private individuals who, except for a conscious contract to create a minimal government, have nothing in common. Our lives make sense in a thousand ways, most of

which we are unaware of, because of traditions that are centuries, if not millennia, old. It is these traditions that help us to know that it does make a difference who we are and how we treat one another. . . . But if we owe the meaning of our lives to biblical and republican traditions of which we seldom consciously think, is there not the danger that the erosion of these traditions may eventually deprive us of that meaning altogether? . . . We would argue that if we are ever to enter that new world that so far has been powerless to be born, it will be through reversing modernity's tendency to obliterate all previous culture. We need to learn again from the cultural riches of the human species and to reappropriate and revitalize those riches so that they can speak to our condition today. (*H*, 282—83)[10]

This sounds very much like a call for reconstituting Christian America!

By placing *Habits of the Heart* within this tradition, I do not mean to disparage the genuine contribution the authors of that book have made. As James L. Peacock points out, the book is a cultural event and has obviously struck a chord in the hearts of many. It may even be, as Bernard Yack and Jeffrey Stout suggest, that the authors of *Habits* read into the interviews they report a diagnosis arrived at prior to the interview. Yet, the authors clearly have their hand on the pulse of many. In that respect the criticism of Stout and Yack is friendly criticism that encourages a modest recovery of the practices the authors of *Habits* also want.

Moreover, I believe the authors of *Habits* are right to argue that often the habits of the American people are better than they can say; or more strongly, the language dominant in our society postively distorts people's experience insofar as they are led to describe their familial and community loyalties as "just their thing." Yet I am not convinced that the authors' call for a return to the republican and biblical languages would remedy that state of affairs. It is by no means clear that those languages, even if they are recoverable or operative, are compatible. The virtues of humility and patience so characteristic of Scripture are not prominent in republican rhetoric.

In this respect there is a hint in *Habits of the Heart* of a functional account of religion that I suspect is antithetical to its authors' profoundest convictions. To suggest that religious traditions provide an alternative to the destructiveness of utilitarian individualism implies that the church is a good because it produces good results for the wider society. Yet the church has just as often challenged societies, which on their own terms could be considered moderately good and stable, because Christians care more about truth than results. From a theological perspective it is not sufficient to suggest that for the church to be an "effective public church" it will need dimensions of church, sect, and mystical types. What is needed is for the church to be faithful to God irrespective of whether such faithfulness works out well for the American public ethos. The use of a common lectionary may well, as J. Irwin Trotter suggests, challenge the individualism that so pervades our churches. But as he also notes, what is at stake for the church is the reclaiming of the Christological focus of our worship. The recovery of such a focus may challenge as much as support a recovery of political community.

To pursue this matter further or to highlight the disagreements among Neuhaus, Beckley, *Habits,* and Falwell, while interesting, is not crucial for my case. Rather, I have attempted to show that the reason Falwell is such a challenge to the Christian mainstream in America is not because he is so different from them, but because he has basically accepted their agenda.[11] The Christian right and the Christian left do not disagree about the religious status of the American experiment. They just disagree about what language or political theory will allow them to accomplish their common goal of making American democracy as close as possible to a manifestation of God's kingdom.

WHAT A CHRISTIAN CRITIQUE OF CHRISTIAN AMERICA SHOULD LOOK LIKE

For most Christians in America, from the nominal Christian, the committed social activist, to the theologian, it is almost unthinkable to theorize outside the tradition I have just sketched. Yet I refuse to support prayer in school because I am outside that tradition. Outside, because I do not believe that the universalism intrinsic to the Christian faith is carried by the culture of the West, but instead is to be found first and foremost in the church (see Hauerwas 1981, 1983, 1987). From this perspective, something has already gone wrong when Christians think they can ask, "What is the best form of society or government?" (Yoder 1984, 154).[12] This question assumes that Christians should or do have social and political power so they can determine the ethos of society. That this assumption has long been with us does nothing to confirm its truth.

That assumption, in short, is the heritage of what John Howard Yoder has called "the Constantinian sources of Western social ethics." And it is an assumption shared by Christians and non-Christians alike: the very logic of most contemporary philosophical accounts of ethics and social theory accept its essential rightness, but do so in secular terms. By calling our attention to Constantine, Yoder has no stake in determining the sincerity of Constantine's conversion or whether it was exactly at that time that a decisive shift in Christian assumptions took place. Rather, Constantine is the symbol of the decisive shift in the logic of moral argument when Christians ceased being a minority and accepted Caesar as a member of the church. It is that logic we must understand if we are to make a genuine Christian critique of Christian America.

The most obvious consequence of the change occasioned by Constantine, according to Yoder, is the composition of the church. Prior to Constantine, Christians had been a minority that required some degree of adherence. After Constantine, everyone is a member. It now takes conviction to be a pagan. As a result, Christians are now forced to develop a doctrine of the "true church" that remains invisible (Yoder 1984, 136).[13]

This shift is of crucial importance for how ethics is now understood. Prior to the time of Constantine, Christian belief in God's rule of the world was a matter of faith. However, with Constantine, providence is no longer an object of faith. God's governance of the world is now thought to be empirically evident in the person of the Christian ruler. The new ecclesiology and eschatology required ethics to change: "because one must aim one's behavior at strengthening the regime, and because the ruler himself must have very soon some approbation and perhaps some guidance as he does things the earlier church would have perhaps disapproved" (Yoder 1984, 137). As a result, the distinctive character of Christian life is now primarily identified with inwardness, since everyone by definition is already Christian.

Once Christianity becomes dominant, moreover, it is now thought that moral discourse must be capable of directing the behavior of anyone. Servanthood and love of enemy, contentment and monogamy cannot be expected of everyone. So a duality develops in ethics between "evangelical counsels" for the motivated and "precepts" for everyone else. Perhaps even a more significant change is the assumption that the decisive ethical question becomes:

> What would happen if everyone did it? If everyone gave their wealth away what would we do for capital? If everyone loved their enemies who would ward off the communists? This argument could be met on other levels, but here the only point is to observe that such reasoning would have been preposterous in the early church and remains ludicrous wherever committed Christians accept realistically their minority status. Far more fitting than "What if everybody did it" would be its inverse, "What if nobody else acted like a Christian and we did?" (Yoder 1984, 139)[14]

With this new universalism comes an increasing need to test moral discourse by its effectiveness. Once the course of history is thought to be empirically discernible, and the prosperity of our regime is the measure of the good, efficacy becomes a decisive test for the moral rightness of our action. Self-sacrifice that is not tied to some long-term account of results becomes irrational. This is particularly important in assessing the validity of violence and the Christian's participation in war.

What is important about Yoder's depiction of the change in moral logic occasioned by the Constantinian turn is that the effects he describes are still with us. With the Renaissance and Reformation, "Christendom" is replaced by the nation-state. Christians, however, did not respond to this change by maintaining the cosmopolitanism of the Holy Roman Empire, but rather now maintained that Christian societies could wage war on one another in the name of preserving their Christian culture. With the Enlightenment, the link between church and state is broken, but the moral identification of Christians with the state remains strong. This is especially the case in America, where

> once the separation of church and state is seen as theologically desirable, a society where this separation is achieved is not a pagan society but a nation structured according to the will of God. For nearly two centuries, in fact, the language of American public discourse was not only religious, not only Christian, but specifically Protestant. Moral identification of church with nation remains despite institutional separation. In fact, forms of institutional interlocking develop which partly deny the theory of separation [chaplaincies, tax exemptions]. (Yoder 1984, 142)

If there is to be a genuine Christian critique of Christian America, I am convinced that this habit of thought, which Yoder calls Constantinianism, must be given up. Otherwise we Christians remain caught in the same habits of thought and behavior that implicitly or explicitly assume that insofar as America is a democracy it is Christian. As a result, Christians lose exactly the skills necessary to see how deeply they have been compromised by the assumption that their task is to rule, if not the government, at least the ethos of America. That is why Christian social strategy in America continues to be caught in a fateful ambiguity—namely, Christians claim that Christianity, or at least religion, should be more present in public life—yet they want to make government itself religiously neutral. The history of the Supreme Court decisions on church-state issues should be enough to convince anyone that there is no easy way to resolve this tension in the American legal, much less the social and political, system (see Goldberg 1984).

I am not suggesting that Christians must "withdraw" from the social, political, and legal life of America. Rather, I am suggesting that in order to answer the questions of why or how Christians participate in the life of this country, we do not need a theory about the Christian character of democracy. I am suggesting, with Yoder, that as Christians we would

> be more relaxed and less compulsive about running the world if we made our peace with our minority situation, seeing this neither as a dirty trick of destiny nor as some great new progress but simply as the unmasking of the myth of Christendom, which wasn't true even when it was believed. (Yoder 1984, 158)

As Yoder argues, since rulers claim to be our benefactors in order to justify their rule, there is no reason Christians cannot use that language to call the rulers to be more humane in their ways of governing. Moreover, if we are lucky enough to be in a situation where the ruler's language of justification claims to have the consent of the governed, we can use the machinery of democracy for our own and our neighbor's advantage. But we should not, thereby, be lulled into believing that "we the people" are thereby governing ourselves. Democracy is still government by elite though it may be less oppressive since it uses language in its justification that provides ways to mitigate oppressiveness. But that does not make democracy, from a Christian point of view, different in kind from states of another form (Yoder 1984, 158–59).

Perhaps the hardest habit of thought deriving from our Constantinianism is the assumption that if we do not govern, then surely society and government will fall into anarchy or totalitarianism. But I notice no shortage of people willing to rule or any absence of ideologies for rule. The problem is not Christians' disavowing ruling, but rather that when Christians rule they tend to create international and national disorder because they have such a calling to make things right:

> [If Christians] claim for democracy the status of a social institution *sui gene-ris*, we shall inflate ourselves and destroy our neighbors through the demonic demands of the claims we make for our system and we shall pollute our Christian faith by making of it a civil religion. If, on the other hand, we protect ourselves from the Constantinianism of that view of democracy, we may find the realistic liberty to foster and celebrate relative democratization as one of the prophetic ministries of a servant people in a world we do not control. (Yoder 1984, 165–66)

But if that is the case then it might well be suggested that for anti-Constantinians, liberalism is the best social strategy—particularly the kind suggested by Stout and perhaps Yack. A liberal social order, even if it has some of the results depicted in *Habits*, is forced by those very results to be humble about its achievements. As Stout suggests, liberalism, unlike the communitarian alternatives, rightly places a limit on the political by the very ambiguity it creates in the soul of every citizen.

Moreover, Yack may well be right that the communitarian critics of liberalism have confused liberal theory with liberal practice. What we must do, as Stout suggests, is ignore the pretension of grand liberal theory in order to concentrate on sustaining those practices that provide for a life in common. Certainly there is nothing in Yoder's critique of Constantinian justifications of America that would exclude that alternative. Indeed there is much to favor it.

Yet I am not convinced such a strategy will work. Not only are powerful economic forces working against it, as Stout himself notes, but I fear such a strategy does not attend to the intrinsic relation between liberalism and nationalism. I think Yack is quite right to suggest that liberalism does produce a community in terms of loyalty to the nation. So liberalism is not antisocial; it creates community at the macrolevel of the nation-state. From my perspective, that is just the problem—namely, as Jean Bethke Elshtain suggests, calls for the recovery of the public good in a liberal society result in a strengthening of the state built on the presumption of war. In that respect Richard Wightman Fox's observation that Niebuhr always assumed the state was the guarantor of justice is telling.

Put differently, Yack is quite right that liberalism does have a story. It is not, however, only the story of breaking from the bondage of the past. Rather it is the story of wars necessary to sustain a common memory among a people who have little else in common. America is a country that literally lives by remembering her wars. Virtues are not absent from such a society, but as Elshtain suggests they are "armed virtues."

It may be objected that there is nothing unique about liberalism, or America, in this respect. Every social order and state wages war. The difference lies in how liberal social orders war for no other reason than for war itself—there is no common good beyond war that can limit what war is meant to accomplish. So the ideal story of liberalism becomes an ideology that masks the necessity of liberalism to maintain patterns of domination in the name of freedom.

On a case-by-case basis I am more than willing to work with Stout to sustain practices for the upbuilding of our life together. But that does not mean I am ready to underwrite liberalism as a social strategy for Christians. This is not because I long for a communitarian ideal, which Yack rightly notes often embodies utopian liberal fantasies, but because I distrust the story liberalism would have us accept as the truth about our lives. America is not our home. It is just one place where Christians find themselves called to the service of the near neighbor.

I am aware that the position I am taking will be a surprise to Christians schooled on the assumption that there is an intrinsic relation between Christianity and America. And I suspect the position will also be unwelcome by many who dislike Neuhaus's call for the recovery of the role of religion in American life. They want people who still use their private time to entertain religious convictions to be willing to work to create a social order and corresponding government that relegates those convictions to the private sphere. That is done, of course, in the name of creating a democratic society based on universal claims justified by reason qua reason.[15] Constantinianism is a hard habit to break even for those who no longer understand themselves to be religious.

From this perspective, the problem with Yoder (and Falwell) is his refusal to find a neutral or at least nonconfrontational way to state the social implications of his religious convictions.[16] That is not playing the game fairly. It makes religion more public than is healthy for an allegedly pluralistic society. After all, there have to be some limits to our pluralism.

Yoder might well respond that he is willing pragmatically on a case-by-case basis to use the allegedly more universal language of our society. But for many I suspect such a pragmatic approach would be insufficient.

It is not enough to be willing to play the game of the putative neutral or objective language and procedures of pluralist democracy, you must be willing to believe that such language and procedures are truly the form of the society any people anywhere would choose if they had the material means, institutional creativity, and philosophical acumen. To challenge that presumption, as Yoder has, is the necessary starting point for the genuine Christian critique of Christian America.

ON BEING CHRISTIAN IN AMERICA

But where does this leave us? If America is not the New Jerusalem, does that mean Christians must seek to make America live consistently with secular presuppositions? In order to clarify the distinction between being Christian and being American, must we side with those who wish to force any religious phenomenon out of the public arena? Should we rejoice in the destructive kind of individualism that is so graphically displayed in *Habits of the Hearts*? Do we not have a stake in sustaining a public ethos that might make the rise of paganism, which might well use the language of Christianity, less likely?

I see no reason that the position I am taking would dictate an affirmative answer to these questions. I believe that Christians should not will that secular society be more unjust than it already has a tendency to be. We have a stake in fostering those forms of human association that ensure that the virtues can be sustained. Virtues make it possible to sustain a society committed to working out differences short of violence. What I fear, however, in the absence of those associations, is that we will seek to solve the moral anomie of the American people through state action or by a coercive reclaiming of Christian America.

Therefore, if I refuse to support prayer in the public school, it becomes all the more important that I urge Christians to learn to pray authentically as Christians. If Christians reclaim prayer as an end in itself rather than a way to confirm the "Christian nature" of our society, we will perform our most important civic responsibility. As Origen argued, What more important public service can we render than to pray that the emperor recognize his status as a creature of God? Such a prayer is no less significant in a society that believes "the people" have in fact become the emperor.

PART FIVE

Response by the Authors of
Habits of the Heart

SEVENTEEN

The Idea of Practices in *Habits:*
A Response

Robert N. Bellah

I am grateful to Charles Reynolds and Ralph Norman for their initiative
in organizing and editing this volume and to the authors of the individual essays for the seriousness and helpfulness of their contributions.[1]
The authors of *Habits of the Heart* very much hoped our book would
stimulate public discussion of the issues raised, and this volume represents part of the fulfillment of that hope.

I want to concentrate on the idea of practices in this response, but
Vincent Harding raises such serious objections to our work that I must
deal with them first of all. *Habits of the Heart* focuses on the language and
practices of white middle-class Americans. Harding finds the limited
focus of our attention to be crippling to our argument and wounding to
the sensibilities of those "left out." He accuses us of being, like those we
studied, unable or unwilling to deal with those different from ourselves.
While several of the authors of *Habits* have learned much from Vincent
Harding and while we take his objections with the greatest seriousness,
we nonetheless cannot agree with his explanation of our strategy.

Harding cannot understand our decision as deriving from anything
but moral obtuseness and therefore never asks himself if there might not
be some other reason. He speaks of "a society erupting all around us in
many colors and conditions—most of them neither white nor middle
class." That is certainly true, but it is hardly a reason to think the white
middle class unimportant.

While a limited budget and a small research team influenced our decision, it should be clear from many discussions in our book that our choice
of the white middle class had a much more substantial rationale. Whether
we like it or not, the white middle class has a cultural hegemony in contemporary America. For good or for ill, this is the group that dominates
our cultural institutions and sets pervasive standards that no American,

no matter how insulted, can escape. While it is not the only point of entry, we believe that in a critical effort to recover a public philosophy in America starting with this group is a defensible strategy. It was not our intention to hold this group up for special praise, nor has our book been interpreted as doing that. Rather we sought to show how this group, despite its privileges, nonetheless exemplifies some of its central difficulties. Among these difficulties is the fact that the premodern traditions of this group, like those of all other groups in America, have been seriously eroded by the pressure of what Max Weber called rationalization. In this sense, too, this group is representative of cultural problems that are general in our society.

Vincent Harding is not alone in his reaction to *Habits*, which is one reason that I do not want to evade his challenge. But it is worth noting that Harding's reaction to the book has not been typical of minority readers in my experience. More commonly I have heard two other responses. One is that we have helped define the majority culture they are up against. The other is that they recognize themselves in the book because the problems we deal with are the problems of all Americans. Native Americans have told me that the manager and the therapist as we analyze them are endemic on the reservation, where well-paid Indian civil servants operate with middle-class values in working with people who live at a subsistence level; for example, an Indian psychiatric social worker diagnoses a young man from a terrible home situation as suffering from "narcissistic personality."

But the reaction that has pleased me most, and that I would have hoped for from Vincent Harding, has been the widespread recognition that *Habits of the Heart* does not claim to be anything more than a beginning, indeed that it invites others to join the conversation, and to bring their own experience in so doing. A Japanese-American graduate student in my department is writing a dissertation on the Japanese-American community in San Francisco, using *Habits* as a model. Another student, herself a Chicana, is investigating the extent to which Chicano identity has become a lifestyle enclave for the Chicano middle class. A group in Afro-American Studies at the University of Mississippi has asked me to bring the insights of *Habits* to their restudy of Allison Davis's classic work, *Deep South*. A Japanese team and a French Canadian research group are using *Habits* as a model for studies of their countries. In short, we did not intend *Habits* to leave anyone out, even though we focused mainly on one group, and we are extremely happy that the book is encouraging people of "all colors and conditions" to join in the discussion of the issues we have raised.

I would like to organize my response to the essays in this volume around the idea of "practices" as developed by Alasdair MacIntyre in *After Virtue*. According to MacIntyre, practices are cooperative activities whose goods are internal to the practices. MacIntyre's examples range from games, such as chess, to medical care and the nurture of families and cities. We argue in *Habits* that practices in this sense are hard to understand in a culture that emphasizes the autonomous individual engaged in strategic action to maximize self-interest, action that rather sharply distinguishes between means and ends. In the culture of individualism, "work" is oriented toward the external rewards of money, power, and prestige, while "leisure" is the sphere of spontaneous emotional fulfillment. Neither work nor leisure so conceived are practices. Yet we also argue that radical individualism has never been the whole story in America. Practices necessarily persist in our lives even when we find it difficult to articulate them. Otherwise our society would be much more incoherent than it in fact is. We locate these persistent practices in those spheres of our lives where biblical religion and civic republicanism still survive.

Seeing practices as central to the argument of *Habits*, one might read Jeffrey Stout's essay as more supportive than critical. Certainly I would affirm almost all of his concluding ten points. Yet differences remain. It would seem that *Habits* takes more seriously than he does the notion that our society has, in his words, "a complicated social and conceptual inheritance." If that is true, then it is incorrect to call our society so confidently as Stout does a "liberal society." Perhaps I do not fully understand Stout's conception of liberalism, especially the idea that individualism is not an inherent element of it. Certainly in the Anglo-Saxon world, with the influence of Hobbes and Locke so massive, utilitarian individualism and liberalism would almost seem to be identical. As we understand liberalism, ours could not be a liberal society *tout court* because liberalism is a theory that is theoretically conceivable but performatively impossible. It is precisely the persistence of nonliberal practices that makes our society viable at all.

Again, Stout seems to be concerned to convict us of a foundationalism in moral philosophy to which we are not in the least committed. Our point about Brian Palmer is not that he lacks a foundation or even that he is is inarticulate. Indeed, he is highly articulate about his ethical views. He expresses himself with vigor and humor in what we call the first language of individualism. He falters, however, when that language proves inadequate to express the nonindividualistic practices in which he is also engaged. We wish he had a more adequate language to think and speak about the practices in which he actually engages not because we think he needs a philosophical foundation but because we think language and action should be mutually reflective and supportive in a good life; also because we think that when language fails, practice too may be imperiled.

Stout's key example comes from a slice of Ann Swidler's interview with Brian Palmer, cited in the appendix of *Habits* as an example of our "active, Socratic" form of interviewing. Stout identifies the following statement as "something resembling a moral principle" extracted by relentlessly Socratic questioning that interrupts Brian's Aristotelian storytelling: "I guess I feel like everybody else on this planet is entitled to have a little bit of space, and things that detract from other people's space are kind of bad . . ." (*H,* 304–5). In contrast to Brian's dramatic narrative of his divorce and remarriage, Stout takes this statement to be less Brian's "first language of self-understanding than it is his language of last resort—a set of slogans he reaches for (with obvious reluctance) when somebody else won't take storytelling or unprincipled talk of habit and happiness as sufficient for the purposes of justification." But when we look at Brian's statement in context, as it appears in the book's first chapter, we discover no foundationalist principle abstracted from Brian's lifestory. Instead we find a part of that story, a socially grounded constellation of images and ideas that frame and help to organize that story:

> "I guess I feel like everybody on this planet is entitled to have a little bit of space, and things that detract from other people's space are kind of bad," Brian observes. "One of the things that I use to characterize life in California, one of the things that makes California such a pleasant place to live, is people by and large aren't bothered by other people's value systems as long as they don't infringe upon your own. By and large, the rule of thumb out here is that if you've got the money, honey you can do your thing as long as your thing doesn't destroy someone else's property, or interrupt their sleep, or bother their privacy, then that's fine. If you want to go in your house and smoke marijuana and shoot dope and get all screwed up, that's your business, but don't bring that out on the street, don't expose my children to it, just do your thing. That works out kind of neat." (*H,* 6–7)

The dichotomy between artificially extracted principles and the actually detailed life-story breaks down. Brian did indeed reorder his loves in seeking after happiness, as Stout observes. But Brian sees his search as an expression of his personal value system, set within the social world like a piece of private property within an affluent suburb, secured by his own hard work and assuring that he can "do his thing" as long as he doesn't do overt injury to anyone else.

What is significantly individualistic about Brian's moral outlook is not the absence of a foundation of ultimate or overarching principles drawn from republican and biblical sources. It is the symbolic cosmos of individual property, autonomy, occupational effort, and minimal noninjury that frames his story of mutual affection, respect, and true love at long last discovered. Brian's minimal ethic of noninjury forbids anyone cheating or raping others, no matter the felt satisfaction such actions may yield the doer. But the autonomous integrity of Brian's own value system, played in his own "little bit of space," means that the comic triumph of his remarriage is objectifiable only for someone who happens to share his personal values. Rooted in Brian's experience of a public world structured by procedurally fair competitive relationships and to pay-your-own-way marketplace, this framework dramatically bears out *Habits'* argument about the overgeneralization of individualism, its institutional grounding, and its power to obscure our vision of practical virtue.

Stout, toward the end of his essay, is closest to us when he speaks of "the uneasy relation between social practices and such institutions as the capitalist marketplace and large-scale bureaucracies." We can only agree when he writes:

> We can, nonetheless, reasonably hope for a world in which the proliferation, distribution, and merchandising of external goods is subject to just political control and in which the goods internal to social practices, including the practice of self-government, are granted the right to life and given room to flourish. The hope that social practices, not simply private bonds and the individual pursuit of external goods, be protected is not an expression of terminal wistfulness, for it is neither nostalgic nor utopian. There are in fact countless specific things one could do to improve the prospects of a particular social practice.

Indeed, it is with just such things that the *Habits* group in its current work on a successor volume is primarily concerned—without nostalgia or utopianism.

Bernard Yack's position may seem to be similar to Stout's; yet because Yack does not share the conception of practices shared by Stout and the authors of *Habits,* I believe it is actually rather different. There is one fundamental problem with Yack's position that he does not even see: Liberal theory is not something merely in the minds of academic theorists but is also present in the shared liberal values that he sometimes mistakenly confuses with practices. Yack tells us that individuals are considered as fundamentally unencumbered in liberal theory but, of course, cannot be so in fact. Yet it is precisely the shared liberal "values" of which he speaks which tell people incessantly in our culture that they are radically autonomous and unencumbered. That is not a contradiction between liberal academic theory and liberal practice, but a contradiction at the heart of liberal culture as it actually exists in our society. It is very hard to tell from Yack's essay what he thinks liberal practices actually are, since his examples are mainly shared cultural values such as self-reliance and autonomy. Even his discussion of contract is primarily in terms of theory rather than practice—yet it is just here where he might have made a case. We would argue that liberalism, if it has practices—which is questionable if you define practices as activities good in themselves— must rely primarily on contractual relationships in which conscious, responsible, autonomous individuals relate to each other in order to maximize self-interest. Even here we would argue, with Durkheim, that contract always implies a noncontractual element that cannot itself derive from liberal premises. Yet we do point out that one of the problems with our society, in its actual practice and not just in theory, is that contract as a social form has invaded areas of life where it is inappropriate, with destructive consequences. On this I will have more to say later. We do indeed believe that "modern individualism seems to be producing a way of life that is neither individually nor socially viable" (H, 144) and that it is only the presence of practices rooted in older traditions that makes our society possible at all. Nor does anything Yack has written lead us to any other conclusion.

One example of a liberal practice that Yack offers is quite breathtaking. That is modern nationalism. He never tells us in what sense nationalism is based on liberal individualism—he merely asserts that they are "mutually reinforcing." We would argue that nationalism may well be a reaction to radical individualism, indeed one that provides illegitimate feelings of *Gemeinschaft* that can be easily used for ulterior ends, but nationalism can hardly be a simple expression of individualism. Again, what Yack takes as a normal form of liberal practice we would see as at least potentially pathological.

Christopher Lasch's essay is a useful corrective to one of the implications of Yack's arguments, namely, that a generic objection to liberalism involves commitment to a specific "communitarian" alternative. What is so particularly helpful is the way Lasch differentiates the argument of *Habits* from a sentimental communitarianism rooted in the ideal of *Gemeinschaft*. The practices *Habits* advocates are not confined to small face-to-face groups; nor do they imply lack of dissent. They include the public world of democratic politics and call for vigorous discussion and argument. In such a conversation, tradition provides us with the shared experience and ideals that orient us to the present, but not with answers to present problems. Both the past and the conditions of the present need to be confronted critically in the effort to arrive at provisional agreements on social policy. Neither an abstract individualism nor a nostalgic communitarianism can give us much help in that process. By differentiating the argument of *Habits* from one important strand in the tradition of criticizing individualism in America, namely, the strand that offers only nostalgic *Gemeinschaft* as an alternative, Lasch has clarified and strengthened what we wished to say.

James Peacock's essay is congenial to us because it derives from the same tradition of social research as our own work. His emphasis on *Habits* as a cultural approach is right if you look at the book from a Parsonian perspective, and certainly Parsons is a major background influence. Yet we prefer to use the word *tradition*, rather than *culture*, and that is a difference worth stressing. We do not see America as "a culture" in a global atemporal sense, as social scientists are often tempted to do, but as the locus of partly conflicting traditions, each of which has a complex history. Also we emphasize not simply culture in the precise sense of symbol systems, but also practices, which are certainly culturally regulated actions but ones that always involve social and psychological components. Rituals are quintessential practices, and if we did not emphasize them enough, then Peacock has rightly corrected us. But certainly Peacock is right that *Habits* is more about culture or traditions than it is about institutions and certainly than it is about individual personality. Yet we did not presume that culture has any causal priority, either in the creation of our present predicaments or in getting us out of them. Indeed, we tried to point out the institutional developments that have made modern individualism plausible, particularly the market economy and bureaucratic organization. We certainly do not imagine that all that is required is a "change of heart" without attention to the corporate economy and the state, though some of our critics have suggested as much. Yet we also believe that there are traditions, communities, and forms of discussion capable of taking a critical perspective on our institutional arrangements and that without them it is unlikely we will in fact transform our society. We will have more to say about these matters in the successor volume.

Peacock is not the first to point out that I come to the study of America from a background in East Asian studies (this is also true of Richard Madsen) and that *Habits* has a comparative perspective, though it is largely tacit. So, our analysis has been informed not only by the axial traditions of Israel and Greece but also by those of East Asia, perhaps particularly that of Confucianism, with its emphasis on the forms and practices of social life.

Richard Fox in his generally sympathetic essay raises several issues worth discussing. I must point out at once, however, that Fox uses the word *liberalism* in a way fundamentally different from Stout and Yack. Whereas the latter see *Habits* as opposing liberalism, Fox sees it as an effort to invigorate it. For Stout and Yack use *liberalism* in the context of modern political philosophy, while Fox's usage refers to contemporary politics, where *conservativism* means a defense of consumer capitalism and *liberalism* means an effort to overcome its defects. All are right in their characterizations of *Habits*. Fox, even more than Peacock, sees *Habits* as standing primarily in the tradition of liberal Protestantism, and that is certainly my own background. Yet, as some readers have detected, *Habits* is much less a Protestant jeremiad than was *The Broken Covenant*. It is worth pointing out that I am the only pure WASP in our group. One of us is Jewish and the other three are of Catholic background. It may be a liberal Judaism and a liberal Catholicism from which we come, but I think *Habits* is less Protestant, certainly less exclusively Protestant, than Fox and some other readers tend to assume. But let me move from Fox's assumptions to his actual arguments.

I believe that Fox falls into the error alluded to by Peacock, that of confusing a cultural analysis with an argument for the causal predominance of culture. Fox characterizes *Habits* as arguing that "the problem lies in language, not in action or in social or political institutions. There are no structural impediments to recovering the biblical and republican traditions." While we do believe that our practice is often better than our language, that is because our practice is embedded in actual communities and relationships that resist the pressure of individualist language. Further, we certainly stress, particularly in chapter 5 but throughout the book, that our individualist, and specifically our therapeutic, culture is rooted in the occupational and market structures of our society. There are institutions and practices that allow us to resist these structural pressures, but we do not imagine that any general reappropriation of the biblical and republican traditions would be possible without structural change. If we were not as clear about that issue in *Habits* as we might have been, we will not make that mistake in the next book.

Fox also gently criticizes us for our "determined hopefulness." This is to some degree in the eye of the beholder—others have found ours a rather dark view of contemporary American culture. If we are hopeful, and I think Fox is right that we are, we are certainly not optimistic. Our hope is embedded in the communities and practices that sustain us and not in any general belief that everything is going to come out all right. To some extent our hopefulness is a rhetorical device (we are, remember, admirers of rhetoric). Hopelessness is not a basis for action, and we saw *Habits* as a practical book intended for an audience far beyond the university. We are certainly not unaware of the features of contemporary existence that depressed MacIntyre or the Lynds, nor are we unaware of the sinfulness (Niebuhr) or brokenness (Tillich) of human life. Yet Niebuhr at his most grim was always invigorating because of his commitment to a belief and an institution that transcend our current difficulties. It is in this that we would emulate him.

Stanley Hauerwas, like Bernard Yack, includes us with a number of others as targets for his shotgun. Speaking only for the authors of *Habits*, I think he frequently misses the mark. The last thing we are involved in is "a coercive reclaiming of Christian America." Let us examine the passage from pages 282–83 of *Habits* that Hauerwas says (triumphantly) "sounds very much like a call for reconstituting Christian America!" The passage begins by pointing out that our lives make sense, even when we are not aware of it, because of traditions that are centuries, if not millennia, old. We then indicate that these include biblical and republican traditions. Those statements are ultimately matters of fact. If we are wrong, then it is up to Hauerwas to show us how we are wrong; for example, that biblical and republican traditions never did help Americans make sense of their lives, or that they are so eroded that they no longer do. We are not unaware of the process of erosion, for we go on to suggest the negative consequences of modernity's tendency to obliterate all previous culture. The passage concludes with the sentence, "We need to learn again from the cultural riches of the human species and to reappropriate and revitalize those riches so that they can speak to our condition today." In fact, this passage finally has nothing to do with America or Christianity specifically. It points to the general tendency of modernity to erode traditional culture everywhere (the "human species") and calls for an effort to reverse that trend.

Actually, Hauerwas shares our concern precisely on this point. He sees the erosion of the Christian tradition particularly in his own mainstream liberal Protestant community and is bending all his efforts to reverse that trend, to recover the genuine substance of Christian faith and practice. So his quarrel is not really with our program but with the fact that we want to recover and revitalize the civic republican tradition and therefore the national community as well. He fears that these tasks are not necessarily compatible, that a recovery of a Christian focus "may challenge as much as support a recovery of political community." That is a serious and not a new argument. Even Tocqueville at times thought that the two were incompatible, that Christianity was too exclusively concerned with the individual's spiritual welfare to develop a genuine civic virtue, though in *Democracy in America* he argued otherwise. Yet Hauerwas is concerned with the opposite danger, that Christianity will be used instrumentally for the sake of creating political community but to the detriment of its own authenticity. This is what he means by Constantinianism.

While we recognize the grounds for Hauerwas's anxiety, we feel there are serious deficiencies in his argument. Following John Howard Yoder, he has constructed a profoundly antipolitical picture of Christianity that consigns most of the history of the church to the dustbin of Constantinianism. He overlooks the fact that Christianity has always, like its parent religion of Israel, been a political religion. Any religion that recognizes God as the creator and ruler of the whole universe, of the economy and the polity as well as the family and the church, will have a profound concern for the orders of creation, among which the political will be prominent. This will not necessarily be triumphalist, though at times it certainly has been. But it would be unfaithful to the biblical vision to imagine a Christianity uninvolved with the issues of public life and withdrawn entirely or largely into the issues of its own inner life. Under present circumstances Hauerwas's position may be justified tactically. Perhaps in much of the Protestant church today the substance is so vitiated that the task is primarily a recovery of inner coherence. Even so, such a position cannot be premised on the abandonment of the world but only on the ground that the church can best be present to the world by being itself.

Our position is more pluralist than Hauerwas's. We believe that we live and work in more than one community and that more than one community deserves our loyalty and our efforts to reform it. Indeed, almost no one in America lives in or is loyal to only one community. There will inevitably be conflicts, but they may be creative conflicts. A church that challenges political community may help to invigorate a better political community. Yet pluralism does not mean chaos. There is a hierarchy of commitments and there are spheres of appropriateness. (I will have more to say about this later.) For the authors of *Habits,* biblical religion is clearly a higher loyalty than politics, even the noblest politics, and so religion should never be used instrumentally for political purposes. At the same time, in a democractic society politics can never be the instrument of a religious organization or any combination of them. Religious groups operate in the public realm only through the normal process of discussion and persuasion. The authors of *Habits* would be the last to argue for a coercive Christian America.

Fortunately Hauerwas's worries about the implication of *Habits* do not seem well founded, for we have not to my knowledge been embraced by any proponents of a Christian America. Similarly, in reply to Jean Elshtain I may say that *Habits* has not been embraced by what she calls "nationalists," either. No one has seen it as a call to strengthen the American empire. Rather, the book has been positively received by just those religious, civic, and peace groups for whom Elshtain seems to be speaking. Nonetheless, I do recognize some aspects of the book that might have been the basis for her concern. One point, made by others as well, is that *Habits* is relentlessly focused on the United States and hardly does justice to the recognition that today no country, not even the strongest, can be thought of outside the context of the world order. Even though we tried to say something about this issue at the end of the final chapter, I believe it is a serious defect, one we intend to remedy in our successor volume.

With respect to the possible perversions of civic republicanism, I think we were as aware of this issue as Elshtain. We did not harp on it because we felt civic republicanism is so little understood and so marginal in America today that it is, at the moment, no threat, whereas what it can contribute is sorely needed. What we mean by civic republicanism is a vigorous life of public discussion and concern, not some Machiavellian willingness to sacrifice the soul to the state. We paired biblical religion with civic republicanism not only because we think they have often gone together in America—indeed the churches have often been the haven for republicanism when liberal individualism prevailed elsewhere—but also because we see biblical religion moderating (unfortunately in fact it has not always done so) the particularism of republicanism by insisting on an ethical universalism. We are quite aware of the tensions between these two traditions (and between various strands of both) and would see a critical interchange between them as vital to the health of a reinvigorated tradition.

Elshtain's final call for "ironic remembrance and recognition of the way patriotism can shade into excesses of nationalism" is one that we would strongly support. Indeed, this is what we meant when we several times insisted that a healthy tradition keeps alive the "dangerous memories" of suffering endured and suffering inflicted. If we did not spell out these dangerous memories, it was in part because we wanted to write a book whose rhetoric was not one of condemnation but of positive encouragement to reform. (We failed in this intent according to neo-conservative reviewers, who largely see the book as hostile to America.) Another reason is that I wrote a book not too long ago, *The Broken Covenant,* that was devoted in large part precisely to detailing those dangerous memories.

The essays of Irwin Trotter and David Hollenbach extend the implications of *Habits* for American religion in interesting ways. Trotter argues that the wide acceptance of the Common Lectionary among Protestants is subversive of traditional Protestant individualism. Yet he welcomes this subversion for helping Protestants regain an understanding of ritual (in ways congenial to Peacock's argument about the centrality of ritual), which they had pretty well lost. For Trotter a deeper understanding of liturgy and of the liturgical year functions simultaneously to enhance a renewed appreciation of community, made visible in ritual enactment. He argues that while Protestants are recovering their true "catholic" heritage they are also gaining some distance from American culture, with which they have been too closely identified, particularly in its individualism now grown destructive. It seems to me that Vatican II is the indispensable background for Trotter's benign view of subversion. It is the nonthreatening atmosphere of openness between the great communions that makes possible a situation of mutual learning.

Hollenbach, though less explicitly, represents the other side of this religious interaction. The idea of participation is certainly close to what Tillich called the "protestant principle," and is not what one would have expected from a tradition that has long emphasized hierarchical authority. Yet Hollenbach points out that the emphasis on participation is deeply rooted in modern Catholic social teaching, and in its American application. It is related to the liturgical reform that culminated in Vatican II and which emphasized the participation of the whole people of God. Just as Catholics have rediscovered their deeply social understanding of ritual and have extended that understanding into the realm of ethics and politics in ways that have similarities to the democratic overtones of Protestantism, so they have in turn helped Protestants, long accustomed to social activism, recover a deeper liturgical basis for it in their own religious communities. Hollenbach is less explicitly interested in relating his position to Protestantism than to contemporary secular culture, but in America that secular culture has been profoundly influenced by Protestantism. Hollenbach sees *Habits* as having a message similar to the American Catholic bishops' letter on the economy, *Eco-*

nomic Justice for All, which indeed in its final draft twice quotes from *Habits.* Others have seen these two documents, which appeared together so close in time, as among the most important recent challenges to the American consensus. I would read Trotter and Hollenbach as providing support for the argument that, if this is true, it is in part because of the vitality of discussion among the major biblical traditions today.

Fredric Jameson brings to bear on *Habits* a perspective quite different from that of any of the essays I have discussed so far, namely, the perspective of a postmodern Marxism. Whether the slippages he detects in our argument are really there or are an artifact of his effort to translate *Habits* into his own discourse is well worth discussing. He finds one of our most serious slippages to be a lack of mediation between character, on the one hand, and abstract ideas or social institutions, on the other. He criticizes us for not using the concept of habit, which appears in our title, for this purpose and suggests how we would have profited from developing that idea along the lines of Sartre's practico-inert or Bourdieu's *habitus.* Yet he never mentions at all our frequent use of the idea of practices, which indeed serves for us both as a translation of Tocqueville's "habits" and as a way of mediating between character, culture, and social structure, and thereby doing precisely what he says we do not do. Jameson's failure to see this is all the more surprising because our idea of practices, influenced heavily by MacIntyre, derives from the idea of praxis in Aristotle, which is also the ultimate source of Marx's idea of praxis. Whatever coherence our book has, as I am trying to make clear in this response, derives from our treatment of practices. By ignoring this idea, Jameson must necessarily discover slippages.

Consider the first slippage on which Jameson comments, namely, his notion that the causal logic of our four traditions is radically heterogeneous, the biblical and republican traditions operating with a cultural causation and the two forms of individualism being primarily an expression of the market and thus of economics. Yet in fact we see all four traditions as being cultural, that is, as languages, but also as rooted in institutions and practices. Certainly the premodern traditions are oriented to texts, the Bible and Cicero for example, but so are the modern individualist ones. It is here that we would want to bring in Locke and Hume and Hume's friend Adam Smith, as well as Ben Franklin and, in reaction, Walt Whitman. Locke's works on education were widely read in America in the eighteenth century and undoubtedly had an influence on character, for example. Yet we do not see the older traditions as purely cultural, as being reproduced by texts alone any more than the newer ones. The texts were carried by institutions that in turn encouraged their embodiment in practices. Churches were very real social institutions and even today, in a society that is weakly organized politically, exercise considerable power. Civic republicanism is quite unthinkable without civic institutions: town meetings, legislatures, committees of correspondence during the Revolution, and the wide variety of voluntary civic organizations that persist to this day. Utilitarian individualism has always been oriented to the market, and expressive individualism makes sense only in terms of the emergence, in large measure in reaction to the pressures of the market, of the modern sphere of leisure and private life, with its particular understanding of the family as a haven in a heartless world. Thus we do not view our treatment of the four traditions to be nearly as heterogeneous as does Jameson.

As what I have said about the four traditions implies, we also do not see the slippage that Jameson detects between an old-fashioned idealistic or philosophical model and a contemporary or postcontemporary model of discourse analysis. Rather, we see them as two versions of the same thing. The early modern philosophers to whom we attribute importance were not arcane specialists cloistered in university departments, as are so many contemporary intellectuals, but rather very much engaged in the struggle for linguistic legitimacy that Jameson thinks is quite modern. Think of Locke's *Two Treatises on Government.* Could anyone have been more centrally concerned with legitimacy but also with intellectual dominance in setting the terms of discourse?

Yet ultimately the differences between us and Jameson are not about culture or discourse but about society. We do not have so vague a notion of community as he charges us with. When we speak of communities of memory (Jameson neglects to mention that communities of memory as discussed in *Habits* are at the same time communities of hope), we have quite specific groups in mind, several of which are illustrated in the second half of the book. These include religious organizations, voluntary associations, and citizens' movements. Much of the audience for *Habits* consists in such groups. When Jameson consigns the second languages to the past, to nostalgia, and holds them completely co-opted by the first language, he is also implying that the living communities that carry these second languages are fossils that can have no significant voice in our society. Instead of attempting to reinvigorate them, as we do, he calls for a third language that will transcend the weaknesses of the first and second. The only example he gives is Marxism and socialism, although I would suggest that in societies where these are still viable they have exactly the same status as our second languages. In America, where Marxism and socialism have little legitimacy (the research university is an exception), they have no social basis other than coteries of left-wing intellectuals. Therefore, Jameson is drawn inevitably to suggest that it is out of lifestyle enclaves that the social basis for effective third languages might come. The authors of *Habits* are ready to admit that the institutional basis of second languages in America is marginal and problematic, but we would hold that lifestyle enclaves are an even more fragile basis for any effective opposition to the dominant structures of power and legitimacy. Perhaps it is just that Jameson and the authors of *Habits* are organic intellectuals for different groups.

One final word on American exceptionalism. We are not as ignorant of Gramsci and Sartre, of Foucault and Derrida, as Jameson presumes. But American intellectuals who cannot speak in an American tongue have small audiences, largely confined to the university. If Marxism is ever to be an effective public voice in America, it will have to learn to speak American. *Habits* points out one moment when socialism did speak American, through the voice of Eugene Debs, and we lament the subsequent failure of a cultural and institutional tradition of humane democratic socialism to establish itself in our country.

Mary Elizabeth Albert's essay on the relation of feminism to *Habits* is challenging. She questions our silence about feminism and attributes it to our ambivalence about the movement. While we were not consciously aware of such ambivalence and made no explicit decision to exclude feminism from our list of significant recent social movements, she is nonetheless correct in her surmise. Feminism is one of our most important recent and continuing social movements, and we should have said so. That active feminists did not turn up in our sample is not an excuse, for the kind of feminism that Albert affirms and Elshtain calls social feminism is very close to our own position. To some extent we made the mistake of taking feminism for granted. Mainly, but not exclusively, in the chapter on love and marriage we accept the fundamental equality of women and the value of women's participation in the public sphere. A significant passage in the conclusion, to which Albert does not allude, attests to our views:

> [In a revived social ecology] the split between private and public, work and family, that has grown for over a century, might begin to be mended. If the ethos of work were less brutally competitive and more ecologically harmonious, it would be more consonant with the ethos of private life and, particularly, of family life. A less frantic concern for advancement and a reduction of working hours for both men and women would make it easier for women to be full participants in the workplace without abandoning family life. By the same token, men would be freed to take an equal role at home and in child care. (*H,* 288)

Here, as elsewhere in the book, we see changes in the position of women in our society entailing concomitant changes in the behavior of men.

I agree with Albert that it is a mistake to think the battles are won or that we can think of feminism in the past tense. To make that mistake is not to see that we are only at the beginning of a great change in the relation between the sexes, one that brings social changes as profound as any in human history. If we made that mistake, it may be because of an anxiety that Albert probably correctly labels as ambivalence. No great change in human history ever goes smoothly. Seldom are there two steps forward without at least one step back.

The authors of *Habits* share a high regard for the family—not the traditional family or the patriarchal family, but the family as a committed relation between spouses who intend to raise children. Feminism involves a critique of older family forms, a critique that we largely share, but inevitably in our society criticism of older institutions and a demand for fuller equality take the form of claims to individual rights without much regard for the new forms of solidarity that would give those rights a secure social support. That is one of the consequences of the domination of our language by individualism that *Habits* criticizes. While supporting the demand for the right of women to full equality, we can still see that an emphasis on rights alone can make any kind of family for the moment more difficult. This is in part because feminism itself is not a unified ideology, as Albert recognizes. If feminism simply means that women will now behave in the same way that men traditionally have, then the family will not work. We have encountered feminists who are opposed to the family as such because they think it indelibly oppressive and because, I believe, they have opted for a radically individualistic conception of the self. But we know that feminists of all sorts are aware of the dangers in that position and are attempting to do what often seems so hard to do in America, to combine the struggle for justice with the building of community, one that would include both sexes.

However, even for those who combine commitment to the equality of the sexes with a commitment to family life and a critical appreciation of tradition, family life is difficult today. We must behave in ways different from our parents. Women must learn to be assertive without losing the capacity to nurture, and men must let down the defensive barrier of the male ego so that they can give as well as receive nurture, not only to women but to children as well. The world of work is not set up to support equality either in the workplace or in the home. In this situation we wanted to emphasize the value and importance of the family as much as the equality of the sexes. In trying to maintain this balance, we gave less attention to the difficult and significant achievements of feminism, or we took them more for granted, than we ought to have done, and Albert is right to chide us.

Chapter 4 of *Habits* is called "Love and Marriage" and not "The Family," and Albert helps us understand why when she emphasizes the significance of the marriage relation more than the relation of parents and children in the context of a renewed social ecology. Marriage is, as Hegel said, a contract to enter a noncontractual relationship. That is an idea difficult to understand in an individualistic culture, but it needs to be recovered today. The relationship between two people who intend to raise children together has a special significance for society. Albert recognizes that we affirm a variety of forms of family other than the classic nuclear form, and she is right. We would affirm the dignity and value of single-parent families, committed relationships between persons of the same sex, groups of adults who have established an intentional living community, and so forth. But the nuclear family, not patriarchal and not isolated from larger communities, signals the commitment of men and women to each other and to the care and nurture of children; this commitment underlies the possibility of all others. Thus we would see the family not as a single monolithic type but as a congeries of types with the nuclear family as its symbolic center. We are also aware that nuclear families today are too fragile to survive without a great deal of support from extended kin, congregations, schools, and public services. The family, we believe, is essential, but it is part of a larger ecological web, and it cannot be made an excuse for the subordination of women. We welcome Albert's challenge to make our position more explicit in this important area.

William May develops a critique of what he calls "the Lockean myth" as an inadequate basis for thinking about the professions in America. While we share his critique, and it is thoroughly consonant with the argument of *Habits*, we would point out that "prudent self-interest" has never been the whole story and that the institutions he cites as operating under that rubric have existed side by side with other institutions, religious and civic, that have modified the insistent emphasis on self-interest alone. We share very much his preference for the transformational over the transactional model of leadership and for a teaching, rather than an adversarial, model of the professions. Without quite using the terminology, May would seem to be calling for the reinvigoration of practices, as defined above, in our politics and in our professional life.

Ralph Potter's argument is certainly at odds with the argument of *Habits*, though it seems to me not entirely internally consistent. Potter is suggestive in linking the four languages of *Habits* to the four dimensions of the Parsonian paradigm, though it was not an idea that had consciously occurred to us. But in making this linkage, he could be fruitfully interpreted as suggesting that these are all partial languages, differentiated in terms of the major spheres of life, languages that we must all use at various times as we function in the different spheres. Yet he defies his own logic in seeing them as languages of four different communities, each adequate to the whole of life. Such a logic does indeed render a zero-sum pluralism but is hardly Parsonian. Nor does it seem to me to describe American reality. If I were to develop the Parsonian interpretation, I would say that the language of adaptation, of utilitarian individualism, is indeed legitimate in its own defined sphere but becomes problematic when, as it has in America, it attempts to account for the whole of life. I would also want to keep the Parsonian cybernetic hierarchy, which Potter wishes unaccountably to throw out, and to suggest that as one moves from utilitarian individualism to expressive individualism, then to civic republicanism and to biblical religion, each language accounts for a wider and more comprehensive sphere of life. But in the Parsonian scheme this relation is not tyrannical or oppressive. Each language has its sphere of relative autonomy.

Moral pluralism is not the cause of the problem of individualism diagnosed in *Habits,* and moral absolutism is not the cure prescribed. The problem lies, on the contrary, in the cultural overgeneralization of individualism in its utilitarian and expressive forms to represent a moral Esperanto into which every moral language can and should be translated, or a purely descriptive and analytical metalanguage to which every moral language should be reduced. So the problem *Habits of the Heart* poses is how to redress the moral imbalance of an institutionally differentiated society in which the two languages of modern individualism are being overgeneralized across institutions to foreclose a cultural conversation that embraces four modes of moral discourse and four traditional perspectives on life's meaning.

The overgeneralization of individualism is institutionally grounded in our experience of the procedurally regulated and utilitarian bureaucracies of a corporate economy and an administrative state, coupled with the expressive fulfillments of middle-class leisure and romance. This overgeneralization is dramatized by the representative characters of the manager and therapist. In ideal-typical terms they are "native speakers" of individualism's two modes of moral discourse, centered on interests and feelings, respectively. But, in fact, no one person or group in a complex society and culture like ours is a native speaker of any one moral language to the exclusion of others. We learn to speak all four languages, however varied our degree of practice and fluency in one or the other. We do so because all four of them inhere in social institutions and activities—economic, political, familial, and religious—in which we all participate, however diversely.

Habits argues that the overgeneralization of individualism into a moral Esperanto is our chief problem. For example, by expanding a vision of public life as a marketplace for competing interests and an administrative center for distributing utilities, while narrowing it as a convenantal community and a forum for debating our common needs, virtues, and ends, we are failing to do justice to one another and care for one another as we should. We cannot adequately understand what it means to practice justice and caring, or sustain these social virtues as attributes of communities, without fuller recourse to the biblical and republican traditions. This holds true, no matter how hard we try to guarantee the rights of individuals, satisfy their interests, and respond to their feelings. Yet this does not imply that we can or should dismiss the moral languages of rights, interests, and feelings. We cannot do without them. We don't seek to replace an overgeneralized individualism with an artificially imposed form of biblical authority or republican debate. Just the opposite. We want to correct the biased vision that individual interests, feelings, and rights in their utilitarian and expressive sense can tell the whole truth about the meaning of a good society and a good way of life.

This conclusion contrasts with Potter's judgment that in the absence of any single moral language to adjudicate our common life, "the interplay between the four living languages in our public life is a zero-sum game" among four ways of life and their separate constituencies. But it comes quite close to his final conclusion that among the contrasting moral perspectives and their distinctively institutionalized forms of social relationship and action there exist both perpetual tension and mutual correction.

What we need then is not a new exclusive first language, but to be genuinely multilingual, to speak all four languages well and to know when each is appropriate and when one takes priority over another. We also need to know when we should use one of the languages to push back the pretensions of the others. We did not say that in *Habits*, but I would be quite happy to reformulate our argument in those terms. I might add that a genuine argument within and between the several American public languages can occur only if the institutional bases of these languages are in sound condition. In *The Good Society*, the successor to *Habits* that we are currently preparing, we will be discussing major institutions and the dilemmas facing them much more explicitly than we were able to do in *Habits*.

What Roland Delattre in his essay calls addiction, consumption, and procurement makes sense in a world where means have come loose from ends and genuine practices are difficult to understand or sustain. Such addictions arise in a world where the results of one's actions are problematic; one is not sure that things will work out, that there will be a payoff at the end. Addictions are not practices at all but shortcut means to guarantee that the ends will be forthcoming, such ends as pleasure, distraction, or numbing amnesia. To make the point, we might consider how some of the objects of addiction can also function in the context of practices. Alcohol, for example, becomes addictive only when it becomes a means to an end, rather than part of the end itself. The compulsive drinker doesn't savor the act of drinking as an aesthetic or social experience; rather, he seeks the anesthesia that drinking can bring. Often he is so guilty about drinking that he needs to get drunk to destroy the feeling of guilt. But remember that Plato's *Symposium* was a drinking party. In that context drinking was part of a practice and was one of its internal goods. So long as it remained in the context of a practice, drinking did not become inordinate, insatiable. *Pleonexia,* the desire for more, that Aristotle saw as the opposite of justice, is what destroys practices.

I think the notion of practices helps us see why technology is addictive, why we have come to speak of a "technological fix." Technology often obliterates a practice and replaces it with a disjunction between an end that we want and a means we do not understand. Albert Borgmann has beautifully analyzed this process in *Technology and the Character of Contemporary Life* (1985). Something like Star Wars is a kind of technological pleonexia, a bottomless pit of expenditure and effort aimed at a final perfect fix. The task then is to bring the objects of addiction, whether alcohol or technology, back into the context of practices and therefore overcome the element of inhuman compulsion.

Ernest Wallwork's paper suggests that psychotherapy can be more of a practice than we on the whole find it to be in America today. I would agree, and I think there are passages in the book that say as much. Fortunately for us, the reviews from therapists and in psychological journals have on the whole not interpreted us as rejecting therapy, as Wallwork assumes, but as calling for a reform, one that many of these reviewers agree is overdue. Wallwork himself concludes that "popularized psychotherapy is radically individualistic," and *Habits* is not examining psychotherapy per se, but the popular therapeutic thinking of the American middle class. Seen as such, "the pervasiveness of psychotherapeutic ideas" is not a cause to be blamed for "moral malaise" or the contemporary eclipse of public virtue, as Wallwork reads the book, but a symptom to be probed. I agree entirely with Wallwork that the various schools for psychotherapy do not monolithically embrace radical individualism, and I entirely disagree that *Habits* presumes otherwise. Neither do these schools equally influence popular middle-class culture in America today. In both respects, Freud is a dubious representative of the cultural and moral problems *Habits* diagnoses. Wallwork himself seems to recognize this when he writes that in spite of Freud's "commanding cultural authority," and his perspicacity on the issues of self-other relations, "What Freud says about these issues is not well known, in large part because he has been misread through the distorting glasses of American individualism." Exactly.

Nor is American individualism confined to California. Wallwork argues that *Habits* draws its conclusions about therapeutic thinking from interviews conducted primarily with Californians. "But California psychotherapy is not exactly representative of the mainstream of the tradition," he objects. Variations in the forms of psychotherapeutic theory and practice, however, have more to do with social class and education than with region. Most of the ethnographic material of therapeutic thinking in *Habits* comes from Tipton's interviews, which were mainly conducted in metropolitan Atlanta, Georgia—not California—among white-collar workers, managers, and professionals who spanned the middle class. They had all grown up and gone to college in urban areas in the eastern, midwestern, or southern states. Most of the therapists were students in or graduates of doctoral programs in clinical psychology. California is not a place but a state of mind, the middle-class American mind, something that not only Wallwork but Peacock, Jameson, and other contributors to this volume might note.

Habits begins by continuing a cultural conversation as old as our civilization, and it ends by inviting its readers to advance that conversation, not merely to follow it. The contributors to this volume have done just that. In so doing, they have enabled all of us to appreciate better what it means to examine our habits and search our hearts in the pursuit of common goods diverse yet practical enough to share. May the conversation continue.

NOTES

Quotations from *Habits of the Heart* are cited in the text prefixed by the abbreviation *H;* page references are to the edition published by the University of California Press, 1985.

REYNOLDS AND NORMAN, "THE LONGING FOR COMMUNITY"

1. For an analysis of why the morality associated with liberal democracy has made desegregation in America so ineffective, see Hochschild (1986), an article that demonstrates why a new moral ecology is required if desegregation is to be achieved in American society.

2. The glossary of *Habits* (335) defines *moral ecology* as "The web of moral understandings and commitments that tie people together in community. Also called *social ecology.*" Unfortunately, this definition omits how narrative is critical for defining moral and social ecology in the book. We use the term *civic ecology* frequently (instead of moral or social ecology) because we think this term better fits the thesis of the book.

3. See the Glossary in *Habits* (333–36) for definitions of these key terms.

4. With Anita Chan and Jonathan Unger, Madsen also coauthored *Chen Village: The Recent History of a Peasant Community in Mao's China* (University of California Press, 1984), which presents a more detailed ethnography and history of Chen, but does not focus on the moral ecology of life.

5. Madsen's footnote continues, "See Steven Tipton, *Getting Saved From the Sixties* (1982). The four styles are: (1) revelational-authoritative; (2) regular; (3) situational-expressive; and (4) consequential." For Madsen, Maoism illustrates the revelational-authoritative, which is the biblical tradition in *Habits;* Confucianism represents the regular, which is the civic republican tradition in *Habits;* the revisionists represent the consequential, which is the utilitarian individualism of *Habits;* and Madsen did not need (3) above, which is the expressive individualism of *Habits.*

6. Robert Bellah (1978, 356) describes Ronald Reagan as "an archetypal liberal." But we worry about the latent damage that may be inflicted on the disadvantaged members of our society by a frontal assault on liberalism. At least in ideal theory, liberalism is favorably disposed to the equal opportunity of all to participate in the benefits of society. Thus we favor the term *post-liberalism,* which allows one to specify which aspects of liberalism one is rejecting and which preserving. We reject the asocial view of the self characteristic of liberal theory, but we affirm the liberal commitment to social justice as the quest for equal participation in the benefits of social cooperation.

7. *Practical reason*, a synonym of *moral reason*, is distinguished from *theoretical reason*, in which the goal is simply to understand something in terms of abstract principles, and from *empirical reason*, in which the goal is to describe or quantify something. Practical reason inquires into what one ought to do, how one can become a good person or create a good society, and how to act justly. Practical reason typically has a narrative structure.

8. This grammar of moral discourse is highly indebted to Talcott Parsons and to his theory of society. To unravel the complex history of its development, however, would take us too far afield. Bellah, Potter, and Tipton all studied directly with Parsons. Potter then studied with Bellah. And Tipton then studied with Bellah and Potter.

9. Madsen (1984, xv) describes the "Socratic quality" of his interviews with Ao Meihua as follows: "The longer we talked, the more she came to 'remember' dimensions of her moral commitments that she had not 'known' before. And I too came to 'remember' ideas about the intimate connections between self-sacrificing generosity and self-righteous arrogance that I had 'learned' but never really understood from books and had experienced but never really admitted in my own life." Madsen credits Paul Rabinow with stimulating these ideas about the "Socratic" nature of fieldwork. This is hardly what Stout has in mind when he criticizes the Socratic questioning of those interviewed by the authors of *Habits*.

10. Lasch's notion of tradition is more dynamic than the one offered in the glossary of *Habits* (335). There, tradition is defined as "a pattern of understandings and evaluations that a community has worked out over time." For Lasch, a living tradition is always unfinished, or "in the making." I think Lasch's concept is truer to the intentions of the authors of *Habits* than their own initial definition, which concludes by saying, "Tradition is often an ongoing reasoned argument about the good of the community or institution whose identity it defines."

11. Although Wallwork focuses his essay primarily on Freud, he notes that the "second language" he finds in Freud is also found elsewhere in the psychotherapeutic literature, for example, in Erik Erikson, Henry Stack Sullivan, and recent object-relations theorists. By focusing on Freud, Wallwork takes on the strongest case of those who argue that this tradition supports an individualistic interpretation of human nature.

PEACOCK, "AMERICA AS A CULTURAL SYSTEM"

1. I am grateful to Warren A. Nord, Chair, Program in the Humanities seminar on *Habits of the Heart*, held at the University of North Carolina, Chapel Hill, 31 January–1 February 1986; to speakers Stanley Hauerwas, Edward Tiryakian, Craig Calhoun, and Jeffrey Obler; and to the seminar participants, representing numerous fields and disciplines. Much of the commentary that I summarize derives from discussion during this seminar. I am also grateful to Glenn Elder for the opportunity to have participated in a discussion of *Habits* in a seminar on the life course, held at Chapel Hill in September 1985.

2. For a related discussion, see Ralph Potter's essay in Part Two.

3. Sociologist Craig Calhoun, who kindly read this essay, points out a more fundamental dimension of the sociological critique: that analysis of the social basis of the culture elucidated by *Habits* is necessary not only for sociological understanding but also for cultural understanding. Specifically, Calhoun argues, we must recognize "the very category 'middle classness' as an important part of that culture." That is, to comprehend the essentially middle-class culture set forth in *Habits*, we must understand the middle class as a social entity. At a general level, this view contradicts the Parsonian strategy of separating cultural, social, and psychological analysis. The Parsonian defense would presumably be that one cannot do everything at once; grounding cultural analysis in social (or psychological, ecological, or biological) analysis is undoubtedly illuminating, but it is defensible and necessary to work at one level at a time, provided one clearly defines that level. The conflict is between a systems approach and a dialectical one.

4. The religious practices of the authors are as irrelevant to our assessment as the accusation by one critic that they are masquerading Christians—actually detached social scientists foisting on us a Christian dogma ("It's not fair for a few prescient scholars, coiled over their word processors, to send the rest of us marching back to traditions like original sin, premarital (female) virginity, and the willful ignorance of biology, physics, and cosmology" [Ehrenreich 1985, 118]). At some level the authors' personal creed is relevant, but our first question must be simply, What do they say?

DELATTRE, "THE CULTURE OF PROCUREMENT"

1. See especially Peele and Brodsky (1975), chaps. 6 and 7, "Growing Up Addicted" and "The Addicted Society."
2. These data were gathered from various sources for an American Studies course I taught at the University of Minnesota, 1978–1980.

JAMESON, "ON *HABITS OF THE HEART*"

1. Which the title, however, significantly euphemizes as "commitment."
2. See, for example, Stuart Hall, "Signification, Representation, Ideology: Althusser and the Post-Structuralist Debates" (1985a); "Moving Right" (1981); "Popular-Democratic versus Authoritarian-Populist: Two Ways of 'Taking Democracy Seriously'" (1980); "Authoritarian Populism" (1985b).
3. One does not have to endorse the general theses of Marvin Harris's *America Now: The Anthropology of a Changing Culture* (1981) to find his account of the "religious revival" horrifying and persuasive.
4. My earlier remarks about the contemporary loss of historicity can, for example, be reread in this spirit.
5. A remarkable and neglected work by Rodney Needham, *Belief, Language, and Experience* (1973), argues just this on anthropological and philological grounds: what we call "belief" is generally other people's belief. Contemporary sociologists have widely come to similar positions on the traditional sociological pseudoconcept of "values."

POTTER, "QUALMS OF A BELIEVER"

1. One has to suppose that it is an editorial mishap that has led to the attribution of agency to the civic and biblical traditions. Elsewhere, it is clear that the traditions will not "reformulate themselves." We must make some contribution.
2. There is one more thing that I cannot do without. I want to take one small step toward realizing, even in academic settings, a community of memory and hope. The names of most of those who have been my teachers in such matters, face-to-face or through the medium of books, are on display in *Habits of the Heart*. Two people who are not mentioned and to whom I wish to express immense debt and profound thanks are Talcott Parsons and James Luther Adams.

I hope we can form our institutions and our selves in such a way that will enable us to engage those who might be estranged if they hear our several voices at a distance—at a rally in the stadium or in a glossy television production. Certain subjects can be treated helpfully only in a particular type of setting. Reflection, reappropriation, self-criticism, and renewal require something like the type of thoughtful interaction we enjoyed in this symposium at the University of Tennessee.

STOUT, "LIBERAL SOCIETY AND THE LANGUAGES OF MORALS"

1. I discuss related difficulties caused by the "structural similarity between the questioning of informants in the field and Socratic probing in philosophy" in *The Flight from Authority* (1981, 212–13).

2. MacIntyre is cited in *Habits* (301) as an exemplary practitioner of social science as public philosophy, and *After Virtue* is cited repeatedly in the endnotes. MacIntyre also served the authors in an advisory capacity (*H*, xii).

3. See David E. Cooper, "Moral Relativism" (1980) and R. W. Beardsmore, *Moral Reasoning* (1969, 35).

4. For related criticisms of MacIntyre, see my "Virtue Among the Ruins: An Essay on MacIntyre" (1984), and J. B. Schneewind, "Moral Crisis and the History of Ethics" (1983).

5. I have in mind, in addition to "The Priority of Democracy to Philosophy," especially these essays: "Method, Social Science, and Social Hope" (1982, 191–210); "Solidarity or Objectivity?" (1985c); "Habermas and Lyotard on Postmodernity" (1985a); and "Postmodernist Bourgeois Liberalism" (1985b).

6. Hence my reluctance to choose between "two concepts of Rawls" (see Stout 1981, 222ff., 232–41), and my decision to focus my criticisms not on Rawls himself but rather on authors like David A. J. Richards and Ronald Green, who take Rawlsian ideas in precisely the direction criticized by Sandel. It is because the metaphysical Rawls caught on with a significant reading public that Sandel's criticisms remain valuable even if Rorty is right about how to read *A Theory of Justice*.

7. On the same page, Walzer writes:

> I don't claim to have achieved any great distance from the social world in which I live. One way to begin the philosophical enterprise—perhaps the original way—is to walk out of the cave, leave the city, climb the mountain, fashion for oneself (what can never be fashioned for ordinary men and women) an objective and universal standpoint. Then one describes the terrain of everyday life from far away, so that it loses its particular contours and takes on a general shape. But I mean to stand in the cave, in the city, on the ground. (1983, xiv)

8. Rorty implies that "philosophical presuppositions" should be taken in this context to mean assumptions "about the nature of human beings" and about "whether there is such a thing as 'human nature'" (n.d., 17). But this explication can be seriously misleading, given the ambiguity of the expression "human nature." So in a note Rorty adds: "I am here using the term 'human nature' in the traditional philosophical sense in which Sartre denied that there was such a thing, rather than in the rather unusual one which Rawls gives it." In Rawls's usage, a theory of human nature is "provided by, roughly, common sense plus the social sciences" and need not entail commitment to essentialism as a metaphysical thesis (or, for that matter, to its negation). Whether this sense should be called unusual is a question I shall ignore. But I do want to ask what is left of Rorty's point once this qualification is entered. Has he simply denied that liberal society needs grounding in an *essentialist* view of human nature? If so, this would leave open the possibility that liberal society still needs grounding in a theory of what people are like, perhaps one gleaned from "common sense plus the social sciences." The point Rorty really wants to make, I think, is that liberal society does not need *grounding* at all. In other words, it doesn't rest on "philosophical presuppositions" in the sense which would imply that something has gone terribly wrong if we cannot produce a conception of the self or foundational principles from which the acceptability of our practices and institutions can be deduced. This leaves open the possibility that it might be desirable for liberal society to receive "articulation" in a conception of the self. It also leaves open the possibility that our continued commitment to particular liberal practices or institutions might depend on our ability to "justify" them in response to specific doubts. And those doubts *might* take the form of questions like, Do we really want to carry on with this practice if such-and-such a view of what people are like is false?

9. Elsewhere Rorty says that "we should be more willing than we are to celebrate bourgeois capitalist society as the best polity actualized so far, while regretting that it is irrelevant to most of the problems of most of the population of the planet" (1982, 210). If the concession tagged onto the end of this sentence is intended only to say that bourgeois capitalist society is unlikely to *solve* most of the problems of most of the population of the planet, Rorty may well be right. But it is hard to see how bourgeois capitalist society could conceivably be deemed irrelevant to those problems, at least as a source of dramatically important unintended consequences, many of them bad.

10. These formulas allude, respectively, to John Rawls, T. M. Scanlon, and Jürgen Habermas.

11. See also Rorty (1985a, 174).

12. MacIntyre discusses medicine in "Patients as Agents" (1977b), though because he exaggerates the extent to which our society lacks agreement on the good, he also exaggerates the extent to which medicine's claims to authority lack plausibility or intelligibility in our culture. For an application of MacIntyre's distinction between social practices and institutions to medicine and a brief analysis of "Patients as Agents," see Stanley Hauerwas, *Suffering Presence* (1986, chap. 2).

13. It should be noted that MacIntyre takes full cognizance of the necessity for a provisional and corrigible conception of the good; see Richard J. Bernstein (1984). MacIntyre's *telos* is not a fixed conception of the good for man, despite the impression one might get from the first half of his book:

> It is in the course of the quest and only through encountering and coping with the various particular harms, dangers, temptations and distractions which provide any quest with its episodes and incidents that the goal of the quest is finally to be understood. A quest is always an education both as to the character of that which is sought and in self-knowledge. (1984, 219)

MacIntyre goes on to offer

> a provisional conclusion about the good life for man: the good life for man is life spent in seeking for the good life for man, and the virtues necessary for the seeking are those which will enable us to understand what more and what else the good life for man is. (Ibid.)

On my account, liberal society embodies the recognition that the good life for us must make allowances for the failure to achieve perfect agreement on the good life. We embrace liberal society as the best set of arrangements under the circumstances and until something better comes along. What matters is the highest achievable good, and this changes along with the circumstances.

14. Jefferson and King play important roles in both *Habits of the Heart* and Rorty's "The Priority of Democracy." Rorty's essay, in particular, calls attention to the ease with which the Civil Rights movement combined apparently disparate moral languages.

15. My thanks to everyone who helped me, in one way or another, in composing and revising this essay—not least of all, to members of my graduate seminar on relativism at Princeton University and a group of graduate students at Princeton Theological Seminary with whom I discussed the paper. Three others, in particular, deserve thanks for useful responses to the first draft: David Bromwich, Joseph Incandela, and Bernard Yack.

YACK, "LIBERALISM AND ITS COMMUNITARIAN CRITICS"

1. That critique is directed primarily at contractarian and utilitarian theory, the most popular versions of liberal theory. In this essay I shall also so circumscribe my use of the term *liberal theory*. There are, of course, other versions that do not rest on contractarian or utilitarian assumptions. These versions—arguments made by philosophers like Montaigne, Montesquieu, Hume, George Herbert Mead, and Dewey or social theorists like Adam Ferguson, Tocqueville, and Georg Simmel—are, in my opinion, less vulnerable to communitarian critiques.

2. Michael Walzer is an important exception among communitarian critics of liberal theory. In *Spheres of Justice* (1983), he attempts to develop a theory of justification and social criticism based squarely on shared social meanings. I do not, however, discuss *Spheres of Justice* here, since Walzer seems inclined in that work to accept a broad range of liberal practices, or at least their underlying meaning.

3. See Maurice Agulhon, *Marianne into Battle* (1981); Jay Fliegelman, *Prodigals and Pilgrims* (1982); Hans Blumenberg, *The Legitimacy of the Modern Age* (1983, 445ff.) and *Die Genesis der Kopernikanischen Welt* (1975, 99ff.).

4. For a brilliant attempt to identify the historical context that provoked the Enlightenment's break with tradition, see Blumenberg (1983); see Yack (1987) for a discussion of Blumenberg.

5. See Charles Larmore (1984), a review of Sandel's *Liberalism and the Limits of Justice*.

6. Sandel cites here the same passage in *After Virtue* (p. 61) that I criticized earlier, to support his view about the relation between theory and practice.

7. Stephen Holmes (1984, 222 and 321 n 11) notes the same internal contradiction in Louis de Bonald's and Joseph de Maistre's conservative communitarian arguments.

8. The great nineteenth-century social theorists recognized the difference between these two forms of dissociation. Thus, whether, like Weber, Durkheim, and Ferdinand Tönnies, they generally approved of liberal practices or, like Marx, disapproved of them, their evaluation of those practices did not grow out of their assumptions about the social constitution of individuals.

9. Modern social theorists, following Tönnies in *Gemeinschaft und Gesellschaft*, have tended to distinguish between *community* and *society* as the distinctive species of social interaction. This leaves no generally accepted term to refer to the genus including all forms of social interaction, a term such as *koinonia* was for Aristotle. Simmel used the term *Vergellschaftung*, usually translated by the coinage "sociation," to serve this purpose; but neither it nor any other distinctive generic term has been generally accepted. As a result, *community, society,* and *association* are all, at times, used to refer to the generic form of interaction among human beings, which makes it very easy to blur the distinction between their generic and specific uses.

10. For an account of the growth of nationalism and individualist values as mutually reinforcing, see Ernest Gellner, *Nations and Nationalism* (1983).

11. Charles Taylor asks a similar question in "Atomism" (1979a, 41). He suggests that the approaches to the explanation of motion and the cosmos introduced by the new physics of the seventeenth century made the analysis of societies into their individual atomistic units seem plausible. I agree that the new physics lent plausibility to liberal justification strategies; but I do not think that the desire to emulate the new sciences completely explains the attractiveness of liberal justification strategies. One has to look at the social as well as the intellectual context in order to explain their attractiveness.

12. See Rogers M. Smith, *Liberalism and American Constitutional Law* (1985, 48–49) for a similar suggestion.

13. Unger shares these problems in using human nature as a critical concept with Feuerbach and the other left Hegelians whose arguments he draws on. Like them he writes a Kantian/Hegelian notion of spiritual freedom into his concept of human nature. See Bernard Yack, *The Longing for Total Revolution: Philosophic Sources of Social Discontent from Rousseau to Marx and Nietzsche* (1986), chap. 6.

14. See Smith (1985, 198ff.) and William Galston, "Defending Liberalism" (1982, 629). John Rawls has recently made clear that his theory of justice is appropriate only for individuals who share a "public tradition" committing them to liberal democracy; see Rawls, "Justice as Fairness: Political, Not Metaphysical" (1985); Amy Gutmann "Communitarian Critics of Liberalism" (1985).

15. Richard Rorty, for example, has defended liberal practice in this way; see "Post-Modernist Bourgeois Liberalism" (1983).

LASCH, "THE COMMUNITARIAN CRITIQUE OF LIBERALISM"

1. The following part of my argument owes a good deal to Jeffrey Stout's essay "Liberal Society and the Languages of Morals," which proposes that a good political order is one that sustains and protects the "goods internal to social practices." I would enter a mild dissent, however, from Stout's further contention that we "barely know how to talk about social practices . . . at all." The sociology of work has documented the "degradation of work," in Harry Braverman's phrase, by the eradication of its artistic and playful aspect, and the sociology of the professions abounds in examples of the way external goods corrupt professional practices of all kinds. The corruption of athletics by the mania for winning at all costs provides another familiar example of the corruption of practices by external goods or as Huizinga put it, by the attenuation of the "play element" in culture. In short, there is a richer sociological account of practices than Stout recognizes, although it does not, of course, very often present itself as such.

A more serious disagreement concerns Stout's attempt to reconcile communitarianism with liberalism. I believe the vocabulary of rights to be fundamentally incompatible with the vocabulary of virtue. But an equally important objection to Stout's position is that a society that tried to make virtues and practices the foremost topic of public conversation would have to make it possible for everyone to take part in that conversation, whereas the social and economic inequalities tolerated by liberalism have the effect of depriving large classes of people of an effective public voice.

MAY, "ADVERSARIALISM IN AMERICA AND THE PROFESSIONS"

1. In this interpretation of the framers and apologists for the Constitution, I follow Gordon S. Wood (*Creation of the American Republic, 1776–1787*) rather than Gary Will or the authors of *Habits of the Heart*. The authors of *Habits* attempt to hyphenate the revolutionary thinkers and the apologists for the Constitution. To airbrush the stark picture of human nature found in *The Federalist Papers*, they cite Madison's comment of 1788: "To suppose that any form of government will secure liberty or happiness without any virtue in the people is a chimerical idea." But this concession to the need for virtue does not appear in *The Federalist Papers* themselves, an omission which, in those papers relentlessly oriented to persuade, reflects better the tenor and mood of the times. Madison recommends the Constitution as a mechanism that accommodates to the facts of human self-interest and vice.

2. Modern terrorism, by the way, might be read as an assault on the Hobbesian state. The terrorist proclaims to the state: "You do not have a monopoly over the powers of death, nor are you able to protect people from the threat of death." At an intense moment in London life, when bombs exploded in the pubs, a public official proclaimed: "From now on, everyone is his own magistrate!" He said, in effect, that London was returning to a Hobbesian state of nature.

WALLWORK, "A CONSTRUCTIVE FREUDIAN ALTERNATIVE TO PSYCHOTHERAPEUTIC EGOISM"

1. In this essay, I use the terms *egoistic individualism* and *radical individualism* interchangeably for the most extreme form of individualism, which holds both that we always only seek our own good (psychological egoism) and that the sole good is the good of the self (normative egoism). *Habits* does not use the expression "egoistic individualism" and it does not define radical individualism, but I believe the preceding definition is close to how radical individualism is used in the book.

Utilitarian individualism is used here, as in *Habits,* for "normative egoism." Finally, *expressive individualism* is used in this essay and in *Habits* for the proposition that "each person has a unique core of feeling and intuition that should unfold or be expressed if individuality is to be realized" (*H,* 334). *Habits* emphasizes the affinity between the culture of psychotherapy and all three of these forms of individualism (see especially, chaps. 3 and 5).

2. See also the survey research of Joseph Veroff, Richard A. Kulka, and Elizabeth Douvan, *Mental Health in America: Patterns of Help-Seeking from 1957 to 1976* (1981) and Veroff, Douvan, and Kulka, *The Inner American: A Self Portrait from 1957 to 1976* (1981).

3. *Habits* extrapolates generalizations about psychotherapy's cultural impact from interviews (conducted by Ann Swidler and Steven Tipton) primarily with Californians, but Californian psychotherapy is not exactly representative of the mainstream of the tradition.

4. I have similar problems with the lack of depth in *Habits'* interpretation of the book's leading spokesperson for psychotherapeutic values, Margaret Oldham. In support of attributing radical individualism to Margaret, the authors quote her as saying, "In the end, you're really alone and you really have to answer to yourself."

> Asked whether she was responsible for others, she replied, "No." Asked whether she was responsible for her husband, she replied, "I'm not. He makes his own decisions." What about children? "I . . . I would say I have a legal responsibility for them, but in a sense I think they in turn are responsible for their acts." (*H,* 15–16)

I interpret Margaret's statement differently than the authors. I think she is speaking on behalf of personal responsibility and against a certain kind of paternalistic authoritarianism rather than evidencing a gross lack of concern for moral obligations to others.

5. The authors of *Habits* tend to equate utilitarian individualism with normative egoism (*H,* 336), but they assume, especially when writing about psychotherapy, that utilitarian individualism is commonly supported by psychological egoism, which holds that human beings always seek their own well-being (see footnote 1). I am primarily concerned in this section with examining the view that psychotherapeutic doctrine favors utilitarian individualism by virtue of what it holds regarding psychological egoism.

6. Freud was attracted to the mixed-motive theory of a professor of physics, G. C. Lichtenberg. He wrote to Einstein:

> This [mixture of motives] was perceived long ago by. . . . Professor G. C. Lichtenberg who taught Physics at Göttingen during our classical age—though perhaps he was even more remarkable as a psychologist than as a physicist. He invented a Compass of Motives, for he wrote: "The motives that lead us to do anything might be arranged like the thirty-two winds and might be given names: for instance, 'food-food-food' or 'fame-fame-food.'" So that . . . human beings . . . may have a whole number of motives . . .—some noble and some base, some of which they speak openly and others on which they are silent. There is no need to enumerate them all. (*CP* 5:281–82)

7. The authors of *Habits* acknowledge that many of the therapists they interviewed appreciate the need for values in psychotherapy:

> In fact, many of those to whom we talked, including therapists, share our uneasiness about "values" [as arbitrary choices] and other ways of thinking about the self. . . . some argue that there are "basic needs," perhaps rooted in biology, that everyone shares. Asked what is *worth* seeking in life, one therapist cites "ten basic things that people want and need: health, clothing, housing, food, sex, love and intimacy, work and mastery, playfulness, spiritual meaning, and security." Armed with this list, she can start to make natural law-like judgments of individual wants: "healthy" versus "neurotic" needs, "lower" versus "higher" developmental tasks. (*H,* 80–81)

8. Each of these psychoanalytic concepts—identification, object-love, introjection, internalization, and transference—refers to complex interpersonal relations. For example, for Freud identification is partly a matter of empathy, in that one imagines oneself in another's shoes, and partly a matter of imitation or modeling oneself on another, but it also involves a component of merging so that the lines between the self and other are blurred through a sense of psychic oneness. Such identification of the self with others not only qualifies the liberal concept of the distance of persons, it subtly critiques it in that here the

self *requires* for its fulfillment and flourishing others with whom it is intimately involved.

9. That the self develops through identification with others in the sense of modeling itself after others is a widely known aspect of psychoanalytic theory. It is less widely appreciated that the self also depends upon the approbation of others. But Freud makes the importance of approbation clear in discussing self-esteem. For example, he writes that "He who has been the undisputed darling of his mother retains throughout life that victorious feeling, that confidence in ultimate success, which not seldom brings actual success with it" (*CP*, 4:367). In "On Narcissism" (*SE*, 14:99) and again in *Civilization and Its Discontents* (*SE*, 21:82), Freud emphasizes that genuine love involves mutual approbation, that is, "loving and being loved."

10. I wish to thank my wife, Anne Shere Wallwork, for helping me revise and edit this essay.

HOLLENBACH, "JUSTICE AS PARTICIPATION"

1. Earlier versions of this essay were presented as The Margaret Lindquist Sorensen Lecture at Yale University Divinity School, 17 October 1985, and as one of The Kellogg Lectures at The Episcopal Divinity School, 6 May 1986.

2. See John Rawls, *A Theory of Justice* (1971); Robert Nozick, *Anarchy, State, and Utopia* (1974); Michael J. Sandel, *Liberalism and the Limits of Justice* (1982); Michael Walzer, *Spheres of Justice* (1983). See also Bruce Ackerman, *Justice in the Liberal State* (1980); William A. Galston, *Justice and the Human Good* (1980); Amy Gutmann, *Liberal Equality* (1980).

TROTTER, "ARE WE PREACHING A 'SUBVERSIVE' LECTIONARY?"

1. Some of my colleagues reminded me of the "multivalency" of culture as well as of Scripture. Perhaps women can relate to this renewed individualism more positively than men. To a large extent women have been the sole guardians of corporate, self-giving family values in our society. The new narcissism is to them in some sense liberating, and many women are rejecting the "earth mother" role. What implications this will have for the Protestant church is a provocative question, since liberated females in the clergy are increasing. Having been to some extent liberated from being the chief nurturer in the family, women are now becoming leaders in the main nurturing community. *Habits* (and Tocqueville) touches on this in chap. 4, particularly pp. 87–88.

HAUERWAS, "A CHRISTIAN CRITIQUE OF CHRISTIAN AMERICA"

1. For an extremely interesting approach to the latter subject, see Mark Noll, Nathan Hatch, and George Marsden, *The Search for Christian America* (1983). In summary, their position is

> a careful study of the facts of history shows that early America does not deserve to be considered uniquely, distinctively or even predominantly Christian, if we mean by the word "Christian" a state of society reflecting the ideals presented in Scripture. There is no lost golden age to which American Christians may return. In addition, a careful study of history will also show that evangelicals themselves were often partly to blame for the spread of secularism in contemporary American life. We feel also that careful examination of Christian teaching on government, the state, and the nature of culture shows that the idea of a "Christian nation" is a very ambiguous concept which is usually harmful to effective Christian action in society. (1983, 17)

2. For Stackhouse's own constructive efforts to extend Rauschenbusch's theory of human rights, see his *Creeds, Society, and Human Rights* (1984). In defense of his position, Stackhouse provides a history of the joining of Puritanism and Liberalism to create the universalistic creed of rights that culminated in the United Declaration on Human Rights. He notes that these principles

> could not be articulated in the particular language of Christian piety which had shaped both the Christian and secular liberal philosophers who had first developed them. Representatives from many cultures and religions would have resisted overt theological formulations in christological or deist terms. The principles had to be stated in "confessionally neutral" terms. But even at this point we see the triumph of the basic assumptions of the Liberal-Puritan synthesis. The state itself should not be "religious." In this view the theologically and morally valid state is one limited by righteous principles and one that allows other organizations to define what is religiously valid. In brief, the "godly state" is a secular state. (1984, 103)

Stackhouse's account seems far too sanguine about how the obvious tensions between the Puritan sense of community can be reconciled with the individualism of liberalism. But even if that were not a problem, one cannot help wondering what has happened that a "secular state" by definition can be called "godly."

3. In fairness to Niebuhr, it should be pointed out that he wrote *The Children of Light* at the end of World War II in the interest of trying to deflate some of the more enthusiastic celebrations of democracy the war had occasioned. Yet Niebuhr remained throughout his life a firm supporter of democracy as that social system which best embodies the Christian understanding of man. As Richard W. Fox rightly suggests in the essay preceding, Niebuhr tried to reconcile the religious and secular but was never successful in doing so. Great conceptual confusion can be hidden in the name of being "dialectical."

4. In *An American Strategic Theology* (1982), John Coleman provides the best Roman Catholic attempt to continue Murray's project. Coleman, however, is much more interested in how Catholicism can act to renew the ethos or civil religion of America than the more strictly constitutional issues with which Murray was concerned.

5. Charles Taylor (1979b, 114–15) rightly argues that no one saw this problem more clearly than Hegel—namely, that:

> absolute freedom requires homogeneity. It cannot brook differences which would prevent everyone participating totally in the decisions of the society. And what is even more, it requires some near unanimity of will to emerge from this deliberation, for otherwise the majority would just be imposing its will on the minority and freedom would not be universal. But differentiation of some fairly essential kinds are ineradicable. Moreover they are recognized in our post-Romantic climate as essential to human identity. Men cannot simply identify themselves as men, but they define themselves more immediately by their partial community, cultural, linguistic, confessional and so on. Modern democracy is therefore in a bind. I think the dilemma of this kind can be seen in contemporary society. Modern societies have moved towards much greater homogeneity and greater interdependence, so that partial communities lost their autonomy, and to some extent, their identity. But great differences remain; only because of the ideology of homogeneity these differential characteristics no longer have meaning and value for those who have them. Thus the rural population is taught by the mass media to see itself as just lacking in some of the advantages of a more advanced life style. Homogenization thus increases minority alienation and resentment and the first response of liberal society is to try even more of the same: programs to eliminate poverty, or assimilate Indians, move populations out of declining regions, bring an urban way of life to the countryside. But the radical response is to convert this sense of alienation into a demand for "absolute freedom." The idea is to overcome alienation by creating a society in which everyone, including the present "out" groups, participate fully in the decisions. But both these solutions would simply aggravate the problem, which is that homogenization has undermined the communities or characteristics by which people formerly identified themselves and put nothing in their place. What does step into the gap almost everywhere is ethnic or national identity. Nationalism has become the most powerful focus of identity in modern society. The demand for radical freedom can and frequently does join up with nationalism and is given a definite impetus and direction from this.

Neuhaus's point is profound, but I do not see how he provides an adequate response since he continues to support the political and economic presumptions that are the source of the difficulty. Roland Delattre's observation (Part One of this volume) that the only way some people in our society have to establish community is through consuming is a particularly stark suggestion that those advocating positions like Neuhaus's must meet.

6. For a similar claim, see Neuhaus (1984, 36). While agreeing with Neuhaus that religion needs to help our society discover or create a moral discourse for the public sphere, John Coleman rightly raises questions about the assumed neutrality or objectivity of that discourse. Thus he criticizes Brian Hehir for requiring Christians to come to the public arena shorn of their particularistic commitments. As Coleman says, he does not think it possible to escape

> the "permanent hermeneutical predicament" of particular languages and community traditions in a conflict of interpretive schemes through the emergence of a common universal language. I fear that this proposal could court the risk of a continuation of the pernicious intertwining of an ethics of deep concern with an ethic of looking out for number one. But finally, and most persuasive for me, I simply do not know anywhere else to look in American culture besides to our religious ethical resources to find the social wisdom and ethical orientation we would seem to need if we are to face as Americans our new context of increasing interdependence at the national and international level. (1982, 197–98)

Thus Coleman, like many Protestant thinkers, calls us to renew the biblical and republican-virtue traditions against contemporary liberalism. This is, of course, the main theme of William Sullivan's *Reconstructing Public Philosophy* (1982). It is a strange social order indeed that makes Catholics so committed to making America work that they accept the project of constructive Protestantism. On the destructive results this process has had on orthodoxy, see Vigen Guroian, "The Americanization of Orthodoxy" (1984).

7. In an unpublished paper, "Democratic Morality—A Possibility," Neuhaus qualifies the starkness of this claim:

> I count myself among the many Christians, perhaps the majority of Christians in America, who have the gravest reservations about the idea of "Christian America." It makes sense to speak, always cautiously, of America as a Christian society in terms of historical forces, ideas, and demography. But no society is worthy of the name of Christ, except the society that is the church, and then it is worthy only by virtue of being made worthy through the grace of God in Christ. (N.d., 6)

8. For one of the ablest critiques of Neuhaus, see George Marsden, "Secularism and the Public Square" (1985). Marsden challenges Neuhaus's contention that religion is the morality-bearing part of our culture, thus denying Neuhaus's statement of the problem:

> Non-theistic secularism also promotes a morality. The problem regarding public philosophy is not simply that of whether or not we have morality in public life. More basically, it is a problem of having competing moral systems and hence less of a consensus in public philosophy than we might like. Putting more religion into public life would not resolve this problem unless we decide first whose religion it would be. In fact, there is even less consensus regarding religion than there is on public philosophy; it is difficult to see how adding more religion would increase the needed consensus. (1985, 59)

9. Neuhaus's criticisms are broad strokes of the much more detailed and refined criticism of Rawls offered by Michael Sandel, *Liberalism and the Limits of Justice* (1982). Yet Neuhaus does not explain how he can at once criticize Rawls on such grounds and yet continue to underwrite America as the exemplification of what a Christian social order should look like. For whether Neuhaus likes it or not, the public philosophy of America is liberal and Rawls in many ways is its most eloquent spokesman. In recent essays Rawls has begun to reinterpret *A Theory of Justice* (1971) in terms of political strategies for pluralist democracies; see, for example, "Justice or Fairness: Political Not Metaphysical" (1985). That may at once make his work less philosophically interesting but more socially significant. Despite Rawls's qualifications, the question still remains whether any account of justice can be intelli-

gibly abstracted from a conception of the virtues integral to the pursuit of goods in common.
That Christian theologians such as Beckley feel the need to adopt Rawls in order to
have a comprehensive theory of justice may indicate that something has already gone
wrong in Christians' understanding of the social and political role of the church. In a
phrase, Christians need a theory of justice when they no longer assume that the very existence of the church is a social stance. Christian thinkers obviously must and can test various
accounts of justice in order to find areas of common cause. But it is quite another matter to
assume that in order for Christians to act politically they need a theory, such as Rawls's, that
claims to order the basic structure of society. In that respect, Beckley's contention that
Rawls's theory does not pretend to comprehend all of morality fails to adequately denote the tendency of Rawls's account to render some goods, such as the family, problematic; see, for example, Rawls (1971, 511–12). I am indebted to Mr. Greg Jones for helping
me see this.

10. For Bellah's more explicit views, see "The Revolution and the Civil Religion" (1976).
There Bellah observes: "Only the biblical religions can provide the energy and vision for a
new turn in American history, perhaps a new understanding of covenant, which may be
necessary not only to save ourselves but to keep us from destroying the rest of the world"
(1976, 73).

For a thorough discussion that raises doubts about the extent of the influence of civic
republicanism in America see John Patrick Diggins, *The Lost Soul of American Politics* (1984).
Arthur Vidich and Stanford Lyman, *American Sociology: Worldly Rejections of Religion and
Their Directions* (1985), document that the birth of sociology in America has been, even in its
most secularized and scientific form, a continuation of the project to form civil society on
the basis of religious values:

> The problems of American sociology emanate from the dilemma and contradictions in the rela-
> tionship between God, the state, and civil society. In America's Puritan heritage there is envi-
> sioned a society composed of a voluntaristic covenant of believers, exercising mutual watch-
> fulness over one another, acceding to legitimate civil authority but recognizing the ultimate
> sovereignty of God over all affairs. The nation would take form as a democratic commonwealth.
> However, in America the promise of this democratic commonwealth was threatened by new
> forms of worldly success and failure and new modes of social differentiation. American socio-
> logical thinkers were the moral successors to the earlier Puritan theologians. Convinced that
> America was destined to be the redeemer nation for the world, these sociologists took as their
> project the inner-worldly perfection of American social, economic, and political institutions. Im-
> plicit in this project was the belief that a convenanted national community could be established
> within the boundaries of the United States. Virtually all the American sociologists converted
> issues of theodicy into problems for sociodicy. Instead of vindicating the ways of God to man,
> they sought to justify the ways of society to its members. (Vidich and Lyman 1985, 281)

They also note that as sociologists observed the inability of Protestant churches to provide a
moral framework for civil society, they tended to center on the state as the only institution
with the moral authority to guide society. Sociology as a "policy science" thus became the
new priestly craft necessary to help the modern bureaucratic state "manage" society.

11. Falwell is particularly interesting when he wanders into questions of international
relations. For suddenly he no longer makes direct biblical appeals but sounds like any good
American realist accepting consequential calculations for determining the right moral
policy.

12. When Christians ask such a question, they assume a majority status. In contrast,
Yoder's view, as well as my own, is that Christians cannot help being a minority if they are
being faithful to their basic convictions. I do not believe, however, this means I am a "sectarian," as David Hollenbach suggests. I certainly do not believe the church can only be
concerned about its own life. Rather I believe the church will find, by exploring how we
serve one another economically, how we might witness to wider society. What Hollenbach
forgets is that the characterization of church-sect types is drawn from a Constantinian
perspective.

13. One should not think that Yoder is committing the genetic fallacy by his appeal to the early Christian community. He is not saying that because the early church was a minority it should always be a minority, but rather, in this context, he is working descriptively to show the change in the logic of moral argument when this occurred. Of course, he will argue that the form of the early church is normative for Christians because what the early Christians believed is true and results in Christians taking a critical stance toward the state. I share that view, but I cannot here adequately defend it.

14. Further, once the ruler is let into the church, then the ruler, not the average or weak person, is the model for ethical reason. Thus the rightness of truth-telling or the wrongness of killing is tested first by whether a ruler can meet such standards. Yoder, however, does not mean to exclude rulers from the church but rather he expects them to act like Christians:

> Caesar would be perfectly free (for a while) to bring to bear upon the exercise of his office the ordinary meaning of the Christian faith. It might happen that the result would be that his enemies triumph over him, but that often happens to rulers anyway. It might happen that he would have to suffer, or not stay in office all his life, but that too often happens to rulers anyway, and it is something that Christians are supposed to be ready for. It might happen that some of his followers would have to suffer. But emperors and kings are accustomed to asking people to suffer for them. Especially if the view were still authentically alive, which the earlier Christians undeniably had held to and which the theologians in the age of Constantine were still repeating, that God blesses those who serve him, it might also have been possible that, together with all of the risks just described, most of which a ruler accepts anyway, there could have been in some times and in some places the possibility that good could be done, that creative social alternatives could be discovered, that problems could be solved, enemies loved and justice fostered. (1984, 146)

15. Most Americans, whether religious or secular, continue to take a missionary stance for democracy. Americans criticize the government's support for nondemocratic regimes around the world to the point of sometimes advocating intervention against them. As Yoder observes "after the 'Christian west' has lost the naive righteousness with which it thought it should export its religion around the world, we still seem to have a good conscience about exporting our politics" (1984, 151).

16. By associating Yoder with Falwell at this point, I do not mean to deny their obvious differences. Yet they both use primary religious language in the public arena without apology. The problem with Falwell is not that he uses Christian appeals, but that his understanding of Christianity is so attenuated.

BELLAH, "THE IDEA OF PRACTICES IN *HABITS*"

1. My response owes much to Steven Tipton, from whose "Moral Languages and the Good Society" (1986) I have drawn paragraphs concerning the essays by Stout, Potter, and Wallwork. The concluding paragraph is also largely his. William Sullivan made some helpful suggestions concerning the essay by Jameson.

REFERENCES

Ackerman, Bruce
    1980   *Justice in the Liberal State*. New Haven: Yale University Press.
Adams, Henry
    1889   *History of the United States During the Administrations of Thomas Jefferson*. Reprint, New York: Library of America, 1986.
Agulhon, Maurice
    1981   *Marianne into Battle*. Cambridge: Cambridge University Press.
Asch, S. E.
    1952   *Social Psychology*. Englewood Cliffs, N.J.: Prentice-Hall.
Bailey, Lloyd R.
    1977   "The Lectionary in Critical Perspective." *Interpretation* 31 (2): 139–53.
Baltzell, L. Digby
    1968   *The Search for Community in Modern America*. New York: Harper and Row.
Barber, Benjamin
    1984   *Strong Democracy*. Berkeley: University of California Press.
Beardsmore, R. W.
    1969   *Moral Reasoning*. New York: Schocken.
Beckley, Harlan
    1985   "A Christian Affirmation of Rawls' Idea of Justice as Fairness—Part I." *Journal of Religious Ethics* 13 (2): 210–42.
Bellah, Robert N.
    1957   *Tokugawa Religion: The Values of Pre-Industrial Japan*. New York: Free Press.
    1964   "Religious Evolution." *American Sociological Review* 29:358–74.
    1970   *Beyond Belief: Essays on Religion in a Post-Traditional World*. New York: Harper and Row.
    1975   *The Broken Covenant: American Civil Religion in Time of War*. New York: Seabury Press.
    1976   "The Revolution and the Civil Religion." In *Religion and the American Revolution*, edited by Jerald Brauer. Philadelphia: Fortress.

1978   "The Normative Framework for Pluralism in America." *Soundings* 61
        (3): 355-71.
Bellah, Robert N., Richard Madsen, William M. Sullivan, Ann Swidler, and
Steven M. Tipton
1985   *Habits of the Heart: Individualism and Commitment in American Life.*
        Berkeley: University of California Press.
Bercovitch, Sacvan
1978   *The American Jeremiad.* Madison: University of Wisconsin Press.
Bernstein, Richard J.
1984   "Nietzsche or Aristotle? Reflections on MacIntyre's *After Virtue.*"
        Soundings 67: 6-29.
Blumenberg, Hans
1975   *Die Genesis der Kopernikanischen Welt.* Frankfurt: Suhrkamp.
1983   *The Legitimacy of the Modern Age.* Cambridge, Mass.: MIT Press.
Borgmann, Albert
1985   *Technology and the Character of Contemporary Life.* Chicago: University
        of Chicago Press.
Bourdieu, Pierre
1977   *Outline of a Theory of Practice.* Cambridge: Cambridge University
        Press.
Bouyer, Lewis
1964   *The Liturgy Revived: A Doctrinal Commentary of the Conciliar Constitution
        of the Liturgy.* Notre Dame: University of Notre Dame Press.
Brown, James E.
1982   *The Spiritual Legacy of the American Indian.* New York: Crossroad.
Coleman, John
1982   *An American Strategic Theology.* New York: Paulist Press.
Congar, Yves
1968   "Sacramental Worship and Preaching." In *The Renewal of Preaching,*
        edited by Karl Rahner. New York: Paulist Press.
Cooper, David E.
1980   "Moral Relativism." In *Midwest Studies in Philosophy III/1978,* edited
        by P. French, T. Vehling, and H. Wettstein. Minneapolis: University
        of Minnesota Press.
Davidson, Donald
1984   *Inquiries into Truth and Interpretation.* Oxford: Oxford University Press.
Dawson, Jan
1985   "The Religion of Democracy in Early Twentieth-Century America."
        Journal of Church and State 27 (1): 47-63.
Debray, Regis
1979   "A Modest Contribution to the Rites and Ceremonies of the Tenth
        Anniversary." *New Left Review* 115:58.
Deleuze, Gilles, and Felix Guattari
1983   *Anti-Oedipus.* Vol. 1 of *Capitalism and Schizophrenia.* Translated by
        Robert Hurley, Mark Seem, and Helen R. Lane. Minneapolis: Uni-
        versity of Minnesota.
Diggins, John Patrick
1984   *The Lost Soul of American Politics: Virtue, Self-Interest, and the Founda-
        tions of Liberalism.* New York: Basic Books.

Du Bois, W. E. B.
1903   *Souls of Black Folk*. Reprint, Greenwich, Conn.: Fawcett, 1961.
Ehrenreich, Barbara
1983   "On Feminism, Family and Community." *Dissent* 30:103–6.
1985   "The Moral Bypass." *The Nation* (28 December 1985–4 January 1986): 117–18.
Eisenstadt, S. N., ed.
1968   *The Protestant Ethic and Modernization: A Comparative View*. New York: Basic Books.
Elliott, Emory
1974   *Power and the Pulpit in Puritan New England*. Princeton: Princeton University Press.
Elshtain, Jean Bethke
1981   *Public Man, Private Woman: Women in Social and Political Thought*. Princeton: Princeton University Press.
1982   "Feminism, Family, and Community." *Dissent* 29:442–49.
1983   "Reply." *Dissent* 30:106–9.
1986   *Meditations on Modern Political Thought: Masculine/Feminine Themes from Luther to Arendt*. New York: Praeger.
1987   *Women and War*. New York: Basic Books.
Evans-Pritchard, Edward E.
1962   *Social Anthropology and Other Essays*. New York: Free Press.
FitzGerald, Frances
1985   "The American Millennium." *New Yorker* (11 November).
Flathman, Richard
1976   *The Practice of Rights*. Cambridge: Cambridge University Press.
Fliegelman, Jay
1982   *Prodigals and Pilgrims: The American Revolution Against Patriarchal Authority*. Cambridge: Cambridge University Press.
Floyan, Gerard S., ed.
1964   *The Constitution on the Sacred Liturgy of the Second Vatican Council and the Muto Proprio of Pope Paul VI*. Glen Rock, N.J.: Paulist Press.
Follett, Mary Parker
1918   *The New State: Group Organization the Solution of Popular Government*. New York: Longmans, Green.
Foner, Philip S., ed.
1972   *The Voice of Black America*. New York: Simon and Schuster.
Fox, Richard Wightman
1985   *Reinhold Niebuhr: A Biography*. New York: Pantheon Books.
Fox, Richard Wightman, and T. J. Jackson Lears, eds.
1983   *The Culture of Consumption: Critical Essays in American History, 1880–1980*. New York: Pantheon Books.
Frankel, Marvin E.
1975   "The Search for Truth—An Umpireal View." Thirty-first annual Benjamin N. Cardozo Lecture, delivered before the Association of the Bar of the City of New York, December 1974.
Freud, Sigmund
        Collected Papers. 5 vols. New York: Basic Books, 1959.

The Standard Edition of the Complete Psychological Works of Sigmund Freud. 24 vols. London: Hogarth Press, 1953–1974.

Fromm, Erich
1955   *The Sane Society.* Greenwich, Conn.: Fawcett.

Gadamer, Hans-Georg
1960   *Truth and Method.* Reprint, New York: Crossroads, 1975.

Galston, William A.
1980   *Justice and the Human Good.* Chicago: University of Chicago Press.
1982   "Defending Liberalism." *American Political Science Review* 76:621–29.

Gellner, Ernest
1973   "The New Idealism—Cause and Meaning in the Social Sciences." In *Cause and Meaning in the Social Sciences.* London: Routledge and Kegan Paul.
1983   *Nations and Nationalism.* Ithaca: Cornell University Press.

Goldberg, George
1984   *Reconstructing America.* Grand Rapids, Mich.: Eerdmans.

Gregory, Ian
1975   "Psycho-analysis, Human Nature and Human Conduct." In *Nature and Conduct,* edited by R. S. Peters. New York: St. Martin's Press.

Guroian, Vigen
1984   "The Americanization of Orthodoxy: Crisis and Challenge." *The Greek Orthodox Theological Review* 29 (3): 255–67.

Gusfield, Joseph
1986   "I Gotta Be Me." *Contemporary Sociology* 15 (January): 7–57.

Gustafson, James
1970   *The Church as Moral Decision-Maker.* Philadelphia: Pilgrim.

Gutmann, Amy
1980   *Liberal Equality.* New York: Cambridge University Press.
1985   "Communitarian Critics of Liberalism." *Philosophy and Public Affairs* 14:308–22.

Hale, Nathan G., Jr.
1971   *James Jackson Putnam and Psychoanalysis.* Cambridge, Mass.: Harvard University Press.

Hall, Stuart
1980   "Popular-Democratic versus Authoritarian-Populist: Two Ways of 'Taking Democracy Seriously.'" In *Marxism and Democracy,* edited by Alan Hunt. London: Laurence and Wishart.
1981   "Moving Right." *Socialist Review* 55:113–37.
1985a   "Signification, Representation, Ideology: Althusser and the Post-Structuralist Debates." *Critical Studies in Mass Communication,* 2: 87–114.
1985b   "Authoritarian Populism." *New Left Review* 151:115–24.

Harris, Marvin
1981   *America Now: The Anthropology of a Changing Culture.* New York: Simon and Schuster.

Haskell, Thomas
1977   "Power to the Experts." *New York Review of Books* (13 October).

Hatterer, Lawrence
1980   *The Pleasure Addicts.* New York: Barnes.

Hauerwas, Stanley
  1981   *A Community of Character: Toward A Constructive Christian Social Ethic.*
          Notre Dame: University of Notre Dame.
  1983   *The Peaceable Kingdom: A Primer in Christian Ethics.* Notre Dame: Uni-
          versity of Notre Dame.
  1985   *Against the Nations: War and Survival in a Liberal Society.* Minneapolis:
          Winston-Seabury Press.
  1986   *Suffering Presence.* Notre Dame: University of Notre Dame.
  1987   *Christian Existence Today: Essays on Church, World and Living In-Between.*
          Durham: Lambrinth Press.
Hawkes, Ellen
  1986   *Feminism on Trial: The Ginny Foat Case and the Future of Feminism.* New
          York: William Morrow.
Hochschild, Jennifer L.
  1986   "Approaching Racial Equality Through Indirection: The Problem
          of Race, Class and Power." *Yale Law and Policy Review* 4 (2): 307–30.
Holmes, Stephen
  1984   *Benjamin Constant and the Making of Modern Liberalism.* New Haven:
          Yale University Press.
Homans, George
  1950   *The Human Group.* New York: Harcourt Brace.
Horowitz, Daniel
  1985   *The Morality of Spending: Attitudes Toward the Consumer Society in Amer-
          ica, 1875–1940.* Baltimore: Johns Hopkins University Press.
Howard, Michael
  1984   *The Causes of War.* Cambridge, Mass.: Harvard University Press.
James, William
  1884   "The Dilemma of Determinism." In *The Writings of William James,*
          edited by John J. McDermott. Chicago: University of Chicago Press,
          1977.
Kennedy, David
  1980   *Over Here: The First World War and American Society.* New York: Ox-
          ford University Press.
Kennedy, Gerald
  1948   *Have This Mind.* New York: Harper and Row.
Kohlberg, Lawrence
  1969a   "State and Sequence: The Cognitive-Developmental Approach to
          Socialization." In *Handbook of Socialization Theory and Research,* edited
          by David Goslin. Chicago: Rand McNally.
  1969b   "Moral Education in the Schools: A Developmental View." In *Studies
          in Adolescence,* edited by Robert E. Grinder. New York: Macmillan.
  1971   "From Is to Ought: How to Commit the Naturalist Fallacy and Get
          Away with It in the Study of Moral Development." In *Cognitive Devel-
          opment and Epistemology,* edited by Theodore Mischel. New York: Aca-
          demic Press.
Kohut, Heinz
  1971   *The Analysis of the Self.* New York: International Universities Press.
Larmore, Charles
  1984   [Review article.] *Journal of Philosophy* 81: 336–43.

Lasch, Christopher
  1979   *The Culture of Narcissism.* New York: W. W. Norton.
  1984   *The Minimal Self: Psychic Survival in Troubled Times.* New York: W. W.
          Norton.
Lears, T. J. Jackson
  1983   "From Salvation to Self-Realization: Advertising and the Therapeu-
          tic Roots of the Consumer Culture, 1880–1930." In *The Culture of
          Consumption,* edited by Richard Wightman Fox and T. J. Jackson
          Lears. New York: Pantheon Books.
Levine, Andrea
  1986   "Questions for Today's Women." *Social Policy* 16 (3): 58.
Lindbeck, George
  1971   "The Sectarian Future of the Church." In *The God Experience: Essays
          in Hope,* edited by Joseph P. Whalen. Westminster, Md.: Newman.
Lynd, Robert, and Helen Lynd
  1929   *Middletown: A Study of Contemporary American Culture.* New York: Har-
          court Brace.
  1937   *Middletown in Transition: A Study in Cultural Conflicts.* New York: Har-
          court Brace.
MacIntyre, Alasdair
  1962   "A Mistake about Causality in Social Science." In *Philosophy, Politics
          and Society,* 2d series, edited by Peter Laslett and W. G. Runciman.
          Oxford: Blackwell Press.
  1977a   "Epistemological Crisis, Dramatic Narrative and the Philosophy of
          Science." *Monist* 60:453–72.
  1977b   "Patients as Agents." In *Philosophical Medical Ethics,* edited by H. T.
          Engelhardt, Jr., and S. F. Spicker. Dordrecht, Holland: Reidel.
  1981   *After Virtue: A Study in Moral Theory.* Notre Dame: University of
          Notre Dame Press.
  1984   *After Virtue: A Study in Moral Theory.* 2d ed. Notre Dame: University
          of Notre Dame Press.
Macpherson, C. B.
  1977   *The Life and Times of Liberal Democracy.* New York: Oxford Univer-
          sity Press.
Madsen, Richard
  1984   *Morality and Power in a Chinese Village.* Berkeley: University of Cali-
          fornia Press.
Marsden, George
  1985   "Secularism and the Public Square." *This World* 11 (Spring-Summer):
          48–62.
Mayo, Elton
  1933   *The Human Problems of an Industrial Civilization.* New York: Macmillan.
Meier, August, Elliott Rudwick, and Francis Broderick, eds.
  1971   *Black Protest Thought in the Twentieth Century.* 2d ed. Indianapolis:
          Bobbs-Merrill.
Meilaender, Gilbert C., Jr.
  1983   "Individuals in Community: An Augustinian Vision." *The Cresset*
          (November): 5–10.

Murray, John Courtney
1953a   "The Church and Totalitarian Democracy." *Theological Studies* 13: 525–63.
1953b   "Leo XIII: Separation of Church and State." *Theological Studies* 14: 1–30.
1960   *We Hold These Truths: Catholic Reflections on the American Proposition.* New York: Sheed and Ward.
National Conference of Catholic Bishops (NCCB)
1986   *Economic Justice for All: Catholic Social Teaching and the U.S. Economy.* Washington, D.C.: National Conference of Catholic Bishops/United States Catholic Conference.
Needham, Rodney
1973   *Belief, Language, and Experience.* Chicago: University of Chicago Press.
Neuhaus, Richard John
n.d.   "Democratic Morality—A Possibility." Unpublished manuscript.
1984   *The Naked Public Square: Religion and Democracy in America.* Grand Rapids, Mich.: Eerdmans.
1985   "Nihilism Without the Abyss: Law, Rights, and Transcendent Good." Paper delivered at 1985 conference on Religion and Law at Catholic University Law School.
Newman, John Henry
1864   *Apologia Pro Vita Sua.* London: Longman, Green, Longman, Roberts, & Green.
Niebuhr, Reinhold
1932   *Moral Man and Immoral Society: A Study in Ethics and Politics.* Reprint, New York: Scribners, 1960.
1944   *The Children of Light and the Children of Darkness.* New York: Scribners.
Nisbet, Robert
1975   *The Twilight of Authority.* New York: Oxford University Press.
Noll, Mark, Nathan Hatch, and George Marsden
1983   *The Search for Christian America.* Westchester, Ill.: Crossway Books.
Novak, Michael
1985   "McGovernism Among the Bishops." *Washington Times* (25 October).
Nozick, Robert
1974   *Anarchy, State, and Utopia.* New York: Basic Books.
Oakeshott, Michael
1975   *On Human Conduct.* Oxford: Oxford University Press.
Parsons, Talcott
1951   *The Social System.* New York: Free Press.
Parsons, Talcott, and Edward A. Shils, eds.
1951   *Toward a General Theory of Action: Theoretical Foundations for the Social Sciences.* Cambridge, Mass.: Harvard University Press.
Peacock, James L.
1987   "Barchester Towers in Appalachia." In *Social Meaning*, edited by Phillis Chock. Washington, D.C.: Smithsonian Institute. In press.
Peele, Stanton
1981   *How Much Is Too Much: Healthy Habits or Destructive Addictions.* Englewood Cliffs, N.J.: Prentice-Hall.

Peele, Stanton, and Archie Brodsky
1975 *Love and Addiction.* New York: New American Library.
Pocock, J. G. A.
1967 *The Ancient Constitution and the Feudal Law.* New York: Norton.
1975 *The Machiavellian Moment: Florentine Political Thought and the Atlantic Republican Tradition.* Princeton: Princeton University Press.
Rauschenbusch, Walter
1917 *Theology for the Social Gospel.* Nashville: Abingdon Press.
1968 *The Righteousness of the Kingdom.* Nashville: Abingdon Press.
Rawls, John
1971 *A Theory of Justice.* Cambridge, Mass.: Harvard University Press.
1985 "Justice or Fairness: Political Not Metaphysical." *Philosophy and Public Affairs* 14(3): 223–51.
Ricoeur, Paul
1970 *Freud and Philosophy.* New Haven: Yale University Press.
Rieff, Philip
1961 *Freud: The Mind of the Moralist.* Garden City, N.Y.: Doubleday.
1968 *The Triumph of the Therapeutic.* New York: Harper and Row.
Reisman, David, with Nathan Glazer and Reuel Denney
1950 *The Lonely Crowd: A Study of the Changing American Character.* New Haven: Yale University Press.
Robinson, Lillian S.
1985 "Treason Our Text: Feminist Challenges to the Literary Canon." In *The New Feminist Criticism,* edited by Elaine Showalter. New York: Pantheon.
Rorty, Richard
n.d. "The Priority of Democracy to Philosophy." Unpublished manuscript.
1982 *Consequences of Pragmatism (Essays: 1972–1980).* Minneapolis: University of Minnesota Press.
1983 "Post-Modernist Bourgeois Liberalism." *Journal of Philosophy* 80: 583–89.
1985a "Habermas and Lyotard on Postmodernity." In *Habermas and Modernity,* edited by Richard J. Bernstein. Cambridge, Mass.: MIT Press.
1985b "Postmodernist Bourgeois Liberalism." In *Hermeneutics and Praxis,* edited by Robert Hollinger. Notre Dame: University of Notre Dame Press.
1985c "Solidarity or Objectivity." In *Post-Analytic Philosophy,* edited by John Rajchman and Cornel West. New York: Columbia University Press.
Roszak, Theodore
1972 *Where the Wasteland Ends: Politics and Transcendence in Post-Industrial Society.* New York: Anchor Doubleday.
Rousseau, Jean-Jacques
1762 *The Social Contract.* Reprint, *On the Social Contract with Geneva Manuscript and Political Economy.* Edited by Roger D. Masters. New York: St. Martin's Press, 1978.
The Sacerdotal Communities of Saint-Severin of Paris and Saint-Joseph of Nice
1964 *The Liturgical Movement.* New York: Hawthorne Books.

Sandel, Michael
  1982   *Liberalism and the Limits of Justice.* Cambridge: Cambridge University Press.
  1984   "The Procedural Republic and the Unencumbered Self." *Political Theory* 12:81–96.
Sanders, James A.
  1979   *God Has a Story Too.* Philadelphia: Fortress Press.
  1983   "Canon and Calendar: An Alternative Lectionary Proposal." In *Social Themes of the Christian Year,* edited by Dieter T. Hessel. Philadelphia: Geneva Press.
Sartre, Jean-Paul
  1976   *Critique of Dialectical Reason.* Translated by Alan Sheridan-Smith. London: New Left Books.
Schneewind, J. B.
  1983   "Moral Crisis and the History of Ethics." In *Midwest Studies in Philosophy VIII/1983,* edited by P. French, T. Uehling, and H. Wettstein. Minneapolis: University of Minnesota Press.
Shi, David E.
  1985   *The Simple Life: Plain Living and High Thinking in American Culture.* New York: Oxford University Press.
Shils, Edward
  1981   *Tradition.* Chicago: University of Chicago Press.
Smith, Rogers M.
  1985   *Liberalism and American Constitutional Law.* Cambridge, Mass.: Harvard University Press.
Spragens, Thomas A.
  1981   *Irony of Liberal Reason.* Chicago: University of Chicago Press.
Stackhouse, Max
  1968   Introduction to *The Righteousness of the Kingdom,* by Walter Rauschenbusch. Nashville: Abingdon Press.
  1971   *The Ethics of Necropolis: An Essay on the Military-Industrial Complex and the Quest for a Just Peace.* Boston: Beacon Press.
  1984   *Creeds, Society, and Human Rights.* Grand Rapids, Mich.: Eerdmans.
Stout, Jeffrey
  1981   *The Flight from Authority.* Notre Dame: University of Notre Dame Press.
  1984   "Virtue Among the Ruins: An Essay on MacIntyre." *Neue Zeitschrift fuer Systematisch Theologie und Religionsphilosophie* 26:256–73.
Sullivan, William
  1982   *Reconstructing Public Philosophy.* Berkeley: University of California Press.
Swidler, Ann
  1979   *Organization Without Authority: Dilemmas of Social Control in Free Schools.* Cambridge, Mass.: Harvard University Press.
Synan, Vinson
  1971   *The Holiness-Pentecostal Movement in the United States.* Grand Rapids, Mich.: Eerdmans.

Taylor, Charles
  1979a   "Atomism." In *Power, Property, and Possessions*, edited by A. Kontos. Toronto: University of Toronto Press.
  1979b   *Hegel and Modern Society*. Cambridge: Cambridge University Press.
Tipton, Steven M.
  1982   *Getting Saved From the Sixties: Moral Meaning in Conversion and Cultural Change*. Berkeley: University of California Press.
Tocqueville, Alexis de
  1835–40 *Democracy in America*. 2 vols. Reprint, New York: A. S. Barnes, 1855. Translated by Henry Reeve. Cambridge: Sever and Francis, 1864. Edited by Phillips Bradley. New York: Vintage Books, 1945. Edited by J. P. Mayer, translated by George Lawrence. Garden City, N.Y.: Doubleday, 1969.
Tompkins, Jane
  1985   "Sentimental Power: *Uncle Tom's Cabin* and the Politics of Literary History." In *The New Feminist Criticism*, edited by Elaine Showalter. New York: Pantheon.
Trachtenberg, Alan
  1982   *The Incorporation of America*. New York: Hill and Wang.
Troeltsch, Ernest
  1911   *The Social Teachings of the Christian Churches*. Translated by Olive Wyon. London: George Allen and Unwin, 1931.
Turner, Frederick W., ed.
  1977   *The Portable North American Indian Reader*. New York: Penguin.
Unger, Roberto M.
  1975   *Knowledge and Politics*. New York: Free Press.
  1987   *False Necessity: Anti-Necessitarian Social Theory in the Service of Radical Democracy*. Cambridge: Cambridge University Press.
Veroff, Joseph, Richard A. Kulka, and Elizabeth Douvan
  1981   *Mental Health in America: Patterns of Help-Seeking from 1957 to 1976*. New York: Basic Books.
Veroff, Joseph, Elizabeth Douvan, and Richard A. Kulka
  1981   *The Inner American: A Self Portrait from 1957 to 1976*. New York: Basic Books.
Vidich, Arthur, and Stanford Lyman
  1985   *American Sociology: Worldly Rejections of Religion and Their Directions*. New Haven: Yale University Press.
Wallwork, Ernest
  1982   "'Thou Shalt Love Thy Neighbor as Thyself': The Freudian Critique." *The Journal of Religious Ethics* 10 (Fall): 264–319.
Walzer, Michael
  1983   *Spheres of Justice: A Defense of Pluralism and Equality*. New York: Basic Books.
Warner, W. Lloyd
  1953   *American Life: Dream and Reality*. Chicago: University of Chicago Press.
Washington, James, ed.
  1986   *Testament of Hope*. San Francisco: Harper and Row.

Weber, Max
1905   *Protestant Ethic and the Spirit of Capitalism.* Translated by Talcott Par-
         sons. New York: Scribner's, 1958.
Wegman, Herman
1983   "Significant Effects of Insignificant Changes." In *Liturgy: A Creative
         Tradition,* edited by Mary Collins and David Power. New York:
         Seabury.
Weisberger, Bernard
1958   *They Gathered at the River.* Boston: Little, Brown.
Westbrook, Robert
1983   "Politics as Consumption: Managing the Modern American Elec-
         tion." In *The Culture of Consumption,* edited by Richard Wightman
         Fox and T. J. Jackson Lears. New York: Pantheon Books.
Wolff, Robert Paul
1968   *The Poverty of Liberalism.* Boston: Beacon Press.
Wright, Richard
1941   *Twelve Million Black Voices.* New York: Viking Press.
Yack, Bernard
1986   *The Longing for Total Revolution: Philosophic Sources of Social Discontent
         from Rousseau to Marx and Nietzsche.* Princeton: Princeton University
         Press.
1987   "Myth and Modernity: Han's Blumenberg's Reconstruction of Mod-
         ern Theory." *Political Theory* 15 : 244–61.
Yoder, John H.
1984   *The Priestly Kingdom: Social Ethics as Gospel.* Notre Dame: University
         of Notre Dame Press.

CONTRIBUTORS

M. Elizabeth Albert is a graduate student in the English Department at the University of Maryland at College Park. She received an M.A. in the Writing Seminars at Johns Hopkins University. She holds a B.A. in Humanities from the University of Tennessee at Chattanooga, where she was a William E. Brock Scholar. Her poems and an essay on Wallace Stevens have appeared in *The Poetry Miscellany*. A chapbook of poems, *Nothing You Can See*, was published by the Glavin Press in 1983.

Robert N. Bellah is Elliott Professor of Sociology at the University of California at Berkeley. His publications include *Tokugawa Religion* (1957), *Beyond Belief* (1970), and *The Broken Covenant* (1975). His most recent book is *Uncivil Religion: Interreligious Hostility in America* (1987), edited with Frederick E. Greenspahn. He and the coauthors of *Habits* are working on completing their second volume.

Roland A. Delattre is Professor of American Studies and Religious Studies at the University of Minnesota. Author of *Beauty and Sensibility in the Thought of Jonathan Edwards* (1968), he is currently working on projects related to ritual and the formation of American culture, religious ethics in America, and addiction and American culture.

Jean Bethke Elshtain is Centennial Professor of Political Science at Vanderbilt University. She is the author of *Public Man, Private Woman: Women in Social and Political Thought* (1981); *Meditations on Modern Political Thought* (1981) and *Women and War* (1987) and is editor of *The Family in Political Thought*.

Richard Wightman Fox teaches history and humanities at Reed College. He is the coeditor with T. J. Jackson Lears of *The Culture of Consumption*

(1983) and author of *Reinhold Niebuhr: A Biography* (1985, 1987). He is working on a study of Protestantism in modern American culture.

Vincent Harding is Professor of Religion and Social Transformation at the Iliff School of Theology at the University of Denver. He is a former director of the Martin Luther King Memorial Center and the Institute of the Black World. Two of his most recent books are *The Other American Revolution* (1981) and *There Is a River* (1981), the latter being the first volume of a trilogy.

Stanley Hauerwas is Professor of Theological Ethics and director of Graduate Studies in Religion at Duke University. His publications include: *Vision and Virtue* (1974), *Character and the Christian Life* (1975), *Truthfulness and Tragedy* (1977), and *Suffering Presence* (1986). His most recent book is *Christian Existence Today* (1988).

David Hollenbach, S.J., is Associate Professor of Moral Theology at Weston School of Theology, Cambridge. He is the author of three books: *Claims in Conflict: Retrieving and Renewing the Catholic Human Rights Tradition* (1979), *Nuclear Ethics: A Christian Moral Argument* (1983), and *Justice, Peace, and Human Rights: American Catholic Social Ethics in a Pluralistic World* (1988).

Fredric R. Jameson is the William A. Lane, Jr., Professor of Comparative Literature and director of the Graduate Program in Literature and Theory at Duke University. His books include *Sartre: The Origins of Style* (1961), *Marxism and Form* (1971), *The Prison-House of Language* (1972), and *The Political Unconscious* (1981). He is a coeditor of the journal *Social Text. The Ideologies of Theory, Essays 1971–1986* will be published shortly. Three other forthcoming books will deal with film, dialectical aesthetics, and postmodernism.

Christopher Lasch is Watson Professor of History at the University of Rochester and chair of the Department of History. His published works include *The Culture of Narcissism* (1979) and *The Minimal Self* (1984). Works in progress include *Essays in the History of the Family* and *Progressive Social Thought*.

William F. May is Cary M. Maguire University Professor of Ethics at Southern Methodist University. He has recently published *The Physician's Covenant: Images of the Healer in Medical Ethics* (1983). His next two works will be titled *The Patient's Ordeal* and *The New Rulers of the West, the Public Obligation of the Professional*.

Ralph V. Norman is Professor of Religious Studies and Vice Provost at The University of Tennessee at Knoxville. He is the editor of *Soundings*, an interdisciplinary journal for the humanities. His essays have appeared in

Soundings and *The Christian Scholar.* He is currently writing a work on the imagination of argument in poetry and the novel.

James L. Peacock is Kenan Professor of Anthropology at the University of North Carolina at Chapel Hill. He has done most of his fieldwork in Southeast Asia, though in recent years he has been doing research among religious groups in America. His most recent book is *The Anthropological Lens: Harsh Light, Soft Focus* (1986).

Ralph B. Potter is Professor of Social Ethics at the Harvard Divinity School and a member of the Center for Population Studies at Harvard. His publications include *War and Moral Discourse* (1969), and his research interests are war and peace, population studies, friendship, ideals of character, and moral anthropology.

Charles H. Reynolds is Professor and Head of Religious Studies at The University of Tennessee at Knoxville. He was the founding editor of *The Journal of Religious Ethics* and coeditor of *Clinical Medical Ethics* (1987). His essays have appeared in the *Journal of Religion, Harvard Theological Review, Soundings,* and other journals. He is coauthoring with David C. Smith a book on academic values and ethics.

Jeffrey Stout is Associate Professor of Religion at Princeton University. He is the author of *The Flight from Authority* (1981). His latest book is *Ethics After Babel: The Languages of Morals and Their Discontents* (1988). His articles have appeared in the *Journal of Religious Ethics, Soundings,* and *The Monist.*

J. Irwin Trotter was a Phi Beta Kappa graduate of Occidental College and received his B.D. degree from Yale Divinity School. He later did postgraduate study at the Centro Intercultural de Documentación at Cuernavaca, Mexico. He is currently Gerald H. Kennedy Professor of Preaching at the School of Theology at Claremont in Claremont, California.

Ernest Wallwork is Associate Professor of Religious Ethics at Syracuse University and expert bioethicist at the National Institutes of Health. He is author of *Durkheim: Morality and Milieu* (1972) and coauthor with Roger Johnson of *Critical Issues in Modern Religion* (1973). He is currently completing a book on psychoanalysis and ethics.

Bernard Yack is Assistant Professor of Politics at Princeton University. He is the author of *The Longing for Total Revolution: Philosophic Sources of Social Discontent from Rousseau to Marx and Nietzsche* (1986), as well as articles on Hegel, Aristotle, and contemporary political theory. He is working on a book on Aristotelian social and political thought, tentatively titled *The Problems of a Political Animal.*

INDEX

Compositor: G&S Typesetters, Inc.
Text: 10/12 Baskerville
Display: Baskerville
Printer: Maple-Vail Book Mfg. Group
Binder: Maple-Vail Book Mfg. Group